A CHANGE OF TONGUE

ANTJIE KROG

A CHANGE OF TONGUE

RANDOM HOUSE

This edition first published in South Africa in 2003 by
Random House (Pty) Ltd
Endulini, 5a Jubilee Road, Parktown 2193
Johannesburg, South Africa
Reg. No. 1966/003153/07

Postal address: P.O. Box 2263, Parklands 2121
South Africa

First published 2003

Edited by *Ivan Vladislavić*
Design and layout by *Abdul Amien*
Cover design by *Abdul Amien*
Proofreading by *Tessa Kennedy*

Produced for Random House by Rosebank Publishing Services cc
Project Manager: *Douglas van der Horst*

Litho imaging by Cape Imaging Bureau
Printing and binding by Paarl Print, Oosterland Street, Paarl

ISBN: 0-9584468-4-9

The illustrations on the cover and page 376 have been reproduced
from a chromolithograph of a flat fish that appears in Volume 6 of
P. Bleeker's *Atlas Ichthyologique des Indes Orientales Néérlandaises*,
published between 1866 and 1872. Random House is grateful to the
library staff of the South African Museum, Cape Town, and in
particular to Brenda Commins and Rina Krynauw, for their help in
locating this image and facilitating its reproduction.

SOME RULES, according to Noam Chomsky, are transformational: that is, they change one structure into another according to such prescribed conventions as moving, inserting, deleting, and replacing items. Transformational Grammar has stipulated two levels of syntactic structure: deep structure (an abstract underlying structure that incorporates all the syntactic information required for the interpretation of a given sentence) and surface structure (a structure that incorporates all the syntactic features of a sentence required to convert the sentence into a spoken or written version). Transformation links deep structure with surface structure.

CONTENTS

*I*t is as if the rain picks you up carefully. As if the rain has got your scent. As if you're holding on to fleeces of mist, as if the rain clears your throat and lightly rumbles down your thighs. The rain drapes you out on the front of its bulk. It encompasses everything. You see nothing except brightening sweeps of mist. Somewhere light sifts through. Your eyelashes drenched. The rain sinks forward, tilts. Your nose scatters a drop or two. Amongst rags of spray you make out no fixed shape. Things of vapour and deluge drift and shift across one another.

Then lightning. And stone reefs strain against each other primordially in the mist. Something creaks, then bursts, flashes away with flocks of fire and then sinks back sodden black into the foaming whirl of water. Something tears. You grip the strong forearms of the rain, your back against its underbelly, as if this is all you have. The rain backs away and dives past the stacks of cloud into open air. You start making things out again. Water trails down the scars of highlands and rocks, and swirls together and gushes over, swirls together, gushes over, backs off, flows through, fills up, streams away. Becomes river. Sluiced in basalt and granite, ridged and haltered by snatches of sandstone, limestone, shale, veiled through with sediment, edged in soft silver drifts of sand. And before your very eyes the sun breaks through. You see wild bush-willows bursting from banks and *fluitjiesriet* frittering out finches. In still hippo-pools, soundless rings slip from fish leaping into the sun. The rain clutches you tightly. It holds you. It hurts you. As if the rain has snipped the wire that draws your insides together.

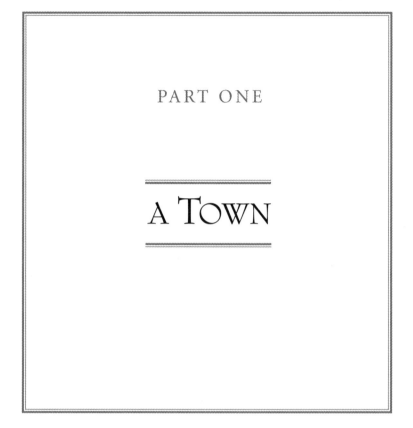

PART ONE

A TOWN

CHAPTER ONE

THE GUNSHOT CRACKS. They lean into the curve. Out from among the white boys shifts the figure of a black child, upright, his fingertips effortlessly upwards at every stride. Down the straight he is way ahead, running with the compelling grace of a top athlete. The pavilion crowd is on its feet. The black schools yelling wildly and pressing up against the railings in front. The white parents cheering, one tossing a hat into the air, and at the finish line a white track official bent almost double by her encouraging screeches.

'Why is everybody happy?' I ask a man in a tracksuit next to me. He is wearing a floppy army hat and takkies. The sunburn on his forehead leads me to suspect that he is a farmer.

'The blacks are happy because it is a black kid beating the whites. The whites are happy because the winning black kid is from a white school and was trained by them.'

It is the Kroonstad district athletics meeting. The programme is running exactly as scheduled. Announcements are made in Afrikaans and Sesotho. Most of the track officials are black, and everyone looks very much at home with the rituals of measuring distance and keeping time, of flags, starting guns and walkie-talkies.

'It was not always so,' says the man in the tracksuit, 'but we have come a long way.' He shifts a toothpick to the other corner of his mouth, obviously dying to tell. He farms somewhere in the district, he says, and had to bring some athletes from his farm to this event. His own child is also participating.

'It was really terrible that first year ... To have athletics with black schools, I mean. We were so scared, I cannot tell you! Each white primary school was put in a league with four black schools and a couple of black farm schools for preliminary trials. The white school was told to organize the event, prepare the track and field, provide refreshments, act as main officials and bring the black teachers up to speed.'

He shakes his head as if he cannot believe it himself. 'Although we had a lot of power in the beginning, we told the kids: bring your parents, bring your grandparents, bring your unemployed uncle, tell your auntie to take off from work that morning. Bring everybody along so that the blacks don't engulf us. We must make sure that at least we are a factor, a presence to be reckoned with, otherwise they might sommer let their own children win everything.

'So I told them ...'

An announcement cuts him off: a new record. The twelve-year-old record for the 200 metres has been broken by the black kid. When the record time is announced, the farmer nods his head and raises his eyebrows. 'That's good. An excellent time.' He writes it down with a Bic pen in his programme.

He continues: 'I told them, I said, "The winning doesn't start on the track, my friends, it starts long before. Let's get a plan in place. Let each school choose its own athletes according to standard times. And here are the rules: nobody may run whose name is not on The List. No school may enter more than four athletes per event. Nobody may run if his ID document has not been verified by us. No event may be delayed to wait for somebody. If you are not at the start when the event is announced, it proceeds without you." But we quickly realized the most important thing: if we want to keep control of the event, we have to hang on to the announcer's job. And the way we do it is to insist on Afrikaans being used. Afrikaans is the language of our schools, and if they have problems with it, someone can sit with us and translate into Sesotho.

'Now, all of this we did. We held ten planning meetings. Ten, I'm telling you. Ten meetings to set out age groups, make lists of participants, emphasize punctuality, check that events don't clash, draw up rosters for officials. In the meantime we prepared our children. Everyone went into overdrive: the teachers set about training the athletes with some zeal for a change, and where they left off, the parents took over. We even invited someone from Bloemfontein to come and help, because nobody felt like making a bad showing against the blacks. I said to them, I said, "Let us be as good as we know we are." At home we warned the kids not to use those toilets on the day, Oom Swannie will bring his caravan on to the premises so that they can go there if they have to. By then we'd heard several stories from neighbouring towns about stabbings and rapes in the public toilets.'

He takes two Cokes from his well-equipped cool bag and offers me one.

'You must remember that over fifteen thousand schoolchildren were involved. More than all the white schoolchildren in Kroonstad put together. Nobody had a clue of the numbers of people expected – can you imagine what will happen if the unemployed from the township turn up? And they just might, because it is all new to them, you know, this New South Africa thing.

'So we slept badly, our children slept badly, and *sowaar*, when we arrived here that morning, everything was already wrong. The pavilion was chock-a-block with blacks. Full. Here and there some seats were still open, but we decided to rather stand at the bottom in front of the pavilion, and sent some of the older boys to fetch us chairs from the school. We were still restrategizing when a black teacher arrived, berating us because the drinks and snacks were supposedly too expensive for the township kids. We tried to explain that the prices were usually loaded a bit to help along the school fund, but he stormed away and simply opened the gates so that the kids could buy from the township traders sitting outside the fence – you know, these people who sell stuff like home-made flavoured ice and cheese curls, positively poisonous with preservatives.

'But okay. We let it go. We were choosing our battles, and the important thing was that our children get their fair due. So we started with the first event. Old Smittie, our school principal, announced the names of the participating athletes over the PA system, but after the third name, thunderous laughter rose from the pavilion. A black school principal jumped up indignantly and rushed to the announcer's booth: "The surname 'Koekoe' is not pronounced *Koo-koo* but *Kwe-kwe*!" According to him, the children could not recognize their own names and did not know who was being called. After half an hour of arguing about language, we realized we had better get under way or we would sit there until that evening and then things might really get out of hand. Because of the dark, you know. We gave the microphone to the black principal, who speaks Sesotho, Afrikaans and English, but when he roared over the PA, "Viva Kroonstad district athletics meeting, viva!" we knew it would be a tough day.

'Just when he wanted the first item to proceed, we heard shouts and saw little flags urgently waving at the starting line. Crisis! Walkie-talkies! The 80 metre starting line coincides with where the 200 metre lanes turn into the straight. The black kids were sitting skew in their starting places. They were clearly focused on the curving lines of the 200 metre lanes rather than the straight lines of the 80 metres, and would therefore collide with other kids when the race got going. Now hell, you don't want to *bedonner* your own child's chances of winning by having him bump into a black kid charging down the wrong lane. So then they sent me because I speak Sesotho. I spelt it out in three languages: "*Dit is die lyne waarin jy moet hardloop.*" And then I walked backwards, waved my arms and said to each kid, "*Matha meleng ena.* This is where you must run in between." They nodded their heads. Then the starter shouted, "On your marks," but you saw, *haai!* this child was still crouching skew in his lane. He still didn't get it.

'The worst were the small ones. Shame, it was the first time they had been set off by a starting gun. So their eyes were like saucers. When they were told, "On your marks," they went into this kind of shaky halfway crouch, like they were skulking behind a fence, and when they heard, "Get set!" they simply shivered their bodies slightly, all the while staring fiercely at the man with the gun. We shouted, "*Kyk voor julle!* Look in front of you!" but they just swiped their faces to the front very fast, and then back. When he fired, you just saw kids running all over the place. When he fired twice for a false start, they ran even faster. Some of them never came back.'

He gets out of his bag a Tupperware box neatly divided inside to keep carved biltong, roasted mealie pips and salted pumpkin seeds, all separate.

'But eventually we had everything sorted out and things could get going. We were only an hour behind, you see, so it was carpe diem and all that. We ran with it, we ran. Until the long-distance events. Flags up. Walkie-talkies. New problem. The black athletes did not understand that they could start off in separate lanes, but then cut to the inside lane after a short distance. We explained in all possible languages, but eventually, to prevent our times from being the slowest in the district, we had to pick them up physically and carry them to where we wanted them. Then some of them angrily ran back to their previous positions, convinced that we were deliberately sabotaging their chances of winning by forcing them to run in the wrong lane.'

My companion battles a piece of biltong between his molars with a toothpick. From the metallic glimpses I get inside his mouth, I suspect all is not well behind the facade of meticulously crowned incisors. 'Despite all of this, sometime during that day, I don't know how, we let it slip. Thinking back, I suspect it happened when Smittie's own child pulled a muscle and he had to go and help her. The black principal simply took over completely and unexpectedly asked some coloured guy, from God knows where, to join him. From then on, we had athletics in full radio-commentary style. When the principal's vocabulary faltered or he became short of breath, the other one chipped in. When the other one was speaking, the principal would accompany him with sounds. We couldn't believe our ears. The athletes were yelled out of their starting blocks, they were shrieked around the corners and roared down the straights. Even the long-distance runners – the two of them brought the athletes in like racehorses, talking them in, talking them in. It was chaos. Everybody was cheering for everybody. The whole notion of competing teams and schools got lost. When my child won the 800 metres, his mates from my black farm school excitedly ran the last stretch with him. In the years before, track officials would have had a fit over this, but it was such a messed-up day anyway that everything became possible. When my chief tractor driver's son won the 11 500 metres, I found I was yelling my tonsils out – I was so bloody proud, because I often saw the little bugger running in the fields, but I didn't know he was practising for something. But fair is fair, and I called Daniel on the radio to tell him his child and my child had won their races and that he must slaughter a sheep for that evening, I will bring some beer from the town.'

He looks at his watch, takes out his cellphone and pushes some buttons. 'Just an SMS to tell my kid to go to the starting line.'

He continues: 'But the day was still not finished! Another crisis was happening at the starting line. We'd obviously stressed the importance of punctuality too much. By twelve o'clock there was not an athlete left on the pavilion. Everyone, family included, was at the starting area. There was such a throng, they were pushing against the athletes already under starter's orders. This could not happen. We tried to work them backwards, but the moment you turned away they were back, some were even standing in front of those in the starting blocks. Then this big coloured *juffrou* arrived. And I mean big. All the officials had to wear white clothes, but presumably she couldn't find anything her size. She was wearing a kind of light-blue tunic, and her ankles bloated out over her shoes so that only the tips were visible. The kids pressed up against her, all around.

'"Can't something be done?" I asked.

'Her eyes sparkled. "Am I being officially delegated?"

'I nodded.

'Then she walked right up to the front, threw her blubbery arms into the air and bellowed in a voice launched from her stomach to crack the air like a mirage: "*Fô-kof!*" Man, I tell you, you could hear that word echoing out over the neighbourhoods of this town, but as true as God, in a flash the track was deserted. Those not staggering up the steps of the pavilion were cowering at the furthest fences. It took the announcers several pleading calls to lure the athletes back to the starting area for the next event. The following year we made her a chief track official.'

He takes out his own stopwatch. 'My child is going to run now.'

We wait. He points out his slightly podgy son. When the gun fires, he presses the button and jumps to his feet. He shouts as if demented. At one stage, I look up right into his mouth: and indeed a complete factory assembly line is clustered there, with pistons and bridles, valves and hooks and clamps holding a few discoloured, shiningly-filled teeth together over cracks and gaps. After the race, he shakes his head, 'His time is a bit off ... the heat, maybe ... You know, now that you think back, you don't know why we were so scared. Just look how well things are going now!'

That I can see. Half the pavilion is full of white parents and teachers, the rest is black children, with here and there a grown-up. Only the coloured school forms a distinct presence. Eighty per cent of the winning athletes are white. What happened?

A few days later, I phone one of the town's top athletics trainers and put the question to him.

'You can ask the people of the town: I am not a racist. They will tell you, no one had more enthusiasm for the new dispensation than me. But I will tell you straight: laziness is a terrible thing. If laziness is in your blood, nobody can do anything about it. When the blacks were still angry and wanted what we had, it was better, because they wanted everything. They were angry and they wanted. They voted us out everywhere, they took up all the important posts, they organized everything when and where it suited them. But once they were sitting there in our places, they found that all these things were actually a lot of work. An athlete, you have to train in your spare time. You have to drive him to sporting events over weekends in your own car, with your own money and without overtime pay. You have to attend coaching courses in your holidays. You have to train your top athletes the whole of December and January. Without extra pay. That is what sport is. Free dedication of teachers to their communities. The success of the athlete is your reward. *Nou ja*. These people, that they don't like.'

'But why were the majority of the officials on Saturday black, if they don't care?'

'No, of course they were there. And did you see anyone without an umbrella or a cooldrink or a chair? Even those controlling the relays demanded chairs and umbrellas. Yes, Mr and Mrs Official were fully equipped. Did you see us whites standing there in the sun just with hats? And if you'd stayed until three o'clock like us, you would have seen that there was not a single black official left after they packed away the lunch. Even the announcer was gone. Because the lunch must be there, oh yes, more discussions take place about the meat and the pudding than about the athletics. But come two o'clock, then this one has to go to a funeral and that one doesn't work on Saturday afternoons and eventually we always have to ask some of the white parents to help out.

And if you say anything about it, they call you a racist. So we shut up and do the work, but the result is that after eight years of mixed sport, the teams are full of white kids.'

A black school principal from Maokeng sees it differently. 'It doesn't matter how things have changed, before you know it, the whites have manipulated it in their favour. When you say that your school does not have a track or long-jump pits or high-jump or shot-put equipment, they say you must stop blaming everything on apartheid. When you ask if you can bring your athletes to their school, they say that they must first get permission from the school board and that only meets next term. And you dare not call them racists, because now they have a few black kids in their school.'

'But they say that black teachers are too lazy to train athletes in the afternoons.'

'They speak easily. Our lower salaries reflect our disadvantaged positions, but now we suddenly have to do more work in much more difficult circumstances. Our classes are double the size of theirs. Our preparation and correction take twice as long. Our parents are less involved, the children less focused and disciplined. Why do you think they do not want to teach at black schools? Because it is hard. It is hard to be a teacher in a township school. On top of that, most of my staff have to do extra work in order to put enough bread on the table for the extended family of unemployed and elderly and orphans who are in their care. And then the whites constantly change the rules. Just when you pick up at the event how the long jump works and you train your athletes accordingly, at the next event it seems that you don't plant your foot *here* anymore but *there*. Both you and your athlete are caught on the wrong foot. And there they win again.'

He sighs deeply. 'Then we heard that after the athletics, they have their own private braai. In the beginning, we wondered why they were just picking at their lunch. We thought maybe it was because we'd made the salad, but then we learnt no, they have their own party that night. Oh, I can go on and on ... you keep on losing out and losing out, you give up eventually.'

CHAPTER TWO

IT HAD BEEN WRITTEN indelibly on our hearts: 'Third World' means bad roads, corruption, dictatorship, means black leaders in shiny suits and sunglasses, surrounded by sweaty, gun-toting soldiers, all sweeping in cavalcade past gaunt-looking women and pot-bellied children covered in flies. The telltale signs of Africa.

The relief was therefore understandable when a slim Nelson Mandela appeared in his festive, loose-fitting shirts, getting out of cars to talk to people in the streets. The optimism grew when it became known that he was wearing sunglasses as a temporary measure, not because he preferred them but because he had damaged his eyes on

Robben Island – the glasses were 'our fault'. Initially, corruption was also something to look forward to: whereas it might take a pile of cash to bribe a white, rumour had it that you could easily sort out a black with a bottle of brandy, a sack of maize or a chicken. However, as the New South Africa became a reality, there was concern and confusion. How to read the codes … To bribe someone, you have to know that the person is competent but corruptible. But how do you know this, when all your life you have believed blacks to be incompetent, when you have never taken the trouble to learn their language, when you cannot 'read' their body language?

'Lukas, you know, Ouma Hannie's son, was told by his farm workers about a particular official who takes bribes for driver's licences,' my host informs me on arrival at his farm in the southern Free State. Peet is my cousin, and he is busy carrying my bag to the house. 'So when Lukas slipped the R500 over the counter along with his application form, the last thing he expected was for Mr Msimela to wave the notes in the air, saying with a loud, stern voice: "Are you trying to bribe me, sir? Because if you are, I will have to report you to the police." Lukas said he could have killed the guy, he was so embarrassed – and beetroot red, of course. But the next day he sent one of his workers, and he got a licence from that same Mr Msimela for R200.'

I hear mad barking. Rina, my cousin's slightly built wife, calls out a greeting and hangs on to the choke chain of her enormous dog. I can hear Nefie grunting and drooling and snapping as the screen door slams behind me.

'Don't you worry about corruption,' Peet continues down the passage, 'at this stage, the blacks only have their hands in the tills, but the Boere are stealing where you still have to open the safe with a password, a wheel and two hands. The Boere are stealing deep, and they won't stop until the coffers are empty.'

This is a stopover on my way to Kroonstad, where I want to do some research for an article about 'Food and Reconciliation' for a Dutch magazine. I managed to convert my initial irritation about the haphazard pairing of two disparate issues into an excuse to come and visit the Free State.

'Food and Reconciliation? You are just in time. We have been invited to Dorsfontein. Ouma Hannie is about to turn eighty and today her children are giving her a birthday lunch.' Rina sees I know what's coming. Ouma Hannie is Peet's aunt and the sister of my grandmother, and in her day was reputedly the best cook in the southern Free State.

On our way to Dorsfontein, we are flagged down at one of the many roadworks I came across on the way from Cape Town. 'Ten minutes, sir,' says the black woman. She is wearing an overall with a reflective bib.

We wait. From up ahead there is nothing. After five minutes, Peet asks her in Sesotho, 'But you don't even have a walkie-talkie or a temporary robot here, how do you know that there are cars coming from the other side?'

She laughs. 'No, it is not that far, I can hear when they call from behind the hill.'

We wait. A huge truck comes to a stop behind us, its engine making such a racket that you wouldn't hear a thunderclap. After ten minutes, Peet says, 'Now I'm going.'

His words have scarcely been uttered when, from the opposite side, a big Land Rover comes hurtling down the hill, barrelling towards the woman controlling the traffic. She stands aside, but the vehicle changes course and heads straight for her. The woman screams and jumps in behind a tar-filled drum at the side of the road. The Land Rover misses narrowly and we just see teeth and red fingernails as the woman behind the wheel erupts with laughter. She is followed by three giant trucks, one with a trailer. They are speeding happily along the specially closed-off, freshly tarred stretch, and from their wheels gravel, flakes of wet tar and traffic safety cones fly. A man in the last truck waves us on with a jolly smile.

When we arrive on the family farm, I greet my way to the kitchen as quickly as possible. Here Peet's overweight cousins are working with the sort of concentration that has nothing to do with gourmet skills, but rests on an absolutely intimate, mouth-watering knowledge of food indulgence. One is busy carving a chicken. She doesn't just saw and cut in order to get good helpings out of the chicken. Her one hand wields the razor-edged knife, while the other lovingly supports the roasted breast. She has the pointed fingertips of a sensitive, emotional, overweight food indulger. The first slice is laid out gently on the platter. Each slice with its curve of brown skin, its piece of juicy filling, is cherished into place. The other cousin is making the gravy. No Bisto or Maizena or soup powder here, but a cup of sherry and thick cream is slowly caressed in, followed by some crumbling Roquefort cheese. The baked potatoes ooze on to clean paper towels. Whole heads of garlic packed in like fragrant roses between the legs of mutton, hams shafted among stacks of pink baked quinces. With tiny tongs, Ouma Hannie lifts something that looks like a nest of stamens. 'Saffron for the yellow rice,' she says as she shakes the bottle. 'Saffron is more expensive than gold these days.' I watch as the yellow rice tumbles out of the pot – not turmeric-yellow, but saffron-golden with big seedless hanepoot raisins steamed in.

At the table, Rina elbows me. Across from us, Lukas's wife Nelmarda takes a seat. Her plate provides new meaning to the idea of full. It is stacked up in layers. We bow our heads, but just before Lukas starts to say grace, Peet chips in, 'Step on it, my brother, last time you prayed so long that Ouma Hannie was nearly a year older by the time you finished.' Lukas glares around angrily, then prays long and sonorously. Next to me, Rina is shaking with suppressed laughter. After the prayer, Nelmarda empties a small glass of muscadel. She wipes her mouth, gives the serviette a final smoothing over on her lap, twists her plate slightly, picks up her knife and fork, and tucks into the top layer: blissful with giddy-headed pleasure; peaceful, like someone preparing to go into rapture. The layers are organized with enviable judgement. She doesn't mess around with a piece of ham here or a piece of offal there: every layer is complete with a different kind of meat, starch, gravy and assorted side dishes.

But this attention to the food doesn't mean that nobody says a word. The bad roads are under discussion. From Heilbron you can now only travel with a 4x4, and the stretch past Reitz has broken up completely. One of the brothers-in-law is involved with road repairs.

'The whole of the Free State is full of roadworks. The guys are laying tar for all they're worth, but the roads break up within a year or so.'

'We just saw how these big trucks break up the tar before it is even dry,' says Peet.

'Those trucks are a curse. They do just whatever they please. They get bonuses when they complete their trips on time. The roadworks are now so common and such a hindrance that the drivers simply ignore them.'

'Yes, Ds Fourie says to me the other day at Bible Study, I must remember he is not in the service of the Afrikaner, he is in the service of Christ. So I said to him, well, Dominee, then you and Christ just have to see how far the two of you can carry the church by yourselves. While I thought to myself, I really hope for Jesus' sake it is not a fifty-fifty partnership.'

Ouma Hannie sits at the head of the table. She talks constantly, right through everyone else's conversations, and in between eating and snatches of talk she is adamant that the sole purpose and mission of the black government is to destroy the Afrikaner. 'If only I could pick up some sign that they are doing it for their own people, but no, they are doing it to eliminate and humiliate us.' She dabs her lips.

'Please, Ouma,' pleads one of the younger cousins, 'please don't credit them with a *plan*, or the successful execution of anything, for Christ's sake.' The talk is peppered with expressions of ruin – the wheels coming off, grinding to a halt, *in sy moer in*, going to pieces, unravelling, *opgefok*. An overwhelming sense of being hounded, deprived and on the edges of chaos rises amidst the aromatic vapours of food.

'We have to have these trucks because the railways are not functioning any more,' Ouma Hannie continues. Implacably. 'All that's left are the empty little stations that used to feed thousands of Afrikaners, abandoned and plundered. They say the squatter camps at Ventersburg are built solely of the plundered building materials from the abandoned railway houses. But what do they care, these politicians? They all go by jet nowadays.'

'I gather that nobody votes NP any more?'

Ouma Hannie puts her knife and fork neatly together and looks me straight in the eye. 'After 1990, there were only two NP members left: your father and F.W. de Klerk. After 1994, only your father.'

'The dessert table is ready,' says one of the cousins, with a bit more saliva in her mouth than is decent. In a big copper pot, *souskluitjies* doze plumply in butter and cinnamon, there is an oozing *malva-poeding*, and the roly-poly groans apricot jam from between its rolls. I break out in a fine sweat.

'Apparently there is corruption at the roadworks ...' Peet tries to get the conversation on to more neutral territory.

'Oh, that I could have told you years ago,' Ouma Hannie jumps in. 'They steal the money in Bloemfontein that is supposed to go for road repairs. They say the people there don't even know what a budget is. If there is money, they take it.'

One of the brothers takes over, the brandy grumbling in his cheeks: 'Ag, shuddup Ma. Apparently they budget enough money, but it is the contractors who steal it. They try to save on the under-layers of the roads. And the under-layer is what makes a road. The tar is just a protection layer. I heard the other day that there is a group of white road workers. They get paid so little that they go and look for work at firm B while they are still employed by firm A. Then they get a salary from both firms for a few months, until A realizes it and fires them. Then they work for a few months at B until they get work with C. When A warns C about them, they go at night and pour water and other fluids into the chemicals so that A's whole roadworks is sabotaged without him knowing.'

'A lot of the smaller contractors have been taken over by farmers who are struggling to survive on their farms,' his brother says. 'That is, if they are not going to America to do contract work.'

'America?' It is hard to keep the disbelief out of my voice: so many things America does not want from us, yet it uses the labour of white farmers?

'Lots of farmers go across to work for eight months on big farms with harvest contracts from coast to coast. These guys live in caravans and move from farm to farm, driving the tractors, harvesting wheat and mealies, driving the trucks ... they say our guys do excellently there. The American farmers like us so much that they book some guys' tickets in advance for the next year. And when a man comes back, he can pay his children's school fees and the interest on his debt.'

'And what is happening on their own farms in the meantime?'

'The women carry on with the farming and the neighbours help where they can. But I must tell you honestly that doing nothing on a farm today has actually become the most profitable way of farming. The moment we plant peanuts, the price falls, when we fatten cattle, pork becomes the favourite, when we go big-time for pork, the price of fodder rises, when we plant fodder, it rains and we no longer need it. The moment you find out what to do, then you should have stopped doing it last month. And a new Department of Agriculture is like a new bride – only when she realizes her limitations does she become useful. But these new guys, they still think you can farm with a Constitution.'

The tablecloth is taken off and a fresh one laid out. 'For coffee,' says Nelmarda. The cakes are brought in: stacks of soft and moistly risen cakes, icing that only knows the terms butter and cream, tarts of milk and honey and lemon. Fluffy flaky pastries. *Koeksistertjies*. Petite little meringues. *Tamboesies*.

'No sugar,' says one of the in-laws, pointing to a gooseberry fridge tart, 'only two tins of condensed milk.'

'Call it what you like, because soon you won't have it,' says Ouma Hannie. 'At the bank there are only these young black girls to help you nowadays. With nails that long and red. When a woman's nails look like that, you know she cannot do a stitch of work. Not typing, not holding a pen, if you ask me they even have trouble scratching their scalps. The other day I said to one of them: Ag, the *oumiesies* she is old, she doesn't hear too well, and she wants a white *oubaas* to help her. So they laughed and dragged old James Toerien out there from the back – I said: Good gracious, James, I said, are you still here? He just rolled his eyes like that: "Yes, Tannie, but I don't know what's going on here any more." You can imagine how they steal from those computers there.'

Between cake forks and teaspoons, Ouma Hannie steams along.

'The other day I went to fill up with petrol and the attendant pretended he couldn't speak Afrikaans. So just before I drove off with an empty tank, I told him that he could keep his petrol for those hundreds of English tanks which pass this *gatkant* of South Africa. Then Fanie, you remember Fanie from Oom Bossie, he called me from the police station later and said that a Mr Mofokeng is there and he wants to lay a charge because I drove over his foot. But he told Mr Mofokeng sommer on my behalf that the *oumiesies* she is old and she cannot see him so well any more.'

'Yes, Ouma, one of these days you will have to start selling all those shares of yours to pay for defamation!'

Before Ouma Hannie can start talking about her shares, Peet gets up for us to leave. Ouma Hannie has lots of platinum shares she bought years and years ago, Peet tells me afterwards. 'But now the old woman complains: "They told me to buy platinum, and now they tell me I'm a millionaire. I don't know what a millionaire is! If it cannot bring the Afrikaner back to power, it means nothing to me."'

'Did you notice' – these are Ouma Hannie's last words to me – 'the black women who read the news on television? They've all had nose jobs. Just see how thin their noses are. They tell me the hospitals are full of blacks who are making their noses thinner. Not one of them with good English has a flat nose, not one of them!'

'How can people eat so well and complain so much? Ouma Hannie is just dripping with vitriol.' We are back in the bakkie.

'Don't let their talk fool you,' says Peet. 'All four of her sons are on their last legs. They had to sell off most of their farms last year, two of the brothers are now living in town trying to make a living by selling pesticides. Ouma Hannie is actually the only one with money among them, and she refuses to part with any of it. So they can't wait for her to die, of course.'

'This area is full of what I call reborn racists,' says Rina. 'A lot of the farmers were initially quite changed by the 1994 election. People thought if we only treat black people humanely, we'll be fine. So a lot of farmers took up the farm schools, drove to the city to buy books, checked on the teachers, the farm wives held clinics on primary health care, and gave lessons in sewing and nutritional cooking. But between then and now a lot has turned sour.'

'Why?'

'It's difficult to say,' says Peet. 'Black people want more than what Rina suggests. The farmers here are saying: you think they want human dignity, then you hear they want *rights*. You think they want rights, then you hear they want *your* rights. You think they want your rights, then you hear they want your *possessions*. And so on. People look at Zimbabwe and realize you gain nothing by giving anything up. So they hold on as tight as they can.'

'All the while talking with such resentment that you would swear they'd already lost everything,' says Rina.

On the main road, Peet throws his 4x4 in a different direction. 'I want to show you something.'

In a haze of phlegmatic digestion we drive half-dozing into the eastern Free State. The last cosmos of the season stands in pink and white sheets next to the road. In the town we drive through, there is a brand new mosque. Its hard yellow-brick walls and green onion-domes shimmer in the afternoon sun.

'Yes, the Indians have moved in here,' Peet confirms, 'Lord only knows why, because this place has practically no commercial life left any more. Most of the shops have closed. There are three white children left in the school. Black parents from villages in the area have bought two houses across the road from the school for next to nothing, and almost sixty children are cared for there by black matrons. Now at least the white teachers here still have work. One day, almost unnoticed, an Indian opened a shop, then another. Then they built this mosque. It caused a whole commotion in the town's *moederkerk*. I heard that elder Gielie Mostert said at the church board meeting: "No, fuck it boys, there are only four coolies in town but they build themselves a brand new church. And here we are, more than fifty souls, and we cannot even keep our own church going. No man, are we worse than them?" Now the amalgamation with the *moederkerk* in Bethlehem has been put on hold.'

The 4x4 turns on to a badly rutted gravel road. We drive through several farms along a stream fringed by late summer grass, reed and a griddle of poplar trees chattering in silver tongues. Eventually we start tilting upwards. Crawling up a twisty mountain track. The vehicle's wheels start edging over the sandstone rocks in independent units.

'Rina, hold on tight!' Peet shouts above the roar of the engine. 'Because she's so small, she kind of sits around too loosely in a bakkie.' Laughing over his shoulder. The mountain is high and steep. I shift away from the cliff-side window and clamp on to the mountain-side handle. Suddenly the vehicle leaps forward and there we are – on top! On a vast grassy plain.

Then I draw a deep breath. Unbelievable. It is as if my eyes and my brain have stopped communicating. My eyes see something that my brain doesn't want to recognize, because nothing in my frame of reference has prepared it for this.

Etched against the wide, clear eastern Free State sky, with its firm white bundles of cloud, is a sandstone construction that my eyes define as a medieval castle, but my brain rejects as impossible in this place. A half-built sandstone castle in the Gothic style. On top of a mountain in the Free State. Can it be?

'Go look!' Peet encourages. I get out slowly. Large blocks of hewn sandstone the colour of honey and grass rise up. Two towers are nearly complete. Specially chiselled lintels form the arches above the entrance. I walk through – and enter somebody's abandoned dream.

In the courtyard there is grass and rusted scaffolding. I climb the spiral stairs to the top floor, where glassless, spear-shaped windows look out on the entire Free State and Lesotho. I almost have no breath. It is immensely silent. Just snatches of children's laughter, far below, and the smoke of dung-fires spiralling up.

I touch the stone, and my hands drown in their silence. The width of plains and horizon and far-off blue mountains draws the world to bone. The clouds leave themselves behind in patches of stream and river. I stand in the middle of the big room. I can see in all directions. I can lay myself over the earth and the fullness thereof. I feel as if I could rule the world.

How did the cement get here? The sand? The tools to quarry the sandstone blocks from the mountain, the pulleys to lift them high in the air? How did the precast Gothic windows get here? Why has everything been left unfinished? Why a castle? Why Gothic? Why here?

Peet and Rina join me. He opens a bottle of muscadel and we sit with our backs against the sandstone foundations and watch the sun set over the mountains. It was a fertilizer magnate who decided to build a castle here with several towers and a ballroom and bedrooms for many guests. The whole thing was to be built according to the design of a real Gothic castle, complete with service caskets or trays that could be hoisted on ropes to take the food from the kitchen on the ground floor to the banquet hall above. All the building materials were brought up the mountain by helicopter, and a whole team of stonemasons worked here. Then the magnate went bankrupt. The chief mason still kept on building for some months, hoping against hope, but eventually also threw in the trowel.

Several pasts roam across our skin in shades of stone and setting sun. I feel at once touched and repulsed by this place draped in the smell of uprooted visions of grandeur and unanchored, wild expectations. And beauty. Silence grows firmly in my mouth. The cool evening air pushing up from the plains leaves our lungs light and fluttering.

Rina takes up the conversation about the farmers in America.

'You know,' she says, 'the Afrikaner will now do any kind of work as long as it's overseas. Your child can scrape toilets clean with his fingernails and eat baked banana peels, but you regard it as special because it's overseas. Children who wouldn't rinse a glass at home are now working as waiters in London. Farmers you wouldn't see near a tractor or a truck here are harvesting through the night in America.'

'But they earn dollars and pounds,' says Peet. 'Besides, you cannot compare the young people in London with the farmers, Rina. It is really tough to do farm work like that. Not only do you work night and day, you are also away from your family for eight months at a time, and this has an enormous effect on everyone's lives. People are really desperate around here.'

'I find it interesting how often the guys who come back comment that rural American women are unrefined and vulgar,' says Rina. 'It means they do definitely look around ...'

'Here in the southern Free State, some of the farmers initially took their sons along, in order to make double the money for the family, but the younger ones didn't last there. The following year not one of the young farm boys went along.'

'To the great worry of the wives who stayed behind,' says Rina. 'Because father and child could at least keep each other on the straight and narrow during migrant-labour periods.'

'Tell about the dog,' says Peet.

'Ag no, some other time.' Rina gets up unexpectedly and walks towards the 4x4. 'We have to hurry, it will be dark soon.'

Down on the main road again, I ask about the dog. Rina sits quietly. Peet starts:

'Half of the farm workers went to town on the Friday to do their Christmas shopping and the other half went on the Saturday. Sambuti, who works for Rina in the garden, went on Friday. So on Saturday he comes to Rina and tells her that he can't work in the garden because he has to go to a funeral that day. So Rina says he can't and he becomes vexed ...'

'No,' says Rina with a sigh, looking out on the dark fields. 'I was busy pruning my roses a bit to have them at their best for Christmas, when Sambuti asked to go to a funeral. So I said the garden didn't get water the previous day because he was away and it was very hot. He should first water the garden before he leaves. I saw he didn't like what I was saying, but this was the situation. So he clicked his tongue, bent down, and picked up the hosepipe to throw it near the tap, but as he bent down I heard this incredible growl and saw Nefie just going for him.'

Nefie is as big as a calf.

'And what does she do? Does she attach the hose and scare off the dog with the water? Does she run into the house and call us on the radio? No,' says Peet, his voice edged. 'She jumps in between Sambuti and the dog.'

'The dog knocked him off his feet and immediately there was blood all over. I lay down over Sambuti so the dog could not get hold of him ... but it was awful. Nefie tore at whatever he could find. I saw a piece of ear go, then I felt Sambuti's leg being savaged, both of us shouting, knowing full well there was no one near the house.

Yelling at the dog, we had to crawl, inch by inch, to the nearest tree, so that Sambuti could get up with his back against the trunk and me in front of him. All the time the dog barking viciously, foaming, lunging at him.'

Peet breaks in: 'I'd gone home purely by chance to get my chequebook when I heard this commotion. And there they were, so covered in blood that I could hardly make out who was who. And both had wounds. My first thought was: fuck it! Fucking Aids! So I fastened the dog, and rushed them to hospital. And yes, of course, Sambuti had Aids. I was so furious, I thought I was going to lose my mind – this kind of stupid, naive caring for someone who is nothing more than a bloody half-drunk, half-retarded, Aids-infested little swaggerer. I wanted to murder him. With her I've given up. She has always been utterly clueless when it comes to blacks.'

'They gave me AZT,' Rina says quietly, 'and I will be tested next month.'

That evening, I sit with my notebook, but later I put it away again. No easy walk between perception and truth in this country.

CHAPTER THREE

I DRIVE THROUGH THE OUTSTRETCHED PLAINS of the southern Free State. Verlatenfontein, Heuningneskloof, Brakspruit, Eensaamheid, Abjaterskop, Erfdeel. Gravel roads thread to unseen farmsteads. One is struck by the sense of an intentional vast emptiness in which far-off hilltops feature as slight draughts of breath. The land-scape feels ancient and clear. Everything human feels accidental and threadbare – a residue to be simply scraped off one morning from the majestic monotony. Nothing ornamental is tolerated. Nothing that cannot endure so much sky.

What effect does a landscape like this have on a psyche? What forms did freedom and democracy translate themselves into on these plains? Have they ever reached here? I remember gathering some stories before the first democratic election, some of them sent to me by Rina.

Apart from stockpiling canned goods and ammunition, she informed me, some farmers from the western Free State had their wives and children sleep in black night-gowns and pyjamas: if the enemy attacked, they could flee unseen in the dark across the veld.

She also told me about a farmer from Smithfield, tinkering on his tractor in the big barn the week before the election, casually asking his labourers: 'Are you going to receive land after the election?'

'Aikona, the land will go to all those on the TV.'

'But if you do get land, will you at least have a job for me?'

Deathly silence. 'You know me. When I come to ask for work, will you take me in and give me a hut?'

Mild giggling. 'Ja-nee, we will.'

'Now what kind of work will I have to do?'

'Work?' one of them asks in surprise.

'Yes, work. Daniël, what work will you give me to do?'

Daniël, pat: 'Tending sheep.'

A moment of silence. Tending sheep rates as the most humble work on a farm. A wild, enthusiastic eruption of laughter.

'No, let him milk,' says another. The gasp is audible. Then more laughter. Milking demands the hardest and most merciless hours on a farm.

'No, let him work in the garden. Hoeing and watering.'

Gardening is working for the farmer's wife. It is to be in the garden when other people come to visit, it is to be the big, strong, mature man they see busy planting seedlings or raking up leaves or digging up earth on the orders of the *miesies*. This meets with raucous laughter.

'No, Baas Pieter,' says yet another. 'I will make you drive. I will give you the car, then I will say: "Pieter, how about it, take me *bietjie* to Cape Town, let's go and check it out there!"'

'Wow!' yell the younger ones, somersaulting in pure abundance, laughing uproariously. Suddenly everything is cut off as if with a knife. As if the same thought is dawning on everyone. Shakily one of the farm workers sinks to the ground. Then another. The farmer emerges slowly from underneath the tractor. So everyone sits on the edge of the cement floor, speechless beside the abyss of their own thoughts, until the first guineafowl comes up to the eucalyptus grove for the night.

✧

The pre-election time ticked away in a highly volatile atmosphere. Everything was both possible and impossible. People did things, heard things, said things they had never imagined before. Big, important events frittered away into nothingness in the face of so many possibilities of change. Small gestures took on a symbolism of great significance.

So it was that Lieutenant Colonel Johan Botha was visited by an angel while he was busy praying. On his knees he was pleading with the Lord to deliver this country from a black government, when he suddenly, inexplicably, switched over to English. 'I don't know why I suddenly started speaking English,' he said in a radio interview. 'It just happened like that. One moment I was praying in Afrikaans, the next moment I asked in English: "God, what do you want of this country?"' And suddenly, there on his knees, he became aware of a presence. A glow. A heat. And when he opened his eyes he saw this angel and the glory of the Lord shone around him. The angel did not touch the ground, according to Lieutenant Colonel Botha, and its face was in shadow. Then the angel spoke. Why the angel spoke in English, Lieutenant Colonel Botha also did not know. 'I want South Africa on its knees,' said the angel via Botha in an English tinged with Afrikaans. 'I don't think it was an angel,' the young son of Lieutenant Colonel Botha said afterwards. 'It was God Himself, because He said "I".'

A week before the election, there was a political rally in Kroonstad. Some comrades were singing 'America – six foot under the ground' one moment, and cheerfully chanting the next: 'Viva pap en boerewors, viva Calvin Klein jeans!' One of the speakers pointed emphatically at the fancy white neighbourhood and said, to tumultuous applause: 'After the election all of this will be ours!'

During this time, I did an interview with the man who had been the foreman on our farm all of his life. First my father's playmate, later his right-hand man. The man who drove us children to school every day and me to Odendaalsrus for violin lessons on Saturday afternoons. After I published the interview, my mother said: 'We all had to reassess our relationship with Isak after reading the piece. None of us realized he cared so deeply about your father.'

I, Sebata Isak Mokokoane, come from Basotholand, but so long ago that I cannot remember it. My father's father lies buried in Basotholand. Your father and I grew up together on the farm. We grew up like each other. We grew up smartly. We spoke Sesotho, and *sjoe! re bapala*. We play, play, play. In the mornings it is still dark night when I go down to the house, then he is already waiting for me, then we play there, we hunt birds with the catapult, we ride horses, we go down to the spruit. We played, we played, until the *oumiesies* came out of the house with her bonnet to look for us.

Like Matjama was, so was I. We ate porridge from the same bowl. One o'clock Matjama gets his plate in the dining room, I get my plate in the kitchen. Then he doesn't eat well. Then *oumiesies* puts his food in my plate, then he sits with me, then we eat together. When he went to school, we went apart for the first time. Until then we were just even-even. We were like each other. Then he went past me, but it could not be the other way – my people were not used to sending a child away to school. So then Matjama only came to the farm on Fridays. Then, then ... the whole week the two of us, we wait for then. When he gets off the car I see his face changes when he sees me. Mine too. On Fridays, I became a person.

Then he went to get clever. Then I became clever on my own. Then I married and I worked in the town. Then the Baas there told me, Baas Willem is getting married in Kroonstad and he wants you. You must meet him in Senekal at the café. So I went there. I was waiting for him. But I was afraid. I was actually shaking. I was afraid that I wouldn't remember him if I saw him. All that I remembered very well was the mark. Matjama had a little mark above his eye from an accident when we were small. One of my sticks cut him. Then I saw this man standing there and I said suddenly, without looking at him:

'Hey, *dumela* Matjama!' Then I saw no, this man's head jerked in the air. Then the man laughed and I saw the mark above his eye. The mark I made. It was him. Then he told me he is getting married on a farm and I must come with him. We must stay together. We must always be together. Then I came. So we stayed together until today.

I know Matjama well. As well as I know myself. When he comes out from the house, then I already know if he is teary or angry. But one thing, he may be Matjama or the Baas, but when he is finished speaking he has nothing left inside him. If he is angry, he will look away, look away, and then when he speaks, the tears hang from your face. He does not like to quarrel and he never swears.

On the farm I looked after milking, sick calves, chickens, every year the coop was full of chicks that had to get ants fed to them, pruning trees, grapes, making drains and diggings, I slaughtered sheep, cattle, pigs, I built with sandstone, dolerite, brick, I put in ceilings, plank floors, gutters. I put on roofs. I drove cars, tractors, trucks. For years I drove you to school, fetched fodder for the farm. If I didn't know how, I looked, looked, and then I saw how. Then I did it. One thing that I am sad about is that all the work that I know does not have papers. I can do all these things but the papers do not show it. Now I'm not what I am.

Land I would like. Just a small bit. I want to know: here I stay. Here I build. Here I sit on my own place. I will build a house. From stone. Plant vegetables, carrots, potatoes. And trees. Apricot and peach trees and a shady tree. Matjama's mother taught me that a person should always have a shady tree. But one thing: I will not let Matjama go. I will let Matjama go the day he dies or I die.

The elections confuse me. My wife Eveline says we cannot vote for Mandela, because he does not live here with us. We stay with you, where you vote, we will vote. I just wish to stay with the Baas. I am old. My efforts lie here. It is Matjama who is holding me upright. I can live, I can eat. I do not need anything. If I need, he helps. I want to die here. I want to die under the Baas. He is all I know.

The night before the election, Beethoven's opera *Fidelio* was performed in Cape Town. In the final scene, a few hours before the first polling booths would open, a light broke out over the stage. From dungeons and cells came people, arms waving, faces turned up to the glorious light. A black Florestan exulted:

Do I not sense a breathing, soft-swirling air?
I see an angel in a rose-coloured glow
Ein Engel
Der führt mich zur Freiheit ...
Freiheit!

The choir broke into a mighty sound: Freedom. In the front row someone leapt up enthusiastically, fist clenched in the air. Freedom.

✧

Polling day itself was rainy in Cape Town, but along the wet streets people showed themselves, became visible, grew into queues snaking across pavements – honourable, tolerant, dignified. Initially, the queue I joined was made up only of the coloured residents of Woodstock. But gradually, as problems were encountered at other polling stations, taxis brought in people from Khayelitsha.

When I unfolded the ballot, the full national choice lay under my hand. For the first time. It was as if a miracle burst open like a small seed-casing in my throat. For the first time I am part of my complete country. My hands neither ordering nor begging. Making the cross, liberation spiking my blood with belonging.

The next day, some ANC comrades who were also election officials called from the Free State: 'You never told us the Boere are so friendly, man. In all the towns, we were received with such warmth. Real warmth, hey. When our car broke down on the way to Steynsrus, we were afraid, and we said to each other: today we will be murdered here next to this very road. Then this big farmer stopped behind us in his bakkie, and we said to ourselves, boykies, this is it. Either we run away in our official T-shirts, or we face our end in this car. But the man was so friendly. Spoke Sesotho. Gave us a lift. Up in front, hey. Took us to his house, sat us down in the living room. Coffee and rusks on a tray with a lace cover. The same cups as them, hey. He even phoned his own mechanic in Petrus Steyn to come and fetch our car. No man, *die Boere is nxa!*'

Rina also called. She had been a monitor at a small polling station. 'Was I scared! Half past seven in the morning on the way there I saw a dead jackal lying next to the road, the blood on him still fresh but his skin in perfect condition. I loaded him into the car. When I got to the polling station, there were black people already queuing for two kilometres and I was the only white and I thought, sister, today you are going to be killed right here. If not for your minibus, then definitely for the jackal skin. I stopped a distance away, but when I walked down past the queue, I saw that I knew almost everyone, because at one stage or another they had all attended the clinic where I worked. Inside the hall I had to monitor proceedings with the PAC guy and the ANC guy. PAC? We checked each other out from the corners of our eyes. One of the first people to come in was this ancient woman. Here and there still a tooth. Fingers stiffened in all directions. Of course, she could not read. She could not write. The official showed her the ballot paper and explained patiently in Sesotho how she had to point to the face of the candidate she wanted to vote for. Her hand hesitated. Then she pointed at ... guess who? At Constand Viljoen. We looked at each other and started laughing. We told her to look carefully. Suddenly her face livened up and she pointed to Mandela, and she laughed and pointed and pointed. Then with the provincial ballot, her hand moved slowly down the list until it came to rest securely on Zach de Beer. Man, then we held each other from all the laughing, but we felt that she knew now how it worked, and so she must have wanted to vote like that.'

A week after the election, Rina phoned again. 'Peet was on his way to Zimbabwe and decided to stop in Pietersburg to have a haircut. The barber was a woman. While she cuts, he asks, just to make conversation, "Now who is your premier in this area?" "*Jis meneer*, now you ask me a thing. Liesbeth!" she shouts to the back of the shop. "What is our premier's name again?" Liesbeth appears in a flash, busily drying a cup. "Ngoako Ramatlhodi," she says. The barber looks at him in the mirror and shrugs: "Yes sir, what can I say!"'

Some months after the election, Sello Thulo and I were sent to the Free State by the SABC to see what progress the provincial government was making under the new dispensation. As a counterpoint to the image of Nelson Mandela surrounded by South African military men during his inauguration as president, Free State premier Mosiuoa 'Terror' Lekota was responsible for one of the strongest visual moments of change on television: the statue of Hendrik Frensch Verwoerd swinging and tumbling on cables as it is lifted from its pedestal and loaded on to a truck.

The new government of the Free State was all fired up. The top political leaders were in charge, and it was exciting to walk in the corridors of power and see comrades in the offices, and coloured and black kids I once taught behind the desks. 'Hi Miss, how could anyone have predicted this?' one of my ex-pupils asked. Although he worked in the Department of Finance, he showed me a card he kept in the right-hand drawer of his desk with this mnemonic written on it: *onmiddellik* (two deeds, two lies) and *interessant* (one ring, two shoes). 'This is what you taught me and I will never ever misspell those words.' My hair stood on end. I had never suspected that one of my students would use my unique Afrikaans spelling techniques to boost his confidence as an economist. But he was filled with the idealism of progress and reconciliation.

'Easy it is not,' he confessed during the interview. 'I mean, how does one create a Finance Department, Miss? The Free State's funding has always been handled at national level, now we suddenly have to open a full-blooded Department of Finance. And people have problems. How much power does the Department have? Who may open accounts for it? Who should sign the cheques? Can you open an account at any bank or does the state have a preference? Exactly how do provincial powers differ from the national ones? What are the priorities? All of this will determine the processes preferred by this provincial government. If development takes precedence, we will have to work out processes to encourage it. What are these? Finances are not merely records of income and expenditure.'

I was impressed. But he had just paused to take a breath, and went on again: 'Before this, you need offices and telephones and furniture. Who should buy this? Should there be tendering procedures? Do you get somebody who has been fitting out offices for years or do you use a new affirmative action group? Are there any requirements for the location of a Department of Finance in a city? Must we be close to the Legislature? In the centre of town? How many people may work in this Department? Then there is the mistrust between officials from the old system and those coming in new. What are they not telling you? Can you go ahead and do absolutely everything you think is important? Or must you wait for instructions from Pretoria? But the most annoying is: the old guard leaks everything to the media. Practices we have inherited from them now leak out into the media like big, corrupt, evil, black swamps – as if we invented them!'

Later that day, Sello and I drove on to Bloemhof, where Cas Human, MEC for Agriculture, was giving a speech to a large group of farm workers. Because the meeting was held in the township, there were no white farmers present, but the hall was packed with unemployed people.

'Our dream is that every person in South Africa should have enough food to eat. And this is possible. If we can give each family one cow, three goats, three African chickens, two hares, spinach, cabbage and carrot seed, one mulberry tree and a couple of silkworms, you will not only be able to eat, you will also be able to send your children to school. You can earn R170 with one cow, less feeding costs. The goats will provide milk and meat, the chickens will lay eggs you can eat or sell, the hares you can eat for the protein, the silkworm cocoons we will export from the Free State to China, and with just one shoebox full of silk spinnings you can pay the school fees of three children.'

The audience sat listening with blank faces. Cas Human is white, but he has a respectable struggle background in the eastern Free State. 'My biggest problem is the hares,' he told us afterwards. 'The people don't want to eat hare meat. I organized a special hare evening with roast hare, potjiekos hare, hare meatballs, hare burgers, but people didn't want it to pass their lips.' 'He calls it hare,' one of his black assistants tells Sello, 'but actually it is rabbit. And the people who slaughtered the rabbits say they are not at all like the veld hare – they are much more bloody and kind of spongy.'

Before the end of the first term, both Terror Lekota and Cas Human had been removed from their positions, and the Finance Department was being kept on a tight rein by Pretoria.

chapter one

To melt into blue. To translate longing into the light blue loosening of sound. To stand looking up at the boy on the steps – and be born into blueness.

School case over the shoulder, looking up, being hauled from drowning in one sweep right up into the clearest, most open heart of blue. Slippery wet and breathing for the first time.

The boy on the steps in the pristine white shirt, the neat school tie, the dark, straight hair, the boy, first and foremost, had eyes.

How does she write the blue? How does she write the boy?

Her life has begun.

chapter two

He sits behind her. He leans over her to point out where her maths equation has gone wrong. He lisps slightly. His thin wrist. His fingers lightsome around the strict line of pencil. His soft cheek hairless. When he looks at her, she reels down into his eyes.

Through the classroom window she notes the airy amphibrach of birds against the sky.

How does she write the stars suddenly in her mouth? The warmth. How does she write light?

CHAPTER FOUR

THE N1 COILS LIKE A SMALL INTESTINE through the northern Free State with villages and towns attached like festering glands. Where Winburg used to be, new RDP houses stand right up against the highway. Ventersburg clings to both sides of the N1. On one side stretches an enormous squatter camp as far as the eye can see. On the other side a tiny collection of plots, houses, shops and garages. How on earth does such a small commercial area carry such a large poor neighbourhood? Where does everybody work? What do they live from?

The closer to Kroonstad, the more my eyes fall into place. I have come to accept that there is earth that never leaves one's soul. My ancestors were one of the first six Boer families who settled along the Valschrivier long before the Great Trek. For eight generations my story has run with this town and this river. My great-grandfather, Danie Serfontein, was the first member of parliament for Kroonstad after the Anglo-Boer War. My family fills the entire district. On the banks of this river, I was made.

I cross the bridge spanning the river like a harp. I turn off to the right in order to go and greet the river before I continue on home. What the hell? ... where are the willows? They must have been chopped down. While I'm looking for them, I almost drive into a tree trunk. An enormous pine has fallen across the road. It must have happened a while ago, considering the weeds growing amongst the roots. I see heaps of paper and tins. I smell before I see the plundered toilets. On the front steps people have obviously been shitting at arm's length from one another. The lawns have vanished under weeds and rubbish. The playground with its ancient slides and swings is decomposing into rusty colours.

I reverse so fast, I get tears in my eyes.

'It's the new town council,' is the answer given to me later. 'The previous council wanted to start charging for use of the facilities at the river, but the new council said it was just an excuse to keep black people out. The park is now in the hands of the people of Kroonstad, and this is what the people of Kroonstad have done with it. Christmas and New Year it is so packed and aggressive there, no white person dare go near it.'

My family now stay in town. Middenspruit, our farm, is being leased to someone with the option to buy, and my two brothers and their wives are working full time. Farming does not pay any more, they say. The new government took away the subsidies, and overheads have rocketed to the extent that one makes almost no profit, and cannot recover from a failed harvest. In addition, theft has had such a negative impact on the value of the land that they can no longer borrow money from the bank. Besides, our farm is so close to town that everything is carried off – mealies, wheat, peanuts, potatoes, sheep, cattle, chickens, pigs, diesel, bakkies. The only thing you can farm with a bit is sunflower. But that is often destroyed by flocks and flocks of doves. A new kind of hybrid racing dove thrives in the silos of Kroonstad, and thousands of them sweep through the sunflower fields of the northern Free State during the day.

While I'm waiting to pay for bread and some fruit at the café, I read a letter by Mr H.J. Nolte in the local newspaper: 'It all started in the sixties, when the money was changed from pounds to rands and my overdraft in effect doubled. Just when I got used to this, they changed pounds to kilograms and my harvest was reduced to half its size. Then they changed inches to millimetres and since then it hasn't rained an inch. Then they brought in a thing called Celsius and from then on it was twenty degrees colder and no mealies wanted to grow on my farm any more. Then morgen became hectares and my farm was suddenly half the size of what I inherited. However, the moment I put my farm on the market, miles became kilometres, and then it was so far out of town that no one was interested!'

Andries and Hendrik, my brothers, have organized that I stay for a few weeks in the rondavel at Middenspruit. There is still a telephone line available for my computer.

I drive out to our old farm. The sign that previously read 'Trespassers will be prosecuted' has been replaced by a sign displaying the head of a leopard, above the words 'Mapogo a Mathamaga'. Slowly I drive on to the *werf*. A bath has been abandoned under a thorn tree. The orchard is overgrown. I try not to draw any conclusions.

A strange black man unlocks the rondavel for me. I carry my luggage inside, open the windows, make myself a cup of coffee and sit on the stone bench outside in the late afternoon sun. I hear turtle doves, sounding as they do only on this farm. Sparrows dart with tiny scratchy sounds from the rainwater pipes. My throat feels thick and ostracized, my chest hurts with the indescribable intimacy of belonging and loss. This is my place. Place that in a way never really wanted me. Place that bore my love so fruit-lessly. For its veld. For its sky. For its spruits. For its grass and trees. For its horizon, which carries every other horizon I have dreamt of. A love that longs for land.

They can sell it, take it, divide it, pawn it, waste it. That will be all right. If only, until I die, I can come and sit here. So quiet. So here. So completely dissolved into where I belong. I will never lay claim to it. Ever. If I can just come and sit here, in the autumn, with my heart so light-headed.

A shadow falls over me. It is the new man of the farm. He introduces himself as Joep Joubert. Joep looks stressed out, the way only a man who has recently entered into thousands upon thousands of rands of debt at the Land Bank can look. It probably irritates him that I am sitting here. Reminding him of how whites can fail.

We exchange a few awkward pleasantries. Then I ask: 'What is that sign there at the gate?'

He sinks into one of the wire chairs. '"Mapogo a Mathamaga" means "the spots of the leopard", but apparently it has to do with a specific colour.'

Then I recall. Years ago, one of my colleagues did a story about a black vigilante group, which had arisen in a township somewhere in response to the police's failure to act after a spate of murders. My colleague's story was about a robbery at the local school. Thousands of rands worth of computers, heaters, radios, a photocopier and curtains had been stolen. After repeated calls, it became clear that the police were not even interested enough to put in an appearance, so the principal called in Mapogo a Mathamaga. Mapogo then drove around the township, with a megaphone mounted on a bakkie displaying the head of the leopard, and announced that if the stolen property was not back at the school by the following morning, Mapogo's men would come and fetch it themselves. When the principal arrived at the school the next morning, the goods were stacked up neatly at the front gate.

'The vigilante group?' I ask.

'Mapogo is not a vigilante group!' he says indignantly. 'It is a black security com-pany that delivers service of the highest quality. All the farmers in the area have joined up.'

'My colleagues tell me that farmers join up because the head of Mapogo speaks pure Afrikaans and still uses the word kaffer.'

'Your colleagues talk nonsense. I personally joined Mapogo because times have changed. It's not like in the days of your family, when a farmer could work with the army to make his farm safe. This civilian watch stuff is just crap. The time is past when you can provide safety with other white people. Now you must work with black people. And the head of Mapogo is a man you can work with. You wouldn't believe how much success he has had.'

An old bakkie with what looks like cages at the back drives up to the yard. Joep jumps up and goes to talk to the driver. When I hear his cellphone ring, I go inside to wash my cup and sort out the computer. But he is back.

'I want to finish my story about Mapogo.' I see he is wearing three cellphones in three separate holsters on his leather belt.

'Right at the beginning, the farmers organized a meeting to listen to the head of Mapogo. He said: "That old Jonas who has worked for your father and your grandfather all these years, that same Jonas who you are sitting with today, it is he who steals. Listen to what I have to say today." We all paid our cheques for a year's membership, and the next week he came to drop off his people here. Three of them. With just a sjambok and a bag of mealie meal. And they were thin, hey. Their skin was that kind of shedding grey colour that only a black who is fucking hungry can have. Those three work together for a month, then he rotates them. To prevent corruption, collusion, factionalism or bribery, Mapogo makes sure that they never work in the same area with the same colleagues again. So they just slept here in the farm-school building. The people here on the farm were very upset when they saw the Mapogo sign, but I told them, "Only the guilty need be afraid."'

'Yes, but remember that in the days of P.W. Botha it was said the police could catch a lizard and beat him until he confessed to being a crocodile. Doesn't Mapogo also work like that? They catch anybody and beat him until he admits his guilt.'

'No, it doesn't work like that. Everybody is so scared of them anyway, they tell you right away who did the stealing, even before you ask. But listen to what happened. One morning, they phoned Klein Neels Uys just as he was about to tee off at the golf course, and told him one of his bakkies had been stolen. And you know Klein Neels doesn't take crap from anybody. So he phoned Mapogo and said, come, let me see now. They say that before Klein Neels Uys reached the ninth green, Mapogo phoned him: we have the man. Klein Neels drove out there and *wragtig* there sits the black man who worked for his father all the years. Old Anneries! You remember Anneries. And then he even confessed to stealing some other bakkies before and selling them to a middleman in Botswana. So you can sleep in peace tonight.'

The new farmer on my birth-ground leans back, takes out one of his cellphones and pushes some buttons.

'Three cellphones?' I ask.

'Ja, to keep my businesses separate. This one is for personal stuff and the farm, and the others are for hunting transport and white-maize transport.'

I don't understand a word. Hunting? Maize?

'I have a small grinder for white mealies. I sell to shop owners in neighbouring countries where there is only yellow maize on offer. People are prepared to pay quite a lot of money for white maize. Actually, I'm just sending messages now to let the buyers know where to wait near the border.'

I leave the legality of this aside. 'And the hunting?'

'Nowadays, it pays better to have game on your farm than cattle. You can earn more for one lion than for a herd of cattle. If you go towards the Kalahari, in those small towns where people used to be really poor, these days you will see only new bakkies in the streets, and the rugby field of the school is packed with private planes, so well off have the farmers become there.'

'How are you involved?'

'If a kudu on your farm pays more than an ox, then it is better to breed game rather than cattle or sheep. So now you get farmers breeding lions, cheetahs, giraffes, white springbok, anything rare. Some also breed birds. Yes, birds,' he answers my sceptical look, 'hunters come to South Africa specially for birds. Birds are big money. In any case, this is where I come in. If a farmer has sold a package of one lion, two kudus and five partridges or whatever, then I transport these items from the game breeders to the hunting farms. At the height of the hunting season, things get so hectic that sometimes I have hardly dropped off the lion when the hunter pitches up to shoot it. Usually we drop the lion off at night. Then the trackers can go to the hunters the next morning and say, come quickly, we have at last found the spoor of that cunning lion. Then they can lead the hunters to the animal by some roundabout route, scaring them stiff with narrow escapes. The same with the birds. You take them in cages to the farms, feed them there for some months, and then take away the cages just before the hunters arrive.'

'But isn't it in some way ... unfair?'

He bursts out laughing. 'Unfair to whom? You breed cattle for hides and meat, sheep for wool and meat, you breed lions and buck for skins and trophies and meat. But more importantly: you are able to keep your farm ...' He says this deliberately. I change the subject.

'Is Isak Mokokoane still on the farm? The one who grew up with my father?'

'Your brothers are renting a smallholding for him near town. Old Fanie Bouwer's place. He lives there now with his children and grandchildren. He didn't strike it lucky with his offspring, though. He has this no-good child who has been in prison twice for stock theft. Two of his other sons have died recently of Aids. Of course, nobody admits it's Aids, because then the funeral policies don't pay out. We call it here "a House in Virginia" – for HIV, you see – if we don't want people to know what we're talking about. Isak still comes around here now and then, completely cuckoo, then he starts hoeing furiously in the orchard or shouts at my labourers for not watering the trees properly or pruning them. I try to explain to him that those days are over. Fruit orchards and dairies don't pay any more. We only do what makes money now. The only one left from your time is Laetia. Her child Meshack drives my tractors and he's the union's shop steward here. A big *meneer* now. Fuck it, and I dare not slip up with lunch hours, overtime or bonuses, or I have the bloody union on my farm. The other day, I'm not joking, Meshack laid a formal charge against me that I swear too much. Can you believe it? He had the cheek to say that they didn't want to be exposed to such obscene language. I explained to him that this is just the way I talk. I speak this way to every-body. Ja, he said, but that word "*drol*" – that is the word that bothers him so much, words like "fuck" and that I can use, but "*drol*" bothers them deeply. I ask you. So I am told by the union not to say "turd" on my own farm. Christ, a man must know his tongue from his turd these days!'

I let the words 'my own farm' go, thinking how could you *not* support Meshack's point of view, when you see how Joep Joubert's tongue shoots the 'd' forward towards his teeth, then revs it up against the 'r', and at last lashes the word out with the 'ol'. In the meantime, two other bakkies have driven up. It is getting dark, and I quickly ask Joep if he knows someone who can link up my computer. As he walks over to the bakkies, he makes a call.

When I open the little fridge, I see that my mother must have been here. There is some wors, eggs, a tiny tub of butter, and a bread she has baked. Although she's moved to town, she goes on living as if she is still on the farm. She buys milk from a nearby farm to churn her own butter in the small hand churn she inherited from my grand-mother. She bakes her own bread and makes her own wors. In her garden, she has planted spinach, carrots, beans, tomatoes, herbs, as well as cuttings from the grapevine her great-great-grandmother brought from the Cape, pips from the orange trees her mother planted in specially drilled holes in the sandstone of Middenspruit, and two cuttings from roses. Special roses brought to the Free State a century ago: the *Rosa odorata* with its golden-crimson loose-petalled buds given to my family by the Hofmeyr family in the Cape, and the Malmaison rose, from Ds Andrew Murray's wife, with blooms the size of saucers, silky light-pink petals folding layer upon fragrant layer. Every season, she bullies these two rose bushes through serious bouts of mildew and bugs, then nurses the few old-fashioned blooms as if her life depended on them.

The man to link up the computer is at the door. His name is Ferdi. With the speed of youth, he plugs and shifts and clicks, while explaining: 'Tannie must know, the whole country's computers are connected to Pretoria and Jo'burg. So one struggles a bit to dial in from the farms.' And he spreads his large hands open like two webs, 'Tannie can ask Oom Joepie.'

When he is out the door, I type in my password. With a ringing and scratching like broken glass, my modem struggles to connect, and in my imagination I see it as a scruffy farm hen peck-pecking at an overloaded wire web, battling to get an opening into the executive chicken stream to Johannesburg. Then I am in! I start downloading my email. After a few seconds, there is a snap like a set of false teeth and I am discon-nected. I run outside and stop Ferdi before he can drive off. He comes back to look, he phones, changes a couple of settings and eventually I am back in, but a single email takes three minutes to download and I see that fourteen more are still coming. By the third message, I am disconnected again. My cellphone also doesn't have a signal from inside the rondavel.

'If you walk up to the barn and climb on top of the platform for the tractor engines, you will get a good signal,' says Joep. When I get to the barn, the missed calls suddenly leap accusingly on to the little screen.

chapter three

The vacation drifts on in one long flotsam of hay fever and too-bright sun. In the morning around ten o'clock she starts to sneeze and itch and swell. By eleven she drinks two antihistamine tablets. By twelve she starts sleeping the long summer day away. By evening she wakes and walks eagerly, like a werewolf, into the cool dusk. So she gets to know the farmyard, the veld under an awning of stars. At night a wanderer, wild and wet with dew. She climbs on to the roof of the barn. Scales the windpump. At the family graves, she sits on the enclosing wall in the hope of seeing the unseen. The moon is caught in the eucalyptus grove. She smells it. But she never sees the unseen. No ghost, no foreign breath.

She stands still in the darkness and observes the homestead. The lamplight, and her enormous family going about its noisy business. That is what the house is. Too full. Too many. Too many voices, too many sounds, too many bodies, too many vegetables, too many demands. Through one window she sees her mother at the typewriter. She knows her mother is writing a serial story for the women's magazine *Sarie Marais*. Tomorrow morning she will shift the typewriter off the work surface of the closed-up Singer sewing machine in order to bath the latest baby. Then she will store the baby bath, and reseam sheets or make clothes and nappies during the day. After dinner, the typewriter will appear once again in its place.

Like her mother, she also writes. Not stories but a diary. Like her mother, she writes at night. Her daily truths, because she lives twice.

Gradually the house becomes quieter and darker. When the last lamp has been snuffed out, she creeps to the rondavel. The lamp she lights shines as if in a treasure chamber. Shelf upon shelf of books. Her mother's German and Dutch books, the Afrikaans books she has already read through. She can say that she has read through all the prose in Afrikaans, she thinks. On the English shelf she started with Balzac. Now she is at Dostoyevsky. But first she makes an entry in her diary. She has been keeping a diary ever since she learnt to write. Small ring-bound maroon books in which she conjures her ordinary life into gripping reports about aggressive boys, backward teachers and furious outbursts between her mother and her. Then she lies on the carpet plunged into the harsh, dark, unfathomable world of *Crime and Punishment*, until the sun rises. She eats porridge, and while her brother and sister break into a rumpus of fighting and screaming, the baby yelling, she looks down at the spoon in her hand and gives her first sneeze.

chapter four

Her earliest memory is of lying on a high white bed underneath bright lights, looking down at her plain brown sandals. She remembers her mother telling her grandmother: 'Stay with her until she goes to sleep. Every night she relates the whole day in the third person, then she cries where she cried during the day and laughs where she laughed. Let her. If she doesn't get to do this, she has nightmares.' She remembers her mother leaving then for a different part of the hospital. Later they go home together: she with a stretched urethra and her mother with a new baby. Then only can she ask about the meaning of the words 'third person'.

No, it's not true. Her earliest memory is of smelling of pee. Of wetting her pants on her way to the bathroom and hiding in the toilets until the school bell rings. And her hands around her father's tie. A navy and white striped tie. And her hands grabbing the tie. And being pulled by a nurse, but clinging to that tie. The grip of her hands on both sides of it. And how she doesn't make a noise, just hangs on to the tie with all her might, holding her face close to the tie and smelling her father, hoping he will protect her. And how a nurse is pulling her away. And her father's helpless face. And how she is moving away from her father's body, but holding on to his tie. Then her hands are torn loose, first the left, and finally the fabric tears away behind her right thumb. And she sees her father's deeply distressed face. It grows smaller and smaller. A powerless speck at the end of the long hospital corridor.

CHAPTER FIVE

'THE MUSEUM IS CLOSED until further notice,' says the beautifully dressed librarian. 'And the key is with the Municipal Manager.' She smiles very amiably and runs a professional hand over her sheaf of dreadlocks.

My mother looks at me meaningfully. We are here to do research on food in the adjoining Sarel Cilliers Museum. She says nothing, but I can see my mother is wondering what is left of the priceless furniture and artefacts that Afrikaners have given to the museum over the years. In what condition are the minutes of the town council meetings from the previous century and a half, the records of the *moederkerk*, the stacks of Kroonstad's local newspaper (started by the British and neglected by the Boers).

'Wait here, let me quickly get my two books for the week,' says my mother and disappears among the shelves. Under the 'new' librarians everything has changed, according to her. Books are not arranged strictly by number any more, things happen a little haphazardly, with special surprises in between. So you don't work as much from the catalogues as you used to, you browse on the shelves, and it is really amazing what you find.

I look through the library's magazine section for something to read. My hand freezes in mid-air. A sticker with neat capital letters reads: DIE SUID-AFRIKAAN. The only left-wing political and cultural journal in Afrikaans, defunct for six years now. Beautiful! If we are behind the times in Kroonstad, we are at least behind with the right, or should one say left, leanings.

I look around. Nowhere a whole armchair to be seen. Most are peeling their upholstery on to the floor, some have had their armrests torn off. The upright chairs are all occupied by young black people sitting at the tables. In fact, the library is packed with black people. Especially during very cold or very hot weather, people spend their afternoons here, the librarian tells me. Most of them attend college in the mornings and work here in the afternoons. While she's talking to me, two white women put down six volumes each to be checked out. Their worn library cards were pink years ago. As the male librarian stamps the books, dust jackets and loose chapters fly all over the counter. The Afrikaans love stories have clearly been read to pieces. An elderly lady comes to the counter to complain that there are only four large-print books on the shelves.

'There is no money,' the librarian answers my questioning gaze. 'You will see that in the children's section, the Afrikaans books are also just a few. Most of them were so tattered we had to do away with them. And we don't have money to buy new ones.'

My mother appears with two German books – in pristine condition! With deep reverence, the young black man stamps the books. At the exit my mother points out two posters. The first reads: 'This is a Book' (picture of a book follows) ... 'This is the Spine of a Book' (picture of a book spine) ... 'This is called the Index' (picture of an index), and so forth. The other poster reads: 'This is a Book about Facts and Science' (picture of a book about the human body) ... 'This is a book based on fiction' (picture of Nadine Gordimer's *The House Gun*). My mother shakes her head. We walk outside.

'Drive down Station Street a bit,' she says.

A few blocks further, I dart for a parking spot among the taxis so that I can focus on trying to believe the unbelievable. In areola pink stands the Jewish synagogue. Prominently displayed on its dome are advertisements for Iwisa and Taxi Cash and Carry. 'Iwisa feeds the Nation.' The Star of David has been removed from the dome and a lean-to roof built all the way around. Next door is Madiba Cash Loan. I get out of the car to explore. The interior of the synagogue now houses a bustling supermarket. From behind the counter three Indian shopkeepers give me uncomfortable looks. Beautiful woodwork is still visible overhead, and on the carved wooden gallery bags of flour and bottles of paraffin are stacked to the ceiling.

'It seems you will have to rely on *my* book about Kroonstad,' says my mother when we arrive home. 'If I remember correctly there is something in there about food.'

In the early eighties, my mother was asked by the city council to write down the history of Kroonstad. This she did in a book thicker than the Bible. But as I page through, I come upon more information about sewage than food.

'Of course,' she says, 'Kroonstad was a reluctant convert to sanitation. The pit latrine system was the standard for eighty years until the Anglo-Boer War.'

'Heavy fighting broke out in 1901,' she writes. 'The first cases of gastric fever were reported. Plague. The English high command ordered that Kroonstad's health services were to be investigated. The following was reported: (i) Water was not properly purified. (ii) Rainwater collection tanks and wells had been dug, would you believe, next to pit latrines, where all the groundwater "cheerfully mixed". (iii) Animals kept in backyards provided a fruitful source of germs. (iv) To crown it all in Crowntown: the main water reservoir was located next to the black location. How can you save a country with a town like this?'

It seems that the British army stationed in Kroonstad made stern recommendations, but the inhabitants of the town were up in arms. Why should they let their cattle and horses graze in the municipal cattle pens, packed full of sickly English horses? But there was one particular sentence they found unforgivable: 'I, Major General Knox, object to the slipshod way in which the sanitary inspector does his duty.' My word! Generations of inhabitants of Kroonstad had been satisfied with the pit latrine system. How dare he demand that each house build a brick lavatory equipped with buckets? Who does he think he is?

My mother records the bitter protest of the sanitary inspector, Mr P. Steyn, as noted in the town council's minutes: 'Where I had to remove rubbish and slop water in the past, I would now have to carry off buckets of human waste as well. And where indeed should I throw all of the above-said?'

The city council decided that the two former policemen who provided sanitary services to the military should henceforth also take care of civilian needs. The buckets were to be removed twice a week at night. Trenches 1.8 metres deep would be dug outside of town and the night soil was to be dumped in there and covered with a layer of sand.

'"Night soil" is such a nice term in my opinion, as if it is something produced by owls. As if when day comes, the soil disappears.' My mother is busy making *souskluitjies*. 'Page to where it mentions old Strecker. So many of the Tommies who fought here in the war fell completely in love with what they called "the Village among the Willows".'

'The black people called this place "Maokeng", the Place of the Thorn Trees. The

Boere called it "Kroonstad" because a horse named Kroon broke its leg here. Then the British came with "the Village among the Willows". What is it called in the New South Africa?'

'I don't know. Something really unpronounceable. And it was Joseph Orpen, the magistrate of Winburg, who named the town "Kroonstad", not the Boere.'

My mother is a staunch believer in the Kroonstad myth: once you put your feet in the waters of the Valsch River, among the willows, you fall under its spell. You will never be released again. Wherever you go in the world after that, wherever you roam or take root, a nameless longing will always slender through your thoughts. And this longing will only abate when you stand once again on the riverbank and hear the sound of the babblers and the doves, see the blond sandbanks lying like ribbons around the reed, the finches flashing like jewels in the tender green interweave of willow, when you wade into the water, with its warm surface and cold undercurrent, and breathe the fragrance of bark and earth. So she says. And that is why she always insists on being taken to the river on the farm after the first heavy summer rains. Down the bank she struggles with her kieries, wades into the water like someone at prayer, and surrenders to the current. When we meet up with her at the drift, she seems filled with peace.

Here is Strecker. 'Mr A.C. Strecker resigns from the military, acquires a cart and mules, and wins the sanitation contract. By night he disposes of the night soil and by day he fishes in the Valsch River. Strecker confesses to long-time Kroonstad residents that a strange enchantment emanates from the willows, that it brings a spaciousness to his soul he has never experienced before in Leeds, where he hails from. After the war he remains in Kroonstad, sells his night-soil removal business and becomes an energetic champion of the river.'

'This is all about sewage and I want to know about food,' I complain.

'The way people deal with each other's toilet habits will perhaps tell you more about reconciliation than food,' says my mother. 'Your brothers told us how the toilets there on the border were set up in a row without any subdivisions. So you and your fellow soldiers sat and shat together, and it was apparently a much better bonding exercise than eating together.'

I continue reading. Where would the buckets for the new lavatories come from? 'Two Jewish brothers, Jacobson and Jacobson, who repaired pots and pans in town, got the contract to make five hundred night-soil buckets, while the builder Morris was able to retire after building hundreds of outhouses in the yards of Kroonstad. After the war, the Afrikaner bureaucrats returned one by one from exile or from where they had been hiding with family in the big cities. By this time they had themselves experienced a whole world of lavatories. Where have you ever seen, asked an indignant J.N. Blignault of the town council, that buckets, filled to the brim with you-know-what, are picked up and carried sloppily from the yard and emptied into a wagon in the street? Proper cities like East London had access lanes behind the yards for the night-soil wagons. The lavatories were built up against the lane with an opening the size of the bucket in the rear wall. The opening had a proper flap so that the bucket could be taken out and replaced directly with a clean one.

'The English forbade people from keeping animals on their property and also went to work on the streets in general. Hotels had to resolder their sewage tanks to prevent leakage. Streets were sloped to the edges and regulations laid down for storm-water drainage. All roofs had to get gutters, all gutters needed downpipes, and all downpipes had to discharge into the sidewalk gutter. The military authorities acquired a water cart in order to tame the dusty streets. Every day, two stunning percherons trundled slowly up and down in the town centre, spraying the streets and releasing a wonderful, intense damp smell from the ground.'

I close the book.

'Your grandfather always told us how strange it was for them that the ordinary Tommies joined the Salvation Army in their hundreds, while the officers were Anglican or Methodist. Don't close the book, read more. There is a piece about how sometime after the war your grandmother made a big meal for some or other prince. There should be a picture of it.'

I look it up. Nineteen twenty-eight. Indeed, there is a photograph: I recognize the big stoep and sandstone walls of the house at Erfdeel, the Serfontein family farm near Kroonstad.

'Read the text,' my mother goes on, 'where I quote the minutes of the town council meetings.'

The first minute reads: 'The Governor General will visit Kroonstad on 12 October, owing to a slight alteration in the itinerary. He expressed the desire to be entertained in a similar manner to Prince Arthur of Connought [sic], and the Mayor submitted details of the provisional programme for the visit.' And the second, from a month later: 'A letter was subsequently sent to Mr and Mrs J.H. Serfontein, expressing this council's grateful thanks for the services of Mr Serfontein in connection with the visit of His Excellency the Governor General, Lord Athlone, in providing a lunch to over one hundred persons and affording such a splendid opportunity for the Governor General to meet the farmers of the district. His Excellency declared himself highly satisfied with the arrangements here.'

'The services of Mr Serfontein only ...,' I muse. 'What happened to Mrs Serfontein? More to the point: I thought Oupa Kootjie was so furiously anti-English that he would rather have died than host a lunch for the British aristocracy?'

'I expect Oupa was very flattered. The legend has it that Lord Athlone, as a seasoned traveller should, made enquiries through his British connections about where he could experience "the best South African cuisine"! He was told by Prince Arthur of Connaught, a cousin who had preceded him as Governor General of the Union, that he had enjoyed an unforgettable lunch on Tant Lenie's farm in the Kroonstad district.

There is a photograph of that earlier occasion too: the Prince, great-grandma Lenie, Ouma Anna – from whom you inherited your name, your stinkwood bed and those velvet-covered poetry books – and old Ds Klomp.

'So when Lord Athlone came, he wanted to visit the same farm and be treated to exactly the same menu. As Ouma Lenie was too frail by then, her daughter, your grandma, stood in for her. Ouma Lenie – that's her here, the third woman from the right – was the source of my family's celebrated culinary skills. She was known as "the woman who cooked for the angels". According to family legend, Lord Athlone said afterwards: "I had not been told the half of it."'

'Still. Why did Oupa allow it?'

'According to your Ouma, the town council first wanted to do it all by themselves. But when the hotels in town refused on grounds of hygiene to host such a big, important crowd for a lavish meal, Oupa was asked to approach Ouma on the council's behalf. Apparently he said: "For the sake of the good name of this town, we must make sure that this lot of lofty Englishmen don't die of a stomach complaint from Kroonstad hotel food."'

'Did anybody record this famous menu for which Princes and Lords traipsed all the way from Cape Town?'

'I know some of the dishes, because they later acquired the tag "which Ouma cooked for the Prince". But Ouma Hannie still has a letter in which someone describes the meal. You could try and get it from her.'

I immediately lose half my interest and study the picture instead.

The event is perhaps more remarkable than the food. Who are the Boers in the photograph and who are the British? How is it possible that aristocrats from England do not sparkle like diamonds among gravel? I never saw my handsome grandfather wearing a tie, but he has one here – and look at his elegant stance! The Governor General with his walking stick, his hat on my Aunt Nooientjie's head, is standing between my grandfather and my overweight grandmother, the latter for some reason dressed in black. What did they talk about? Nobody could really speak English. The sentence that intrigues me most is Lord Athlone's remark: 'I had not been told the half of it.' Which half? The barbarian half or the civilized half? The resentment half or the bending-over-backwards-to-please-the-upper-class-British half? Which half does one discover over a plate of food?

But a lot is also not evident from the photograph. Suited and stockinged, hatted and tied, calm and amiable, there they all were, standing on the stoep; but you can bet your bottom sovereign that the yard behind the house, under the eucalyptus trees, was teeming with blacks, busy cleaning and washing, scrubbing and plucking, poking fires, keeping away flies and cats, peeling and cutting – and one of them undoubtedly looking after my two-year-old mother. What did they, the unacknowledged victims of the war, officially robbed of any claims to their country, make of all this?

'What do you think of Koos de la Rey Joubert?'

I haven't noticed my father coming in from town, and so I'm taken aback. Who is he talking about?

'The man who rents the farm.'

'You mean Joep Joubert? I don't know – he seems a bit shady, but he's obviously geared to make it work.'

'Ah,' says my father, 'don't judge a man by his jacket. He's got important blood flowing in his veins. He's related to the Nels on the other side of the Swartbergpas, just when you come down the pass, the first farm on your left-hand side. This Nel had a sister who was the mother of the Voortrekker, Louis Trichardt. Her daughters were the mothers or grandmothers of three formidable men: President Marthinus Steyn, and Generals Louis Botha and Koos de la Rey. If you want to go back even further: the freed slave Lijsbeth van de Kaap, daughter of Abraham and Pandoor of Guinea, was the fore-mother of two presidents and two generals: Kruger and Steyn, Botha and De la Rey.' This is as direct a bloodline as my father is prepared to take with him into the New South Africa.

As a very successful sheep breeder, he is a firm believer in bloodlines. Next to his bed lie his Bible and the two-volume *Geslagsregister van die Ou Kaapse Families* by De Villiers and Pama, which charts the genealogies of Afrikaner families. He understood the country best when it was run by the bloodlines he knew or could tease out. Long before a minister, president, newspaper editor or Reserve Bank governor took over, my father had already predicted his rise, as well as the focus of his term, and sometimes also his downfall. All based purely on bloodlines. He absolves many an Afrikaner scoundrel with the words: But bear in mind that he had a remarkable mother, she was from the Swartse of the Overberg (or the Vloks from Sutherland, or whatever). On the other hand, the name of many a top Afrikaner is accompanied by a soft snorting sound through his nose. Then you may assume that his family were either *verraaiers*, joiners or *hanskakies* during the Anglo-Boer War, or supporters of Jan Smuts in later years. The day the Cabinet began to feature more surnames starting with M or N than anything else, he lost interest.

After lunch, I leave my parents to take their afternoon nap and drive over to the township. The road is worse than I remembered, with potholes and washed-out stretches. My car crawls down to the new Maokeng library, where there is a small monument to the fallen comrades of Kroonstad. For some reason it is dusk inside. Behind the counter sits somebody I know. It is Ike! Ike of all people!

Ike from the march (this is what flashes through my mind when I see him sitting there): the make-or-break school march in the late eighties. That whole day the school-children had been confronting the police, pelting them with stones, then running away, burning tyres, then running away. Suddenly, from where I sat marking essays in my classroom, I heard: '*Senzenina* – What have we done? What have we done? Our only sin is the colour of our skin.' But this time sung slowly, with such determined fierceness that my blood ran cold. I stormed from my classroom, bumped into my colleague, Denzil Hendriks. 'We must stop them,' he said. We ran into the street.

The first child I recognized was Celestine Wilson from my Standard Nine B class, who'd got eight out of ten for her essay that very morning. From the corner of my eye, the police were spreading out, taking aim, while a megaphone warned that any child who crossed the line of the stop street would be shot on the spot.

As if in slow motion I saw it happen: how their feet marched closer. Celestine half hidden by the 'Free Mandela' banner, the clever young Ike singing as if his voice was ridding him of his fear. Closer and closer. It felt as if something wanted to tear loose from me forever in order to escape the relentless progress of time. Paralysed, I saw their feet hesitate at the line, heard the song. My eyeballs pulsating against my eyelids.

A metallic click from a gun. I grabbed Denzil's arm. The children did not look at anyone, they focused far ahead of them – on the black neighbourhood over the rise. Then they did it. The battered shoes and bare feet stepped over. They crossed that line. And they kept coming, walking fearlessly, death-defiantly in front of the loaded guns. Denzil and I sank shakily to our haunches. I felt nauseous.

The whole of the next day I was in a state of shock, bewildered by the strongly contrasting emotions the incident had evoked in me. The fear and the anguish, the cowardly hope that they would cross the line, the shame of knowing that if the police shot them, I would never be able to live with myself again. Worse was the thought that these children had crossed a boundary which I had not. Never again would I be able to tell Ike: 'You must do your work, otherwise you will have no future.'

He is smiling from ear to ear. He is the librarian here. Everything is brand new. He shows me the children's books, a whole long shelf of Sesotho, another of isiXhosa and Setswana. Three shelves filled with beautiful Afrikaans children's books. Neatly covered in plastic. Brand new. Ten shelves with some of the best English books. He takes me to the poetry shelf. I shake my head in disbelief – it must be one of the best collections of poetry in the country. I recognize a rare volume by Sankie Mthembi-Mahanyele, the Minister of Housing, published outside the country under her MK name. Work by two of my favourite poets, Keorapetse Willie Kgositsile and Mongane Wally Serote. Every single black poet is here. Also many of the English classics. There is poetry from the Caribbean, from the Horn of Africa, Egypt, Mali, a thick collection from Ghana, several Nigerian poets, and a whole shelf devoted to Ngugi wa Thiong'o, Wole Soyinka and Chinua Achebe. What an absolute treasure of books! Ike smiles proudly.

A young boy with a neat school blazer is busy taking out the books one by one, opening them and putting them back.

'He's looking for a particular book, but since our index system is not online, you cannot search for a title by number. You must go through them one by one.'

The library in town is full of people studying. But here there is nobody?

'With the big rains, some of the roof collapsed.' I notice the caved-in corrugated iron for the first time. 'During the night hundreds of books got wet. Now the power is not working and it is too dark here to sit and read.'

Not fixed in three months?

'We've reported it a few times, but the province hasn't sent anybody yet.'

Well, I think as I'm driving home, at least one can see that the Free State provincial library services are buying books – even if they end up in places where they cannot be read. But where the new town council is spending its money remains a mystery. In the white neighbourhoods the streets are full of potholes, half the street lights don't work, the river looks like a pigsty. Large amounts of commercial space are standing empty. On the flyover, weeds and grass grow knee-high against the wire fence, and there is a healthy harvest of mealies, wheat and even sunflowers in the cracks and holes. Where has all the money gone?

Back at the rondavel I discover that all the farm telephones in the area are 'offline'. The problem has been reported, but we will have to wait, says Joep, it could take as long as a month to fix. Probably the cables have been stolen, and they take much longer to repair than to steal. If I want to send something, I should put it on disk, take it into town and send it from there.

Cut off from any contact outside of Kroonstad, I work on the 'Food and Reconciliation' piece at night.

chapter five

It is Sunday. The Peugeot station wagon stops under the karee tree and amidst fighting and reprimanding all the children tumble out. She greets no one, but slinks away immediately behind the barn. Eight hundred metres from her grandfather's house lies the old orchard, between dam and stream. 'The Forbidden Garden' is what she calls it. In the dilapidated stone wall is a gate. Without touching anything, she slips with a long, light back through the almost-opening to the inside.

All at once it is as if she is embraced by cool pelts of leaves, the smell of dam water and damp irrigation furrows. Her feet become lanky as a goat's. She stands and smells ... luscious undergrowth, ferns, moss, overripe fruit, rotting leaves, nuts. To the left against the embankment lies the fig-tree avenue like a dark tunnel. She flees through the frank flavour of coppery figs, the leaves rough as sandpaper. Wild geese shoot skyward. Chattering. Until the tunnel opens out into a holy space filled with shafts of fern-green light. In the middle a white stinkwood soars above the other trees and sprays out into the blue. She folds her body intimately around the pale, smooth trunk. Embraces its coolness, flattens her arms along the branches, heaves her head behind leaves. She becomes tree and bursts upwards to sky.

Next to the water she sits. She will sit here until she sees something unusual. Something will come to her from life if she waits long enough. She sits silently. She spots little creatures on the surface of the water which she will later recognize from a poem by C.M. van den Heever as *waterhondjies*, whirligig beetles. The clouds move like mica sails across the dam. She waits. She doesn't stir. Is this how time dies? This place that will quietly breathe on, even if she leaves or disappears? She sits for so long that she sees a tiny flower open as the shadow moves from one side of her foot to the other.

A couple of paces from her he comes sliding lithely from the reeds. His forked tongue in bright-red, moving streaks. His little eyes, beady and old as the world, stare at her as if she has become a tree. With a plunge he disappears softly into the water. She leans forward against the trunk of a willow. She has seen a wonder. It has been revealed to her.

CHAPTER SIX

'I CAN PROMISE YOU that the municipal regulations and systems in place today are a hundred times better than anything we've ever had in this country,' Oom Johnnie Malan assures me. As the former treasurer of a town in the southern Free State, he was 'given a package' by the new regime. But he now earns double his previous salary as the Special Government Budget Advisor to municipal councils. 'Kroonstad has amalgamated with smaller places like Viljoenskroon, Vierfontein, and so on, and is known as ... man, I'd rather not say it, because if you can't click your tongue on the "q", it sounds like a swear word. Moqhaka. And that is exactly what the whites think of the new dispensation here in Kroonstad: a bucket of Moqhaka.'

'What makes the new system better than the old one?'

'In the old days, you had to let your municipality develop organically. Therefore job descriptions, legal responsibilities and all kinds of regulations about contracts developed their own definitions. So every municipality was different, which made sustained policies impossible. Now a whole structure has been worked out which each municipal area has to conform with. For example, now for the first time you can give a training course to the person in each area responsible for service delivery or the payment of accounts.'

Initially, his task was to train municipalities to work out their budgets. Those were difficult years, he says. You plan a workshop over two days. Everyone shows up, but within the first hour, you realize that most people cannot work with a decimal point on a computer. So you spend the whole first day on computer training. Then the initial course has to be followed by a second one to cover the actual work.

'But Oom Johnnie, when I passed through Ventersburg, I wondered how such a small spot of a town can support such massive squatter camps. It's surely impossible!'

'It isn't necessary. The government looks after the squatters.'

My mouth falls open. What does he mean?

'The state pays for the housing, water and electricity of each unemployed person – the "indigent", as they are called. Municipalities receive huge amounts each month for the poor. When a mayor says that he cannot pay his officials because the poorest of the poor are not paying their rates and taxes, then he is lying. The state is paying for the poorest. If a town is bankrupt, it is not because of the poor.'

'Then why?'

'Ask them yourself. Tomorrow is the town council meeting and it is open to the public.'

It is news to me that the country's government is paying for the poor. Actually, I am flabbergasted. Why do we not hear about this?

At my parents' house a strange car is parked in the street. It is Ouma Hannie. She is in town to see the 'specialists', who are attached to a special private hospital in a neighbouring town that treats whites only. Some nurses who were unwilling to move from the old white hospitals to the Boitumelo Hospital in Maokeng bought an old house and fitted it out to the highest standards. You can now have your operations done in the private clinic in Kroonstad, and then recover in the town nearby 'among your own people'.

I'm determined to escape Ouma Hannie. I walk around to the back and sit in the sun to continue reading my mother's own sewage story. She writes:

I was the inspiration behind my father's decision to install a flushing toilet. Ever since I was small, I had been hysterically afraid of hairy worms. Our corrugated-iron outhouse then stood close to a big pepper tree and at certain times of the year the tree was covered with striped hairy worms. Some of them always wandered off and ended up inside the outhouse. And on summer days when the iron sheets would suddenly get too hot for them, they would plop down next to you on the seat. It was terrible to sit in such a trap, already in a state of utter terror about falling backwards into the pit.

My mother lectured me about it: worms are edifying creatures, it is nature's way of getting rid of carrion and germs. Now that I am older, I have come to the conclusion that the youth of today would have a greater respect for life and fear of judgement in the hereafter if they saw more worms. Because what kind of worms do they see anyway? Maybe a skinny little shape in the boarding-school porridge or an insignificant mite larva in the raisins. But when it comes to the real, old-fashioned maggots of yesteryear, operating in their masses and rising up like dough from a dead animal, nobody knows anything any more.

I remember that on my cousin's farm was a deep quarry pit where they disposed of any horses that died of horse-sickness. When I went to visit and we knew that a horse had died, we often went to look inside the pit. Then we staggered back home on unsteady legs, talked in low voices, made up with our enemies, did our homework, sewed on the buttons of our school shirts and helped with the dishes. And promised never ever to go and look again. But next time the call of death would once more prove irresistible.

My final tussle with worms actually occurred when I was visiting my cousin one holiday. Somebody had gone to the toilet the previous night and accidentally dropped the torch into the pit. By the next morning it was still shining lustily down there at the bottom. Of course, we looked down with great fascination. We had to drag each other out of there half in a faint. Because for the first time we had come face to face with the monsters that keep to such dark pits. I swore never to sit on such a toilet again.

Nothing escaped my father's sharp eye. He came to ask my mother: 'What is the child always doing out in the veld and behind the kraal walls?'

Then the story came out. And then I discovered that my father also had a great fear of worms; that my fears were not abnormal, but a legitimate and decent family trait. It was then that he decided to build a water closet.

✧

The next morning I sit in Kroonstad's smart new council chamber and cannot suppress a feeling of pride. All the comrades are here. There is Mamukwa, who arrived at my door years ago, poverty-pale, with a whole string of children in her care, to ask if I would read my poetry at the first 'Free Mandela' rally. Here she sits now in an exquisite white dress. There is Bongani, whom the police assaulted with rifle butts right in front of my eyes during another terrifying march. He has a suit on (the cuffs are perhaps a little too long). Peter Lebase, who spent months in solitary confinement. And so I can pick them out. The mayor is Mr Lebona. I know him from the first democratic national parliament, when he was serving in the Senate.

'I was redeployed to Kroonstad by National,' Mr Lebona says to me in an interview afterwards. 'All the mayors were appointed by the top structures of the ANC, to avoid unnecessary argument and factionalism.'

This innocent comment carries a bloody history. As the new dispensation unfolded after 1994 and the majority got access to the country's resources for the first time, the power struggle in the countryside intensified. If you couldn't make the national parliament, if you couldn't get into the provincial legislature, even as a clerk or a cleaner, then the local government structures were your last chance. Colleagues in KwaZulu-Natal, one of the poorest provinces in the country, told me that people killed to get on to the ANC's final list of local councillors. Imagine. Someone from your godforsaken area has to be on the list. You and the other candidate have been in the front line all these years.

The one who doesn't make it will join the ranks of the unemployed. Have him killed, and you secure the future of yourself and your descendants. This was the context in which the ANC, amidst great criticism, decided to appoint premiers and mayors in each province.

'So, I am responsible firstly to Pretoria for delivery,' says Mr Lebona. I learn afterwards that Ivy Matsepe-Casaburri, another powerful former citizen of Kroonstad, had been sent down specially to berate the municipality over its sloppy attitude and failure to deliver. Apparently, you could hear her shouting at them from the street outside.

I plunge straight in. 'Why is the river looking so bad? It is the only place black people can go and relax for free, where children from impoverished communities can experience the luxuries of lawn and cool water and shady trees.'

'The problem is money. The streets are run-down, the sewage system is collapsing, the entire infrastructure of this town demands enormous maintenance costs. There is no money, it is as simple as that. The reasons are manifold.'

'For instance?'

'Let me start with the previous dispensation. When it became clear that the ANC would achieve a landslide victory during the '94 election, the previous council adopted a slew of resolutions. Among other things, they greatly increased their own salaries as well as their pensions and medical schemes, their travel and other allowances. Before they left, they would gather as much as they could. So when we took over, it was big news – wow, the mayor gets a travel allowance of twenty-five grand a month! But that was not instituted by me.'

'Yes, but people say that the previous mayor did all the work by himself. Now you have appointed three additional people who draw big salaries.'

'Unlike my predecessors, I am a full-time mayor. I do not have any other work that demands my attention. Also, I not only have this town, but three other towns and countless farms under my supervision. I must keep all of this going. To run the financial side, I appointed an economic assistant. To make sure we are up to date with the political demands of the provincial and national governments, I appointed a political assistant. Then I also have a duty to transform Kroonstad, so I appointed a black administrative assistant. Or would you rather have me dismiss the white assistant, with her long years of service? She now works for one of my colleagues.'

The phone rings. He gets up and asks his secretary to hold his calls, as he is busy with an interview. Just as he's sitting down, she calls him outside – the call is urgent. Relieved, I switch off the tape recorder. It is difficult for me to ask these questions, and I am not quite sure why. Perhaps I battle to find a way of making him understand that I am on his side. That my criticism is a sign that I care, that I want him and this town to succeed. Then again, how legitimate is the criticism contained in my questions? If the state of the river bothers me so much, why did I never ask former white mayors why the river close to the township had no facilities, or why sewage was being pumped into it in that vicinity? In fact, I never thought to ask the former apartheid mayors anything. The corruption of white officials, the state of township streets, the lack of libraries and a swimming pool – none of these things prompted me to publish interviews with the mayor of Kroonstad. Now Mr Lebona has to be accountable. It is hard to find a legitimate space to criticize from, but it seems harder still for him not to feel victimized by it. He comes back.

'Should I go on?'

I nod.

'I was telling you what happened here before we took over. Take this: the whites adopted resolutions that contracts for all civil work – engineering and architectural work, medical and catering services – should in future go to specific firms only. They shouldn't be evenly spread among doctors and architects and engineers, no, they should go to those very firms that had been doing work for the council for decades already. The last white council entrenched that privilege. When I asked if they hadn't heard of legislation governing competition and tendering procedures, they told me that these laws don't apply to local governments. One can only laugh. National laws apply everywhere except in Kroonstad.'

'It's true. When I was growing up, Attie Bloem got all the architectural work from the council. For a few years, he made a special ceremony of throwing all the bottles of alcohol he received from builders and clients and officials into the Valsch River. He'd stop on the Sarel Cilliers bridge in his smart Mercedes and you'd just see boxes of Johnnie Walker and KWV brandy falling down into the water. For months afterwards, the schoolboys of the town would be diving there.'

'Well, his closest friends were the town clerk, and a prominent lawyer who also just happened to be big in the Broederbond. When you're that well connected, you don't need to take bribes.'

Tea is being brought in.

'Another reason we're in dire economic straits is that the previous councillors were business people. The council was so closely interwoven with business interests that the waters got muddied, also for the bureaucracy. We have several cases here of maladministration, even theft of government property. You know, the workers from the sewage installation used to work in the gardens of councillors and officials, using the council's lawnmowers, fertilizers, pesticides, spades, picks. The council's equipment belonged to everyone. Some councillors were involved with insurance companies. To evade taxes for the council, they started paying premiums to these companies. We were barely in office when the Receiver sent us an account for over a million rand. None of this could have taken place without close cooperation between council officials and people from the revenue services.

'One of the town's biggest freeway fuel-stops was built on council property. The whole transaction is still shady today. You know, I haven't even been able to acquire a complete asset register for the council. We don't know how much of the land that is being farmed so lustily here around Kroonstad belongs to us.'

'But surely you can demand to be supplied with such a register?'

'Yes, and you get one, but always on the understanding that it may be incomplete. Another thing: during the last couple of years before we took over, people started doing two jobs. A person would leave, but his position and salary would remain and be taken over by others; so you had two riders and three horses. It took us a long time to sort this out. Unfortunately, you can't just stop everything and say: wait guys, let's first get the whole municipal system in perfect order before we carry on.'

'So everything is the previous government's fault, and in the democratic era you haven't been able to recover at all?'

'That's not what I'm saying. We have made many mistakes. I admit that.'

'Such as?'

'The first black mayor bought up a whole lot of smallholdings, at great cost, and while everyone was waiting for the legislation on land to be finalized, he allowed councillors to use these plots. They in turn, without ever having paid a cent for the use of the land, began subletting to all and sundry, and now it's becoming a squatter camp. Everyone there uses free power and water, and we have to carry the burden of the poor and homeless.'

'But that cannot be. The government pays for them. This is the money that keeps a lot of councils going. Apparently, it's the officials, the teachers, the police, those who actually *do* work, who *do* earn a salary, who do not pay. And I hear that you let this happen, otherwise they will vote you out in the next election.'

Mr Lebona looks at me with something like pity.

'No one can vote me out! I was sent by National. You can't blackmail me by threatening not to vote for me.'

'Okay, okay, so the council pays for the poor and homeless.'

'We call them "indigents". But they have to register with the municipality first, so that we can prove to the state that we have so many indigents. And the problem is they don't register. They refuse. Our people are in squatter camps, but they refuse to be labelled poor and homeless.'

'Why?'

'If they are on that list, they are not allowed to open any accounts. They cannot buy an oven or a bed or a fridge on hire purchase. So now you get a house with water and electricity, but you can't buy anything to use in it. We really struggle to put the numbers together, while at the same time we have debts of more than seven million.'

'It seems, though, that the council has not made an example of people who could pay but don't.'

'That is so ... but where do I start? Do I start with a white business? White businesses in town do not want to pay rates and taxes any more, because they say the infrastructure is collapsing. But in actual fact they have been paying too little over the years. If you have a big house or a business in town, where there are tar roads, parking spaces, pavements and proper sewage, then you should pay more than people with big houses and businesses in the township, where all these things are lacking. The businesses say the town has gone backwards so much that they have lost most of their customers, and if we increase anything, they will also leave. So we've had to make some compromises.'

I'm thinking to myself that if he arrests a teacher or a prison warder who could pay rates and taxes but doesn't, he will have a revolt by the emerging black middle class on his hands, which also won't go down too well with 'National'.

'Another problem: how to get the ward system up and running. The whites are not used to consulting anyone. They just appoint people in their own circle. On the other hand, the township is so bent on consultation, that nothing happens there either. They'll be consulting until doomsday. And then the Reformed churches do not want to be represented by a Catholic, nor the Afrikaans churches by an Englishman, nor the black churches by a white ...'

'Whew. So there's no good news?'

'The good news is that the whites have slowly realized that they have to work with us – especially since Marthinus van Schalkwyk signed that cooperation agreement with the ANC. Before then, they told us straight: you wanted everything, now you have it, so go ahead and mess it up, that is all you blacks can do anyway, but leave us alone. Nowadays, they seem to understand that if this place doesn't work, they also lose everything. Everyone must put in his share. In Setswana we say: "*Khumo le lehuma di lala mmogo.*" Wealth and poverty go hand in hand. However, the problems are with the young ones. They do not sound like me. They are in a hurry. They ask, how long are we going to accommodate the whites? It is time we put our foot down and took what is rightfully ours.'

Despondent, I leave the mayoral suite. There seems to be no solution and hardly any enthusiasm for trying. The secretary greets me with a warm handshake. Outside the sun is bright. I phone Oom Johnnie Malan: 'If everybody pays their rates and taxes in Kroonstad, can the town survive?'

He laughs. 'Remember that the backlogs and restructuring of town facilities will take some time and a lot of extra money. I assume the state knows that some towns will never be able to sustain themselves. All I can tell you is that it will be a long process.'

At the robot, someone flashes his lights at me. I recognize the bakkie of my elder brother Andries.

'I'm having lunch with Hendrik at the river,' he says. 'Want to join us?'

'But it is a mess there!'

'Come on, man, don't argue.'

Since my arrival, I haven't found time for a proper conversation with them. So I lock my car and get into his bakkie. First he stops at a tiny shop called The Pot and comes back with cartons of delicious-smelling curry.

'Shin,' he says, 'the best in the world.'

I am surprised. My brothers have always regarded only mutton chops and leg of lamb as meat. To them, ribs were no better than vegetables and shin was dog food. But I don't ask. Everybody is entitled to change. At the Sarel Cilliers bridge he turns right towards the Alexandra bridge and heads for a part of the river where we seldom go. I am pleased to find lots of trees and the grass recently cut. Several people sit fishing. A black family is having a picnic next to their car. Small children run around.

'The owners of the flats here on the banks organize the upkeep of this small part. So it is quite nice here.'

'I am in need of good Kroonstad news.'

'The town is full of surprising secrets, you just have to know how to look. The other day I was driving past Jukskei Park when I saw something that made my eyes pop out. At one of the sandpits where they throw the jukskeis, there was a well-built black boy throwing the *moer uit* with his skei. I stopped to watch. Not just him because he was so bloody good, but the whole group, actually, because it was so bloody ... normal. So I went inside and saw Annatjie there at the gate, Annatjie who was with you and Rina at school, and she tells me this guy Andile or Sandile Nqulwa or something from Khayelitsha is one of the top players in the Western Cape junior jukskei team. So there you have it!'

I love being with my brothers. Both have a keen eye for detail and are masters at turning a phrase. The two of them holding forth around our long dining-room table is one of my most vivid memories of the farm.

Hendrik comes speeding up. From far you can see he is agitated. He jumps out, talking so excitedly that some of the anglers turn around with disturbed frowns. Hendrik is the family's maths boffin. Practically every school holiday, one or other matriculant in the family stays over with him and gets maths lessons twice a day. He is strict and demanding. But our family has achieved a remarkable number of maths distinctions given the fact that we are famously unconnected with numbers. Now Hendrik is so full of story that he will hardly let me embrace him. And he goes on talking while we sit down by the water. Andries and I forget to open the cartons of curry listening to Hendrik's well-worded tirade.

'You know *mos* these right-wingers, they have created a little school for themselves so that they can stay white. But they don't really have money, so they battle to find teachers. The beginning of the year they phoned me and begged me to come and teach maths twice a week until they can find a teacher – as a big favour – and I thought, ag, let me do it. So I take Standards Six to Eight for two and a half hours without a break. But these are obviously children who couldn't make it in a normal school anyway. So you wouldn't say the sparks are flying there. The way you get the maths into them is a deadly affair. So I scold and drive and carry on.

'But this morning, quarter to eight, my child calls me. She says there is a man on the phone. I say just take a message, but she says no, the Oom is too angry. He says he wants to speak to you *now*. Well, then one must try and find out why this guy feels so strongly. I pick up the phone. He says it is Manie van Pletzen on the line, but I still don't quite catch on. He says, do I teach maths at the Afrikaner Support School? Yes, I say. Then he asks: Did you tell my child yesterday that you will donner him? I don't keep a record of these things, I say, but that sounds like my style. So what is your problem actually? No, he says, I can't tell his child that I will donner him. Oh, I say, did he not tell you that I also said I would kill him? Because that I do also say. When I say donner, then I say kill in the next sentence. No, he says, he didn't tell him that. So, I say, that doesn't bother you then? I can kill him, as long as I don't donner him? Is that why you are calling me this morning?

'No, but I must remember that his child has a lot of problems, he put him specially in that school because he is a fearful child. So then I say, but I *want* him to be fearful of me, that is the whole point. I want him to be shit-scared of me, so that he'll do his work. There's no other reason. I see him only once a week, so there must be no doubt in his mind what will happen next week when I get there and he hasn't done his homework.

'Then Manie says, how can I use such language in a classroom? Now by then I had worked out who he was. And I say to him, but very slowly, Manie, let's not you and me bullshit each other here. In your house, the word "donner" is at the bottom of the scale. If we talk about "poes", then we are more or less in the region where the language in your house flaps around. So don't come and tell me this nonsense that I mustn't use strong fucking language. But I get so angry, you know. I say, if you don't like it that I tell your fucking child that I will donner him, then go tell the fucking principal, man! Because your little school is too pathetic to pay me to stand in front of those kids, and now *you* want to come and give me shit! I tell him: you have only one reason to phone me ever again, and that is to say, thanks very much, pal, for helping my child! Otherwise, I say, don't bloody call me ever again!'

chapter six

The sunlight smells of bark. The water tumbles in crocheted waves from the sandstone ridge into the pool. Millions of red-pink willow veins branch along the brook's bed. It is a bright sandstone pool. 'It is the place of a god,' she thinks. On the bank she builds herself from stone and clay a bold god to look across the water. Then she picks flowery tassels from the thorn tree for the sacrificial bowl at his feet. She bows deeply towards the opposite bank. Somebody calls from the house for her to come and eat. 'I will eat no more, I will drink no more, I will serve you now,' she mutters with her mouth against the stone. Before she goes home, she takes off her wristwatch and lays it solemnly down on the flowers.

The whole week at boarding school, the god sits like a warm tongue inside her. 'He will never leave me. He will remain standing because he is god.' She stops reading her Bible and praying. She serves the god of earth and stone and tree. She abhors the God of law and punishment.

The next Sunday, she runs breathlessly to the pool. The god has tumbled forward into the water. The stones lie on the bottom, with the wristwatch gleaming golden amongst them.

'This child is really careless beyond belief,' she hears her mother tell her father. 'She has dropped her grandmother's beautiful little gold watch into the water.'

chapter seven

She lies on her back in the water. Her long hair floats heavily around her. She is offered up to the pool. She pretends her wrists have been cut and she is bleeding out into the water. Suddenly she becomes aware of movement and sees a herd of cattle coming towards the pool to drink. She hears a whiplash. In a flash she draws herself up into a hollow in the sandstone bank and hopes that the willow boughs will hide her face. The cattle drink. Among them walks a black man: Malebo, her grandfather's cattle herder. He opens the fly of his overall. Her whole body stiffens in an anguished warmth. He pees an arc into the water. It is the first time she has seen a grown man's penis. He tugs on the foreskin, then pulls it back and closely inspects the pink tip. Can he see her clothes on the opposite bank? He puts his penis back into his overall. Then he herds the cattle up against the bank to the luscious welts of lucerne field. She is shaking as she climbs out and puts on her clothes.

chapter eight

She is disenchanted with her diary. She also suspects someone is reading it. She dare not write about what really disturbs her. She fears the breaks at school. When she walks out of the classroom, she feels struck down by sunlight. Her whole head whirls and throbs in the light blanching from the school walls. She holds her arm up like a shield and tries to find a shady place where she can sit, her hands covering her face, her eyes streaming with tears. Her mother has given her a pair of old sunglasses. Amidst the taunts of other schoolchildren and the smiles of teachers, she wears them to calm her paralysing headache. She is also the only child with sandals. When the principal sent her home to get properly dressed, her mother came to the school and told him: 'Let the other children's feet stink in their stuffy shoes, but my own child's feet will breathe.' But school breaks have become even more menacing because of a boy named Jannie Lubbe. He has decided that she looks like a maid and therefore should be treated like one. Every break, he smells her out wherever she's hiding, and then roars threateningly: 'Come and clean, *meid*!' She has improvised a broom of twigs to sweep the little cement stoep he and his friends dirty with gravel and rubbish, while they roll on the grass with laughter. Once, she tried to hide in the toilets, but what she saw there was worse than death. She is often absent – stomach pains, chickenpox, measles, bladder infections, burns, faints – until Jannie Lubbe gradually forgets about her.

Then her grandmother dies.

The farmyard is transformed into a gigantic funeral service. All the grandchildren wear white and stand beside the grave. It is the first time she sees her mother crying. And her grandfather just sits and stares. She feels bad that she can't cry. But actually she never cries. Even when she gets a hiding, she bites on her lip and goes to her room, locks the door and starts breathing rapidly, while she stretches her eyes very wide. And then it passes. That evening, she first uses the words 'rend' and 'bewilder' in her diary.

When she reads the entry again a few weeks later, a terrible burning pain shoots up into her chest, as if to wrench her heart apart. And then she cries. She cries for her grandmother. Much later, she puts the book down and pushes her face into her hands and feels her body starting to shake with a kind of ecstasy. The words have not lost their power. The words have kept their content like bottled fruit, and every time she reads them she will experience her grandmother's funeral again. She will never lose it. For the first time, her grandmother's death is really part of her.

chapter nine

It is bitterly cold outside. She has to set the table. Her mother comes in from outside with an armful of wood. She pushes the back door closed with her hip and stacks the wood next to the fireplace. The winter wind jerks at the roof sheets and the windows. Her mother stands at the window and says mysteriously: '*Wie roer aan my deur so vertroulik sag? Kom binne maar vreemdling, dis awend, dis nag ...*'

'What are you saying?'

'Poems. I'm saying poetry about winter. "Who stirs at my door, whose touch is so light? Stranger, please enter, it's evening, it's night."'

'Do you know any more?'

Without turning, her mother says:

Twigs are swerving, branches swaying –
'tis the winter wind a-blowing ...

There stands a mother with her child
lonely in the wind so wild –
and no one there to see her tears,
and no one there to calm her fears.

Die twye swenk, die takke swaai –
dit is die winterwind wat waai ...

Daar staan 'n moeder met haar kind
allenig in die winterwind –
en niemand wat haar trane siet,
en niemand wat haar trooste bied.

She feels as if she is somewhere else. Something else. Not in this kitchen without running water, not her mother, not herself, but in another realm. That night, her mother reads her the whole poem.

✧

In history at school, they learn about the heroism of Japie Greyling. 'Oh, the way they do it is so ... un-visceral!' says her mother, and takes out a book with a poem about Japie Greyling. She reads the part where the British commander tries to force Japie to betray his father's commando: '"Wijs, wijs met jou hand waar die Boere-mag trek, / Of ik skiet jou daar dood waar jij staat, op die plek."'
'Show, show with your hand where the Boer forces band, / Or I'll shoot you stone dead on the spot where you stand.' // 'I'll shoot!' roars the brute, filling his gun with lead, / 'Shoot,' says Japie, 'yes, shoot then dead!'
'"Ik skiet!" brul die wreedaard, en mik al sij skoot.' But then her mother lifts her head and says in a very quiet way: 'En ... "Skiet," seg Japie, "skiet dan maar dood."'
She is completely enchanted. 'Why does the poet say "shoot then dead" and not "shoot me dead"?'
Her mother looks at her as if she is seeing her for the first time. 'If he said "shoot me dead" it would be an ordinary sentence. You have remembered it precisely because of the "then".'

✧

Her mother opens the volume of poetry (it is *Die Vlakte* by Jan F.E. Celliers). This is written on the flyleaf in black ink:

Anna Delport
5 Augustus 1915
Pretoria

Suid-Afrika – 'n moeder in haar weë
wat aan die wêreld 'n nasie gee

'n Boom is geplant

South Africa – a mother in her labour pain
who gives the world a nation

A tree has been planted

'Your grandmother bought this book on the day she participated in the famous women's march to the Union Buildings in Pretoria, to plead for the release of General Christiaan de Wet after the rebellion. She always told us how thousands of Afrikaner women walked in complete silence along Church Street. She used to say that this march had a holy power.'

chapter ten

Pencil in hand, she reads the Bible. She is reading through it from the beginning and underlining every passage she finds striking. 'One doesn't scratch in one's Bible like that,' her grandmother scolds. 'One only marks the passages that cast light on one's life path.'

She is as far as the life of David. She marks these verses: 'And he sent, and brought him in. Now he was ruddy, and withal of a beautiful countenance, and goodly to look to. And the Lord said, Arise, anoint him: for this is he.'

She marks the text where David dances in front of the ark: 'And as the ark of the Lord came into the city of David, Michal Saul's daughter looked through a window, and saw king David leaping and dancing before the Lord; and she despised him in her heart ... Therefore Michal the daughter of Saul had no child unto the day of her death.'

She learns by heart the song of Hezekiah: 'Like a crane or a swallow, so did I chatter: I did mourn as a dove: mine eyes fail with looking upward: O Lord, I am oppressed; undertake for me.'

She shows her mother the following verse: 'And thou shalt eat it as barley cakes, and thou shalt bake it with dung that cometh out of man, in their sight.' Her mother says: 'The Bible finds no action too base, no theme too unimportant to write about, it pays attention to the smallest detail as well as to the most important question: why we are on earth.'

But it is the word used in the farewell between David and Jonathan that haunts her. The verse in Samuel reads: 'And as soon as the lad was gone, David arose out of a place toward the south, and fell on his face to the ground, and bowed himself three times: and they kibsed one another' – *hulle het mekaar gesben*, the Afrikaans text says – 'and wept one with another, until David exceeded.'

What does '*gesben*' mean? What is it that men do with one another when they are crying? Or if they love each other but that love has no place? Her imagination takes flight. *Gesben*. Men are doing something wonderful to one another that is all locked up in that single word. A word that comes to her as new. That can unlock a world for her. In the rondavel, she looks in the dictionary: *gesben*; *ges-ben*; *ge-sben*? Nothing.

'What does "*gesben*" mean?' she asks her mother, who is patching a torn shirt.

'There is no such word,' she says, without looking up from her needle.

That is even more wonderful. Of course it is a forbidden word. She will have to look deeper. In the study of her uncle, a doctor, she tries several books. The word remains closed.

When the big Afrikaans *Companion to the Bible* is eventually published, she turns with great anticipation to the text. And so she discovers that her edition of the Bible contained a printing error: '*gesben*' was meant to be '*gesoen*' – 'kibsed' was nothing more than 'kissed'. They kissed each other and wept bitterly.

chapter eleven

She pricks a circle with an arrow sticking out of it into the skin of her thigh. She rubs ink over it. She is a man. With this she lays down all weakness and softness, vulnerability and emotion. Impenetrable. The fallen willow tree becomes her ship, from which she wreaks death upon thousands; the pool her holy territory, where she awaits the cattle with a flaming reed sabre. She starts moving around mysteriously and observing people. She finds a slimy balloon-like thing on top of her father's wardrobe. She sees her mother playing the record of 'Fauré-lieder' and staring out of the window with tears streaming down her face. She sees her standing at the coal stove and burning stacks of typed sheets. She hears her mother say: 'Men ought to be like library books: divided up according to type. Then you could go and take out a handyman one week, then a historian, at planting time you could get a farmer, and when everything is peaceful, a nice romantic one.' She hears her brother say to his black playmate: 'Show my mother your hands, you are turning white. See, your hands are completely white, your soles as well. You can stay with us from now on.'

chapter twelve

Everybody sits on top of one another in the car. Because she is the eldest, she always gets a window. When the car fills up with breath and need, she stares outside and tries to draw her soul from her body. Then she floats above the car and looks down on everyone. How small and ridiculous they are. Then she flattens herself up against the mountain. Her gigantic cheek caresses the rock. Over the sunflower fields she turns the breasts that must still come to the sun.

chapter thirteen

Her essay has won a national prize for the age group under eleven. She wrote about Elijah praying for rain. When she complained that she was supposed to write an essay titled 'In an instant ...', but nothing had ever happened to her in an instant, her mother told her to take a story from the Bible. 'Pretend that you are somebody else. Take somebody's life and colour it in with your own.' She chose Elijah, and put him in the middle of a Free State drought, looking across the plains, the grass, the dust. And she included the line 'Where your northern wind tumbles the weeds and chases them across the chapped, brackish plains of Africa' (a verse by D.J. Opperman that she had copied into her diary). 'That is very clever,' said her mother.

So she receives a prize of R5. With the money she buys herself a small white hymn book.

chapter fourteen

'Why does your history book look like this?' asks the Standard Four teacher.

'I got it like this, Miss,' she lies. 'I showed it to the trainee teacher at the beginning of the year, but she said I could still use it.'

She's lying. She knows she's lying. But she has her principles. It was she who used ink to blot out the face of Lady Anne Barnard from her history book. Lady Anne is the only woman mentioned in the history book in her own right. But all she did, according to the book, was to host large parties at the Castle in Cape Town. This is simply not good enough. She may have been a flawless beauty, but she doesn't deserve a place in a book of history if she was unable to do something worthwhile with her life.

What she also did was to cut out the picture of the utterly handsome John Fairbairn, fighter for the freedom of the press, to keep in her Bible.

CHAPTER SEVEN

THE TOWN CLERK and municipal manager of Moqhaka is Matshidiso Moadire. Originally from Mafikeng, he arrived in Kroonstad with a formidable weight of experience. I must understand that he has been here only for a month, he says, but he will answer my questions if he can.

'A council sets its budget according to the money it expects to receive from its ratepayers. So if the ratepayers do not pay up, the council cannot deliver services, it is as simple as that. The big problem in Kroonstad is the attitude of its residents. Everyone tries to find a reason for not paying. They think if they don't pay, they are getting it for free. But this is not so. It just means that the poor, once again, are paying for those with money. But it is very difficult to get people to pay. To cut off someone's power or water is a cruel thing, but at least it gives you some leverage. People need water and electricity. But what do you do when people refuse to pay municipal taxes? As soon as a road is tarred in the centre of town, there is unhappiness in the township: we will not pay taxes, because you only tar the roads of the whites. Now this is a perception I need to change; after all, the centre of town belongs to everybody. If the streets and services in the town centre look good, and attract business and investment, it benefits all of us. Then there's the other side of the coin. The moment you tar a road in the township, the white businesses complain: you are tarring roads in an area where nobody even owns a car, while my clients practically need a 4x4 to get to my shop. I won't pay taxes.'

'But I've been told that the old tension between a politically driven council and a civilly minded municipality is still prevalent in Kroonstad,' I say. 'If the municipal manager cuts off the services of a councillor, policeman or principal, they start to organize against the ruling party. If the manager wants to seize and auction off the defaulter's assets to pay for his debts, the mayor derails the proceedings to protect support for his party. I hear that many towns just drift deeper and deeper into debt, until the state has to intervene. How does one prevent this?'

'There are mechanisms. If I find the council or the mayor interfering with my duties or even trying to blackmail me, there is a special provincial structure I can go to. But the issues are complex. You must remember that the real struggle in South Africa is happening here in the ordinary towns and districts, where access to resources is being worked out. The national politicians go about their business, things are sorted out in the provinces and the big cities, without making much of an impact on the lives of ordinary individuals. They simply hear the names of the politicians changing, as they come and go. But at the level of the town or district, you touch the lives of each resident. And it is going badly.

'What I personally find the hardest to handle is the way people fight blindly to hang on to what they have. They don't have another plan to offer, they don't come forward with proposals, they just undermine everything. They refuse to believe that they may gain by cooperating. And it doesn't bother them that they may lose everything. This includes blacks and whites. One white man told me straight, "Not in my lifetime will I lose what I have. And my children are already overseas." The black salaried worker says, "You can try and take from me. But remember that the youth do not believe this nonsense about sharing and reconciliation. If you take from me, they will rise up and take everything. Because the country belongs to us.'"

His secretary brings us tea. She is white. As he's putting in sugar, I say, 'There are stories that the previous town clerk refused to vacate his post and now the town has to pay both his salary and yours.'

He sidesteps the comment. 'I said to everybody in the beginning: I drive the delivery bus. Those who are at the back trying to stall the process – I will pull them along; those who hang on to the sides trying to divert us – I will pull them on board; but those who stand in front wanting to stop the bus – we will crush them, we will not stop, we will run them over, it doesn't matter what colour they are. We want a better life for all. The hardest fight is here on the ground. The challenge of resources.'

'Now why does the river look so bad?'

'Yes, can you imagine,' rolling his eyes, 'that one could let such an asset go to waste. Look at the towns in the Free State. Those that thought "Tourism", like Clarens, are providing work for hundreds of people. It is a thriving town. Kroonstad is close to Johannesburg. So why would anybody stay over here or drive out here for the day? Because of the river! We are next to the N1, there is an airstrip. If the riverbanks and the amazing dams were properly developed, you could create a refreshing little paradise here. Kroonstad is busy setting up black farmers and this might encourage visits from school groups. The town has so much potential, but people fight each other over a rubbish bin here or a pavement there. My biggest task is to convince people that Kroonstad and its river are for all of us.'

'People say the town is "Africanizing". Would you say that's a fair description?'

'Look, I know what they're trying to imply – that it is deteriorating, becoming dirty and falling apart. But I say the town is "Africanizing" in that it's transforming into a place that reflects the past of all its inhabitants and their dreams for the future. This requires an important shift, which people, both black and white, find hard to accept at times. We, as blacks, cannot and need not fit in with the dreams of whites any more. They, living in a town where most people are black, have to fit in with our dreams. And we have incredible dreams for Kroonstad as a home to all of us.'

⟡

The pharmacist Braem Schmiedt is standing outside his pharmacy. Ablaze with fury. 'You see, I arrive at my shop this morning seven o'clock, my usual time, and here I find a woman sticking her home-made poster on my shopfront. I said to her: take it off! Do you see any other posters here? This is my shop and I am proud of how it looks and I don't want anything stuck on it. I am going to write a letter to the newspaper that people have no pride in this town!'

Once upon a time, Braem's father, Cyril Schmiedt, charmed the town with his sign-board: C. Schmiedt and See Better. In the late forties there were eighty-four Jewish families in Kroonstad. Concerning the community life of Kroonstad Jews, the famous journalist and newspaper editor Joel Mervis wrote in the *Zionist Record*: 'I believe what affected me more powerfully was the Synagogue, which was a monument to the intense, almost fanatical Jewishness which Kroonstad's Jewish elders had left behind them in places like Kovno and Motol. The Kroonstad Jewry had a two-tiered society: foreign parents and local-born children. By the time the children were ten they were better educated than their parents. My idea of a hundred percent, bona fide, genuine Shul is the kind of Shul we had in Kroonstad. This has affected my attitude to and my judgement of Jewish ritual ever since.'

According to council minutes of August 1903, the Jewish community had asked for a cemetery and land for the building of a synagogue. 'The Jews became a very blessed influence on Kroonstad after the war,' my mother writes in her book about Kroonstad. 'As penniless residents they opened their little shops with government subsidies gener-ously doled out to the English. And they didn't differentiate. Boer and black man were treated on the same footing. In addition, they did not see it as their personal respons-ibility to transform the Boers into English people. While some could not read and write, they could mostly speak Afrikaans and Sesotho, and their servants Yiddish. They didn't send their children away to private schools like the English, but to school in Kroonstad, where Hebrew was a high-school subject until the mid-fifties.'

'We are four Jewish families left in Kroonstad,' says Braem Schmiedt. 'We had to sell the synagogue and bring people in from Johannesburg at great expense for the cultural events to make up the quota of ten for the minyan. My children want me to sell everything here and go and live with them in the Cape. I have thought about it a lot, but you know, it is my place here. This shop here in the main street was set up by my ancestors. This is who I am, this ...' and he indicates the pharmacy around him. 'For generations, we have been looking out of this door on to this main street. On these riverbanks I came by my wits. I can't ever go away. This is my place. If they just don't stick this crap on my shopfront!'

He takes me to the ordinary three-bedroom house in Moll Street that has been turned into a kind of mini-synagogue. The Star of David cut from the dome of the synagogue-turned-bazaar has been welded to the front door. A beautiful stained-glass window with the Star of David motif opens to the street. Inside, what was formerly the living room has been furnished with the old synagogue's beautiful wooden pews, and there are richly beaded velvet drapes with tassels. Braem beckons me. Turning several combination locks, he opens a safe: I blink my eyes. In the bland February daylight, in this prefab suburb with its ordinary sounds of vacuum cleaners and dogs, maids chatting and children playing, the precious colours of long-cherished treasure suddenly glow: the Torah, the holy word. 'One of the scrolls is here, the other is being kept elsewhere until we need it again.' And Braem holds the scroll, as if he feels loved by merely holding it; and the scroll, one feels, has always loved to be looked at. To be touched. Both of us stand soaked in this ancient luminosity of providence. And the day gets its depth. He puts it back reluctantly, carefully, and the afternoon turns ordinary. The small bedroom is a vestry, hung with portraits of well-known people who have played an important role in Kroonstad, as well as a series of photographs of Rabbi Cyril Harris, the Chief Rabbi of South Africa, closing down the old synagogue.

'We are four men, of whom two are already too ill to attend Friday evenings. But the two of us who can, come regularly. When I went to Johannesburg for my bypass surgery, I phoned Wally and told him: "You have to go, please man, you must go. Even if we are one, we have to go. We have to go. If we don't, we are letting go of Jewishness."' His voice quavers. 'Go to the cemetery. See how they have plundered the small Jewish funeral parlour. They have ripped out the washbasins and toilets and simply shattered them. If they took these things for themselves, something would make sense, but I find it hard to stomach mere destruction.'

'What is the matter with us Afrikaners?' asks my mother when I tell her about the visit to Moll Street. 'If you don't go, you let go of Jewishness! My God, how I envy them! Can you imagine an Afrikaner ever saying a thing like that? Oh no, we are only too glad to get rid of Afrikanerdom.'

It is four o'clock and we have coffee and warm rusks fresh from the oven, which my mother and I eat with dripping Marmite and my father with apricot jam.

'I'm trying to get a grip on the idea of criticism. When and how does one give it and what does one do with it? Were you criticized when you came to power in 1948?'

'What are you talking about! "Criticized" is much too mild a word – we were ridiculed, derided, disdained, reviled. It was simply a continuation from the Anglo-Boer War, when we were described as hairy barbarians, *takhare* and backvelders. Everything we were was worthy of ridicule, our language, our political leaders, our intellectuals, our newspapers, our universities, our music, our literature or what we dared to think of as one, even our bodies – fat, coarse women and bearded, spitting men. Nothing we had was worthy of respect. We were simply lazier, more stupid, more corrupt than any English person.' My mother closes the Marmite jar and puts a doily over the jam. 'It is hard to describe now, but you felt that you were thought of as a one-dimensional being, as if you had no ancestry, no culture that would be able to give you real depth. If you did something worthwhile, it was purely by chance, and tomorrow it would be exposed as stolen or mistaken.'

I haven't encountered my parents like this before. 'But wasn't this a kind of inferiority on your part, and not really the fault of the British?'

My father sighs. 'I'm sure that played a role. But if inferiority is a given and you want a well-run country, you have to make the removal of inferiority part of your plan and not tear into it with such venom.'

'Yes, make no mistake, those old English journalists were absolute masters of the craft of humiliation. Their tongues could assassinate a person. They had these adjectives, you know, hissing like snakes through the paragraphs, and they could make you smart. *Jissis*, you'd limp forever when they were finished with you.' My mother in her dramatic mood.

'But how did you deal then with criticism in the fifties and sixties?'

'We minimized contact with it. We stopped reading their newspapers – why should we expose ourselves to daily ridicule? We didn't go to their universities, we didn't listen to their radio programmes. If we had a need for something, we created it ourselves, our own films, our own books, our own history, our own Afrikaner businesses and millionaires. We appointed our own people to build up our own confidence. We looked after our own poor. If it wasn't for that, we'd still be skulking around feeling inadequate.'

'But that means that when the English press started to warn South Africans about human rights violations and oppression, you didn't even notice.'

They look at each other – both realizing, perhaps too late, where this conversation is going. My mother gets up to take the tray back to the kitchen. 'Listen here, nothing we did was ever good enough for them. So the warnings you're talking about were just part of this enormous spout of derision about our so-called incompetence.'

✧

I go out to the farm, where it appears that the area is back 'online'. Joep Joubert comes beaming into the rondavel.

'I see you're downloading,' he says innocently.

'Yes, and it didn't take a month at all, did it?'

'And because why? Because I phoned my only pal still left in Telkom, and he gave me the cell number of the guy in charge of this area. So then I phoned Mr Kakhetla and I said to him, "Sir! do you want half a sheep? Neatly cut into chops? If you restore my phone line before tonight, half a sheep is yours." And here you are!'

I can't believe my ears. 'I never asked you to start bribing people on my behalf! Maybe I'd rather be without a line than know that you've turned Mr Kakhetla into a corrupt person.'

'I didn't do it for you at all!' he says sarcastically. 'I did it for myself. You live down there in Cape Town, safely tucked away among the whites. We here in the rural areas, we have to find out what's moving the coalface, so that we can survive in this country, because the coalface is no longer white, see. All of us here on the farms are in close contact with white farmers in Zimbabwe, and we study them and their options, and we learn! Maybe the biggest thing we learn from Zimbabwe is that the peaceful route does not work. And look at our government. No land reform plan. No real one. More farms are for sale than ever before in the history of South Africa. Do they buy them? No. Do they buy land for people who want to farm? No. Do they hand out municipal land to new black farmers? No, because the municipalities are so bankrupt that they'd rather rent land out to whites to get some money. Do they redistribute army land? No. State land? No. Do they assist those already on the land? No. Look at the smallholdings next to this farm. Bought by the new municipality for millions, and now people simply squat there. Do they plant anything? No. But they chop things down, oh yes, they tear things down. So I tell you: government is deliberately stalling on land reform to create frustration at the grass-roots level. While expertly using Mugabe and Nujoma to do the inciting for them, they swear in the name of holy capitalism that such things will never happen here ... Yet they are carefully preparing the soil for it. And let me tell you one thing, the peaceful way is not the answer ... *Groot kak* is coming. In the meantime, you may use the line I got through corrupt means.' He turns on his heel and walks out.

I go to pour some wine. A bakkie revs angrily outside and then shuttles down the dirt road. I feel bad. The man has been doing me a favour by letting me use the rondavel, and enduring my critical eye. Politics is the last thing I wanted to discuss with him.

One of the downloaded emails is from Rina. I cheer up immediately. She writes from London, where she is visiting her cousin Katrien, who is a nurse (like Rina herself). Rina knows how to tell a story, so I read it first:

It was the last few minutes in the departure lounge. The rest of us were already boarding, when they streamed in. Recent farewell-takers. All Afrikaners, you could see that. The eyes of the young men red-rimmed, the young women burying their sobbing faces in a coat or scarf. One young girl was holding on to a railing and howling like somebody shot through the kidneys. Behind me in the queue, an Afrikaner girl was crying into her cellphone: 'Why do I always feel like such a bitch when I leave here? Give Ma a hug for me.' Further back in the queue, I saw two with swollen faces excitedly showing each other CDs of old Afrikaans children's songs: 'Almal dra 'n jas', 'Kammalielies' and 'Tjoeke-tjoeke-paf'. Then there was a real Afrikaner couple, the man with one of those suntans you get from wearing a hat all the time, his khaki pants ironed neatly. I heard him asking, 'Have you got the biltong?'

The plane seemed to be packed with Afrikaners working in England or parents visiting their children. Inside I landed up in front of Mamma, Pappa and Boetie. Boetie was about five or six years old and under the strict supervision of Mamma, Pappa and pure Afrikaans. 'Fasten your seatbelt there, *bulletjie* ... Slide your window shade closed ... I'm only telling you once,' and so forth.

'You and Bertus had a good time playing on the farm, hey, *my ram*?'

'Yes, we played shop-shop the whole day.'

'That is very nice,' in a condescending, grown-up tone. 'What did you sell?'

'Guns,' came the answer, 'to all the *kaffertjies*.'

Mamma and Pappa were momentarily dumbstruck. When the plane took off, Boetie started crying broken-heartedly. They reprimanded him, but eventually it broke through: 'I want to go home. I want to go home now!'

'But we *are* going home now. This plane is flying straight home.'

Then furiously, at the top of his lungs: 'I don't want to go with you. I want to go home to Ouma's!' After such defiance, I couldn't help but peek through the seats, just in time to catch Mamma's eyes pooling with tears.

After dinner they made Boetie comfortable and started reading to him. My heart skipped a beat. You know what they read? Alba Bouwer's unforgettable rhymes: 'Little boys who've been at play / the whole day without pause / begin to smell around midday / of mallow and tobacco sauce. // Of wild wormwood, warty toad / and really crusted pap, / Dutch drops and paregoric, / kitten's-paw and strong janlap.' 'What is Dutch drops and paregoric? What is ...?' Mamma and Pappa had their work cut out for them, but they managed to explain words with the most primordial of Afrikaans roots. I felt quite proud of them!

Klein seuntjies wat gespeel het / die heeldag aanmekaar, / dié ruik so teen die middag / na twak en kiesieblaar. // Na wilde-als en padda / en aangebrande pap, / harmansdrup en paregorie, / katjiepoetjie en janlap.

At the airport, blossoming Boer children ran up to greet the farm couple. I wanted to observe their reunion, but realized at that precise moment that my bag with my passport, tickets, credit cards and everything had just been stolen off my baggage trolley, right here in crime-free Old England.

Katrien says people joke that the crime rate has increased in London because so many South Africans live here now. She says the words you most often hear on the streets of London are Afrikaans and go something like this: '*Fokkit, maar hoe skaaf hierdie skoene my nou!*' ['Fuck, these shoes are really chafing me now!']

It is frightening to see how people here cling to an Afrikaner identity that has long ceased to exist in South Africa. I told Katrien, you know, those of us who have remained behind, we adapt, we die, we sacrifice, give way, compromise, we fight a bit too much here on the off side, a bit too little there on the on side, but hell, we know how to change from mean-whiskered bully to arse-kissing poodle, from God Almighty to Father Christmas. Whatever is required at the moment. Our children go to mixed schools, read from books about Bongi and Thandi, we click our clumsy tongues around Ngconde and Nongqawuse and Xolile, and we know how to make ourselves scarce.

I said to her, the danger is that one day you suddenly realize you've kept faith with an imaginary country, a country constructed purely from your longings and your memories. Has the South Africa of which you speak not disappeared already? You long for and want to go back to a place that doesn't exist any more, and that makes you a bit like a refugee who cannot go home again.

But Katrien said she preferred the refugee kind to the Afrikaners who try to assimilate. They have an obsession with the bad news from South Africa, they keep the negative stories alive like babies in incubators, to justify their leaving and their staying away.

I write back: Dear Rina, you remind me of the day I had to wait for a translator at Cape Town International. You could tell immediately which of the disembarking people were from South Africa. The white men walking off with big, self-assured strides, hailing taxis with broad gestures and loud voices, are from America and Europe. In South Africa, white men have not walked like that for a long time now. Head down humbly on the chest, shoulders drawn in to avoid attracting attention, ego wilted, he slips into the parking area before you're sure that you've seen him. A black Cabinet minister apparently said recently: 'I like white men: they come so cheap and they work so hard.' My own husband believes that the only people who can really work hard are white men and black women. He says this country would be better off if they were allowed to run everything!

✧

It's been two days since Joep Joubert has spoken to me. I really feel bad. I take one of the good red wines I brought from Cape Town and walk to the house. When I stand before the front door, I inexplicably want to cry. No, it's not crying, I realize, my body is in need of *howling*, and I don't know why, because I have been here since my parents moved out. Behind the security gate the double doors of heavy teak have been parched by the elements. I put my hand through the bars and knock. Here I am. Here I am, knocking at the door which all my life I have simply opened. Always, when I closed it behind me on blinding hot days, it sealed me off in air cool with stone and silky with wood. Over this threshold I walked from nowhere to somewhere as a child, a teenager, a student, a lover.

Nobody comes. I walk round to the door into the dining room. The security gate is open. I knock again, but walk in as if drawn. Of course, the long yellowwood dining-room table is gone, but in its place is a Formica-topped table and some white plastic garden chairs. Joep lives alone, I reproach myself, what should I expect? I put the bottle of wine on the table. My throat contracts and grief comes to me in a searing way. I feel the cool draught coming down the sandstone passage. My heart hangs dazed on her hinges. It is as if the breeze wants to say, hi, I'm so glad you've come. I remember you as you remember me. I wish we could go back, the two of us, and recall every room on some similarly silent day. I want to touch something, hold something, resurrect all the wholeness that once was mine. But the stones have been painted over, the woodwork has not seen turpentine and beeswax for years – it is only the draught that comes to me and hovers like a mandate at my shoulder. I grab the wine and flee.

In front of the rondavel on the wire chairs, I find Joep in deep conversation with a black man.

'Meet my neighbour, Petrus Sithole.'

Surprised, I hand the bottle of wine to Joep. 'I know Petrus,' I say, as we shake hands. Actually, everybody in the neighbourhood knows Petrus – as the man to take note of. For nearly thirty years he was the only black foreman or farm manager, to use a more distinguished term, in the district. He controlled the magnificent Hugo farms on his own. His fields were always impeccable, his harvests plentiful. When Petrus sent his ploughs in, the neighbouring farmers wondered, what does he know that we don't? There's *mos* still no sign of rain. But Petrus would scarcely have finished, when the first rains would start to fall. Then, while everybody was ploughing, he was already planting. Sometimes it rained, but Petrus wasn't ploughing. What does *he* know? Is it the sangomas or the ancestors? And you could take a bet that the next rain would be slow in coming that year.

When the New South Africa dawned and the farms near the town were being plundered on a daily basis, many farmers started to sell their land. The only man who was prepared to farm next to Maokeng township had been farming there for many years already. In 1997, Petrus Sithole and his long-time boss went to the Land Bank to borrow money for Petrus to buy the farm.

'All the farmers here know that I work well, my fields are always clean. When the people knock off at four o'clock, I bring in another team who work until eleven at night. Then I get in there and work until the first team comes back at four. But I know it is only for three weeks, so I don't worry, because when I'm finished, I see: no, my work looks good. I repair my tractors myself when they break down, I make my own trailers, I welded a ripper on to my planter so that the ground is ripped up deep and planted at the same time. When I heard Baas Chris talk about land, I said yes immediately. And he helped me at the bank and he lent me tractors, his welding machine, planters and plough. He is a good man.

'When I got the land, that day I slaughtered a cow to say thank you according to our beliefs. I cut open the jugular. Many relatives were there. That night we left the cow there for the ancestors to come and eat during the night – the land had been returned – and the next day we feasted. Also the people who stayed next to me came.'

Petrus avoided a lot of traps. He didn't build a new house for himself on the farm. He kept on living where he had lived for the past thirty years, in a ramshackle old house among the other black farm workers' cottages. Did their attitude towards him change when he suddenly became their boss?

'Yes, they are very angry with me. It is hard for me, because I love them. All these years, I loved them. My wife has divorced me and taken my children to the location. So these people around me are all that I have. But they disconnected my water, so I must go fetch water from the town. When their pumps are broken, they come to ask me for water, then I give them. When I said I would fix the pumps for free so that we can use the water together, they didn't want to share. They want my water. When I was just a foreman, it was better. But when it became my land, it got bad. Although my relationship with the white farmers is getting better and better.'

Petrus's farming isn't going well. In the beginning, he struggled to fulfil his role as owner of a farm as well as foreman of the remaining Hugo farms.

'In the first year I couldn't harvest, because I had to finish the Baas's own fields. By the time I got the tractors it was too late, I couldn't put anything in any more. And the bank doesn't wait. So I started an overdraft. Then I sold my seventy-five cattle to pay the first interest. Then the people from the location came to ask if their cattle could walk in my fields, because I didn't have cattle any more. Then they didn't pay me, because they said the grass would just have been there anyway. So the next year was my chance. I bought tractors and all those things, I worked carefully at the right time and it rained – I planted sunflowers. They only steal a little bit of this for their pigeons, so it is safe.

'It was really nice to harvest that first crop of sunflowers. The first thing I did was to go to the bank to pay the year's interest. The second year when I went to pay the debt, I saw how their eyes got big. Is this man going to pay every year? Now the third year, I take a letter to ask a little extension of the time. I cannot pay. I was in Swaziland to sell the flour mills for Baas Chris and I organized that my wheat is stored in the barns of one of the farmers until it is dry. But they did not stir it every day, and when I came back, it was rotten. At least the Co-op helped me by buying it, but for a very low price. But then I heard that now I must pay two years' debt and they give me until June month. And Lord, it is just around the corner. I am worried. Very worried. I see now the farming is going to beat me. I will lose this farm. Not because I don't know how to farm, but because I can't keep ahead. I farm with cash. I don't want to make debts at the Co-op. Now when I see that I must send in the rake to break up the weeds before the young plants come up, I know that I don't have money for diesel. I see my harvest doesn't come up well, because I didn't have money for enough fertilizer. Now I take stupid farming decisions because I can't keep ahead. If I can just get the diesel, seed and fertilizer for one year free from the government, then nobody will stop me again, not ever. No, it will be very sad if I have to stop now.'

Obviously, Petrus will realize sooner or later that maybe he need not pay back his debt to the Land Bank. Who will ever buy a farm so close to the township? Who can farm here? But Petrus is not there yet. As a desperate measure, he has offered to enter into a sharecropping contract with recently settled black farmers. The government has helped these farmers to buy land and start up their farms. But they have no implements and no experience. Petrus will sow and harvest their lands for part of their income.

Apparently, the government can only help him if he forms part of a group of emerging farmers. All of this does not make a carefree man of Petrus Sithole.

'Weekends I can't go and visit. Fridays I work, Saturdays I work, Sundays I maintain my equipment. My workers, they just want to knock off. So it is lonely. I can talk to nobody about my farm. Before it was better for me, because I didn't worry so much. But if I fail now, who will back me up? I have always worked hard. But now I work hard because the crocodile is in front of me. Everything is up to me. Baas Tattie Crous at the Co-op asked me the other day: how's the farming going? So I said: no, it is a bit difficult. So he said: how can it be difficult when it is raining? So I saw he doesn't understand my difficulty. I don't know what is happening with the other farmers. I hear from Baas Chris if the price of wheat has gone up or down.

'I like it that a field is planted properly. When the clean rows stand next to each other. In the afternoons my brother sometimes comes and helps me. He is a principal, but then he helps me and we take the harvest in. I don't meet with other people. My meetings are at night when I go to sleep. I think by myself until I am prepared for the next day. Then I know exactly what I have to do the next morning. If a tractor gives me trouble, I think at night till I know where the problem is. When I get up I go straight to the problem. I have all my meetings at night. This I like. But it is just the thing of the R4 000 that I must pay June month. Actually R12 000 altogether. And I can't figure it out. I almost do not know how to write it down. In the sixty-one years of my life there has never been so much money against my name.'

✧

That night Petrus weighs heavily on my heart. What are the changes in this country worth if they cannot offer somebody like Petrus a breathing space? An opportunity to shoot upwards from generations of meagreness and deprivation, from years of back-breaking labour, to breathe in peace, in the name of the ancestors. To walk the veld of one's dreams, among grazing cattle, to covet with one's eye freshly ploughed fields and feathering sunflowers. Where does the fault lie? Does he need help with financial management? A bigger overdraft? Agricultural guidance?

'With so many white farmers going bankrupt, how can Petrus even think he will make it?' Joep says to me, when the man with the vexed face has waved us goodbye and driven off in his battered bakkie. 'Farming has become impossible. I don't want to repeat what I said the other day, but does government help Petrus? No. It is only the biggest farmers who can survive in these unsympathetic circumstances, with rising diesel and fertilizer prices, theft, lack of safety and falling land values. The joke is that the aggression is aimed more and more at those farmers who have many farms. As if this is a matter of showing off rather than simple survival.'

The man sounds bitter, I think to myself. He is one of those Afrikaners whose forefathers, despite their Boer War bravery, lost their land during the Depression, and for whom land, over years and generations, has become a mythical ideal representing the ultimate of freedom, the ultimate of independence, the ultimate of being human. I have land, therefore I am. It is not for nothing that the old Afrikaans literature is filled with poetry and novels about land and landscape.

Is ownership of land all that can name one? All that links one to this breathtaking earth?

chapter fifteen

While her mother weaves the second plait, she says, 'Soon the time will come when you start menstruating. I have bought you a packet of sanitary towels and a belt. They are in the drawer next to your bed.'

'The other girls in the hostel wear tampons and plastic underpants.'

'One doesn't push all kinds of foreign objects in between one's legs, you'll hear from them again when they have growths and miscarriages and additional bleeding. And really, if you prefer to sit sweating into plastic underpants, I will buy you a pair.'

The package of Dr White's sanitary towels and the belt lie on top of a book: *It Is Time That You Knew.*

Oh dear. It is a difficult matter to broach with her mother. When everyone in her corridor of the hostel started wearing bras, her mother took her to Harding and Parker and insisted on a cotton Maidenform bra. 'One only wears cotton and wool. These synthetic fibres make one sweat and smell.'

Out of anger and frustration, she refused to speak to anyone in the house for two weeks. Wearing her cotton bra the way a fed-up waitress would carry a tray. 'You make me sick,' her mother says, and takes her to the fancy make-up counter at Harding and Parker: 'Put some make-up on this child, so that she can get some professional advice about it. As you can see, it is not one of my strong points.'

'But I don't want make-up!' she interjects.

'That's strange, I thought you wanted to look like everybody else? You have been giving me hell ever since you became so clever: you want sharp-toed school shoes like everyone else, and not round-toed Harley Streets, you want a briefcase like everyone else and not a rucksack, you want a nylon tunic and not one made of serge ... Then I thought: I give up! The Good Lord gave me a child who longs to be like everyone else. She wants to melt away into the grey mass of complacency and become one of those women whose hairdressing account is bigger than her book account.'

Her mother presses her own hair to her head and cuts it off with the kitchen scissors. Her mother doesn't shave her legs or armpits or upper lip. Her mother has thick calluses under her feet from walking barefoot. Her mother looks like no other woman she knows.

When she gets into the car with her heavily made-up face, her little brothers yell into their seats with laughter.

chapter sixteen

A woman in the street congratulates her mother on the beautiful essay in *Sarie Marais*. 'I read it to Attie and we laughed so much. One's children can really lead one a merry dance!'

Her ears prick up. One's children? At home she hides the *Sarie* in her bedroom. When everyone is sleeping, she pages through the magazine. At first she sees nothing. She pages a second time, and now she sees her mother's name but with a different surname, her maiden name:

Journeying with Children and Cooldrink – A Sketch by Dot Serfontein

She reads the opening line: 'Our first day in Cape Town a couple of years ago is something I will not easily forget.' She feels her heart beating faster. It was a terrible vacation, and she remembers little of it other than endless travelling, arguments and a variety of vile smells. Like a stranger, she reads the story, in which she recognizes everything, but can confess to nothing.

As a housewife I don't have much to pride myself on, but there is one virtue I have: and that is the ability to protect my husband's jackets under the most difficult circumstances from melting ice creams and chocolates in the motor car. Because my children chew the corners off chequebooks and road maps, or draw stick men on them, we now take these along in a briefcase. When we stop in front of a hotel, we send him through the front door like the dove of peace, the very picture of refinement, briefcase in hand. I could write a book about the faces of hotel managers, who come beaming through the front door, with a string of waiters and my suite-booking husband in tow, only to lay eyes on the small dull motor car with its dust-caked windows, the troop of dusty, barefoot children unravelling beside it, followed by a wind-blown woman tugging at her rumpled dress and pressing her little brown hat on to her head.

Then the unpacking starts. There is always a collapsible pram giving trouble, a cretonne nappy-bag from which dubious smells rise, pillows with dirty footprints, shoes of all sizes, sour baby bottles, naartjie peels and bread crusts, empty cooldrink bottles ... Lastly, struggling out with a moan, is someone we refer to on our trips as 'Our Nanny', but who in fact is Eveline, our laundry maid with big farm feet and a head cloth.

For a number of years it was impossible to go anywhere without Eveline. Otherwise, within a few hours of our arrival, the flower arrangements in the hall would be lying on the floor, the water closet would be blocked, the lift would be out of order, the hotel dog would be hysterical, and one or more children would be missing.

To our credit I can mention that when we leave such a hotel, my children are always moved to tears when we take leave of the hotel staff. While the hotel manager nods them an icy farewell from behind the reception counter, my sons share their last sweets with the waiters, give them their empty bottles as a farewell present, bury them in a flood of Sesotho blessings, promise them work on the farm, and lean halfway out of the car, waving to them until we disappear around the last corner.

She breathes deeply. It is them. Us. The family. And she feels how the swamp of their vacations, as she usually experiences them, acquires the sharp edge of definition. From the murk, things are being pulled up like fish, shining with such colour and flavour and movement that the turbid water disappears completely.

That day in Cape Town there were luckily only three children, with a fourth conspicuously on the way. When we pull up at the hotel behind an imposing black official car, I say to my husband, 'Look, it is almost ten. The children haven't eaten anything this morning. While you check in and unload, I'll quickly take them to a café. Lunch time is still a very long way off.'

We agree – my husband quite unwilling and worried.

'Don't go far. For heaven's sake, don't get lost. Don't forget the hotel's name. Make sure you don't let go of each other's hands.' By then our little boy, the youngest, is already around the corner, the two girl-children behind him, giving chase.

So this is how she enters the written word. As one of 'the two girl-children' chasing after their naughty brother.

He is atrocious. He refuses to take our hands, he ambles along two steps behind, and if one of us dared to take his hand, he would fall flat on the pavement on his stomach. Meanwhile, we see no sign of a café. How's that for the great Cape Town! My second eldest, always the practical one, tugs on the sleeve of a passer-by: 'Uncle, where can we find a keffy, Uncle?'

'Good restaurant, fourth floor of the department store right here. And your uncle is not an uncle, little one, he is just a coloured mister.' And he pats her sympathetically on the head. 'From the Transvaal, *mêdêm*?' he asks me.

'Is the Uncle a Boy then, Ma?' the eldest asks bewilderedly as we walk into the store.

It is perhaps not the time to explain South Africa's complicated social make-up. Neither is it necessary, since as we walk into the store the three spot an escalator. And they know escalators. There used to be one in Bloemfontein in those days. One storey high. And here the escalator staggers luxuriously from one floor to the next, as high as the eye can see. They charge forward with a cheer.

She, the eldest, remembers nothing of this. She also didn't know that the place they eventually ended up in was called Stuttafords. What she does realize is that her mother is funny and that she is writing a story about herself.

Our kind coloured Uncle wasn't exaggerating. It must be a very popular restaurant, because people are trampling one another to get in. I know that the Cape is something special, but that the Cape women toff themselves up like this for a Tuesday morning's shopping, I couldn't imagine. We ourselves journeyed sleeplessly all night through the Karoo in a small car, and there is nothing to hide the hard facts.

'That will be seven-and-sixpence, madam,' says the cashier.

Heavens, must you pay in the Cape even before you sit down! If ever there was a time to turn back, it is now. But the touch of disdain with which her eyes sweep over us brings out the old pioneer's blood in me. I pay as coolly as a cucumber.

And there the four of us stand. The place is packed. No sign of an aisle. Everywhere there are extra chairs. People sitting shoulder to shoulder.

And everyone is English. I could never have imagined that the Cape was such an English nest. And not just ordinary street English. The real old blue ones, as my father always said.

Of all the eating places in the Cape, we had to discover the most popular one! But thank goodness, with the help of a waitress, we find room at a table squeezed into the corner.

'Your order, madam?' she asks impatiently in Afrikaans. Can you believe such an expert in knowing who speaks what!

The children tap me on the arm and point to an old lady at the table next to us. They want to eat what she is eating.

She is eating waffles. I hesitate. I didn't mean to order anything more involved than tea and scones. Then I remember the seven-and-six at the cashier. We must recover our outlay, I feel.

'You must order quickly, madam, because once the show starts, we won't be able to do anything,' says the waitress.

'Show?'

'It is a fashion parade, lady, for the National Council of Women. I can bring you a pro-gramme if you like.' Fool that I am. That I couldn't work out that something out of the ordinary was happening here!

We must get out of here immediately! I want to jump up, but my chair is so squashed in that even Wolraad Woltemade, with a big strong Boer horse, wouldn't have been able to move me from this human ocean.

'Please bring me some waffles with tea,' I say resignedly.

'And Coca-Cola,' my little son adds. Of course. What century do I think I'm living in? Then the waffles come.

And this I will say for those waffles: they were crisp, fragrant, with a big pot of cane syrup and a glass bowl of fresh cream. All complete with cutlery and paper napkins.

And when the waitress puts it down in front of us, my children relax completely. They tuck in with gusto, they spread syrup, they slice, they swing their elbows and their legs, they applaud the models and pull faces at the English children. The youngest sticks his waffles together like a sandwich and bites into it so that the syrup droops in golden strings between his dirty little fingers. Now and then he stands up on his chair to get a better view. And wherever he touches the furniture, the syrup makes a sucking sound when he draws away his hand.

I defend. I coax. I dab my handkerchief in the black tea and wipe away syrup as far as I can. I stop those who would scald themselves on the teapot. I make sure that they don't talk louder than the muffled music accompanying the fashion models. I check that they don't fight, that they don't knock the hats off the heads of the people in front of us ... Eventually, I am drenched in sweat.

If it had been an Afrikaans event, I am sure there would have been some practical Boer woman removing a damp dishcloth from her handbag. Or some fellow with a sense of these things would have tapped my son on the shoulder and said, 'Listen here, if you don't behave yourself, Uncle will throw you to the lions outside.' Or some Afrikaner offi-cial would have helped me forge a way through to the outside by way of the kitchens.

But no. The English people have an entirely different way of handling these things. They just ignore it. The naughtier, the more unbearable the children become, the less they appear to notice. Those sitting closest to us turn their heads conspicuously, their entire torsos turned away from us, or look straight through us as if we were invisible.

Finally we finish eating. I am just congratulating myself that we have come this far, when my son announces for everyone to hear that he wants to go and make a pee-pee.

We try desperately to focus his attention on the fashion show, but he remains insist-ent. He becomes cantankerous and moany. And I know that he will soon start crying. That will, of course, be the end. So now to see what we can do. We make him stand between me and his sister, we pull his trousers to half mast and hold the Cola bottle for him. It works like a charm. I thank the Dear Lord that he isn't in need of more substan-tial relief. I put down the bottle between my feet and make sure no one knocks it over on to the thick, expensive carpeting. Another milestone reached. Thankfully the show has reached the stage of the evening gowns. I start hoping for a speedy release.

But nature is a contagious thing. Soon number two is also in terrible need of relief.

'You will keep it in,' I hiss in her ear. Because now we are trapped. Bottles won't work for little girls. The poor child's eyes stretch wider and wider, in a true panic. But I remain rock solid. What cannot be, simply cannot be.

But eventually I am forced to tackle this emergency too. I squeeze anything that is a paper napkin into a ball. She is to crawl under the table, squat on her haunches and aim at the bundle of paper. Oh, that I have to endure such misery in what I took to be the cradle of civilization!

Half past eleven has come and gone by the time we emerge. I smile tenderly at each waitress we squeeze past, because I know something about our little table that they have yet to realize.

Downstairs at the entrance I am directionless. I look in shop windows, observe the traffic, anything to head off the rising panic in me. Because I have forgotten the name of our hotel. I am overwhelmed by the most terrible feeling of hopelessness. For years, of course, I have been one of those women who forget about meetings if their husbands don't remind them, who leave cakes in the oven if they don't set an alarm clock, who write letters and forget to post them, who, when measuring something, forget if there are already five or six or seven spoons in the mix, who forget their own telephone or post box or registration number. But this must be the ultimate.

'There is our hotel,' my youngest calls enthusiastically as we come round a corner.

'Is not. Our hotel is the Grand Hotel, you baboon,' says my eldest loftily. 'It is around the next corner.'

I hunch myself over in deep humiliation. See, this is the advantage of having a whole lot of children. There is always one gifted with what's necessary to deal with the crisis at hand.

When we reach the hotel, I see three men huddled in a panicky little group – my husband, a constable and the hotel manager. No one is happy to see us.

'It is now five to twelve,' my husband says with forced calm. 'At exactly twelve, the police were to take to the streets to search for you. Two hours! Do you realize that?'

It is wonderful how nature at times blesses even someone like myself with a little extra. I smile lovingly at each one in turn. 'Were you waiting? I am terribly sorry. We were just at a fashion parade.' And what a lovely uplifting of my battered self-image it was to see the three of them crumple like tomato stalks drenched with a bucket of boiling water.

She switches off the light, but remains sitting upright in bed. Hundreds of thoughts mill through her head. Throughout the entire piece, she rebelled against what she was reading: not true, not like that – but the last sentence took her breath away. A bucket of boiling water over three tomato plants. Why *tomato plants*?

The next morning she finds her mother kneading dough.

'Things didn't happen the way you wrote in the *Sarie*.'

'Like what?'

'Like the English. There were other Afrikaans people sitting next to us.'

'I wasn't giving a factual account of what happened that morning, I wanted to say some other things in an amusing way.'

'What things?'

'That the ways and means of a poor Afrikaans family are also heroic, that you don't have to be embarrassed among the English. Things like that.'

'And when we got to the hotel, Pa wasn't angry. He was relaxed and reading on the hotel balcony, and when you saw him you burst into tears and for days you didn't speak a word to each other.'

'Every story must have an ending. This was the ending that I made.'

'Then why tomato plants and not pumpkins or dahlias?'

'Because there was a tomato plant at your grandmother's back door and I once saw her emptying a bucket of boiling water over it.'

'And what if I don't like you writing about me?'

'Look,' she says, and covers the bowl of dough with a blanket so that it will rise further. 'Some children's mothers drink, other's steal or abuse them, or sit at home with empty heads or spend hours at tea parties talking nonsense. Your mother writes. And like hundreds of children across the world, you will have to make peace with the fact that your mother writes and that she writes about what happens around her.'

'But what if I feel you can write and everything, but me personally you must leave out of it. I don't want to be part of your writing.'

'If you feel that I'm twisting things, you can write your own story and correct it. I don't deny you that right. But if you really don't want to be part of it, I can take you out. Then I will just write about my three children instead of four, and you will disappear. You will be missing from the family.'

'And say I don't mind disappearing?'

Her mother stands quietly for a long while, her head forward on her chest.

'I mean, you actually abuse me in your version of ...'

But before she can finish the sentence, her mother, in one single swoop, picks up an empty Pyrex dish and, with an extra twist in her back, smashes it into a thousand pieces against the wall above the stove. Eveline comes in through the screen door, eyes wide. Her mother closes the door in Eveline's face.

'Shall I take my things and leave?' her mother screams. 'And fuck off somewhere where my know-it-all child and my husband who secretly reads everything behind my back don't crap all over my writing? I am so sick of you all! So goddamn *sick* of you!'

She has never heard her mother speak like this before. Is this 'rage' or 'fury'? Her mother bends over and speaks into her face. Her eyes two burning black coals.

'It is the only bit of my life that I keep for myself. What do you know about the courage it takes to write something down? What do you know about the personal battlefield strewn with corpses which I leave behind every time I finish a piece? What do you know about giving it up – only to buy your typewriter back from the pawnshop the next day, because you cannot do without it? What on God's earth do you know, you poor, stupid child?'

Her mother turns and walks out. She is light-headed and uncomfortably triumphant. That she could drive her mother to such an outburst.

chapter seventeen

It is dark in front of the hostel. When she turns around, he grabs her arm and kisses her. Before she knows it, she is in the hostel's passage. And she only remembers his desperate hands, his Standard Six stubble and his slimy tongue.

chapter eighteen

She wins the prize for the best essay in the arts competition.

'You take after me,' says her mother, 'you don't have a head for figures.'

'Why do you write under a different surname?' she asks.

'Because I am two people. The one uses her own surname and writes her own stories and earns her own money. The other one has a husband and children.'

'Which one do you like being the most?'

'The one who is content with having a husband and children.'

'Then why not just be her?'

'Because I'm not good enough. The writing is so that I can make peace with the fact that I am not the apron-mother or the I-had-my-hair-done-mother.'

'So why don't you rather just write?'

'There is nothing, no book, no prize, no fame that I would exchange for my life on this farm amongst the cattle and the sheep and the chickens and the children and the trees. Your father and I have a highly interesting life together. It is not something you will understand, even though you imagine yourself to be a little Inquisition all on your own.'

CHAPTER EIGHT

THE WHOLE FARMYARD is holding its breath.

It has gone absolutely quiet.

The five oxen move their heads nervously, whisking a tail in the sunny winter air. My uncle lifts his rifle. He holds it, holds it ... The shot rings out. One animal thuds to the ground. With death in their nostrils, the rest shy blindly away.

Then the farmyard comes alive.

I jump from the bakkie to get close, to see. Isak Mokokoane doesn't need to test the blade. He cuts the throat and opens the jugular. With a silky sound the most vivid of blood, in a red that is alive, spurts into the air. Expertly, Isak turns the wound to the ground and shows us the other: a bullet hole right in the middle of the forehead. The workers murmur with approval. My uncle is a prize shot.

I breathe the blood into my lungs.

With luxurious abandon it spreads itself across the yard, it unfurls, it evens out, it moves ever so lightly, utterly without sound, it flows into a broad, rampant velvet carpet that covers the ground. In the heart of the flat, stretched-out Free State winter, it is the only colour, the only abundance any of us have seen for months.

Wild piercing squeals cut through the crisp morning as Isak stabs the pig just below the neck into the heart. One of my father's old razors lies waiting on the cement slab. My father himself left early this morning. He does not own a rifle and hates this kind of thing.

The skin of the red ox unfurls into a cape of fat, glowing satin. The bulging, blue-green stomach is carried away to be cut open for the poultry, the intestines are taken to be cleaned.

The yard turns into a whirl of smells. Coriander scorched and ground with pestles, thyme crushed and cut, lemon squeezed for the gut, tubs scrubbed for biltong and brine. Some are frying fat, there is a whiff of tomato and onion relish. The air bristles with laughter and jokes and stories. Big pots are steaming on stoves and outdoor fires – food must be provided for the day.

I sit for a long time with my hands on the keyboard. I am trying to write about 'Food and Reconciliation'. The slaughtering of an Afrikaner ox was a bloodthirsty ritual of sharing, a spectacle of skill, an abundance of impressions. I remember it all so well, and God, how I miss the unsafe spaces of my youth.

The yard is alive, watched over by my mother, wearing an apron and velskoene, with a very impressive knife in her left hand. Our own Commanding Officer. She looks at the amount of fat on the stomach and taps it, clearly satisfied. It is a young Afrikaner ox – a veld ox. That is the only meat she will touch. (In later years, when we have to slaughter Jerseys or Brahmans, she will be revolted and offended, and will often refuse to lend us her knives. 'Look at the stomach fat of these foreign cattle,' she will say, 'it is not a healthy white, but this yellow kind of trash.')

While the ox bleeds, Eveline collects some of the blood in a bowl. In the kitchen she stirs it with a stainless-steel spoon until the blood forms threads. She pours it through a sieve. 'Now it is pure blood,' she says, 'the soul of the ox has stayed in the water.' With flour, salt, egg and baking powder, the mixture is put into a flour bag and then into a pot of boiling water. After an hour and a half it has swollen to double its size. 'This is for us old people,' she says. 'We eat with the *badimo* ...'

While the farm workers are skinning the ox, Isak rewards himself with a 'puff adder': chitterlings stuffed with finely chopped onion, pork, kidney, heart, liver, bread, lemon, salt and sage, and roasted on the coals.

The quartered ox is hung in the *vleiskamer*. While all the black workers go off for a breakfast cooked on the coals, my mother cuts out biltong and steaks. Every biltong has a name and she teaches me: this one is called 'the eye', that one is 'the red *meneer*', here is 'the round one' and there the soft, threadlike '*garingbiltong*', which she gently tears from the backbone. A shuddering, compact hump of meat becomes a layered basket of muscle, names and textures – embroidered with fat. The glands are cut out like blue beans, the hip-knobbles lie moist and slippery in transparent knuckle fluid. As the morning progresses, all the women join in the activities of the *vleiskamer*, cutting fat and silver sinews from sausage meat, minced meat, corned beef, oven cuts, cooking meat, biltong meat.

The cutting up of the meat loosens our tongues. In the vleiskamer we are all women. The men have done the killing and have left. We are providing for the days to come. We talk about children, we gossip about the latest romances on the farm; some of the new young wives are being taught how to sharpen a knife, the difference between the meat for sausage and the meat for mince, how to treat sore eyes. And we laugh a lot.

'What does "*makgoa*" mean?' I ask Eveline, although I know it is the Sesotho word for 'whites'.

While she laughs somewhat respectfully, one of the younger ones interrupts, 'Baboons!'

'*Hayi suka wena*,' scolds Eveline, 'it means "whites" in Sesotho. In Northern Sotho it means "those on whom we spit when we see them".'

'Why baboons?'

The young one explains with a giggle, 'Because baboons always look over their shoulders, because they look one way but walk the other way, because they do nothing, they just check out, check out, check out – the whole day.'

My mother comes in with the spices and we change the subject. The spicing of the sausage meat is a sacred moment. My mother uses the recipe of my great-grandmother Lenie, who cooked for a Prince and a Lord. Over the meat she sprinkles first pepper, then salt (only Swartkopsrivier salt, not Cerebos, nor anything else), thyme, scorched coriander and grape vinegar.

'Is that all?' eager young housewives have been known to ask, after they have eaten the sausage and pleaded for the recipe. 'No nutmeg, no cloves?' At the mention of these absolute no-nos for spicing boerewors, my mother will merely close her eyes for a few seconds as if to overcome a painful moment, then say: 'No, for Afrikaner beef that is all you need.' I remember the horror on her face once, when the wife of a neighbouring farmer added some tomato sauce and Worcestershire sauce to the sausage meat at the church bazaar.

It is time to stuff the sausage. This demands military precision. We all take our places. Laetia rolls evenly-sized balls of mince and stuffs them into the funnel of the sausage machine. Pantjie rinses the lengths of gut, finds the openings and passes them to my mother, who pulls them over the nozzle. I put the sausage into plastic bags. And start to giggle at the condom-like gut, pulled over the nozzle, at the slow turning of the wheel by Eveline, the spurt of meat which is neatly caught by my mother and then rolled into spirals and placed in plastic bags. All these women stand around the shrine of a sausage machine, turning Afrikaner beef into long, smooth coils of edible wors.

'All of us around this ... spout,' I mumble.

'You are misinterpreting the situation,' my mother says, unruffled. 'A nozzle is a device. Men make war and cause trouble with it, we make food with it.'

I grew up on the beef from Afrikaner cattle, and on the stories about them. My grandfather was one of the most renowned breeders of Afrikaner cattle in the country. For years he was the main adjudicator of prize cattle at the Rand Easter Show in Johannesburg, leaving for the city at four o'clock every morning and making the two-hour drive back to Kroonstad again every evening, simply because he did not want to spend the night in what he called 'that English den'.

My grandfather loved Afrikaner cattle more than he loved people. He never kissed me or picked me up or touched me – or anybody else, for that matter. He also seldom spoke to me. Yet he would chop up pumpkin for the old cows he kept near the house, and talk to his stud bulls as if they were his equals, often tenderly stroking the bridges of their noses, playfully tugging at their jowls, lovingly caressing their humps and horns.

A family legend recounts how my grandfather, then in his mid-forties, walked into the arena at the Rand Easter Show to receive the championship prize for the best bull of that year. Farm workers led the other competing bulls by means of nose rings and iron shafts. But my grandfather walked in with his beloved Arend at his heels. The huge beast, with its enormous hump, the notched neck, the long white horns like two wide flashes of lightning, the delicate forehead and soft jowl-skin, the satin-smooth flanks and massive rump, followed him like a friend. The crowd applauded wildly. 'When I saw the two of them, I got gooseflesh,' my mother told me.

I go through the notes and sources on Afrikaner cattle given to me by my father. How reliable they are, I will have to check when I am back in Cape Town. It is dark outside and very quiet. Now and then a mosquito buzzes or a moth thuds dully against the screened windows.

Afrikaner cattle are an indigenous species. Their ancestors migrated down Africa along with people. The cattle that Jan van Riebeeck bartered from the Khoi at the Cape were Afrikaner cattle. Cattle continue to play a very important role in indigenous rural cultures. In the past, different groups of breeders focused on different characteristics and thus produced different breeds. For some, colour was the overriding factor, because the skins were needed to make shields, which were typically black and white. For others, it was important that the animals' backs were white, so that they would be easier to spot in overgrown, bushy areas; and that their horns were short, so that they would not become entangled. A protruding mouth meant that the animal would be able to eat the short grass in winter, and the quantity of milk produced was always an important consideration.

By the end of the nineteenth century, three different breeds of Afrikaner cattle could already be distinguished in South Africa: the *bakhoring* (bow-horn), the *draaihoring* (twisted horn) and the *keepnek* (notch-neck). White Afrikaans farmers preferred the latter, began calling them 'Afrikaners' and specialized in breeding the 'correct red colour'. Oom Joseph du Plessis of the Free State was one of the most famous breeders. According to oral history, Oom Joseph took the core of his Afrikaner cattle stock and fled with them during the Anglo-Boer War to Bechuanaland, the Kalahari or the Northern Transvaal – nobody quite knows where. Throughout the war, he lived and fled with his herd. They were trained to obey a variety of whistles: to stand and wait, to follow, to be quiet, to lie down. A member of the family came across Oom Joseph all alone in the bush, and thought he had lost his cattle. 'Shh,' Oom Joseph held his finger to his lips, then made the sound of a commando bird, and suddenly, out of the grass, without a sound, the whole herd of cattle rose. After another kind of whistle, his chief bull, Generaal, came out of the shade as if to receive his orders.

After the war, the British imported large numbers of cattle in order to populate the devastated countryside with sufficient livestock. But, as a matter of honour, many farmers continued to breed only Afrikaner cattle.

This is a problem, I realize. Most sources give only one side of the story. I try to go on to the Internet to find a mention of cattle in, say, African-language poetry. The computer is so slow that I am able to make myself a cup of tea while it whirrs and groans on its own. The modern sound of a team of cyberoxen pulling one into the unknown, and yes, it finds a piece by John and Jean Comaroff, as well as some poems. I add to my notes:

In Setswana, cattle are known as *modimo o nkô e metsi* – god-with-the-wet-nose.

Among the Basotho, cattle are not merely a sign of wealth, but an expression of the collective self. The bigger, the more fruitful, the more beautiful and pure your herd, the more clearly these cattle say something about your humanity. A Tswana saying claims: A fool who owns an ox is no longer a fool. Cattle make a human being of you. They enable you to marry and to trade, in other words, to be fully human.

Cattle are also signs of the promises and agreements made between giver and receiver. When you give away your cattle as lobola or loan them to the poor, when you trade cattle with the headman or take them from someone during a conflict, you are weaving yourself into a new social fabric. When your cattle are walking with the herd of your in-laws or the headman and they multiply, you earn spiritual interest. In a poem about cattle, some verses focus on their ability to bring nourishment even to strangers:

> Cattle – they who draw assegais to themselves
> > Malenkhu a marumo
> they who produce warm milky milk
> > seapaa letoutou
> they, the wet-nosed gods
> > modimo o nkô e metsi
> with their intense nourishing drink
> > mogodungwane o molelo
> have cream that scorches the whiskers of men
> > more o fisang banna ditedu
> the whiskers drip with cream that they did not plaster on themselves
> > dinya mafura di sa a tloteng
> there is enough – even the mouths of foreigners shine with lustre
> > selo sa mosimane wa Mokalaka

In Sotho culture, the *seriti* of cattle – their dignity and spirit – is almost as strong as that of humans and can be communicated with. Black cattle have the strongest *seriti*. The relationship with cattle is personal: each animal has a name and is visited daily and talked about. Precise terms are needed to describe the physical characteristics of cattle down to the finest detail. Where English would require a descriptive phrase, Northern

Sotho has a single exact word: white with black markings is *pududu*; white with red markings, *kebja*; black with some white markings on the neck, *kgoopa*; and red with white markings on the back, *thamaga*. There are in the region of sixty words just to describe the colours of cattle.

From Xhosa poetry it appears that the cattle pen or kraal is the holy of holies, and a proverb states that the beauty of a Xhosa man lies in his cattle. Old, blackened kraal dung is the best dung, since it includes the dung of famous and well-loved cattle of the past. To be black kraal dung is to be fully anchored in the best and proudest of the past. That is why in one of the famous Xhosa praise poems, King George V is called the dung-coloured man, the star of the blackest dung from the depths of the kraal.

Cattle help to form the poet. It is amongst cattle that many aspiring praise poets learn to distinguish themselves as potential *iimbongi* or praise singers. By singing the praises of your father's cattle, you not only get to know them well, but you also learn to express your observations in captivating language. The opening line of an Ndebele praise song is always: 'Take the cattle!'; while Sepedi praise songs start off by announcing: 'The cow's udder is bulging! Who will milk her out?'

During the apartheid years, cattle were used as a heart-rending metaphor for the oppressed by H.M.L. Lentsoane, in his well-known poem about the Soweto uprising:

> rumours of unrest and revolt are thrown up by motley black cattle that are dumb
> cattle that are not sullen, although they obey the rules
> cattle that are carefully kept under watch
> cattle that murmur in muffled voices
> against those who boisterously announce ideas of contempt
> eventually they are strung up – they, the motley black cattle
> the time of the covenant with the ancestors has arrived

> E gorogile melaetsa ka kgonono,
> E hlatswa ke thomo ya semuma,
> Thomo ya go hloka matepe.
> E tsitsinketswe thomo,
> Ya fetlekwa ka lepopodumo,
> Ya ahlaahlwa ka megopolo ya lenyatso
> Mafelelong ya fegwa,
> Kgauswi ya ba kgweranong le badimo.

I have lost track of 'Food and Reconciliation' completely. While I'm trying to go back to my original script, the computer becomes extremely tardy in completing my commands. Suddenly a message flashes: 'You have committed a fatal error.' Fatal, my foot!

How I hate this thing which is a machine but loves to talk back as if it's human or determines fate. I click here and there, but eventually everything freezes up. I hope I won't lose anything. But just in case, I run up to the barn and stand on the platform for the engines to call, by the light of the moon, the computer guy.

'Ferdi, everything is hanging like that.'

Ferdi doesn't ask any questions. He already knows: he's dealing with a digiot. 'Just switch it off nicely and bring it in tomorrow eight o'clock, then we'll check it out.'

As I walk back to the rondavel, I contemplate this phenomenon in my life: the computer guy.

He. The one you must have if you are older than forty-five and think you can warble along on the Internet. The one you phone when 'things start hanging', when your recent documents have suddenly disappeared, when strange messages threaten you with 'fatal errors' and being 'shut down immediately'. The one whose cell number is pasted up next to your bed. The one you phone with more desperation and hope than a prospective date for the Standard Seven hostel party.

The only problem with this 'guy' is that he changes so often. Over the years, he has taken many forms in my life. Recently, he was a family man whose child clambered about on his lap and didn't want to leave alone 'the nice lady's crystal' (for bad karma, cancer, blood pressure and things). Before him, it was a dedicated dagga-smoker who only came if he needed money for the weekend, and whose memory (long- and short-term) was just as flaky as my computer's. Somewhere in between there was the Clearasil special with too many or too few fingers (whether there was one missing on the one side or one extra on the other was never clear because of the tremendous speed with which his hands flew over the keyboard).

At this moment in my disembodied life in Kroonstad, it is Ferdi. And this Ferdi is still a child. But he has the calm confidence of a seasoned vet birthing a calf for an old cow.

I sit down at the computer. Perhaps I can copy the day's work out by hand? But the computer will not budge. Then, before I can switch it off, a message flashes beside a red cross: 'You may think you are somebody, but you are just a big old shit.' I start to breathe violently through my throat, and push the off button.

The next morning at half past seven I'm already at the computer shop, the 'box' wrapped tenderly in my swimming towel, my eyes resting hopefully on the youth.

Ferdi advises me to go for a stroll while he quickly takes a look. I amble about in the main street. The small shop that used to sell quality porcelain and glass has closed down, and so has the bookshop. The fabric shop, which once drew clients from right across the Free State, has survived. Behind the counter is Beatrix. She went to school with me and married someone who became a diplomat in Germany. 'Gerrit was retrenched after 1994,' she says. 'We bought this shop with his package, but things are not going well. People no longer make their own clothes or curtains, you know.' Gerrit, in his mid-forties, is apparently very depressed. He sits at home doing nothing. Even the German books sent to him regularly by a shop in Bonn, he refuses to look at. She takes them to the local library from time to time. I walk past La Vogue and remember somebody asking me once whether I had seen the nice clothes at 'La Fok-You'. I see that Rautenbach's, the family outfitter, has closed down, that the OK Bazaars no longer occupies the same prominent corner, and that Greg's Muti Shop has doubled the size of its premises. I see it all, but it hardly registers.

I go back to Ferdi. In the friendliest voice, his eyes sparkling as if he is telling me that this cup has English tea and that one rooibos, he says: 'The whole hard drive has been wiped out by a virus, Tannie, I'm installing a brand new one for you.'

My heart stops beating.

My lungs stop breathing.

My eyes stop blinking.

'That cannot be, Ferdi,' I say in a voice outdoing his for evenness, a voice more neutral than the road between Welkom and Kroonstad.

'Did Tannie not make back-ups?' he asks cheerfully.

Back-ups! I sink to my knees.

Fuck me – fuck you! Back-ups!

Back-ups!

For God's sake.

I sit deathly still for the next three minutes while everything that I should have backed up tumbles through my brain. In raging waves the destruction washes over me. Still crouching on the floor, I feel the blood draining from my body. I have lost everything. My epic address book. New poems. Lectures, essays, creative pieces spanning nearly ten years, the chapters on poetry in African languages, the half-finished Afrikaans translation of Mandela's *Long Walk to Freedom*, a recent play in pentameters ...

I want to hit Ferdi. I want to assault him. Crush him. In the absence of the swine who gave me the virus, I want to murder Ferdi.

And Ferdi knows this. He watches me from the corner of his eye. He says not a thing. He sits there on his bar stool, far too young to understand that there are things in one's life that one simply cannot lose. Dare not lose. He seems confused by my desperate reaction.

'Tannie,' his voice falters, 'I can give it back to you, but it is completely destroyed.'

I take the thing and cradle it like a dead body, while Ferdi pushes one disk after another into a new big box he is lending me, to charge it up.

With my empty memory on the passenger seat beside me, and my destroyed memory in the boot, I drive out to the farm. My insides as numb as my computer. I see nothing. I hear nothing. I drink a glass of red wine as if it is milk. Among the moths and mosquitoes, I sit like a fool in front of my computer. When I load up the word processor, there is no file, no folder, just Drive C.

After a while I try to prepare some food, but I feel completely incoherent as my head churns the process of loss over and over. Eventually, I sit down again. New Document, and I write:

To be wiped out.

> Let me set it down tonight in black and white (so that it exists in ink on paper and not floating around in some nebulous cyberspace): I have lost more on a computer than everything the entire Old and New South Africa, plus the Receiver of Revenue, plus old age, plus illness was able to plunder from me.

My fingers find their own way.

> Savage and seething, I sit here. Spitting coals and venom. Raging. Burning with fury. Vengeful. Strangling. Middle finger up. I am murderous with frustration. A heretic of hatred. On the verge of slashing my wrists. To lie down in the middle of the road, yelling from my gut: drive over me, yes, speed over me, trample me, ye taxis and 4x4s and beer trucks – yes, trash me the way you trash the roads, do what you like, because I am already dead. I am without memory. My life has been taken from me. All that is needed is the second obliter-

Before I can add the final -ation, my left arm suddenly shoots upwards – like the claw of a bird. I force it down to the keyboard and aim for the 'a' – but my whole hand collapses on to the keys. I try again, but my third, fourth and fifth fingers are hanging like dead lumps. Yes. You see. That's what you get for wanting to write everything down … Traitor. Spiller. Distorter of the Truth. You have been stopped. Go to bed. Abide.

I get up and walk slap bang into the doorpost. I seem to be drunk. In bed I try to read, but my left eye will not focus properly. I throw the book against the wall and switch off the light. I fall asleep immediately.

The next morning when I wake up, I realize that something is terribly wrong. The blood is thundering in my veins. My left hand cannot help me to make coffee, and in the shower my face feels as if it is in both cold and hot water. My tongue recognizes no taste.

I decide that the best test will be to see if I can still balance on my head in a yoga pose. I battle a bit to get up, but then stand on my head without effort for four minutes and immediately feel better. But within half an hour I feel worse than before. I drive into town to the family doctor. 'You look okay to me,' says the receptionist, giving me the once-over, 'if you're still poorly this afternoon, do come around again. Doctor is very busy.' I drive off, and realize I am half off the road on the gravel most of the time. Let me try the Emergency at the nearest hospital. I sit there for two hours on a chair all by myself, nurses passing cheerfully to and fro, refusing all eye contact and shrugging off every attempt to ask for help. At last I recognize a doctor in the passage who went to school with one of my brothers, and plead with him to check whether anything is wrong with me. He takes my blood pressure, gives a shout, and immediately has me put on a bed, where pills are administered to me.

'My God, woman!' Braem Schmiedt says with a merry laugh as he makes up my prescription. 'Only three weeks in the Third World and you need pills for high blood pressure! Welcome to Kroonstad, my dear.'

The next day my condition is unchanged. I am sent to Bloemfontein. My younger brother takes me in the elder one's new BMW. Halfway there, Andries phones: 'How's my car doing?' 'I can tell you,' Hendrik laughs into the cellphone, 'we are not driving to Bloem, we are flowing!'

I spend the afternoon in the waiting room at the Brain-Scanning Unit. The main colour is maroon. The main reading matter is *Matieland*, Stellenbosch University's alumni magazine. All of us waiting here try to look as if our brains are the last places that need scanning. We each keep a shuddering hand, a staggering foot, a twitching eyelid under icy control.

We don't cause trouble. We sit on the maroon precipice of the Great Unknown: The Brain.

On a broad maroon notice board I read: *Alle rekeninge is onmidellik betaalbaar* – All accounts to be settled imediately. '*Onmiddellik*' is misspelt. One of the words I was so careful to teach my students to spell. It takes me some time to notice the mistake. It is nothing, I say to myself, given what may be wrong in one's life, it is absolutely nothing. But my eye keeps straying from the *Matieland* and I start wondering under whose guidance the sign was put up. Is it possible that phalanxes of well-travelled neurologists and radiologists and money-grubbing cash-ologists have not picked it up themselves? Aren't they bothered enough to replace it or – granted that money might be scarce because people don't pay their accounts 'imediately' – to correct it with a felt-tip pen. Maybe no one can spell around here? Maybe no one cares!

Ah, I see, it was done on purpose. It is a test. If you point out the mistake, your brain functions are obviously fine. They give you a discount. Or they dismiss you as neurotic.

I leave the clinic with the information that I have suffered a mild stroke in the brainstem.

On the way back, we have company. While he was waiting for me, my brother bumped into Eben Swart, an old acquaintance from Kroonstad, and he wants to catch a ride with us. Eben's wife is from one of the richest families in Kroonstad, but he bankrupted her land from under them and now sells policies in Bloemfontein. 'And how's it going with the land barons?' he asks, the sarcasm obvious.

'No, it is hard for everybody who still has land,' Hendrik counters.

'Not if your surname is Schoeman. Those people have land as far as the eye can see. Their wives operate with a budget not even the Minister of Finance can muster. The last time my wife came back from one of their parties, she was in a daze for a week.'

He shifts in his seat, preparing himself for a big gossip. 'This was Miets Schoeman's birthday party. It was before the election, in the middle of winter. My wife says those marble and yellowwood and stinkwood tables were loaded with meringues and berries and cheesecakes and pavlovas and what-have-yous, and smaller tables had been set for a sit-down for fifty women. Do you know how many tables and cups and saucers and knives and forks you must own to provide tea and cake for so many women? Just when everyone was laughing and chatting nicely, the kitchen door opened and the black kids from the farm school came filing in. One of the ladies had organized them to come and sing happy birthday to Miets. They had to stand all round the room against the walls, and someone accompanied them on the accordion. They had to sing "Happy Birthday, *Miesies*", and my wife says you could see them shivering in their thin clothes, unable to keep their eyes off the food and the silver and the porcelain. "The Lord is going to punish them for this," I told my wife. "The Lord is going to punish."'

'And you actually want to know how the Lord has punished the Schoemans?' Hendrik asks.

'There you go,' Eben answers.

My brother sits without words, I sit with my stroke. Because the Schoemans still have all their land, one of the few successful farming units in the district.

✧

It is the day before I return to Cape Town. The pills for high blood pressure are slowly taking effect. On the way to fetch the letter about the royal meal from Ouma Hannie, I stop at Suidrand, the primary school across the river which all my children attended twenty years ago, in order to pick up a parcel from the secretary for her daughter in the Cape. Just let an Afrikaner hear that somebody is travelling more than two hundred kilometres, and they want to send a parcel along. I park in the open field next to the playground where I used to wait for my children every afternoon. Mine is the only private vehicle. All the others are taxis, row upon row of them, with their drivers chatting cheerfully through the open windows.

When the bell rings, the children spill out across the street. Little black girls strolling along with breezy plaits, neat little socks and tunics bouncing pertly. A group of little boys wrestling along happily. Among them is a white child. He says goodbye and walks down the street to where he lives. The taxi drivers pack in the school bags and one by one they leave in the direction of the township.

The secretary is in the library. Here there is a long queue of black children checking out books. She shows me the stacks of library cards. The number of books being taken out has quadrupled since black children started attending the school. Books about aeroplanes and houses are popular – but they read everything.

Another teacher comes in. I ask her: 'Was it difficult in the beginning to teach black children?'

'Terribly,' she admits. 'And the problems were legion. The main problem was hygiene. We made up rhymes and songs that go: "When I cough, I make my little hand a fist; when I sneeze, I make my little hand flat; when I yawn, I hold my little hand in front." Otherwise it would just be all over the place. We had to spend time demonstrating how to flush the toilet, how to use the paper, brushing your teeth, blowing your nose. How you have to wash before you come to school. How your clothes must be clean. We had to have a meeting with the parents to agree on hair rules, to explain the necessity of homework. A lot of the kids would go straight home from here, tidy up the house, look after the younger ones back from crèche, and then start cooking supper. Because both their parents work. But now this cannot be, in the afternoons children must study.'

'What about sport?'

'It is difficult for the children to come back in the afternoons for sport. It is an extra trip. So now we coach the various sporting codes during PT periods and break times. Sometimes children stay a bit after school. But the children have so much talent here, that we leave the other white schools far behind with the medals. The only black swimmers in the Northern Free State team are from this school.

'The biggest problem, of course, was language. The children arrive here and can speak only Sesotho. Now we are suddenly forced to present Maths and Science and such things in English, and our English is not always too good. We struggled. Now it is better, since children who come from the kindergarten levels have at least mastered the basic vocabulary of sit and stand.'

'For me the most difficult thing in the beginning was to touch them,' confesses a kindergarten teacher. 'One knows that the little ones still need a lot of physical contact and I was very nervous that I wouldn't be able to. I was afraid that I would flinch when I touched their hair.'

'Don't talk about hair,' says the teacher who takes the Special Education classes. 'One day I could see that these children wanted something from me. Then it came out: they wanted to touch my hair. They'd heard that whites' hair is like that of a cat. So I agreed. They came closer and touched my hair and asked if they could comb it. And then, very pleased with themselves, said that I could now touch *their* hair.'

Did the kindergarten teacher overcome her inhibitions?

'Just the second school day a little girl came running down the corridor, but between her and me there was a little set of steps. And I saw her throwing up her arms and I realized, God, the child thinks I am going to catch her. And then she jumped. And I grabbed her in my arms and saw the expression of joy on her face. I actually kissed her on the cheek.' The teacher's eyes are filled with a confused vulnerability.

Some of the others nod. 'It is unbelievable to teach them.' 'You should see the Valentine's Day cards I got from black children in my class!' 'Every day you can unlock entire worlds for them.'

'My husband can't believe that I touch them. I must wash my hands when I get home.'

'Four hundred of the four hundred and seventy pupils are now black,' says the principal. 'And it was difficult to manage the changes. After 1994, the school kept on losing teaching posts because our numbers were shrinking. I started taking in black children so that people wouldn't lose their jobs. First in separate classrooms, just with certain teachers, so that things could be sorted out in an unthreatening environment. But then I realized that tension was building up among the teachers. Whenever there was a commotion, somebody would say: it is your children who are making the noise. So I decided to make all the teachers part of this, and that was difficult. The more black children came in, the more the white ones left. And that was the top students, the children of the white elite – the children of poor white parents remained behind. In town, I was introduced by other principals as the head of the kaffir school. But over the years we've become so well known for our results and our discipline that nobody can do without us any more.'

'Are there any black teachers here?'

'No. But there is enormous pressure from the parents. My entire school committee is black. And I feel that the first post that opens up must be filled by a black teacher, so that the children can start to have black role models too. But the teachers are still very opposed to this. They feel that they have a good relationship with the children, that there is mutual respect and love, and that a black teacher might spoil things. Because we can't speak Sesotho, he could easily incite the children against us. Or what if he was lazy or drunk or molested the young girls, which we hear often happens in the township, how would we get rid of him without making a racial incident out of it?'

As I walk out I glance at the honours roll. A few names below that of my daughter, there it is: Sophie Mothopeng. Dux pupil 1999.

On the way out to the farm, I come across two white children walking home from school with their mother, and I give them a lift. Yes, they walk five kilometres to school every day. Her husband is unemployed and she works in the hospital laundry. No, it is not a hassle. She would like the children to be in another school, because there are so many blacks in this one. But it is too far. 'Anyway, I tell my kids, if you do not do anything to them, they will not do anything to you. If you just treat them like normal people, everything will be okay.'

chapter nineteen

She feels fat. She feels dumb. She feels that she is wasting away daily from an unknown anguish. How people look, how they speak, how they pronounce their words, how they build their sentences, it all crunches her apart. She lies on her bed for hours while something like hurt washes over her in waves.

Maths classes are the worst. Most lonely. Most intensely lost. She feels annihilated. Her eyes stare without understanding at the scribbling of figures and she clings desperately to words, to 'prove', to 'theorem'. It is as if she cannot break through. Through to calculations, to the others, to herself. During breaks, she sits alone against the wall of the shooting range. She closes her eyes and stares with her inside at the sun.

Every day, break time confirms her unbearable non-existence.

chapter twenty

Her mother calls her to the rondavel. In her hands she holds a big yellow book with a charcoal drawing of a cow on the cover.

'Listen to how beautiful this is ...'

Her mother reads aloud to her. She sees her mother's strong shoulders and neck locked together in a kind of wonderment. Her voice almost a whisper:

sleep now, stooped over intensely, as if listening to our secret bed
the eyelashes relax   the balled eyes have fences
around the closed-up monasteries of the pupils
whirled together in one bright cone of life, a chalice of light
the scream of living, the pain of knowing, you live
a moment

slaap nou, vooroorgebuk intens asof luisterend na ons geheime bed
die wimpers ontspan versluier die gebalde oë, heinings
om die geslote kloosters van die kykers
saamgekolk in een helder tregter van leef, 'n kelk van lig
die skree van lewe, die pyn van wete, jy leef
'n oomblik

...

you are a delicate flower of pulsing ivory
you are deep like a gardenia   silent like an arum lily

sleep now, stir, you break the light with your hands
how narcotic the whelms in the depths of your collarbones
for you I offer these hands full of air, take
   eat   drink   live
take my hands also   and the juice from my body
laugh once more in your dreams   my flower   my fruit
do you not hear? how the night gnaws at the eaves

Her mother closes the book and shakes her head.

'It's just bloody unbelievable, this volume. Look at what he does here.' She shows her daughter a poem called 'Jousting' that consists only of sounds. They try and work out how one would read it aloud.

Kleng jaa tjeng tjang tjeng kleng
Ai joei tsji tsjan bik sjoeing tjôrrr
Fuut tjeng wam kieng oo ssssip
...
Touché

Aaaaaaaaaaaaaaaaaaaaaaaaaaaaaaaaaaaaaaaaaaaaaa
  (ek voel sy swaard soos 'n graat in my gorrel)

'But just look here! The very first poem.'

let the sly bitter ducks shit on my grave
in the rain

They both laugh with exhilaration. It is the first time they have seen the word 'shit' printed on paper. *kak*. In a volume of poetry in which there are no capital letters.

'Who is breyten breytenbach?' she asks.

'I don't care,' her mother says as if she knows exactly, and gently closes *die ysterkoei moet sweet*, holding it like something precious in her lap.

chapter twenty-one

She hangs her music bag on the handlebars and pedals slowly back to the hostel, with the dramatic opening notes of the Beethoven piano sonata on which she has just been tutored lingering in her mind. She turns off towards the river, where the lawns lie autumned on the banks between the frayed golden willow branches. At her favourite tree she drops her bike, takes off her sandals and climbs high up to a branch that makes a seating-fork before it stretches out over the water. This is the branch of wellness, she decided long ago, when she came here during her first weeks in the hostel demented with longing for the farm. Before she sits, she has to stand without holding on to anything, in perfect balance, and say: 'Let me be well. Let me be filled with wellness.' Until she feels accepted. Then she sits down.

The water is ginger green and reflects a quiet clemency of clouds. Slivers of red ochre and copper sift from the willows into the water. She closes her eyes and lets it wash over her. This morning. Third period. Maths. Mr De Haan is returning the marked tests, starting with the best results and working his way down. The boy with the blue eyes behind her gets his first. Mr De Haan hands out the papers and reads out the marks. Half the class has theirs. Three quarters. Then Migal Moller, then even Wouter Cornelissen who is already nineteen ... Lastly, he throws hers on her desk. 'Nought,' he says, 'pathetic, absolutely pathetic.' Remembering the words burns away her chest. Throttles her. She breathes with difficulty, but lets it spend itself. She recalls the face of Mr De Haan and dwells deliberately on his disapproving mouth as he said the word 'nought', the way his eyes dismissed her, the place on his chin where he had nicked himself with a razor, his thumbnail with the prominent grooves holding her test slashed with red. The humiliation of that. That feeling.

Then she grabs the face of Mr De Haan with both hands, takes a deep breath and dives down in her head. She dives through different glowing strata of water. It becomes colder and darker, but she perseveres. Mr De Haan's face is deathly pale in her hands, his hairy ears slimy, he cannot control the corners of his mouth, air globules bleed from his nostrils. His thinning hair drifts like sediment from his blotched scalp. The purple rims of his eyes half-closed. At last she reaches the trunk. She opens the lid and throws in the head of Mr De Haan and his voice and his words. In the bottom of the trunk she sees Jannie Lubbe, her mother's face moving around while saying, 'A monster is what you have become.' The PT teacher. She shuts the trunk with a bang. She clicks the lock shut. She cuts herself loose from the waving knotting waterweed and shoots to the surface. When she opens her eyes, she knows it will never enter her mind again. She stretches her arms into the flaming light and repeats: 'I am filled with wellness. I am well.'

chapter twenty-two

A writer comes to visit. Her mother has to fetch him from the station, because he doesn't drive. For dinner she bakes bread and opens *nastergal* jam. She realizes that the man is special to her mother. If she likes somebody, she opens jam with whole orange pieces; if she wants to impress somebody, she opens her green-fig jam bottled with copper pennies; but *nastergal*, bane-wort, picked with endless patience, a batch never consisting of more than a cup or two, takes first prize. This is for really special people.

That first night, the writer breaks a lamp chimney but tells no one as he writes through the night by the small flickering light. The next morning he comes to the breakfast table with only half his beard shaved. He lost interest when he was halfway through, he says.

Her father takes a picture of him sitting on the ironstone wall reading. The writer looks up, sees her father and says jokingly, 'You can offer the photograph to the newspapers the day I win the Hertzog Prize – it will be the only photograph of me in existence.'

This is the first writer, other than her mother, that she has met in real life.

'Is he not terribly conceited?' she asks.

'He is a brilliant man. One can feel that. And he is merely eccentric, not conceited,' her mother says. 'You must remember that to be able to write, to believe that you have something to say which other people will want to read, always requires some kind of ego. And often the bigger the talent, the bigger the ego; but at the same time, the greater the insecurity and the need to be affirmed. The trick lies in managing that ego in such a way that you can live a normal life. Otherwise, what will you write about?'

'But he doesn't seem to me to lead a normal life. Not driving. Not eating meat. Not talking if he doesn't find the conversation "worthwhile".'

'We will have to see what he writes ...'

A few months after his visit, the book appears. She waits impatiently for her mother to finish reading it. Then, for the first time, she reads the language of loneliness: 'Inside the circle of lamplight it was as lonely as the streets of this deserted autumn. He wanted to write, but he was not able. The things that touched him – leaves that turn the colour of ochre and flame, swans in Vondel Park, the sickle moon behind the clouds – could yield nothing more than the verse of occasion ...'

And right at the end: 'And it stayed with him. The loneliness. On every plane, in every airport, in every street, even in the circle of lamplight on a faraway farm, it stayed with him.'

Within a year the book is awarded the coveted Hertzog Prize. The Sunday newspaper uses the photograph taken by her father.

chapter twenty-three

When she arrives back from her piano lesson, her mother is waiting in front of the hostel. 'I've come to fetch you, they have killed Dr Verwoerd.'

The next morning the Standard Six Afrikaans teacher takes her aside. Her cheeks are red and her eyes almost wild. 'The staff have decided to dedicate the whole school yearbook to Dr Verwoerd and we want it to open with a powerful poem about him. I want you to write it. You have to understand that it is a very important assignment.'

She has never written a poem before. She has never even imagined that she *could* write a poem.

One about Dr Verwoerd? She remembers sitting on her father's shoulders while a crowd of people from the town waited for him to pass by on his way to Bloemfontein. His car pulled over next to the road and he greeted some of the people amicably. The man with him called her father forward and described him as the 'force' behind the party in Kroonstad. Then her hand was also ceremoniously shaken. But that is all she can remember.

How could she colour his life with her own?

And who is saying she *is* a poet?

'First write a poem about something you do know,' her mother says on Friday afternoon, 'and then read it aloud. It mustn't sound fabricated.'

She writes three rhyming stanzas about Ruth, who could not have children. She finds it so easy, as if it had already been written elsewhere. She also finds it easy to imagine the biblical Ruth. She doesn't know why.

She likes her first effort so much that she writes a longer poem that same evening which does not rhyme: it is addressed to a blind friend and describes the joys of seeing. She feels the images rising from the page and realizes that she can hear what she writes clearly. But the poem sounds phoney. 'Of course it does,' her mother says. 'Aside from that morose blind piano tuner, you know nobody who is blind. You also cannot know what Ruth is feeling, mind you, but in this poem you are merely telling a story.'

'So can I write something about Dr Verwoerd?'

'A Standard Six child? I don't think so.'

That evening she reads Lorca and wishes she could write something like:

Oh, white wall of Spain!
Oh, black bull of sorrow!
Oh, hard blood of Ignacio!
Oh, nightingale of his veins!
No.

She tries. But her hand becomes unbearably heavy, as if the pencil makes it wilt. Her fingers wither from her senses. She leaves writing and starts reading insatiably. Love poetry. She devours everything. She goes on a poetry binge. She writes down, she annotates, she learns by heart in Afrikaans the words of Van Wyk Louw:

Your eyes have become attentively quiet
in the midst of our words,
as in the vineyard when the wind dies down

Jou oë het aandagtig stil geword
in die middel van ons woorde,
soos in die wingerd as die wind gaan lê.

She writes everything down in a separate book. This is the only thing she will serve. For the rest she cares nothing. She refuses to do Maths homework. She fails Science. She sits alone like a cold seething fire. She doesn't care. During breaks she sits by herself at the far edge of the school grounds to read poetry. Or to write. Diary and poems. She shudders at the sight of other people. She loathes the teachers when she sees them sitting with their little hats and lunch boxes and cases. She makes a point of not talking. At home she is dumb at the table, but there is always such a commotion that no one even notices that she has become someone else.

chapter twenty-four

They return from deep inside Lesotho. That night she writes a poem about mountains with fields that look as if they were carved out with a razorblade. Next door she hears her mother typing. In the morning, when her mother takes a walk, she quietly goes to read at the typewriter.

'When you say: Lesotho, you say: mountains, you say: Maluti. He who sees the Maluti turning white in winter, who sees silver slivers of water cascading down her green flanks, will never untangle himself from that beguilement. As if the umbilical cord of South Africa had been cut there in Lesotho, steaming lava bulges up high into the air from the squashed mountain folds. A spectacle it is when the mountain ties to her body the snow blanket that she loves. Majestic and untouched as she rises from the mist and rain, guarding over the summery sounds of children's voices and goats in the sun.'

She sits in wonderment. That her mother is so good.

When she tears up her own attempt, she realizes that she is fiercely jealous.

chapter twenty-five

In the bright lights of the stage her right hand looks lean yet purposeful. She hesitates before it alights on the upper G key. She is intensely aware that the hall is absolutely quiet. She feels the power flowing in her arm, flooding over into the final cadence. When she bows for the applause and receives the cup for the best competitor in piano, joy squirts through her. A camera flashes. Her name and photograph appear in the local newspaper for the first time.

chapter twenty-six

The German teacher calls her aside. 'Are you a child of the Lord?'

'How do you mean, Miss?'

She holds her forefinger in the air. 'Just answer my question. Are you a child of the Lord?'

'Yes, Miss, maybe not the best child ...'

'That was not my question,' the teacher interrupts her. 'I read your work in the yearbook. When one has received a gift from God, one has to give it back to Him. One must use it to His honour.'

She walks away astonished. The one poem was about Ruth, the other about a blind friend. How on earth could they have exposed her as an insincere child of the Lord?

chapter twenty-seven

His hands dig in under her dress. When she stops him, he pushes them into her bra, snorting wetly in her ear, and it is just beard and breath and sweaty fingers. She pulls away and starts running. The next day he is walking with the girl with the gorgeous legs.

What is it? He cannot even string two intelligent words together, but he wants to get under her clothes. What is wrong with them? They read nothing, they know nothing. If they ask you to folk dancing, it is to make out. If they ask you to the bioscope, it is to make out. If they sit next to you on the bus, it is to make out. And evenings are filled with bouts of endless wrestling.

chapter twenty-eight

She hates her mother. When she had to do the hem of her school tunic, she made it nice and short. 'Unpick that hem,' her mother said. 'Or do you want to look like a slut?'

chapter twenty-nine

'Yes, you nice privileged white children – spun into your little cocoons,' says the new History teacher, who has an anchor tattooed on his enormous upper arm. Evidently he used to be a sailor. 'While you are driven to school in your thick winter clothing, black children your age are digging for food in the rubbish heaps a couple of miles from here. But what do you care?' he says, and continues with the lesson.

It is Friday afternoon. At home, back from boarding school, she puts down her knife and fork next to her plate. 'I can't eat such a plate of food when there are children in town who have to dig through the rubbish heaps for scraps.'

'And where do you hear such nonsense?' her mother asks in the way that shows she has her full furious attention.

'It's not nonsense, old Koos Matroos sees them every morning when he drives to school.'

Her mother gets up. She goes to the telephone and speaks to somebody. Then she calls her: 'Come here and speak to your uncle. Since he's the mayor of the town, he should know what's going on.' Then she speaks into the handset: 'Pieter, please explain to this child what the black children are doing on the rubbish heaps.'

Her mother gives her the handset and she puts it to her ear. '*Og*, my child,' booms Uncle Pieter, 'these black kids are collecting things. You know that white people are *mos* very indifferent about what they throw away. We are spoilt. Now some merchants have organized these children to scour the rubbish dumps for valuable items and they pick up teaspoons and knives and beautiful jewellery. These are not poor children you see there. On the contrary.'

Uncle Pieter speaks loudly enough for her mother to hear. She looks up into her mother's eyes. And for one terrible moment she knows that her mother knows that she knows that Uncle Pieter is lying. But that it would be easier for all of them to just live with it.

That Monday she is moved to the B class. Now she has History with Mr Boshof. She does not know anybody. She just sits and stares in front of her. Break time she goes to the library. The next morning she walks reluctantly to her new class. At the top of the stairs a boy is sitting. 'You dropped your eraser yesterday,' he says and holds his hand out to her. She takes it and when she looks up she steps into his eyes. Blindly, she keeps staring and staring. She turns hot and then cold. As if she is being washed with blue.

In class he sits across from her. He takes out his pencil case, which is covered in labels.

'Who is that?' she asks.

'The Beatles ...' He looks a trifle shocked that she doesn't know what he is talking about.

'This boy's in love with you ... and that one will make you cry,' he sings softly, lisping his tongue and swaying his body a little. She is blinded by his eyes and graceful lankness.

chapter thirty

That night she looks fervently through all her volumes of poetry, quotation books, collections. What she wants to tell him, she cannot find in her books. She takes up a pencil:

'slaked by your eyes
I walk my heart
and hum your name'

Everything inside her comes together. Fits. Each open synapse melts perfectly into her pencil and her entire being finds its balance. Her whole body feels light and infused with sound.

'your eyes are wind blue and it spreads like heartache'

That whole night language flows from her.

'let me break through blue
oh see the white jessamine I gathered for you'

She crosses out 'white' and adds 'have'.

chapter thirty-one

She unfolds the little note:

The pain of loving you
Is almost more than I can bear

I walk in fear of you
The darkness starts up where
You stand, and the night comes through
Your eyes when you look at me
                    D.H. Lawrence

She is utterly delighted. That he is so smart. That he is so beautiful. That he is so unmoveable. That he can find poetry with which to express himself. He sends her: 'How you murdered your family / means nothing to me / as your mouth moves across my body' (Leonard Cohen). And: 'Blackbird singing in the dead of night / Take these broken wings and learn to fly' (Paul McCartney).

chapter thirty-two

'everything is ending'

(She writes as if it all comes by itself. As if somebody is saying it to her.)

'also me, also you, also this year.
that you will leave me soon
I cannot bear'

That evening she writes another poem. And that Saturday and that Sunday.

It is a whole handful of poems that she takes in her suitcase back to boarding school on Sunday evening. During the week she does not find time to write, but the poems lie like something warm and glorious in her cupboard under her shirts. The next weekend she writes them all out neatly in a small notebook that she carries in her case. Every day during the first period she sends him poetry. And sees the soft down on his peachlike skin. She sends him what she is reading.

Beautiful youth of reed
Wide shoulders, narrow waist
Skin of apple at night
Sad mouth, enormous eyes
With nerves of burning silver
Patrols the slim street.

Lorca

chapter thirty-three

Suddenly school is bearable, she manages to survive the overfull hostel with its hairy, steaming bathrooms, its matted-together, well-built farm daughters, its cabbage and disinfectant smells. He explains the maths to her. Teaches her how to draw perfect biology sketches. When she comes back from piano lessons, he is waiting for her on his bicycle. They walk on the banks of the river back to the hostel. Their feet ankle-deep in dry autumn leaves. He turns the colour of winter. His thin wrists. His scrawny body in a long brown jersey. Orange bell-bottoms. Bony feet. His lush brown hair. The willows with their brown whips in the water. His body is light and free. His thoughts in many places.

That evening she writes:

'move your feet through the dry leaves
move them, move them'

chapter thirty-four

One Friday afternoon a strange boy and his mother are at the table. They speak English. Mrs Read is a journalist from the *Farmer's Weekly* who wants to write an article on her father's sheep. Mrs Read's hair is dyed so black, she hears her mother say later, that the colour is actually starting to seep down her forehead. The boy is chubby and full of pimples and stubble.

Everybody rides on the back of the bakkie to the kraal where the stud sheep are waiting. Isak Mokokoane leads the prize ram through the crush pen. She sits on the wall with the English boy. She is suddenly ashamed of the farm workers' worn overalls and ragged shoes.

'I don't know why black people should be treated like this,' she says, suddenly.

He turns to her in surprise. His sulkiness forgotten. A fire burns in his eyes. 'Me too! I think black people are the equals of whites. I think black people should rise up in revolution and take their country back. This country belongs to them.'

Somewhat surprised herself, she nods her head. 'I belong to this organization,' he says, muffling his voice, but his mother bids him with a sharp voice to fetch her camera from the bakkie. The rest of the time the woman sees to it that he does not strike up a conversation with her again.

chapter thirty-five

An hour before her violin exams, the bridge of her instrument snaps. She struggles to repair it and then sees that she is late. In front of the hostel she stops a man on a motor-bike and asks him to drop her at the church hall. Her mother's eyes are black with fury when she arrives amidst clouds of exhaust fumes and engine noise, with her violin case and a strange man.

chapter thirty-six

She walks into the barber's shop to have her hair cut. 'We only cut men's hair,' the barber says. 'I want my hair cut like a man,' she says. The rest of the time neither the barber nor the men waiting say a word to one another.

chapter thirty-seven

She decides that she does not believe in sin. Sin is all in people's heads. You are getting too big for your boots, her mother says.

One day she will be somebody, she says. She might even commit murder, just to be somebody.

'What a terrible, monstrous child you're becoming,' says her mother.

She refuses to wait for anybody. If a teacher is not in the class, she gets up and goes to the library. If one of her parents or Isak is not waiting outside the school on Fridays, she starts walking out to the farm. She will not allow anybody to waste her time.

'I cannot believe this child's obsessive selfishness,' her father complains after he has had to drive up and down the route to the farm searching for her.

'The Light of Lichtenburg, the King of King William's Town, that is who I'll become, and then nobody will think that my mother writes my poetry for me.'

'The way you're behaving now, you will become nothing more than the Baloney of Benoni,' her mother snipes, and both her parents crow with laughter.

'One day people will know you as *my* mother and nobody will dream that I am supposed to be Dot Serfontein's daughter!' But before she even finishes the sentence, she starts laughing herself.

chapter thirty-eight

Aunt Enid comes to visit for the weekend. She is a psychologist. Saturday morning, Aunt Enid and her mother go into the rondavel and lock the door. She knows that they are talking about her. All through the previous evening, they were looking at each other meaningfully, as the books say, every time she opened her mouth. She walks past the window of the rondavel a couple of times, but can hear nothing. After persistent eavesdropping, the next afternoon she hears her mother telling her father: 'Enid talked a lot of nonsense. It was really a stupid idea of me to get her. She suggested such ridiculous things as safe surroundings so that the child can open herself up to experiences, now I ask you – a sixteen-year-old girl opening herself up to experiences, for crying in a bucket. And we should allow her to daydream. According to Enid, Freud said it is an essential component of creativity – daydreaming. But when I asked her what she meant by daydreaming, did it mean drifting off in maths classes for example, she became very vague. She gave me some sheets of exercises for developing the ability to make imaginative leaps and link unexpected things. I find it all so silly!'

'And her lying?'

'Enid says we should make a distinction between lying and imagination. So I asked her, tell me, is it lying or imagination when a teacher compliments you on your child's heart-rending speech about the terrible car accident you recently had in Cape Town. In the meantime, you haven't been to Cape Town for years and never had an accident in your life. But Enid has nothing better to offer than that we should ask her about it and help her to understand the difference between reality and imagination. I mean, what kind of nonsense is that? She knows the difference all too well, she'll just say she coloured something she read with her own life to get a good mark or whatever.'

'But how should we discipline her?'

'According to Enid, we should actively encourage her ambition. She says many people are creative and talented, but most find it too hard to make something of it. They're too afraid to take the risk. She says that to tap the inner walls takes courage. And then she moved to her favourite topic: women. Especially gifted women. She says research has shown that gifted women often try to escape the demands of their talent by marrying a creative or potentially creative husband instead. A gifted woman will rather support her creative husband than be brave enough to live out her own creativity. I said to Enid, the women in my family are not like this – we will never hide behind such bullshit!'

'Now why do you think it's nonsense?' Her father has never sworn. A word like 'shit' will never cross his lips.

'Man, I told her the child is one of four children in a family struggling to make ends meet on a farm staggering under debt. In this household, one child is not, and never will be, more special than any other. This is a full, busy household where everybody has his or her own talents and ambitions. There is really no room here for anybody to be a prima donna warranting special attention and terrorizing the rest with whims and delusions. I said to Enid: in this house everybody knows his place and carries his fucking weight. You bloody well fit in. And you live out your writing in the way other women bake cakes or make clothes.'

Then her mother goes for a walk and returns long after dark.

chapter thirty-nine

'I am writing a poem for you, ma'
(she writes that evening)

'without fancy punctuation
without words that rhyme
without adjectives
just sommer
a barefoot poem –

because you raise me
in your small halting hands
you chisel me with your black eyes
and pointed words

I am so sorry ma
that I am not
what I so much want to be for you'

chapter forty

The riverbank is a profusion of colour and light. All along, strings and strings of Christmas lights are streaking the water with colour. The big pine trees have lights woven even into their highest branches. The lights of a gigantic yellow daffodil and a blue and white windmill beam across the sprawling lawns, and at the playground enormous balls made of hundreds of lights twirl in the summer-night air. The suspension bridge looks like a fairy path strewn with lights. The river boat chuffs up and down leaving slashes of blurred colour shimmering in its wake. At the Chinese garden, among a flurry of red lights, children are jumping from stone to stone – past water lilies, over small stone bridges and around fountains. Families have spread blankets on the grass for picnics. An end-of-the-year party is taking place at the braai area. At the pavilion there is a session, where young people with long hair and chunky jewellery are twisting and shaking to the music. She sits between his legs in a little rowing boat. He rows serenely and with ease. They do not talk. She is only aware of his legs against her thighs, his chest against her back. At times he stops rowing and draws his hand through her short, boyish hair. She feels how they melt into colour and moving water. From a radio on the banks Françoise Hardy sings towards them in her husky voice: 'All over the world, people must meet and part / There's someone like me, feeling a pain in her heart.' He rows in under the hanging branches of a willow. They are softly closed off by fragrant fringes and the smell of willow bark. He bends over, kisses her neck and puts his hands on her breasts. In the dark she sees his hands on her blue granny-print top. 'That thumb,' she thinks, 'with that thumb he broke his sandwich in half this morning to share with me.' 'If you move, we will capsize,' he whispers in her neck and ear, and she feels how blood shoots like ice into her nipples. When he rows out she feels him swollen against her back.

chapter forty-one

'Aaaah!' she moans aloud, snapping the book shut, sinking to the floor. Too late she realizes she is among people in a bookshop. She puts the new *Groot Verseboek* quickly back on the shelf and walks out with a stiff back. She is both exuberant and devastated. For three years now she has been trying to find the exact words, the precise image to describe waves rolling on to the beach with their spray flying backwards in the wind. She has tried everything to capture the forward movement of the wave, the backward movement of the spray, the darkness of the wave, the whiteness of the spray. Until a moment ago, browsing through this latest volume of Afrikaans poetry, she came across a new poem by D.J. Opperman: like porcupines the waves storm the beach. Porcupines. Oh my dear God and Lord of Lords and King of Heaven and Earth! Oh, to have that kind of eye – an eye that is like a magnet for plucking the right words from your soul.

CHAPTER NINE

I take my grandmother's letter to Ouma Hannie out of the envelope. I know her broad, placid handwriting so well. She writes:

> We have had a hard time of it with the Governor General's visit. First the council let us know that thirty people would be coming, and then again later fifty. In the district there was also great argument over who was invited and who not. And all I could think of was: We are dining with the enemy. We are feeding those who have starved us. I will be smiling at those who broke my people's heart.
>
> Mother Lenie was still very weak. But she had installed herself on Aunt Sannie Leeukuil's chair, while we darted about carrying out her instructions. She made Aunt Stoffies from Rivierplaas come over to make the puff pastry for the venison and chicken pies, milk tarts and jam tartlets. Aunt Stoffies, as befits a doyenne of puff pastry, moved into the spare room a week before the occasion to supervise the purchasing of flour, the churning of butter, the scrubbing of the rolling pins and marble slabs. Because of her hands, they say. Aunt Stoffies is reputed to have perfect puff-pastry hands. They say she gets up at four o'clock in the morning to roll out the dough. In midsummer, she locks

the door and takes off all her clothes so as not to perspire – puff pastry does not respond well to sweaty hands. On cool slabs of specially carved marble, she will roll out the dough. I have to tell you that because of this rumour of supposed nakedness, Kootjie now refuses bluntly to eat anything resembling puff pastry. When I asked, 'What do you think would happen to the dough if she ...?' he just got up and walked out of the door.

Old Aunt Anna-jannie, old and toothlessly shuddering as she is, had to come and make her koeksisters in front of Ma Lenie's eyes. When she mixed the syrup, she chased out everybody except Ma, who pretended to be crocheting while Anna-jannie mixed the ingredients. And so, at last, as you might have gathered, we have discovered that it was not ginger but a knife-tip of cream of tartar that gave her syrup its unmatchable taste. Can you believe it? Ma Lenie always suspected that something was missing from the recipe.

But you wanted to know about the menu.

The Governor General had a choice of pies, venison and lamb, Afrikaner hump in brine with sweet mustard, three turkeys stuffed with prunes and figs, five geese stuffed with cumquats from the colony, three enormous hams with their skins in crackling shards in separate dishes, six larded legs of springbok marinated for a week in butter-milk, accompanied by two buckets of funeral rice (yellow rice with raisins), a bucket of pumpkin with cinnamon and aniseed, a bucket of green-bean bredie stewed with sheep's tails, a cauldron overflowing with baked potatoes, and twenty bowls of Ma Lenie's famous tomato salad. After much debate, the stewed quinces were put in an old unused trough (the Guest, however, never touched them). But as you have guessed, the pièce de résistance was the plum pudding, specially cooked for the Governor General in a caul-dron. Klasie presented this enormous pudding to him in a newly painted wheelbarrow. With the coffee we served milk tart, koeksisters and Aunt Stoffie's feather-light jam puffs and paper-thin slices of guava marinated in port. As an unexpected surprise, Ma Lenie ordered biltong and cream for the aftertaste. All of these were served by the young women of the district wearing white dresses.

'I never knew that grandma was such a compelling writer!' I say surprised, but know my mother's answer in advance: Writing, like music, runs in families. It is nothing spe-cial, it is genetic. Some families can cook, others can write. All the same: I am thrilled to be drifting among so many female texts.

✧

I greet my parents in the small hallway of their house in town. I am leaving very early the next morning for Cape Town. I hug them and feel how frail they have become. I want to extend some tender gesture or make some promise to allay their confusion, but the sound of blood through my head is overwhelming. Clearly, the pills have not kicked in completely yet. On the stoep, my mother says: 'Across from us a coloured family has moved in. The man seems to be a policeman. But he and I are the only ones in the street who work in our own gardens. So we greet each other these days, and yesterday he came to ask me how I get my gardenias to be without yellow leaves.'

Before I leave for the farm, I stop at the house of my friend and former colleague, Sheridan Jooste. Since we last taught together at the coloured high school, he has completed a master's degree in business administration and has been employed in the civil service.

Sheridan and I have come a long way together. The most memorable moment I shared with him was when his choir was declared overall winner in the national Coloured Choir of the Year competition, and the children carried the two of us – choirmaster and accompanist – on their shoulders from the Cape Town city hall out on to the Parade.

Sheridan was also with me in the first and only truly inclusive march in Kroonstad. During the eighties, all mass protest in Kroonstad was ruthlessly suppressed. Then a march was organized from the coloured area to the centre of town, to say: this is our town too and we demand equal rights here. We were a few hundred people from the coloured and black townships in a column eight abreast. Right in front walked the tiny dominee of the mission church, his cassock flapping in the dusty August wind.

Surrounded by our pupils, Sheridan and I toyi-toyied along. They showed us the latest styles. 'No, Miss, you must lift your legs like a young comrade!' There was an emancipating aggression in the air. From this day forth the town would belong to all of us. That was the purpose of the march. To tell the town: take notice of us, acknowledge us. This is also our town. We want to share in it.

So there we stood, aligned as ordered, and waited. Up in front, serious negotiations were taking place. We waited. The comrades were getting restless. Then the message came down through the ranks. The march would be shot to pieces if it tried to enter the white town.

'But what must I do with the pent-up energies of the people behind me?' Ds Jantjies apparently argued. 'If I call it off now, people will go on the rampage and then you will have much more trouble than if you just let them march a little.'

All right, the police decided, we could march up to the small flyover where the industrial area began. What! That is barely eight hundred metres! Well, it's that or nothing, and we don't really have any more time to waste. Ds Jantjies consulted down the line. Look, it is better than nothing. Let us march!

Everyone in position, but suddenly we saw the police deploying. They spread out so that they could cover the whole procession as well as the adjacent veld with their weapons. You could hear them cocking their guns. Others patrolled us with dogs.

Sheridan and I were standing next to a steel wall of yellow armoured cars, and from the corners of our eyes we saw the bandoliers glimmering with finger-thick bullets. We looked ahead, while slit-eyed policemen let the chains of their attack dogs slip so that they raged up, possessed and foaming, right next to us. We could smell their breath. We felt more and more thin, I more bleak, more pulsing, more alone in the cold sooty air blowing over the township. The merry bravado of earlier had turned to silence. We were sharply aware of the ash, the waste paper fluttering disconsolately amongst us. And of being up against a cruel, indestructible force.

We linked arms. We stood arm in arm. Suddenly it was as if the whole landscape stopped breathing. Then we started walking. It was a march in complete stillness. Your heart started to spin dully inside you like an overripe pear. But after a few steps, we felt the power flowing through us. We marched, therefore we were.

A hundred metres or so from the flyover, the procession halted abruptly. I stretched to see through the ranks. Just past the flyover, without a care in the world, Oom Piet Buffel was herding his cattle back from the town pen. He was halfway across when he became aware of the spectacle. He looked back, then this way, then that, then suddenly pulled himself up straight, tilted his hat a little on his head, and carried on with his cattle, sauntering as if he went about his work every day under the fearful gaze of hundreds of people, surrounded by loaded guns and Casspirs.

The moment the march resumed, one of the young oxen took fright and crashed into the police lines. A dog broke loose. Others barked furiously. Then shots, orders being yelled. We scattered across the neighbourhood. In total panic, hundreds of us ran to the nearest houses. Before me somebody fell down. I saw blood. Some jumped cat-footed over an asbestos-sheeting wall, others dived in behind wire fences or wrenched open garden gates. I took cover behind someone's woodpile. A whitey in the woodpile, it flashed through my mind. How long it was before I realized everything had gone quiet, I don't know. I found my way back to the school. There the others were waiting on school desks that they had carried out into the sun. And they laughed. And shuddered. And giggled with fright. The march discovered it had a thousand eyes. Each telling their own version. Three were wounded, none were dead – except for one of Oom Piet's cows. We screamed with laughter. We related the day's events over and over to each other. We kept on touching each other – in wonder, in rapture. We stretched out our arms in the sunlight, we sniffed the winter air. Somebody went off to buy vetkoek and snoek. Sheridan laughed nervously: 'Miss Antjie, when I looked down, I saw that you were *pumping* those Adidas of yours – the gravel was actually flying!'

It was Sheridan who fetched his television set from home, bunny ears and all, when we got the message through the ANC underground to watch F.W. de Klerk's speech at the opening of parliament. The television was set up in the school's singing room and we all squeezed on to the choir benches for the occasion. Finally, the moment arrived. F.W. spoke. We listened. Then it was all over. 'Now what the hell did he say?'

We put our heads together: he has unbanned the ANC and announced that Nelson Mandela will be released. No? Yes!

'How can he say such unbelievable things as if it is nothing!' a teacher cried out. 'As if it is just another announcement that only affects him and the whites!'

Somebody went to listen to the news on his car radio and reported back: it was true! It was genuinely true! The school day was forgotten. We decided to go and have tea at the Wimpy Bar in the main street. Everything was *mos* now desegregated. Everything was now equalized. Everything was now ours too. People were arriving at the Wimpy proudly wearing T-shirts that used to be banned. SACP. Nelson Mandela. We packed the place to the rafters. The black waitresses serving us with huge smiles.

At one stage I looked outside. Everything seemed ominously normal out there. 'Do you see what I see, Mr Sheridan?' He looked down the main street. 'Everything might be different, my friend, but let me tell you, in this street everything still looks suspiciously the same. Here nobody gives a damn what we are celebrating.'

'No, Miss Antjie, things have changed forever, don't you worry.'

More than a decade later, it is indeed true. Most of the big stores have disappeared. Lots of 'Space to Let' signs are up. Before, Reitz Street was the dividing line: black above, white below. Now the whole town is black, its street image is black. Well-dressed black people bustle across the intersections, buy at the shops. At the traffic lights, I study the faces. Intelligent. Good-natured. Most seem relaxed. Here and there a white figure appears. Sunken with stress, visibly poor to the point of seeming retarded. Why do so many of the whites look like this? Only later, I learn that the parking attendants in Kroonstad are all disabled whites. It is a church-run project to provide them with an income.

'Terrible poverty among the whites,' says the social worker. 'And it is almost as if they are degenerating because of the poverty. You know, as if they are becoming inhuman. There is much greater deprivation among black people, but there are also such amazing support structures: you will always find help somewhere, someone sends a little money, gives a little flour or a jersey. Even though people make a living off the rubbish dump, a sort of humanity remains. I don't know why that is. But the levels of dehumanization among whites I have never encountered among blacks.'

Rubbish dump? Did I hear correctly? She takes me. The dump looks like a big sore festering with shimmering plastic bags, smoke, broken glass, and scores of people, mostly women, but also children and men. In the midst of great squalor, they wait to storm the lorries in the hope of finding something to survive by. The leader of the scavengers says the municipality pays them if they manage to salvage paper and cardboard, bottles and tins. It makes the retrieving a little bit easier if it is already sorted out. The only things that have no value are the plastic bags.

Sheridan is doing well. Even though his children are at white schools, he hasn't moved out of the black neighbourhood. He has made some additions to his house and drives a new Mercedes. 'I think it is necessary to remain in your community in order to strengthen it.' When I arrive, one of his colleagues from the Education Department, whom he introduces as Thabo, is visiting. They are talking shop.

It appears that the education authorities have been monitoring a particular black school in a town near Kroonstad. For years, the school had a very low pass rate – under ten per cent. So the authorities sent in a team to observe the school for two weeks, and then a list was handed to the principal about all the irregularities, ranging from the absence of a timetable to the absence of teachers. After a year, nothing had changed. Then the entire staff was summoned to Bloemfontein and given a thorough dressing-down.

'Why are you not wearing ties?' the Director-General of Education apparently said. 'Can we assume that the lack of respect you are showing us, your superiors, you also show to education in general?' And then they took the teachers one by one. 'Mr Molefe, why should the Department pay your salary when not a single child in your class has passed Maths? Explain it to us.'

By the end of that year, the school's pass rate had shot up to more than thirty per cent, the year after to more than forty, and in the most recent exams to sixty. Thabo is chuffed.

'Have you managed to set up timetables?' I ask. From experience, I know that some black schools have only a partial timetable, a 'sort of' schedule. A teacher who feels like teaching will simply step out of his classroom and call whichever class happens to be sitting in the sun outside to come in and do a bit of his subject. Physical Training, Religious Instruction or Career Guidance are seldom taught. At one school where I worked, some teachers were incapable of teaching after the break on Fridays, because they had already started drinking. Many were absent on Mondays with a babelaas. Then there was the teacher who refused to teach Maths after twelve, because the children were too tired. So she sat in the sun and smoked, or munched from a well-stocked lunch box.

'Well, every school now has a computer with special software that works out a timetable in the blink of an eye,' Thabo says with a fleeting smile.

'And how are things at the white schools?'

'In general, very difficult. You can't budge them. They sit in their little kingdoms as if they are made of gold. Even the smallest change is accompanied by endless discussion and eventual blackmail. And then they slip through your fingers anyway and do things the way they want to. In one school, Afrikaans is being used to keep black children out. Another school that does use English in its teaching, only takes enough black students for one class – between thirty and forty. They have heard somewhere that if a school becomes more than one third black, then the ethos changes. Oh, and that dare not happen. The result is we now have black kids with a good primary school education – from the old "Model C" schools – who cannot be accommodated in a high school. In addition, the white principals of the mainly black primary schools refuse to appoint black teachers. When you speak to them about it, they just stiffen their faces like this. We will have to start leaning on them soon.'

'But things have changed a lot, haven't they?'

'Not really,' Sheridan says. 'The whites still have everything and the blacks still have nothing.'

'That isn't true,' I say. 'Look at you. You couldn't even attend university when you were young, and here you're a DG with a master's degree.'

'In spite of the changes, not because of them!'

'But what are you comparing things to? Ten years ago, your children would have had to go to school here in the township, you would have had to go all the way to Vista to study. No white principal would have given Thabo the time of day. Now he can put pressure on them.'

'None of the principals listen to me, anyway. But that is not the point. The changes you see are in places where they don't make a difference. On television black men are suddenly drinking whisky, black women are doing their own laundry. In Kroonstad a black man wears the mayor's chain, there are black children in the white schools. But these things don't matter. As soon as black people take control of something, that thing loses its power. *Sjoep!* Suddenly the power is gone, and you look around and see that the whites have twisted things here and there, and taken the power with them. It is somewhere else again.'

'Oh, please. Where does the power lie in Kroonstad? The state gives millions to the municipality – which is run by blacks! – to look after the poor. But instead of doing that, they pay themselves big salaries and employ double the number of officials. Whose fault is that? Where have whites taken the power? As I see it, the whites are the only ones paying their rates and taxes.'

Sheridan is jogging his foot, a nervous habit I remember from the past. He says:

'If a black mayor arrives in a white municipality, then he is disempowered from the word go. They put a spoke in his wheel, they patronize him, they pay him off, in short, they try to work him through the ears, because they and their buddies want to keep things as they are. Their positions, their abuse of council property and privilege. Now such a mayor has to create a black municipality before he can reach the poor.'

'The problem is maybe that there are not many examples in Africa of people who've got their hands on the money, but kept their priorities focused on the poor.'

'You see!' Sheridan is getting excited. 'One can't have any discussion in this country. As soon as you make a point, you are bombarded with examples from Africa!'

'Well, it's not as if anyone has been distancing themselves from these examples, loud and clear.'

He pours the tea that his wife has brought in. He is angry. I regret my words, but also realize that our good relationship is bound to have its tensions. Our lives have diverged over the years.

Thabo is shaking snuff from a small tin. Then he takes another container from his pocket, filled with sugar-free tablets, and puts three in his tea.

'Something else may be missing here,' says Thabo. 'Before 1990, we all had distorted images of each other. Whites are like this and blacks are like that. From 1990 to 1994, we realized with growing astonishment how many things we actually do have in common. How much is shared between Afrikaner and African. How little Ubuntu Communism and Boere Socialism differ from one another, how much of an old-fashioned Christian ethic underscores all our comings and goings. That is why the elections were such a success. Because of what bound us together and what future we envisioned.'

'And what was that?'

'I would say: in spite of our different colours and languages and incomes, we accepted that we are actually of each other, we care for one another, we will stand in queues together and vote, because we grant each other a future in this country.'

'What you forget,' Sheridan interrupts, 'is that the vision of the future as embodied by Mandela and Tutu and perhaps De Klerk is like one of those electronic advertising billboards that keeps changing. Each person who comes along sees a different ad. In the beginning, whites were relieved, because they started to realize that they wouldn't have to lose anything if they went along with the plan. Blacks bought in, because it seemed as if they would get the power to change everything. It is only now that we've woken up and realized that you don't take the whites out of power so easily. Their white skins protect them everywhere in the world. If you touch a white person it has international repercussions. And that is what I resent most. We are not dealing with real fellow citizens here. Whites have the universal sanctity of the white skin.'

I pick up my handbag. I don't have the nerve for this. I made black friends in the difficult years of apartheid, despite the limitations on my side and the sacrifices on theirs, and I'm not prepared to lose them now in overheated debates about delivery. Surely we have gone through too much together to throw it away in one afternoon?

'Don't walk away,' Sheridan orders, and pulls a book from his shelf. 'Listen to one of your heroes:

'"An historic opportunity has arisen now for white South Africa to participate in a humanistic revival of our country through a readiness to participate in the process of redress and reconciliation. This is on the understanding that the 'heart of whiteness' will be hard put to reclaim its humanity without the restoration of dignity to the black body.

'"We are all familiar with the global sanctity of the white body. Wherever the white body is violated in the world, severe retribution follows somehow for the perpetrators, if they are non-white, regardless of the social status of the white body. The white body is inviolable, and that inviolability is in direct proportion to the global vulnerability of the black body. This leads me to think that if South African whiteness is a beneficiary of the protectiveness assured by international whiteness, it has an opportunity to write a new chapter in world history. It will have to come out from under the umbrella and repudiate it. Putting itself at risk, it will have to declare that it is home now, sharing in the vulnerability of other compatriot bodies. South African whiteness will have to declare that its dignity is inseparable from the dignity of black bodies."'

Triumphantly he flaps the book shut. 'Njabulo Ndebele. And where are you in this?'

'Please, Sheridan. Not once, but hundreds of times, I have confirmed that, but you don't *hear* me! You don't *want* to hear me! You, Sheridan Jooste, have run away with me from the bullets of the South African police, yet you prefer to put me back into your convenient "white box". If I am a stereotypical white, then you can avoid the complexities of good and bad whites, and good and bad blacks. You can avoid complex moral decisions, and continue to serve your middle-class black interests with a clean conscience.' I stop talking. It is terrible what I have just said.

Thabo clears his throat. 'I'll come back to what we said earlier. Before, we had a vision of a country that is better for everyone. We had white and black leaders who formulated it and embodied it. That vision is now gone. Why would a black principal ensure that his staff do their work? Why would a white principal accept black children? What are they working towards?'

'I thought the African Renaissance is the vision,' Sheridan says snootily.

'It is supposed to be, but the government hasn't been able to make it a day-to-day concern of black people, let alone whites.'

'All I'm saying is that I'm tired of realizing time and again: in order to change something, I have to get past one or other unwilling whitey. And I'm tired of the fact that whites keep setting my agenda. I can't break away from them.'

'Maybe you prefer to forget that I also can't break loose from you,' I say. 'My whole definition of who I am, what "white" is, where I live, where I come from, what my future looks like, is bound up with you. But now you have power. You can change things!'

'After 1990, were we really in a position to say: hey, you know, actually we don't want to share a country with whites? We think we'd rather be alone here on the southern tip. After 1990, could we really say: now we will redistribute everything? Everyone will get some cash and a piece of land. Could we? No, we had to bend over backwards to say: hosanna to the whites! Hosanna to the free market! That's why we keep quiet about Zimbabwe. Zimbabweans have simply acknowledged that they have that choice. And we envy Mugabe for creating the conditions where people can exercise that choice, while we here are being squeezed like lice between the fingers of America and Europe.'

There is not much left to be said. I get the goodbyes out of the way and drive back to the farm. On the way, I realize that I have forgotten to give Sheridan my presents for his children. I turn around and head for the offices of the Education Department. As I turn into the parking lot, I am confronted with a scene that astounds me: an enormous heap of school desks and chairs in various stages of disintegration. As far as the eye can see, they lie fallen over, heaped up, thrown down, left behind. Thousands of them! It is so bizarre that I cannot keep my eyes off it. Judging by the height of the grass sprouting among the bent and broken pieces, they have been here for a while already. From where? Why? How could any self-respecting person walk past here every day and not feel that he had failed completely somewhere? That he was not responsible enough to deliver these things to the schools that need them. That he could not even get it together to have them dumped at a scrapyard.

When I question the receptionist behind the counter, she just shrugs her shoulders, without missing a beat of her chewing-gum rhythm. I leave the parcels with her.

Back at the farm, Joep Joubert calls me. 'I want you to see something before you go.' I actually don't feel like this. I am dog-tired. The blood racing through my veins feels and sounds like froth – light and fast, as if the valves in my arteries have given up against the stampede, and lie open like abandoned gates. My thoughts have no time for looking back, holding on, they race blindly along to stay ahead of the thundering pack at their heels. Joep drives me up to the fields where a group of women are hoeing. 'Do you see that one there in the front with the fancy pink hat?'

I see.

'She isn't one hundred per cent "full", as we say, a bit retarded, and with a real scoundrel of a husband. I had to take her into town the other day to collect her disability and child-support grants. She came home with R420. And suddenly she has a hell of a status on the farm, even her husband gets all attentive and flirtatious.'

'Are you showing me this to confirm that Minister Zola Skweyiya does good work and that grants are finally being paid even on the most forgotten farms in the countryside? Or are you actually trying to say that you've helped her to apply for the grant?'

He rolls his eyes. 'I'm doing it to show you that she bought a bloody fucking hat with half of her money. And now she's working in the fields with it! And I can promise you, she will have a child every year as long as she can keep herself in money. These are the people that we are sharing the country with! *Transformation?* You don't understand half of it.'

I clasp my lame left hand to me as he drives me back. I think about the woman – how her face glowed as if light was collecting on her skin underneath the pink hat. How, while we were looking, she raised her one hand softly, as if she was touching something very special, and pulled the hat forward on her brow.

✧

It is my last night on the farm. In the meantime, my husband has arrived. He is to drive me down to Cape Town the following day. He watches me like a hawk with his steady blue eyes. 'How's your hand? How's your foot? Your face seems normal.' As he checks the car and disconnects my computer, I go and sit up at the cement dam, in the soothing smell of the eucalyptus trees with their chafed white trunks. The dam water is lukewarm in the white blade of moonlight. The yard lies desolate and strange, while so much of what I remember burns through in this night.

'I prefer a heart attack or cancer to a stroke,' the doctor said. 'You can recover from the others or die, but a stroke changes you into what you never were.' He explained that there are two kinds of stroke: the first one, which is caused by a clot, is like a tree falling across a stream – the part behind the fallen tree does not get water. The other one is like a flood – a vein becomes flooded and destroys what lies in its path. The fallen-tree kind is easier to treat by thinning the blood and preventing clots. The other kind is more difficult. 'If you'd had one of those, and then went and stood on your head, you would have brought on a massive stroke,' he told me, as I was leaving with medicine to bring down blood pressure, thin the blood and lower stress.

I look at my left foot. In the past week I have sprained two of the toes bumping into things. My whole left arm is covered with bruises. But it is my hand, my neglected clumsy left hand, that I want to spread out and look at and touch and bathe and infuse with care. It lies on my lap like a wilted lily. I start stroking each estranged finger, of me and not of me.

I have a sudden urge to kiss open my left hand, from the palm outwards, the way a lover does. To bury my nose in that chalice of lifelines, and say: there's no echo of song, my left hand, that you have not gathered to me. You have taken me to the closest sound of touch, I know no more vulnerable place on this earth than this left palm I so nearly lost, I know you have always ached to touch like the right hand. All your life, you too wanted to behold beloved jawbone, fondle collarbones of stars, coddle scrotum or soft, newborn head. But your lot was to lie next to, to balance, to cradle in the lap.

As I sit beside the water under a bushel of stars, I am keenly aware of how much I, so fixated on skin, have taken my body for granted. Assumed that it was strong and fit and healthy. And now my ears are turned inward to uncover signs of betrayal or weakness. I hear my heart thundering away, driving new clots to my brain. I want to untangle it carefully from its web of stress and anxiety, and whisper into its thudding chambers: be calm. You have brought me tonight to this hem of light. Shush now. Never again will I send draughts of anguish down upon you. I will settle my body in peace. I will let her grow old in love, surrender her to wisdom's loose skirt. For a long time I sit like that until the windpump trails some water into the dam.

At the rondavel my husband has packed the car. He insists on making the padkos, and sits me down in a chair.

'Read me what you've written – oh, sorry,' he bites his lip. 'All gone with the hard drive ...'

'I'll read you something else. For some reason I've been seized by this morbid scatological interest here in Kroonstad.'

He frowns at the word.

'Preoccupation with excrement. How we deal with what the body has purged, the rubbish cast aside after transformation, the outward signs of the internal change, or something to that effect. Let me read you the last chapter of Ma's first book of essays. "Father Builds a Water Closet."'

While he puts eggs in a pot to boil, cuts up tomatoes and cheese, I read:

During those days it was a big innovation – even in town they were still working with the night-wagon and mules. With great effort, my father got hold of the instructions for building a septic tank and ordered the necessities from Cape Town. One should know that my father was a man always in search of the principles of a thing and never unnecessarily interested in the detail. Therefore, he scratched out on the sketch plan all kinds of things which he thought superfluous.

'This French drain business is unnecessary,' he said then. 'I will rather make the tank twice as big as what they specify here.'

'But it won't work like that,' my mother said. Not that she knew anything about it, but she was one of those people who very piously look after the details others think so little of.

My father, of course, did not pay any attention to her. He built everything neatly with his own hands and blew out a veritable Pit of Daniel with dynamite. He laid it out beautifully with sandstone, plastered it and cast a solid concrete roof over it.

'Well, our generation, in any case, will not live to see it full,' he said with satisfaction.

It was the talking point in the district. The neighbours all came to have a look. We little ones had to go and brood on it, and the results were flushed away with great drama. Paper bags, matchboxes, everything at hand was thrown in to test the strength of the mechanism. Once, I found a little girl rinsing her handkerchief in the lavatory bowl. 'Little girl,' I said, 'one washes ones things here in the basin.'

'No, don't worry, little girl, I've finished. I can reach better here in the lower basin.'

For the rest of its existence, however, the flushing lavatory remained something to be reckoned with. It became blocked at every opportunity. We did not know about inspection eyes in plumbing. Therefore my father chiselled neat holes here and there in the pipes and installed wooden plugs that could be removed during times of crisis, so that the fault could be hauled out with barbed wire.

And only we residents could flush it. It required a special flourish. It was something terrible to see the embarrassment of the guests as their jerking and clattering with the handle only caused a sickly sprinkle of water until the cistern was empty. Then they had to wait for it to fill up again before they recommenced their sawing. Eventually they would have to appear with their tail between their legs, and call the smallest, which was me, to come and sort the thing out.

My mother was the first to discover that all was not in order with the septic tank. She said nothing to my father, but just assiduously started rationing us. Don't flush if it's not strictly necessary, and if possible, go behind the woodpile. But eventually the truth leaked out. The gigantic septic tank, in spite of all measures taken, was completely full.

I will never forget how my father pushed back his empty plate at the breakfast table that morning, let his blue eyes rest frostily on each of us, and said: 'I see you've filled him up. The lavatory's tank.' As if we'd done it from sheer extravagance, with premeditation.

An expert was called in and his pronouncement was to the point: the fall is too great, that's why it gets blocked, and a French drain was supposed to have been put in. My father argued with the man for hours, but finally had to construct the French drain under the most unpleasant of circumstances.

When my mother and he moved to my mother's family farm in their old age, he also had a flushing system installed there. A breathtaking masterpiece of construction, this time with a cylindrical tank, but once again without a French drain. We tactfully pointed out the omission.

'Look,' he said, 'this time it is only Ouma and myself. We will not drive bundles and bundles of paper down there like you lot in the olden days. It will see the two of us through. Those coming after us can dig their own tanks.'

Again, he was not spared the humiliation of seeing the pit fill up once more. I remember how aggrievedly my mother complained to me: 'Now your father says it's my fault. Meanwhile, he never understood a thing about machinery in his life.'

✧

We set the alarm clock and go to bed.

In the small hours of the morning I wake up with a start. It is pitch dark, not even a shimmer of moonlight. But for some unknown reason, I am filled with a sickening dread, a kind of choking anxiety I've never experienced before. I turn to my husband, shaking him awake: 'Take me away from here. Now. Let us go immediately, before we're trapped in this place forever.'

He gathers me to him, as I go on pleading. 'I want to be where the phones and the computers work properly, and the lights and the roads. I don't want to battle to find a doctor, or have my medicine shipped in by 4x4s from Bloemfontein. I want to stay informed about the country's intellectual debates and not find myself constantly drowning in a quicksand of racist arguments and conversations. Please, let's leave. Please. I don't want to die here.'

He rocks me slowly. 'We *are* leaving, we'll take a nice slow drive back to Cape Town and you will get completely well again ...'

'And fix the crashed hard drive ...'

'Sh ...'

chapter forty-two

It is Eisteddfod time again. She enters for everything. 'Don't just enter love poems, make sure you offer a balance,' says her mother. She makes up titles for all the poems, arranges them into cycles. Adds verses here and there. She puts more work into the ending of the love poem:

'What has remained of this time of blue and grace?
A page of maths, the imprint of your face?
No. Where we were once together
only the raw place'

She puts together several protest stanzas, in which she experiments more freely with rhyme, and calls the poem 'My Beautiful Land'.

'look, I build myself a land
where skin colour doesn't count
only the inner brand

of self; where no goatface in parliament
can keep things permanently verkrampt

where I can love you,
can lie beside you in the grass
without saying "I do"

where black and white hand in hand
can bring peace and love
to my beautiful land'

She also puts in the poem for her mother.

She contemplates the title of the prescribed essay: 'Then the evening wind rustles through the leaves ...' 'What a pathetic, old-fashioned theme to give to children who grew up with the writers of the sixties,' scoffs her mother. 'You will struggle to do something original without insulting the cliché of the title.'

She doesn't quite understand what her mother means. She has just finished reading Émile Zola's 'Abbe Mouret's Transgression', in which a priest meets a girl in a beautiful garden. Their sexual discovery then becomes the original sin of Paradise. She decides to use this in her essay. Zola's garden becomes her grandfather's orchard, with its stone wall and gate, and she is the girl.

'I become vulnerable.

'Suddenly something slips up against my ankles. A narrow head slides over my calves, up my legs, and hesitatingly harbours itself in the dark triangle of my body. My heart turns athwart, my breath shudders. The little head coils across my stomach, lisps its tongue in the bowl of my navel, curls on to my chest and stares up at me with a strange white fire in its eyes. Its skin is cool like a mountain stream, its tongue breathes over my body. When I collapse with a shriek, it slips away over my shoulder.

'Then the evening wind rustles through the leaves ... and I hear the voice of God.'

chapter forty-three

Her cousin is getting married. She has an engagement ring and a chest filled with her trousseau. Her cousin spends hours paging through a scrapbook with pictures of wedding dresses, cakes, bridesmaids. She is left cold with disdain and disgust.

All those contributions that received A's at the Eisteddfod are going to be published in the school yearbook.

chapter forty-four

She goes for a walk. It has rained lightly a little earlier, and just before the sun sets, thousands of flying termites burst out into the sky. 'Like flaming angels,' she thinks. They were bred specially for this moment. They have waited inside their nests in a heightened state of excitement. Impatient. When it stopped raining, the workers broke a hole in the wall of the nest. The moment the light pierced in, they swarmed out with their delicate rustling wings, to be met by thousands of others whose nests had opened at precisely the same time. She knows this from *The Soul of the White Ant* by Eugène Marais. Far into the fields, in the red grass, she sits down. She takes off her clothes. She lies on her back. Within a few seconds the first termite lands, shrugging off its gossamer wings. Then more and still more. The whole sky crackles with wings and pale ochre, the damp red grass is flushed with fragrance, and it feels as if hundreds of little shoots are growing from her spinal marrow and taking root in the ground. She feels completely covered by mating termites, boring into the ground to establish new cities in the darkness. Thus it is to be part of the earth, she thinks. She closes her eyes and lies for a long time like this, intoxicated by earth and grass, silky termites and growth and power. She opens her eyes again. The sun is setting majestically. She feels that she is on the edge of giddy discoveries – with nothing to betray or threaten her.

CHAPTER TEN

Back home in Cape Town, I work systematically through any information on transformation I can lay my hands on, but the concept does not seem to have received extensive philosophical attention. Linguistically, I find a lot.

Transformation [(O)Fr., or late L *transformatio(–)*, f. L *transformat-* pa. ppl stem of *transformare*: see prec., -ATION.] **I 1** The action of changing in form, shape, or appearance; metamorphosis. LME. **2** A complete change in character, nature, etc. L16. **3** *Theatr.* More fully *transformation scene*. A scene in a pantomime in which (part of) the scenery is dramatically altered in the sight of the audience; *esp.* (now *Hist.*) one in which the principal performers became the players of an ensuing harlequinade. M19. **4** A woman's wig. Now *rare.* E20. **II** *techn.* **5** *Math.* A change of any mathematical entity in accordance with some definite rule or set of rules; the rules themselves ... **6** Natural change of form in a living organism; = METAMOR-PHOSIS 3a. M17 ... **8** *Electr.* Change of a current into one of different potential, or different type, or both, as by a transformer ... **12** *Ling.* The conversion of one syntactic structure into another by the application of specific rules; a rule convert-ing deep structure into surface structure.

Okay, okay, okay! Keep it simple. The word consists of two parts: the prefix 'trans', which is the Latin for across, the other side (as in Transkei, Transvaal); and 'form', which means to give structure to, to create, to bring forth. In its deepest structure, then, the word 'transformation' means: to form the other side, to start creating where you are going.

But 'trans' also appears in words like transfigure, transfer, transcend, transaction, transgress, transience. And it is embedded in the Dutch *hemeltrans*, where it means 'firmament'. One could say that in order to create the other side, one has to remake the firmament – no mere change of structure or exterior, but of the guiding essence.

The more I listen, though, the more I hear people using the word 'transformation' as if it has a generally agreed meaning. They also use it interchangeably with 'change' and even 'metamorphosis'. I phone around. I spend hours with dictionaries and linguists.

I begin to see a kind of hierarchy: change ... metamorphosis ... transformation. The latter includes the former, whereas 'change' implies neither metamorphosis nor transformation.

This is confirmed by the industrial psychologist I consult. Change and transforma-tion are not the same thing. You may appoint a new manager, or get a new name for your firm or your country, without changing direction, without changing 'the firma-ment'. Things have been changed but not transformed. Transformation means that the same unit undergoes an internal change. Replacing white people with black people is therefore not transformation in itself. If these newly appointed black people bring another vision with them, or the white people already employed by the firm develop a new vision or attitude because of a name change, then transformation is taking place. If black people replace white people but the same structures, systems, visions and attitudes are retained, you merely have change.

'This is why black people say *nothing* has changed and white people feel *everything* has changed,' says Prof. Guy Smith, who runs an NGO that assists businesses in their efforts to transform. 'Black people are appointed in positions, and then everybody assumes that the firm has been transformed. See! We have a black face here, and two white women. These new black appointees often find themselves caught up in the existing structures and ways of thinking, which causes them to behave not very differently to the whites. That's why you often hear black people saying that those at the top have sold out. It isn't true. The faces have changed, but the company has not been transformed. In order to deal with the lack of transformation, the newly appointed blacks often say that they have no power: the whites who appointed them took away the power of these positions, or the previous incumbents somehow took the power with them.'

We are sitting in the professor's house in Rondebosch, in a room overflowing with books. He has several files on rural towns which have been transformed from hostile racist fiefdoms into successful centres that benefit all their inhabitants.

'The whites, on the other hand, see that they are being replaced by blacks. They do not have the same convenient access as before, because they do not have the connections with black officials that they used to have with the white ones. For them, everything has therefore changed. But they also confuse change with transformation. They are convinced that because everything has changed, it has also been transformed – and look what a big mess it is. Blacks are incompetent, they say. They have all the power, but they can't get anything done with it.'

Transformation processes tend to follow the same pattern. There is a specific agent for bringing about the change, and this agent follows a specific route. The route usually crosses a boundary, leading from one domain to another, and creates a new structure, which may be very diverse or uneven.

An academic at one of the business schools in the Western Cape has identified three phases in which transformation takes place.

To begin with, resources have to be unlocked. Society must be opened up to all who have previously been excluded from it. This 'liberalization of resources' often has unforeseen results (unrest, power struggles, violence).

'You can read F.W. de Klerk's 1990 speech as such an opening up and liberalization of the previously privileged position that whites were in. The unforeseen unrest and violence you find in the fact that more people were killed between 1990 and 1994 than during the previous ten years. On the one hand, there was violence; on the other, a constitution was being drawn up to create a new shared vision for the country, a statement about who we are and what kind of society we want to live in. The opening up of resources is always accompanied by violent tensions.'

The second phase also has two facets: there is full participation in processes and power structures by everybody, and there is a demand for accountability to the people represented. 'Full participation was ushered in by our election in 1994. We learnt that everyone has an equal voice.'

The third phase involves the consolidation of democracy at all levels: economic, political and social. 'It is here that transformation is still needed most. At a national level, democracy has already been socialized. Parliament is an excellent example of this. People of different backgrounds, persuasions and parties sit together in parliament, and listen to each other, and shout and heckle. They also work together when they have to. The same cooperation takes place to a lesser extent at provincial level. But it is in the rural towns where the problems lie. Political socialization takes place with difficulty, because people live apart from one another, work apart from one another – mainly as master and servant – don't go to church together, don't listen to the same music, often don't buy in the same shops. Economically, culturally and socially the country has not been transformed. Changed, but not transformed. Not in Johannesburg. Not in Vierfontein. Some schools, some universities, some neighbourhoods are making progress, but generally phase three of true transformation still has to happen.'

Marx had another definition of transformation, the Internet reminds me. The superstructure can only change if the underlying economic base changes. This normally takes a revolution. The difference between a revolution and a coup d'état is that in the second instance only the rulers change, not the systems or structures. Some would argue that what we have had in this country is more like a coup d'état than the quiet revolution we hear so much about. Others claim that the days of revolution are over, as no country has the freedom any more to change its entire economic base.

'You dare not be blind to global modernizing processes,' Prof. Smith lectures me. 'Along with the computers that people now have for working out the timetables in their schools, there is an accompanying management system and work ethic. In a world where human rights are taken seriously by many countries and people are migrating across borders all the time, you cannot just decide to stone an adulterous woman to death. If an economic system dies out because it doesn't work, you cannot really decide that this is precisely the system you want to bring back. These things have nothing to do with race, but with the ways of a world in which computers are put to work to make mines – and education departments – effective.'

He looks out of the window. 'In Zimbabwe a lot has changed, but I would say little has been transformed.'

The next day he sends me an email containing this quotation:

The chief characteristic of flatfishes like the sole is that one flank really functions as the underside of the fish ... The juvenile fish are built perfectly normally and have to go through certain kinds of *transformation* and *metamorphosis* [my emphasis] before the function of the flank is determined. At the same time this is happening, other forms of morphological asymmetry take place. The eye of the underside migrates to the other flank, which will now be functioning as the upper side. The mouth becomes oblique, the nasal and gill openings are removed to a different position, various skull bones develop asymmetrically, and on the upper side a dark pigmentation develops.

The mouth becomes oblique, the skull changes, the upper side turns dark.

'We do not use the word "transformation" in psychology,' says the psychiatrist I interview. 'We talk of personal growth or development. We assume that a person cannot transform, actually *should not* transform, or change his essence. That would make him no longer himself, make him lose his sense of self and disintegrate, fall apart. Accommodate a variety of identities, yes. Transform, no.'

It seems, then, that one can transform an institution or a country only by changing its essence. This essential change takes place on different levels and in different phases. As for the people in these institutions and places, they cannot transform, but they can change by integrating several social identities: you are no longer only white, but also South African and African.

I receive an email from Rina. She says she heard about my setback in Kroonstad and thinks of me often. Her HIV test was negative. She ends with a quotation from Susan Sontag:

There is something about facing mortal illness that means you never completely come back. Once you've had the death sentence, you have taken on board in a deeper way the knowledge of your mortality. You don't stare at the sun and you don't stare at your own death either. You gain something from these painful experiences but you also are diminished. There is something in you that becomes permanently sad and a little bit posthumous. And there is something in you that's permanently strengthened or deepened. It's called having a life.

chapter forty-five

It is Friday afternoon. She is practising for the final piano exam when the telephone rings. She hears her mother's voice rising to an upset pitch it seldom reaches. She walks down the passage on her toes to eavesdrop. 'But the child is still only in matric! You can't do that. I demand to speak to the editor ... Do you want me to take you to court?' And then later: 'Mr Pienaar man, I'm really begging you now. Can you not just leave it all out? These are only the ramblings of a schoolchild and the whole of her final year lies ahead ...' and so it continues, on and on. Her mother telephones Cape Town, Pretoria, Johannesburg. Friends, enemies. She pleads, she threatens. Promises biltong, revenge. She turns around: 'Somebody from Kroonstad complained about the explicit nature of your work in the yearbook and it is going to be a back-page story in the Sunday newspaper.' Her mother does not sound angry with her.

'What are they complaining about?'

'Apparently some of the parents think it is "twisted", and old Frank Boswell said that it is blasphemous and that he will take it all the way to the Director of Education. Two religious ministers said that it defies the basic principles of the country. Old Mrs Spies, coward that she is, said that these poems don't belong in a publication, but she would rather not say anything, since she knows the family and they are good people. The principal tried to save the situation by saying that you are very humble and child-like, with a religious background. He said that you write so well they were still unsure last year whether it was your own work.'

She and her mother look at each other, somewhat astonished. Then her mother sniffs: 'I suppose it will take a while to die down, but let us not lose perspective. Go and practise your scales.'

She practises and hears how solidly her heart is beating.

chapter forty-six

Saturday is the sports day in Senekal. They sit next to each other on the bus. She tells him. He just laughs and puts his arm along the back of the seat, tugs softly at the muscles in her neck under the collar of her hockey top. She scores a goal, but feels very strange, as if she is breaking into two pieces. When the bus stops at the school in the late afternoon, a string of bakkies is waiting to drive them out to Lydia's farm for the class party. All the girls get dressed in one room. She tightens up from embarrassment and discomfort. Her large cotton panties and bra. It feels as if everybody knows and nobody knows. He waits for her outside on the lawn in a long white shirt and torn jeans. He puts his arms around her from behind.

Bessie plays guitar, her favourite song from the film *Katrina*. 'As sad as the darkness with each break of day / as sad as the sunlight / as it too can't stay ... sad is the girl / sad is the boy ...' Others play touch rugby on the grass. The food is carried to the tables. Somebody comes to call her to the telephone. It is her mother. The editor of the Sunday paper, Schalk Pienaar, phoned to say that he is moving the story from the back page to the middle, and that they showed the poems to the poet Ernst van Heerden and he said they were very good, and that the whole affair will therefore blow over very quickly. Her mother's voice sounds thin and unconvincing. 'It's just me and the little ones here at home, with your father out of town, as usual.'

She walks out to the stoep where everybody has started dancing. They look happy and jolly. It feels as if she is standing alone in a large room. As if everybody is miles away from her.

He dances near the light with a freedom and abandon that tugs at her throat. 'Eloise ... are like the stars that shine ...' His lips form the words, his eyes are closed. Doing the twist with another girl. 'Back in the USSR.' His spare hips swaying sensually between his wrists. He twists down to the ground. His shiny hair reflecting the light. His eyes shining shards of blue.

She stands in the dark. If she evaporated, no one would notice. 'In the end, I'm actually always alone,' she thinks. 'Like my mother.'

Like a sleepwalker, she turns to go.

Somebody grabs her arm. 'Where are you off to?' It is him ... She has no words. 'Let me show you how to play darts.' He keeps his arm around her waist. He shows her how to aim.

She cannot dance. She does not like to dance. She does not want to let her body follow another. She finds dancing more intimate than making out. He puts his hand on her back and starts waltzing. Slowly. First his face is light, then his face is dark. His eyes like velvet cloths near her, his mouth in her hair. She closes her eyes. Maybe everything will stay like this forever. He does not let her go once. He holds on to her until she gets off the bakkie with the others at the hostel.

chapter forty-seven

At one o'clock that night she climbs through the window of the dining hall and walks down Reitz Street to the Waterloo Café. Ten cents in her hand. The Sunday newspaper should be there already. As her footsteps echo along the street, she looks down at her feet in their flat navy shoes on the pockmarked tar. The feet of an ordinary schoolchild, she thinks. These are ordinary feet, ordinary legs, an ordinary body, an ordinary mind, an ordinary heart. When she walks back on this same road, everything will have changed. Nothing will be like it was.

The moon is frigid and clear as a pestle.

Mr Costas looks at her with a frown. The newspaper is not in yet. She walks back and falls asleep in her clothes on her bed. It is still dark when her mother walks into the room. She has driven in from the farm. Her eyes are thick and tired. 'Costas tells me you were there in the middle of the night.'

Her mother opens the newspaper on the bed and starts reading. But it makes no impression. Not the compliments, not the complaints. Not the accusations of pornography or politics. Nothing finds a way in. Without a word they drive home. Her mother walks to the telephone determinedly and pulls the line from the socket. She closes her bedroom door. She lies on her bed and stares at her feet. She lies like somebody waiting.

In the afternoon, he arrives out of the blue. He plays for her, 'Oh my love for the first time in my life ... my eyes can see.' She lies dumb in his arms. Somebody knocks on the door. It is two men from the *Sunday Times*. He grabs her hand and they run out of the back door to the dam. He holds her close. She presses her fists into his armpits and he moans in her neck.

That evening her mother says: 'The journalist even claimed that his name was Fairbairn Pringle – as if I would believe a name like that.'

She says: 'I don't think I'm going to school tomorrow.'

'Nonsense,' her mother says. 'It is actually not so bad. If you look closely, it is really nothing. It may be a headline large enough for the Second Coming: "Town buzzes over poems in school yearbook." And they do quote all the passages about dark triangles and raw places and it may look terrible next to your chaste prefect photograph, but Prof. Van Heerden is quite flattering, so it is all okay. The biggest challenge is to let it blow over – it mustn't be stretched out with departmental investigations and follow-up articles. So we'll pretend that nothing has happened and won't speak to anybody else. In the meantime, it is important for you to realize that it is absolutely nothing. Tonight they will wrap their fish and chips in it and tomorrow you're just another matric girl."

chapter forty-eight

In front of the school the next day there is a gathering of people with cameras, and the principal is trying to get them off the school grounds. Her mother turns into a side street and drops her at the back of the school. 'You speak to nobody. You say nothing. You just do your work.'

She gets out and walks to the Biology class. It is as if everybody's eyes flinch away from her.

She sits stunned. For days. In between articles and photographs and headlines. 'Storm brews in churches about schoolgirl's poems.' 'Last poems by distressed school-girl?' 'Poems cause furore in O.F.S. town.' The latter story is by Fairbairn Pringle. Somebody leaves an entire bag of telegrams and letters on her desk. Some simply addressed to her name and the town. Schalk Pienaar sends her mother a cartoon by Connolly from the English newspapers showing a mother, a father and a little girl. The caption reads: 'She's written a poem that begins "roses are red and violets are blue", but it's got a shocking ending.'

She gets no more marks for her essays, just the remark: very good. No one speaks to her. She is aware that the teachers' eyes are following her. She does not know how to behave. Everything feels disturbed. Each and every relationship that exists around her is affected, and neither she nor her classmates nor her teachers and principal know how to transform them into something new.

At home her mother says that a publisher has called to find out whether there are enough poems for a volume. They say that D.J. Opperman wants to see whether it ought to be published.

It's as if she wakes up to reality for the first time. 'Then I'm definitely not going to school for the rest of the week,' she says. 'I want to finish the volume and find a title and so forth.'

'You will go to school, even if I have to get the police to come and fetch you,' her mother says.

'Oh, and wouldn't that make a wonderful newspaper headline.'

'I won't let myself be blackmailed by a little puff of instant fame. You will live your life like any other seventeen-year-old girl.'

She feels herself flushing. 'But I want to write! And I don't learn anything there any more, it is a waste of time!'

'In order to write you must first have a fucking life!' her mother shouts. All the calm of the previous days suddenly gone. 'If you want to waste away as an anaemic, meagre little writer, then you must withdraw into an ivory tower. You first have a life to live – the writing, if you are worth it, will come by itself. A talent that is pampered will die into itself.'

Without her knowing why, she is suddenly also blind with rage.

'I will not go to school!' she yells. 'I have nothing else. I can do nothing else but write. I won't go! I'll take my savings and go to Paris or Spain like Breyten Breytenbach and André P. Brink and everyone else who is worth anything.'

This is a mistake. Her mother bursts out laughing. 'Oh, you poor snot-nosed kid! Shows you what you know. If you have to go to exotic places to write poetry, then you may as well give up now. Then you are nothing. If your talent is not big enough to make poetry from the ordinary things around you, then you don't have any. Then you are nothing but a ball of noise without a matric certificate. If you want to fuck up your life because you imagine that you have talent, then you can do it when you are twenty-one. But as long as you live under my roof, you will go to school and do the things a matric child does. And that's all I've got to say on the matter.'

'Then it would be nice,' she says, 'if you would just shut your mouth and not speak such shit to the newspapers about how my political poems are naive and how I experiment with themes like other girls with lipstick and that I am ...' She gets no further. Her cheek burns like fire, her mother's eyes are like two embers. She turns away to her room.

chapter forty-nine

One of the letters that she opens comes from somebody who calls himself Saul Radunsky: 'I want to congratulate you on your brave stance. Those who fight for liberation will never forget this.' Another letter reads: 'In the name of Nelson Mandela we thank you for opening the eyes of your people!' It becomes a surge, these letters. Every day there are more. Every day she hears her mother fighting into the telephone: No, she is not a liberal. No, she is not from a liberal home. No, she was not expelled from the school. No, we don't think it is terrible. No, we don't think that she is against apartheid.

chapter fifty

Daily she experiences attacks of verse. The poems float in her like driftwood. She picks them up as she hears them.

She puts a volume together. Her mother helps her to divide it into sections. One Sunday afternoon in the veld she finds the poem that will later become the title: 'Daughter of Jephthah.' Next to 'Contents' on the envelope she writes in large block letters: MANUSCRIPT. She mails it.

chapter fifty-one

She is called to the rondavel. On the desk between her mother and father lies a pile of papers. A newspaper with the headline: 'Dar es Salaam: Schoolgirl's poem is used against our Country.' She recognizes some of the letters she wrote. The one to Saul Radunsky lies on top. She sees her notebooks and even a diary or two. Where did they get all of this? She mailed the letters herself.

'You are in contact with people from an underground communist cell,' says her father, blinking his eyes as if he doesn't see very well. It appears that he has been called in by the Broederbond to explain where she came by her political ideas. Confronted with documentary proof.

'I will make contact with whoever I want,' she says.

'No, you will not. And all these things will stop now. I will not allow my daughter to destroy her life like Stephanie Kempf. You can go now.'

'Just remember,' her mother says to her back, 'no amount of literary acclaim is worth betraying your country or destroying the people around you. The more you do that, the less what you want to say will be worth.'

She walks out. Who is Stephanie Kempf? Who is Nelson Mandela?

chapter fifty-two

They walk slowly across the suspension bridge. The air is entirely sweet from tender green willow leaves and whitish blooms. Suddenly, she pulls him underneath the weeping branches and pushes him up against the tree trunk so that the bark crunches behind his back. She unzips his fly and puts her hand into his underpants. He gasps and in his eyes his black pupils wash across the blue.

'What are you doing?' he asks hoarsely.

'I think I want to rape you or hit you or something.'

He pulls away from her hand and his eyes are acutely cold.

'When I started loving you, you were nobody. Today you are somebody. And just as much as I never tried to dominate you, just as little will I allow you to dominate me.' He fastens his zip and gets on his bicycle.

'So you can do what you want, but not me,' she calls after him. He speeds away, his shiny hair straight in the wind. Suddenly he brakes and she hears his tyres on the tar. Then he turns around and comes riding back, upright. He puts down his bicycle and comes to stand before her.

'In our relationship I have never done what I wanted. I think differently about relationships and you know that. If you think you can use me or abuse me, you are no better than all those who have a mouthful to say about you.' He takes her formally by the shoulders and kisses her full on the mouth.

'In your head a revolution has happened, not in the heads of everybody else. But if the revolution means that you want to play the master – find someone else.'

chapter fifty-three

That afternoon a telegram is lying on her bed: Opperman recommends publication of volume. Letter to follow. Congratulations. Human & Rousseau.

*Y*ou stand up between the nubs on the head of the giraffe and look out across the plain. You are small and insignificant and you can see far. Animals rush across the plain. Steenbok spiky as devil's thorn. Eland with rippling dewlaps and backs of glazed lilac. A plash of springbok swells past, from which a few, one after the other, leap like dandy white tufted stars nicked open by the wind. An ostrich runs along – its eyes riveted like washers to its knobkierie head. Nearby zebras are grazing – their tails swishing across the soapy clefts between their thighs. But of them all, you love the giraffe the most. For its big soft eyes, its clumsiness, its skin swept by fire around so much intimate gentleness. You love it for its far-sightedness. Its intense nearby-ness. From a wag-'n-bietjie tree the giraffe nibbles fine foliage, its volatile lips gliding unharmed from thorns to the youngest green. Through the eyes of the giraffe you see a man. He is carving into a stone near the river. From the hands of the man the tender legs of the giraffe flow into stone. And you and the giraffe and the man and the stone breathe through one another. Through the ears of the giraffe you hear that the universe is inscribed in the body of the man, that the giraffe snorts from the stone, that you yourself gleam in geometric patterns across its hide. You sense that the man feels himself at one with the sky and the birds and the veld and the animals. That he reads the entire creation in his body. That while he is chiselling away there, he feels the giraffe's long silky neck slide up into his own bone marrow, feels his heart staring with the big soft eyes, the nubs leaping up like short flames on his skull. The man chiselling there knows that the knees of the giraffe crack like lightning, its breast tautens like a bow. For the man and you and the giraffe and the stone there is no end, because everything carries the word of the other in its body. You are only heard because your word is embodied by them. Through them everything comes to you. The earth is your parent, the stars are your children, the moon carries every heart that has fallen. The shadow-bird is your friend. The giraffe your playful soul. As the giraffe rocks back and forth, you cling on tightly and sink down to hang dizzyingly over the cool rippling river. The giraffe drinks. The water smells of willow and earth, and you see red and yellow finches suspended like jewels in the fluitjiesriet, cat-thorn stippled with berries. On clumps of sweet-thorn bloom tufts of bees and cicadas. A great white cloud anchors its shadow in the red grass. You embrace a fiery blond horn in both of your arms and decide oh! to become it.

PART TWO

A HARD DRIVE

THE WORKSHOP WHERE THEY RECOVER MEMORY has neither a signboard nor a name, just a heavy barred gate on which I rattle. A thin, tired girl buzzes me in and calls the chief technician. He listens sympathetically.

'In this thing are two pieces of information that I have to recover at all cost,' I say. 'The one piece is about the Boer War. It was written by my mother, and I have been preparing it for publication. The disk on which she sent it to me has been lost and the only copy of this piece of work was on my hard drive. The other piece is an interview with Deborah Matshoba, following up on the Truth Commission hearings.'

But apparently it is not that simple. They will first have to establish whether the problem is indeed with the hard drive and not with the processor or maybe the motherboard. 'The hard drive is only the memory of the computer,' he explains when he sees my eyes glazing over. 'The fault could also have been in the brain that controls how all the systems and programs access the memory. Or in the spine or brainstem, that is, the motherboard, which ties all these things together. Only then will we be able to tell whether there is anything salvageable.'

He disappears into the back with my hard drive. I remain sitting in a worn-out armchair. On the coffee table is a collection of computer magazines. Why do computer and financial magazines always have such dull, unimaginative covers? It's as if the number crunchers, the money men and computer guys are saying with pride: we despise the aesthetic, we spit on beauty – unless it has tits.

While I'm waiting, I work on the tendons in my left hand with the exercises pre-scribed by the physiotherapist after the stroke. I think about Deborah Matshoba. She was the subject of a television documentary about reconciliation, chosen first and fore-most because she spoke good English and could therefore discuss the subject without the need for interpretation. Although she had been arrested and tortured, her story was far from the worst heard before the Truth Commission. Yet, when I interviewed her, the extent of the damage done to her by these 'less severe brutalizations' impressed upon me how deeply maimed our society is.

Deborah is a beautiful woman. She met us in the slick, high-tech building where she works as Key Accounts Manager for an insurance company. Smart, composed, briefcase in hand. The cameraman and I followed her out into the crowds on Commissioner Street. The golden afternoon sun caught her skin, her gold-rimmed glasses and the slight movement of her lips as she turned homewards among hundreds of other commuters. The street was filled with them – ordinary black people going about their daily business. Deborah took a bus, with the cameraman and I still follow-ing. In the bus she kept her briefcase on her lap. At one point, a fat white man sat down next to her. She looked out of the window. It was only afterwards, when we were reviewing the footage, that we spotted the clenching of her neck muscles as the man shifted his heavy body next to hers. Two blocks from her house she got off and walked the rest of the way. In front of one house a white man without a single tooth in his mouth was watering his garden. 'Afternoon Deborah!' he called out. She struggled a bit to unlock the security gate, and there was a weariness in her shoulders as she pushed open the front door and invited us in. In the living room: a television set, a hi-fi system and a carpet, two plastic garden chairs at a plastic table. The two bedrooms jumbled with bedspreads, frills, soft toys, posters, feathers, clothes, make-up. While Deborah took off her shoes, I went to the kitchen to make some tea. There was a kettle without a cord. In the fridge, a plastic bottle with the last dregs of cola and a saucer with a cube of margarine. Otherwise nothing. No bread, no milk, not a single edible thing. The cameraman fetched orange juice from the car.

She lived alone, Deborah said. Her son stayed nearby at the place where he worked, her daughter was with her sister.

The technician calls me to come and look. In the workshop several young boys are sitting, and I cannot help but remember the first time I was delivered into the hands of the computer boy (a more youthful incarnation of the computer guy). This was during the summit of the Non-Aligned Movement in Durban, which the SABC covered. Our technicians there simply could not get our computers linked to Johannesburg. They blamed the overzealous security systems which had been installed next to us at the International Conference Centre to protect the communications of the Foreign Affairs Department. After three days, I threw a tantrum, demanding the absolute best computer brains in Durban, and two pimply schoolboys were brought to me. One still had his blazer on. I despaired. But, indeed, after a mere two and a half hours, we were in smooth contact with Johannesburg. I have also learnt, however, that young people are not perturbed about memory. They cannot imagine that anything in the world could be irreplaceable. The more clean memory capacity they offer you, the bigger the favour they think they're doing you. After all, when one is not burdened by memory, it is easier to communicate within memory-less cyber-communities.

The casing of my hard drive has been removed. I see that I have a green motherboard, full of little squiggles and knobs and bars and buttons and bulges and lights. The motherboard glitters with metallic prongs. The processor itself has been twisted away. 'This is the hard drive,' says the technician, and holds out a square steel cigarette case on the palm of his hand. It is connected to the motherboard by an endless flex of multi-coloured wires. 'And these suspender-like things?' I ask. 'Those are the ribbon cables,' he says, 'that connect the whole lot up with each other.'

He tells me he will now connect the hard drive to a testing station, where special software will strip out the viruses, and then he'll see what's there. What is my fax number, he will send through what he finds. He cannot promise anything. If it's only the directory structure that has been destroyed, they will be able to take things off piece-meal. If the file partitions have been destroyed, everything will appear in a great big stew. And if everything has been corrupted down to ones and zeros, then the entire transformation will have to occur digit by digit. Most clients then take their stuff over-seas – in London there are people with specially designed software that is able to do it.

I return home despondent.

✧

That evening a fax arrives:

☐☐☐☐āāā¥u¥☐☐☐āāā¥☐☐☐āāā☐☐☐āāā¿¿°T/r/a¥u¥ ma is being carried over from generation to generation by words, memories, body language, silences and per-sonal scars. 6%%. God visits the iniquities of the fathers upon the children unto the third and fourth generations of those that displease 000fāāāand reject Him, but shows mercy unto generations of those that love Him and keep His commandments. God banished the israelites to the desert for forty years, because he did not want those who KNEW the past, knew slavery to build 00// the \\ »»promised 0 0 ÿ ù land ÿāo.☐☐☐ ☐āāā☐☐☐āā☐☐☐āāā☐☐☐āā

This is not my computer, I let them know. I have never done work on the wrath of the ancestors. Another message. Apologies, wrong fax number. Different client.

I wait. At eleven the next morning I phone them. Sorry, the damage is bigger than they initially suspected. They will get back to me within an hour. At noon a fax arrives:

DO YOU RECOGNIZE THIS?

☐☐☐☐āāā☐☐☐āā...@ When I look around, %Imarvel é^+at how we battle to be normal – and no one knows how shattered we are inside.+= ☐☐☐☐āāā☐☐☐āā

This is mine! Or rather, these are the words of Deborah Matshoba, whose story I documented in *Country of My Skull*: 'On Tuesday they started beating me up, they strangled me with a towel – I collapsed. When I came to, I was lying on the floor and I was all wet – they must have poured water over me. This Roy Otto threw a pack of sanitary pads at me. When I went to the bathroom, I realized that I was menstruating and I wondered how he knew that.'

Yes, this is mine. Do I have to come over? 'No, it's not necessary. We will send things through,' says the technician.

By that evening, long reams of fax paper covered with text lie disgorged from my fax machine.

□□□□āāā□□□□āā¢ 00@ I was awake, suddenly and completely awake in my bed. It was very dark, but I sensed someone bending over me ... then these cold, dry hands around my throat. I started shouting, fighting and hitting out, while the grip tightened at my neck. Then by chance my hand touched a prickly, shorn scalp and I realized immediately it was my bloody old great-grandmother!

She was an ordinary woman. Or so we, her family, thought. The fact that she had shaved her head ever since the Anglo-Boer War and always wore a kind of skullcap was regarded as a sign of healthy mourning. And the death of two of her baby girls, born after the war, seemed part of her somewhat tragic life. But after the attack that night on one of her great-grandchildren, she was sent to an institution.

Years afterwards, we found remnants of a diary which contained the following entry: 'The storm raged throughout the night. The mortuary tent was blown away. This morning they lay there. Row upon row of drenched corpses. Hair wild, and eyes and mouths distended under the scorching sun. Among them we saw the red plait of Aletta.'

Aletta was great-grandmother's firstborn. Then it struck us that at least one of the babies who died had also had red hair, like my great-grandmother herself – and like me.

How does one reconstruct a society after conflict? How does one cut a community loose from the destruction of the past? Is it possible to rebuild a post-war society when those required to weave the new social and moral fabric are themselves maimed? Add to this the well-documented fact that men who have been brutalized in conflict bring violence and abuse into the domestic sphere. How then is maleness to be reconstructed? How does one prevent destroyed identities from affecting the third and fourth ° ° % ~~`□□□□āāā□□□□āā□□□□āāā□□□□āā

My mother's piece on the Boer War breaks off and something else starts.

+\\ || Ä É □□□□āāā□□□□āā Don't call it a tragedy, it's a genocide!' There's irritation in the voice of the woman who saw three of her children hacked to death. 'Don't use safe phrases like "the child was decapitated"! What happened to that head? What happened to that torso? That artery!'

'Where were the writers *before* the genocide? What good does writing do after the event?'

Four years after the genocide, feeling themselves compelled to write about it as a duty of memory, a group of African writers and film makers visited Rwanda. Now they have returned in the new millennium to present and discuss their films, plays and novels.

The writers squirm a bit. Most of the Rwandans sitting among us suffered family losses. The soft-spoken Rector of the University of Rwanda, Emile Rwamasirabo, lost some forty family members who were living in Kigali. The young student next to me, demanding justice for the victims, 'political as well as literary', is the only survivor of an extended family of twenty people.

Seventy-five per cent of Rwanda's Tutsi population was killed during April 1994. When the slaughter started, South Africans were preparing for their first democratic election, and the attention of the world media was focused on the success story of Africa – while the heart of the continent was tearing itself apart.

Catherine Coquio, a specialist in Comparative Literature from the University of Paris, puts it this way: 'For us in France, Rwanda only started to exist through the genocide – the day Rwanda turned against itself. Genocide is always a question and never an answer. It is unthinkable and yet it was carefully thought out. It is only the memory of death that will stop death from getting lost again.'

A white writer now living in Belgium, Monique Bernier, recalls the paralysing fear that ruled Kigali that night of 6 April 1994. The President's plane had been shot down at dusk, and within an hour Hutus started killing their Tutsi neighbours and relatives. With frightening speed, nearly a million people were killed in a hundred days – mainly with pangas. The killing rate in Rwanda was nearly three times as high as that of the Jews during the Holocaust. It was the most efficient mass killing since the atomic bombings of Hiroshima and Nagasaki. Monique Bernier was trapped in her house in Kigali, and heard over the radio how her friends were being murdered. She was eventually evacuated to Belgium.

A hand shoots up: 'Why did you leave? Do you know that a white priest who stayed behind saved the lives of hundreds of children he'd taken into protection?'

'I didn't have a choice: I had a small child,' she says, clutching a pack of cigarettes and her recently published book, *Shame*.

'It doesn't matter where I live, whatever happens in Africa profoundly affects me,' says Ivorian writer Véronique Tadjo. 'When I saw the front page of the *Economist* calling Africa "the Hopeless Continent", I was sick on my stomach for days.' Tadjo wrote a book about the Rwandan genocide: *Imana's Shadow: Voyage to the End of Rwanda*.

The woman who lost three children also published a book: *Death Doesn't Want Me*. 'That night when the President was shot down, my husband called me at the hospital where I was head nurse. When I arrived home he was sitting on the floor against the wall, his arms over his head, crying: "We are all going to be killed." I said, "Utter nonsense!" Then my brother entered the room with some petals in the palm of his hand. "This is what is going to happen to us." He blew the petals in one soft whiff to the floor. "Except you," he said, "because death doesn't want you."'

The face of Yolande Mukagasana is swollen from crying while extracts from her book are being read. Suddenly an attractive young Rwandan student confronts Mukagasana: 'I am sick and tired of you throwing your victimhood in our faces. How dare you order these writers how to write? This is all we've heard since arriving here: I this, I that ... Words should be immersed in collective consciousness ... when you use the word "I", you sink into selfishness ...' She is stopped by the chair.

Mukagasana is emphatic: 'Do you want my life, my girl? Do you want to be in my shoes? You can have it – every single minute of my life, you can have. I have not chosen to be a survivor of a genocide. So long as I am alive, I'll speak on behalf of the dead, on behalf of those whose arms were carried around in Kigali by dogs – and insist that what was done to them is not glossed over by anybody. The only thing I can tell you, my dear, is that you don't know what it's like when the relationship between you and your enemy is the foundation of the world.'

Afterwards the student explains her anger and irritation to me.

'I was in exile when the genocide happened. So every time she uses the word "I", she cuts me out of victimhood, survivorhood and sacrifice. I resent that. I have suffered in another way and I want literature to go beyond what has happened here to individuals – to transform everything into an opening instead of a closed wall.'

'Where is the literature warning us that Rwandans would kill on this scale? Where is the poem about a panga and the inhumanity of m # a ÿ n %%}{☐☐☐☐āāā ☐☐☐āā

$^$^$ÿÿÿ'-,☐☐☐āāā☐☐☐āā'It is early October 1899. At a farmhouse people are laughing, dancing, having a party. On a koppie nearby, from nowhere, suddenly, the lonely figure of a horseman appears. No sound. The next day war is declared between England and the two Boer Republics.'

This is how the War entered my consciousness (the terms 'Anglo-Boer War' or even 'Boer War' were never used in my family, for us it was simply 'the War'; forced to be more explicit, my mother would say 'the Second Liberation War'). Through the first paragraph of *Ruiter in die Nag*, a book for young readers written by Mikro, the image of the lonely rider watching over the injustice done to my people became part of my identity as an Afrikaner. It was only after reading this book as a child that I realized the extent to which the Boer War was already a presence in my life. As a point of reference, as explanation, continuity, backdrop. Seldom the suffering itself, only the statistics, often the betrayal, always the bravery, and never, never the stories in which the Afrikaner was not central.

During my first year at school, there was a boy in my class called Hennie Nagel. My father would tell my uncle: 'She's sitting next to one of the Nagels.' Whereupon my uncle would nod knowingly: '*Kopskote* – they were the best marksmen ... used them to silence the gunners.' To which my father would add: 'After the battle of Sannaspos, Oom Chris van Niekerk specifically measured the distance – from a thousand yards, with open sights, the Nagels had shot every single gunner, one after the other, right between the eyes.'m # a ÿ n %%}{☐☐☐☐āāā☐☐☐āā}{☐☐☐☐ āāā☐☐☐āā m # a ÿ n %%As long as I can remember, my mother collected Free State war stories and diaries. Some she told us, some she simply kept. I remember in particular a graphic description of a man's first moments under fire. The Kroonstad burghers had all been to Natal, and they came back with ears finely tuned for storytelling and a healthy disregard for the honour of the fatherland – a combination that made for vivid stories.

During that first battle, one was so bloated with fear, they said, one could hardly breathe without farting. 'Six feet to my right lay a man with a face like a freshly washed potato. He stacked his bullets in front of him, tested his Mauser's muzzle, took out his watch, put it next to the bullets, followed by a neatly folded handkerchief and a packet of peppermints. Then he got rid of all the small stones under his body, put his Mauser in place and started scanning the landscape with his binoculars. On my left someone was stuffing himself with chewing tobacco like a madman.

'Spewing tobacco juice, he asked me if I knew how to distinguish between a cannon shooting *away* from you and one shooting *towards* you. *Nee my magtig*, how should I know? He knows, he was in the war of 1880. It's simple: when the noise goes *zoeiing zoeiing zoeiing ka-tchla* it is firing away from you; and when the noise goes *ka-tchla zoeiing zoeiing zoeiing* then it is firing towards you.

'I cleaned my sweaty hands on my trousers and put my Mauser bullets next to me. Would I be able to tell my *ka-tchlas* from my *zoeiings*? Then the first English bullets kicked up dust around us. I shot back, blindly. First this side, then that. Before the dust could lift, I saw a rinkhals coming towards me – behind him short tongues of fire flickering where a cannon shot had hit in the grass. I slapped desperately in front of me with my hat until the snake swerved away. My ears were deaf, my hands were shaking so much I could hardly get the bullets into the magazine. I glanced over at the man who knew all about the direction of cannon shots. He was lying turned towards me. From a small hole in his head came a stream of blood. His eyes were staring past me, his mouth hung open like a finch nest around his tobacco-stained teeth. The man on my right had disappeared, only the packet of peppermints remained. Something to my left again caught my attention. Two big bluebottles had settled on the dead man's mouth ...

'... It had become very quiet around me. Someone touched my arm. I looked up. "You arsehole, pretend you're dead so that I can pick you up." I raised my arm in protest. He hissed, "Quiet, you stupid fool, I'm here under the white flag to pick up the dead. If you're alive, you have to go that side as a prisoner of war." I fell forward. He threw me on to a cart. I was with those who had died. Body after body was piled in around me. The stench of death, urine, sweat, blood. The wagon creaked away. I was vomiting. I recognized some of the faces squashed between the bodies. I was convinced I was dead.'

Did all of this happen to one man? Was it true? I never asked, because in a way it didn't matter – I sensed that all these tales were playing themselves out in front of a vast backdrop, part of a drama that would never be documented officially and comprehensively. More importantly, because nation-building and reconciliation prevented the production of any official version depicting all sides of the war, the issues were left largely to the devices of the storytellers within the different communities. āāāā¥āā 'ā"āā

□□□□āāā□□□āā□□□āāā□□□āā

ü æ – å å å å å å 00000000000000000000000000000000It is completely confusing to enter Rwanda. The first person one meets is the customs officer – kind, soft-spoken, charming. Did he? Is he one of the killers? Or is he a surviving witness? People look back at you without expression. I want to meet a Hutu, a perpetrator, I told them before I came, but nothing has happened. They explain to me that there's no difference between the Hutus and the Tutsis – they speak the same language, share the same culture and religion. In South Africa, it would be like the AmaPondo killing the Thembu.

'I'm African. I'm Rwandan. I'm unavoidable,' states Senegalese writer Boubacar Boris Diop.

The first duty of memory is to find words to bear testimony, the second is to try and explain what happened, then it's time for cleansing, and finally for transforming words into oxygen. 'I believe in the sun although there's an eclipse,' says Véronique Tadjo.

The writers start off tentatively by emphasizing the need for all thinking to move beyond the dualities brought in by colonization and Christianity. According to the highly respected academic, Prof. Elikia M'Bokolo, Eastern and Central African societies had a variety of structures that dealt successfully with ethnic tensions and lack of resources. In pre-colonial times, Rwandans were ruled by a monarchy, and diverse administrative, artistic, religious, military and other structures were shared by Hutu and Tutsi alike. These multiple structures were mainly destroyed by the dualities embedded in Christianity (body/soul, sinner/saint, heathen/Christian). As nearly all Rwandans (98 per cent) converted to Catholicism during the twentieth century, people were trapped in a bipolar world of colonizer and colonized, Hutu and Tutsi, crop-farmer and cattle-farmer, administrator and peasant, from which they seemed unable to escape. Added to this was the Belgian colonial authorities' policy of issuing identity cards classifying tall people with thin noses as Tutsis, worthy of top positions in the colonial administration; and squat, solid people with flat noses as Hutus, worthy of manual labour on the land.

I take a walk through Kigali. A strange city. Lush. Green and heavy with birdsong. Spread over hills. 'Rwanda' means: 'a desire to expand.' I see men in pink clothes building a big double-storey house. They are prisoners. After the genocide, the Tutsi government arrested 130 000 Hutus suspected of involvement in the killing. They are now in jail, packed so tightly that they have to take turns standing. Why these pink uniforms? Rumour has it that pink cloth destined for the gays in Nazi concentration camps somehow ended up in Belgium, where someone said, 'Pink! My God, send it to the colonies for the negroes.'

These participants in the genocide have already spent more than seven years in jail without being brought to trial. What to do with them? The fact that they don't riot to get out of the overcrowded prisons is proof, some people believe, that they know they are guilty and therefore better off inside than outside.

The Rwandan participants at the conference are adamant. They want justice – retributive justice. People should appear in court, go to jail or be hanged. 'Don't talk to us about amnesty – it is a despicable option.'

A lively discussion takes place at teatime: is retributive justice only for the rich? After the genocide, Rwanda was declared the poorest country in Africa, because everything had been destroyed. If there is money now, should it be used to rebuild the country or to pay lawyers and judges? What about restorative justice as an alternative in the South? Is it merely some kind of comfort in the face of impunity? Or is it in fact the *only* option, something countries in the North could take note of instead of always pursuing the perpetrators, thereby creating an endless cycle of violence.

Gruesome stories have become part of everyday conversation. Like the one about the survivor who fled to the border. When he bent down at the lake to drink, he had to push the dead out of the way to reach the water. For a while there was a ban on fish caught in Lake Kivu in the markets of Uganda, because someone had found a finger inside a fish. 'We ate some Tutsis last night,' people would joke after a meal of fish. The Tutsis are exceptionally tall. 'It is time you felt what it's like to be as short as I am,' a Hutu would say, systematically hacking off parts of his Tutsi victim's legs. Cutting him down to size. There are stories of Hutu wives who killed their Tutsi husbands and children.

I put down a cup of Rwanda's famous coffee – it suddenly tastes of blood – and am reminded of the adage that Africa is not kind to its gifted. Nearly two thirds of the speakers at this gathering no longer live on the continent. The scourge of Africa is ethnicity, says the journalist from a newspaper in Kampala. Clans fighting for scarce resources. Mugabe is fortunate – he still has an outside enemy to blame, a few white farmers camouflage the real ethnic division in that country.

'I have given up on Africa,' says one of the writers.

'I will never,' says Nocky Djedanoum of Chad, the organizer of the event. 'We have written a history as Africans, maybe we should now write one as humans. And then let it be a history which helps people to exist, helps them to live.' ooooº º☐☐☐☐āāā ☐☐☐☐āā º º º º☐☐☐☐āāā☐☐☐☐āā

^^^^^@^^^☐☐☐☐āāā☐☐☐☐āā#W*h*at is notable about Afrikaner records of the Boer War is that sacrifice and the bravery formed part of an official history written by Afrikaners, whereas the betrayals, the failures, the exceptions, the really gruesome testimonies were often found only in oral history or other neglected sources of information. General De Wet compiled a comprehensive report based on first-hand testimonies, intending to make a case against Britain for violating the Hague Rules of War. After the war, however, he was ordered by President Steyn to drop the case in the name of reconciliation.

So what happened to the stories of the war? Because of a less than honourable victory, the English had to bury theirs in official files in England. The Afrikaners turned theirs into a myth of exclusion. In the absence of a comprehensive account of the war, the stories had no choice but to be choked out orally from generation to generation.

Colonel Thring of Kroonstad, an Irishman who fought on the Boer side, told the following story. After a battle, a wounded British officer asked him where the Boers were. On having them pointed out to him, the wounded man said, 'No, no, I mean the Boers.' Thring replied, 'Well, here they are,' pointing to the same men. The officer said again, 'No, no, you don't understand me – I mean the wild, savage Boers, the people they say look like the orang-utans.' 87ÇÇ-^ `-□□b□□□□□□□□□□□□□□□□□ □□□□□□□□□□□□□□□□□□□□□□□□□□□□□□□āāā□□□āā□□□āāā □□□āā□□□āāā□□□āā□□□āāā□□□āā□ôÜ`-;000During a late-night discussion about colonialism, we explore the question of how the victim can become the perpetrator. PowerPoint technology allows the effects of racism, as formulated by Frantz Fanon, to be set out on a screen. We are at the University of Rwanda, close to where thousands of students were murdered. Before the discussion the audience was asked to be silent while the names of the murdered students and lecturers, and the faculties they belonged to, scrolled across the screen. It took thirteen minutes.

The professor talks to us about the brain and the psyche. What happens to you shapes not only your personality, he says, but your very brain functions. He discusses four of the psychological consequences of racism.

The first is 'intense intra-psychic pain'. It is caused by internalizing the racist messages of the dominant group. Simply put: it hurts to be part of the dominated or persecuted or despised group. This is a constant pain, a constant awareness of the self being different, not being 'like them', not being good enough.

'That pain never leaves you, it pervades your getting up, how you wait in a queue, your whole bearing during the day, how you go to bed, what you dream, and you deeply desire to get rid of everything that causes you this pain of being regarded as different.'

This desire to rid yourself of what you have been told makes you different leads to the second set of consequences: you try to defend yourself against the racist message. But those in the dominant group are seldom vulnerable, can seldom be attacked as the source of distress. They live protected by their privileges, whether near you or in far-away countries. It is then that the dominated turn inward against themselves and their communities. Men, humiliated in their jobs, internalize their impotence, and then turn on their wives and children. Often wives allow the abuse because they are acutely aware of the rage of hopelessness burning away in the men. Hence the high levels of all forms of abuse evident in many oppressed and marginalized communities.

'"I took that with me into my own family. I bashed my son. I almost killed my son. Today he is overseas as a musician ... But his sister saw him go up – he was about six – trying to hang himself in a tree, because I used to bash him so much. When I sent him to the shop, I would spit on the floor. You must be back before the spit dries. My son would run. My boy would run ... and then I would worry. He is too short, they won't see him at the counter. Maybe someone will kidnap him. Maybe he'll die. And when he came back, I would take the sjambok – I would beat him, beat him, beat him – until the neighbours jumped over the fence and stopped me. And this son of mine, this one so close to my heart, I heard him say to his friends: I don't know suffering.'"

The third consequence of racism is the 'psychological double bind'. This happens when it is expected of the dominated group to be 'agreeable' – agreeable in the work-place or neighbourhood, and in the larger arena of nation-building. 'As part of a new dispensation, a white group appoints a black person. But they have carefully selected him. He is not aggressive, he knows his place, he will not make waves, he is more like them than the other applicants. They make sure that the appointee knows this. Now he is in a double bind. He must be "agreeable" even – and especially – when confronted by incidents of racism. The moment he is "agreeable", however, he knows that they think he is subservient, docile, and acquiescent in his own oppression. This he desper-ately wants to avoid. On the other hand, if he is not "agreeable", he will be labelled problematic, angry, aggressive, dangerous and even racist, which again feeds into the stereotypical representations of the dominated, as part of the racist message.'□□□□ āāā□□□āā

āāāÉç0'āāāāI was a pretty little thing in a tutu – the only daughter of a well-off family. We read, we talked politics. Then this was destroyed. My father was jailed and tortured. Our home became cold and needy. Me and my mother ... for me there was a real war against my mother. We were so clumsy with each other ... I felt so unloved by her. I was abused by stick, by mouth, by neglect ... āā'.=

□□□āāā□□□following message appears on the screen: 'In the works on psycho-pathology, there is agreement that "double bind" experiences of any kind are among the most psychologically disruptive a human being can ever be confronted with.'

I think about South Africa and how scarred we all are, how fraught these fragile new relationships and partnerships must be. But the professor continues.

'One of the outcomes of this double bind is what is called the "killing rage" – the fourth consequence of racism. The repressed anger builds up in an individual until he starts lashing out in spurts of uncontrolled violence, either towards other victims of racism or towards members of the dominant group. Or it can turn inward and mani-fest in addiction and other destructive behaviour patterns.

'It all eats away at you. It is a fire that consumes your soul.'

The Rwandans seem irritated. What happened in Rwanda was not racism, at most it was ethnicity, because there is no real difference between Hutu and Tutsi. Most fam-ilies have intermarried, most of them have mixed blood. You cannot tell the one from the other.

'This is part of the problem,' says Ugandan novelist Goretti Kyomuhendo, 'people here need to acknowledge the racism within their ethnicity and how it has manifested in their personalities.' +"",□□□□□□□□□□□□□□□□□□□□□□□□□□□□□ 000^^6^6^6 □□□āāā□□□āā It is remarkable how many of the stories of betrayal involve horses. People stole horses. 'I could not find my horse, but was told by the *veldkornet* that no horse could have got away. I gave the whistle which I always give when I have his fodder. There was this sudden commotion. A man swore and pulled the reins, but the horse reared up into the air. It stormed towards me. No longer with four white hoofs and a blaze, but definitely my horse. When I touched his nose, there was shoe polish on my hand.'

Horses also got horse-sickness. The Boere remedy was: a bottle of human urine down the left nostril. But two burghers refused to stoop to that. They stayed with their ill horses. Desperate. Nothing helped. That afternoon, one of them loaded his gun. 'I cannot endure it any longer, I'm shooting her.' The other sighed. Then he took a bottle and unbuttoned his fly. 'Are you really going to do it?' He filled the bottle. Slowly, he poured the lukewarm urine down the horse's nostril. He made sure that it was the left nostril. A quarter of an hour later, the other burgher did the same.

But let the first burgher take up the story: 'An hour later my horse's fever broke. Again I filled the bottle and my friend did the same. We did so every hour, drinking water so that we could fulfil our duties. By dusk my horse was really better, but the other horse not. "Please man," my friend asked respectfully, "give me a bit of your pee. It must be a weak kind of thing which I'm churning out." "Get me some coffee, then," I said, "I'm dry as a bone." He came back with buchu brandy. The shock of the alcohol produced miracles. An hour later, we started walking the horses slowly, step by step. What we didn't realize was that the others at the campsite were watching our efforts with keen clinical interest through binoculars. My homeopathic potential became a legend, and all through the war I've been bothered regularly for a contribution.'

This notion of betrayal by the world and by one's own blood (or urine) forms a crucial substance of the Afrikaner consciousness. Betrayal by one's own is unforgivable, no matter the circumstances. 'Why did we lose Natal and therefore the war?' is a question the Afrikaner has never tired of asking. In his book *Commando*, Deneys Reitz gives one answer. It was a crucial moment after the battle at Nicholson's Nek. Ten thousand British soldiers were in disorderly retreat before General Piet Joubert's men. Reitz describes how he was standing close to Christian de Wet, and heard him muttering under his breath: '*Los jou ruiters* – loose your horsemen.' Everybody was waiting for General Joubert to pursue the English and drive them out of Ladysmith. But he held back. Apparently he explained afterwards, 'When God holds out a finger, don't take the whole hand.' In my family, the story was told differently. Joubert said to his commando, 'Leave them, one never shoots a Christian in the back.' And the story would always conclude with this moral: those very same Christians later turned around and killed 266 000 Afrikaner women and children. All of them Christians.

The war taught the Afrikaner a few things: the world can and will turn against you. You are on your own. More importantly: you will have to do things the outside world regards as ghastly and impossible – fighting a mighty empire, shooting Christians in the back, making and enforcing racist laws – to safeguard your survival. Such thinking was never part of any official narrative, but substantially informed the way the Afrikaner|$%^&0☐0☐0☐0☐0☐0☐0 ☐0☐0☐000 0 0 0 0 0 0 0 0 0 0 0 0 00 ☐☐☐☐ āāā☐☐☐āā00000000000000000000☐☐☐☐āāā☐☐☐☐ā

✧

I knock carefully on the door. The little passage is stacked to the ceiling with keyboards, printers, screens, heaps of motherboards and ugly posters filled with digital lettering. The code for accessing the memory has been found and it has been left up to Moses to print everything out for me. Moses is terribly fat. His little office conspicuously grey and empty. On a dusty cloth spread out on his desk lies what I suspect must be my hard drive. Next to it lies a tool kit with several little screwdrivers, tubs of screws, a brush, tweezers and a chip-grabber (he calls it) tucked neatly into it.

I'm here because I'm still looking for the interview with Deborah Matshoba.

'Why do you keep *vroetel-ing* in the past?' asks Moses. His eyes glinting with either disdain or discouragement.

'I'm not digging around in the past. I want the stuff on my hard drive back.'

He nudges his mouse around with his fat fingers.

'Why don't you forget, like this whole country is forgetting, and start afresh?' His face is immobile.

'And find myself surprised too by the high crime rate, the violence in families, the moral chaos in South Africa – the whole of Africa, actually? If you don't know where things come from, you won't be able to deal with them.'

'You misunderstand me. The only valid reason to keep your hard drive intact is to get a kind of moral immunity for yourself. It goes like this: because this suffering is recorded on my hard drive, I may do as I please. Because I suffered, I may now make others suffer and you dare not do anything to me.' Noting my surprise at the direction the discussion is taking, he goes on: 'My father was arrested during the apartheid years. To this day, I hate to see him. He still has that look of surrender and humiliation, and I cannot stand it. I refuse to live my life in this state of victimhood. I have bought him a separate house. Out of my way. But what I hate most is when I lash out against whites, and he says, all whites are not like that, and wants to tell me about some kind prison warder or other who gave him a newspaper. A newspaper, for God's sake!'

'But maybe he knew whites in a more intimate way than you. He could distinguish between good whites and bad whites. You work here in a coloured business. How many whites do you know?'

'That is not the point. He is too soft on the likes of you. We, the children of that generation, we are more realistic. We are not interested if maybe there's a wonderful white person out there somewhere. We don't care. We want a country without whites.'

'Because you want to forget the past. Before you can wipe your eyes out, you'll be behaving like a racist towards coloureds and Indians – or should they also leave? The solution doesn't lie in forgetting or ignoring the past, because then you run the risk of becoming a racist yourself, and having a future no better than the past you've just struggled to overthrow. Like a drug addict with a destroyed memory. Because he cannot remember, he cannot imagine a new kind of life for himself.'

A smile flits across Moses' face. He hands me another piece of paper and says with some disdain, 'I'll fax you the rest.'

□□□□āāā□□□āāP Win4 // (-°] Afterwards we are taken to the school, which has become a graveyard for thousands of skeletons. On shelves, on tables, on the floor, in heaps. The remains of people, stripped of all that makes us different. The neatly stacked, mummified bodies are no longer man or woman, white or black, they are inescapably, incontrovertibly, unhumanly human, slaughtered at the hands of those who were already dead.

We who have had so many words to say during the past few days grow more silent, until by the end we are speechless. When the bus travels back through the dark plantations, it's as if we can see how easily death could trot through these fields, without a sound, without a rustle, just now and then a sudden clip of metal. Death trotting along in the footpath, in sole and cartilage, trotting along one godless night in April.

Until a long-held-back scream screamed.

And the hacked ones fell in embraces of blood. There she tumbled, a mother with her child carved into her pelvis, here is another with a pair of pink panties notched into her femur, a string of beads drooping over a wing-thin scapula, babies mortared to a prickly-pear mash. The skeletons stalled in movement. Every limb averted, every skull shunned, every arm inventing its own silence. Three hundred and thirty deaths an hour.

The hills around Butare awoke that morning into a sediment of blood, and the wide, unseemly spectacle of bones. Bones. So many bones spoke in the banana plantations, so many bodies rafted down the banks. Coffee, avocado, honeybees, dogs, a complete firmament of crows fed on blood. AeûāT□□□□āāā□□□āā

The next day Moses faxes me part of an email.

Sāā –á{!!¢ÿ
>The human interaction between Brit and Boer

>never formed part of my collective memory,
>but somehow the interaction between Black and Boer
>was part of my private memory.
>My grandmother often spoke of how her mother would go down
>from the caves where they were hiding,
>and how the old black man staying on the farm
>would sit for hours with a knife at the spruit to spear a fish for her.
>She would whisper to me: if it wasn't for him,
>we would have died.
zD¿zz'k /wh..

This is followed by something else Moses clearly feels I should take note of:

'An individual's identity involves a complex interplay of multiple spheres, such as the interpersonal, the ethnic, the occupational, the economic, the political, etc. These parts of a person coexist dynamically to create a continuous conception of life from past through present to future. Ideally, the individual should simultaneously have free psychological access to and movement within all these identity dimensions. Exposure to trauma causes a rupture in the personality so that the person no longer has free or easy access to these dimensions.'

'Ja, ja, Moses,' I fax back, 'get me my interview!'
    Obstinately, he replies: 'To heal, the person has to integrate the trauma in all of life's relevant dimensions, not only the personal or communal but also the national.'
    I know the book he is quoting from – probably using it for a Unisa course. But before I can reply, he sends it. The interview as I wrote it up after the documentary film had been edited:

|$%^&0□0□0□0□0□0□0□0□0□0□000 0 0 0 0 0 0 0 0 0 0 0 0 0
□□□āāā□□□āā000000000000000000000□□□āāā□□□ā ā
□□□āāā□□□āā000000000000000000000Do you trust whites?'
    'As a group?'
    'As a group, yes.'
    'Being Deborah: no. No, I don't. Being Deborah Matshoba, born in Munsieville, bred in Kagiso, went to prison for three years, got banned for five years: no, it's not possible. Individuals here and there, yes, but as a group? No.
    'I come from the Matshoba clan, and my Dad would have told you, we have always fought injustice when we meet it. My Dad comes from Queenstown, from the rural area of Hewu. He moved, he trekked to Kimberley, then to Lichtenburg, where we settled after the killing of the Israelites at Ntabelanga by Jan Smuts.'

In her testimony before the Truth Commission, it sometimes seemed that her political choices came naturally, buttressed by personal bravery, but now I see that they were deeply informed by a solid thread of behaviour from generation to generation. Deborah's family survived the Bulhoek massacre. Her ancestor Samuel Matshoba was Enoch Mgijima's right-hand man.

The prophet Enoch Mgijima established his own church in 1912. His followers – among them the Matshobas – were known as the Israelites, and his holy village at the foot of Ntabelanga ('The place where the sun rises') was near Bulhoek in the Queenstown area. The prophet himself designed the church uniforms: white tunics with fezzes for the men, black dresses with white roses for the hair of the women, and small brooches showing his portrait.

In 1919, Mgijima had a vision which prompted him to summon all his followers to Ntabelanga. People came from all over Southern Africa, occupied land and began to establish a self-sufficient community. This alarmed the neighbouring farmers. The Israelites' defiance of the law alarmed the authorities even more. Mgijima and his followers refused to move. After a long stand-off, the police attacked the village and nearly two hundred Israelites were killed. The inscription on their mass grave at Bulhoek reads: 'Because our people chose the plan of God, there was no place for them on earth.'

I ask Deborah what role the memory of the massacre played in her own political life. 'I grew up to accept that tone ... the tone of resistance, the tone against political oppression.' When she was detained in the late seventies, she had to draw on these resources just to survive.

'The worst was not the torture, the solitary confinement. When I was inside, unbeknown to me, they had killed Steve Biko. And when I heard that, it was like they had taken the soul out of me. There was also a certain sense of fright in me that I was never going to go out of that cell again. If they could kill him, they could kill anybody and everybody.'

As Deborah is talking, she sometimes closes her eyes, very slowly, like someone on medication. According to the literature on the effects of torture, the experience leaves no part of the victim's life untouched. Torture victims display a wide variety of symptoms – depression, anxiety, sleep disorders, sexual dysfunction, irritability, physical illness. Their capacity to cope is usually overwhelmed, their trust in humanity eroded and sense of self destroyed. After being released, they feel alienated from others and may have enduring difficulties in forming relationships.

'Sometimes she would just be alone, you know,' says Deborah's brother, who lives in a township close by, 'alone, and you can see her crying and you ask what for? And you can see she is far away, far, far away, and when you touch her she just becomes violent. And then my mother would say, no, you know what, let her just take it gradually, gradually. Even right now, she is not fine. You find her crying ... she cries from the chest, you know, not like crying from the mouth or the eyes.'

'How do you see reconciliation?' I ask her.

'For me reconciliation is "*uxolelwano*". When Jesus Christ was on the cross, he said: forgive them, because they don't know what they are doing … that is how I understand it – forgiveness is creating a culture of ubuntu, humaneness, *medemenslikheid* …'

'In what way are you combining ubuntu with reconciliation?'

'When a man has done wrong and asks for pardon, he has to be pardoned; he has to show that he deserves the pardon, and the other one has to show that he has the ability to grant it. My mentor, Steve Biko, always said that out there in the world, as much as there are good white people, there are also bad, bad black people. What we have to do is to identify who the enemy is. So when you talk about bitterness and anger, one has to determine who the anger is aimed at.'

'What is it in whites that will make you say: that is why I don't want to live in a country with them?'

'Things like – and I'm just mentioning a few – they don't know that we only started having a democratic vote, a democratic government in 1994. Oh really! Were you oppressed? You were arrested? We didn't know that! You couldn't get a management position? You were in jail? What for? They don't know that they used to put the National Party in power. That is irritating, very, very irritating.'

'After you were appointed at Old Mutual, you bought a house in Witpoortjie. Why did you want to live away from your family in a predominantly white suburb?'

'Because it is my country. I fought for this dispensation and nothing will stop me. It is my country and I am going to live anywhere I want. If I want to live in the bundu, or in Sandton, if I want to live in Ventersdorp next to Eugene Terre'blanche, I will live there.'

'Do you find this area with its burglar bars, guard dogs and racist whites worth your decision?'

'Yes. I've made my mark. And I've found acceptance, which I haven't actually sought. You know, my neighbours also have to seek acceptance from me here. If they feel they don't need acceptance from me they might as well go and live in Canada.'

Deborah is on the board of the neighbourhood watch. One night her neighbours, who are members of the Afrikaner Weerstandsbeweging – the Afrikaner Resistance Movement – noticed someone creeping into her yard. Bokkie Erasmus and her husband stormed next door and trapped the burglar as he was breaking into Deborah's house. When I interviewed Bokkie, she was surprised to hear that Deborah had been in jail.

'I will be the last one to judge,' Bokkie said. 'If she was in jail, there may be reasons. I also had family members in jail.'

'Deborah was in jail for political reasons,' I said.

'You mean she was a terrorist?'

I drew up my shoulders. Bokkie sat on her couch contemplating the news, her feet nervously flicking in her slippers. Finally she said, 'Then she has changed. I promise you, I think she has changed.'

'And have you changed?' I asked.

'We still have friends who are staunch AWBs and they are astonished to hear that we live next to blacks. No, never, you can never live next to them, I promise you, they can't accept it. Martiens and Rentia can't believe it, because they are AWBs. I tell them it is wonderful, you have less trouble with them and they are friendly and you can trust them.'

Before I left, Bokkie proudly told me another story: 'My daughter had to dress up for a special cultural day at her work. We borrowed Deborah's dress and head cloth and earrings and things. The people are still talking about how my child looked.'

Deborah bites on her lip for a long time. Her lip bears a scar.

'I believe in President Mandela and I believe that he's got foresight, that he is looking into the future. He is not thinking about the bitterness, the anger that some of us are having, he is thinking about the future of this country. That is why he avoids the cycle of revenge. He is thinking about the future.'

'Are you saying that whites are essential for the future of this country?'

'People. I believe in people. I believe in the human kind ... basically, I believe in ... humanity ...'

These last words are a kind of shuddering. It feels almost heartless to carry on, to ask such questions of this woman whose eyes are almost permanently brimming with tears.

'Often one hears that it is impossible to forgive the unforgivable. That you cannot forgive on behalf of the dead. That you, Deborah Matshoba, cannot forgive on behalf of Steve Biko.'

She sits for a long time with her eyes closed, rocking herself back and forth, and then speaks with enormous effort. 'I think the underlying point is that one cannot forget. One has lost a lot of friends, and unduly so, it was not necessary. When you look at the circumstances and you say: Steve died at the age of thirty. The contribution he was making, when you've known these people, when you've eaten from the same plate with them. You know, this is how we've lived with Steve, shared the same piece of meat with Mapetla Mohapi, with Onkgopotse Tiro, you know, it is not easy ... it is not easy ... they did not know what they were doing.'

'And if I brought Roy Otto to you now, what would you do?'

'Roy Otto? I think I would go and raise my Dad from his grave and say, here is Roy Otto! I've found him!' Her face, which she has kept impassive with immense self-control, is crossed by a slight, sardonic smile, which dissolves immediately into one of the most painful expressions I have ever witnessed, as she says, 'You died looking for him. Because he hurt your daughter. He hurt your daughter, he hurt your manhood where you could not even protect her. He hurt my son, he hurt my family ... I know that it is impossible, but I'm saying to you, I will go and call my Dad and tell him: Tata, here he is ... I found him ...'

It is so quiet. Deborah sits with her eyes closed.

We make tea on the stove. Ubuntu. The most profound opposite of Apartheid. More than forgiveness or reconciliation. More than 'turn the other cheek'. It is what humanity has lost. Through the back window I see Deborah's swimming pool, a shambles of stagnant green and debris. On the washing line, a colourful peach scarf flutters in the wind scurrying through this ordinary □□□□āāā□□□□āā□□□□āāā

ā□□□□āāā□□□□āā□□□□āāā□□□□āā□□□□āāā□□□□āā
□□□□āāā□□□□āā
□□□□āāā□□□
□□□□āāā□
□□□□

*S*o the moonlight glides. Loose. Lightly breathing. In silver chevrons the river rapids downstream. And you would have skipped this place, would have flown past, whirling into deeper pools, if it were not for the hippopotamus. It rose unexpectedly, a flutter of silver spray and hiss. With the moonlight now you catch the water-clumsy hump lumbering away from the sandbank. You spill into its tracks. You light up the soapy water left behind in the hollows where people did their washing on the sandstone slabs earlier that day. You hear the splintering of wood and then the sound of the animal devouring something – pumpkin, watermelon. Then, with the moon, you hit the squat roof of the church, tingeing the corrugated iron with light. You blush down the whitewashed walls. Imperceptibly, the moon leaves you behind as it sifts across the drag-trails through the dusty streets, the treads of wheels, the tracks of horses. You stay standing in the shadow of the church, with the pale sandstone blocks like huge, still-tepid bars of soap against your back. Around you it rustles. Eucalyptus. Young white trunks denuded by the moon. The village seems deserted. Then a horse snorts, a hoof sounds sharply against stone. The cross-streets peter out in stubbly veld under a sky weighted down by stars. A handful of houses, two shops are sunk in litters of deep shadow. The entrance gate of the house across from you is latched inside an arch of silver-knobbed rambling roses. Behind it you see the moon stooping in the gleam of saddles and bridles. Everything doused in fragrance. From rose you filter to karee, from sweet-thorn to eucalyptus, you sweep from peach to prune, to pit latrine, to pepper tree, to quince-tree lane, from horse manure to cart, from mule wagon to municipal cattle pen, damp with dung and milk and snout. A man coughs in an outbuilding. Someone sashes a window open. You catch up with the moon on its way to an even smaller settlement across the ravines. The thorn trees here are meagre, the houses smaller, the smell of smoke and dung-fire hovers. You drag along with the moonlight until it alights suddenly on the forehead of a man, a man you have not noticed until now. He has a blanket over his shoulders and is holding a stick. He does not move. He stands and watches the village. You slip along the roof of a pigsty, you leap from shard to shard, you lick the thorns of trees with milk and bless their resin with silver. The Southern Cross cants. Then the moon picks up a figure coming across the ravines, a woman kicking her long skirt open at the hem with each step. She does not look at the man. She walks straight to the house which

---

stands with its door to the river. She goes inside and for a moment something flashes steel or tin. The man waits a while, then leans his stick beside the door and goes in after her. When the last ripple laps into the reeds, after the silent drifting in and sinking away of the hippo, you withdraw with the moon. You loosen your eyes sluggishly from a dressing table and a silver hairbrush, your fingers from a desk. You let drop from your sight a map drawn by magistrate Joseph Orpen, showing subdivided erven in the bow of a river. The moonlight dims on Orpen's signature, as it does on the letter from Chief Mamogale of Rhenoster River, complaining about the theft of the land. You and the moon yield to the day.

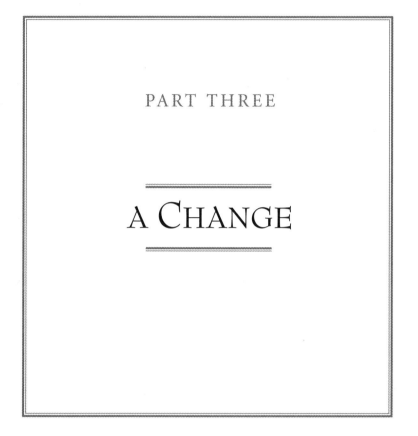

PART THREE

A CHANGE

CHAPTER ONE

I OPEN THE FRONT DOOR. A young black woman, accompanied by a couple of teenage children, wants to speak to me privately. She motions me into the garden and speaks very softly. She is Mamukwa. She has come to inform me that 'the Struggle in Kroonstad' needs me. It is 1987. A 'Free Mandela' rally will be held in the township this coming weekend, and I must come and perform a poem about Mandela. Sunday afternoon in the hall of the Roman Catholic Church. She dares not give me any more details, but I should be there around two o'clock. If anyone asks me about it, I should just say that it is an ordinary church meeting. The Chief Poet of Kroonstad would have come to ask me personally, but he is under surveillance by the police. He could not phone me either, because the comrades from the post office warned him that my phone was being tapped. And off she goes.

My head is spinning. Who exactly is Nelson Mandela? I know and I don't. In any case, I do not know nearly enough to write a poem about him. Equally important: can a poet write under orders? Without something compelling you from inside? Or maybe the most important question is: why has my inside not compelled me yet to write a poem about Nelson Mandela? Although he was jailed when I was seven years old, should I not already have an entire file of poetry on him?

The matter is also more complicated than this. It is against the law to quote Mandela. It is positively dangerous to attend a political rally, never mind to perform a poem about Mandela. However, the request throws up the kinds of questions poets and writers are faced with at times in this country: why are we writing? For whom? In South Africa, art for art's sake seems like an escape, an indulgence, a lie in the face of tortures, killings and a growing fury. Is it more important to write a poem that helps someone, quite literally, to survive what is happening, to stay sane for five minutes, or should one rather be trying to write a poem with universal appeal? Is it a case of the 'political now' versus the 'universal'? Is one doomed either to be 'a member on the panel discussion of Social Relevance' or to 'crochet doilies for the gilded armchairs in the Palace of Art', as Margaret Atwood put it. The ideal, obviously, would be to write a poem that is socially relevant but has universal appeal. So I start looking for examples.

I go through my poetry books. After two days I'm quite desperate. Nothing really works for this specific occasion. 'Everything or nothing. All of us or none' by Brecht? Not really. 'Liberty' by Eluard? 'When the sky falls, raise it; When the world goes wrong, right it' by Mao Zedong? Russian poetry, poems from Cuba, South America? No.

I stumble upon Aimé Césaire's *Return to My Native Land*, in which he celebrates being black as being everything that whites regard as unimportant:

(my ancestors are)

Those who invented neither gunpowder nor compass
those who tamed neither steam nor electricity
those who explored neither sea nor sky
but those who know the humblest corners of the country of suffering
those whose only journeys were uprootings
those who went to sleep on their knees
...
My negritude is neither a tower nor a cathedral;
It plunges into the red flesh of the earth

It doesn't help me. It doesn't resonate for me with the little I know of Mandela, and I'm
not sure what kind of slant a white mouth will give to it. Should I rather use: 'I want to
rediscover the secret of great speech and of great burning. I want to say storm. I want
to say river. I want to say tornado. I want to say leaf, I want to say tree ... The man who
couldn't understand me couldn't understand the roaring of a tiger.'

Perhaps I should simply say: I want to say Mandela. I ask around. I consult students
and activists. But it is clear: Mandela is simply a symbol. Nobody knows what he looks
like, nobody knows exactly what he has said. We just know that he is imprisoned on
Robben Island for the freedom of us all. So I imagine him here – in our breath, on our
tongues, staring out from our eyes. Yes, I see Mandela in a coat on the banks of the
Valsch River, among the reeds we see him, we hear him stirring in the sirens, we sit with
him behind the school desks, we see his tracks in the dusty streets of the township.
Mandela breathes among us like the thorn trees and the grass, he wrestles into the taxis
and the buses, he eats in the outbuildings, he raises his fist in the prisons. From the
dusty winds blowing across the plains, he will come to us and set us free.

The morning before the rally, I fall into a panic of a more practical kind. What does
one wear? Jeans, T-shirt and takkies? I'm already aware that the comrades object to the
fact that whites who actually have more than enough money, a nice house and two cars
always dress down when they come to the townships. As if they don't respect the people.
To church or the theatre they wouldn't dress like that, but in the township suddenly
they have to show how simply they live. A dress? Silk stockings? I decide on somewhere
in between.

When I get out of my car, a Free State wind of blood-red dust has picked up, and
dead leaves and plastic bags hang in the air like kitchen rags. The event has been moved
into the open field next to the church, because there are too many people. I realize three
things simultaneously. Firstly, hundreds of policemen are peering over the concrete
fence – their heads like a string of beads. Secondly, the sheets of paper on which my
poem is neatly typed out will flutter so much in the wind that I will be unable to read.

And thirdly, I am dressed inappropriately. Ghangha, the Chief Poet, is decked out in feathery tassels in the colours of the ANC, worn with a weathered tracksuit and his Sunday-best shoes.

I indicate that I won't be able to read from the sheets of paper. 'You poets of the page,' he rebukes me amiably, and in the blink of an eye has the two sheets taped neatly, one below the other, to a piece of tomato case with a few Band-Aids from the first-aid kit.

When I see that there is no microphone, just a megaphone, I break out in alternating bouts of sweating and giggling. What on earth have I let myself in for! After hours in the sun and dust, my turn comes. The crowd has already been driven to the edge of hysteria. I take the megaphone with a kind of disbelief, hold the tomato case in my shaking left hand and stammer the first line. Ghangha comes and stands next to me, he shouts the first line loudly and gestures to me to repeat it. I get the idea. I yell the first line into the megaphone. My voice sounds as if it comes from another planet. There is loud cheering. Ghangha yells out the first line yet again and I repeat it and the cheering doubles. By the third line, the crowd joins me rhythmically in Afrikaans: '*Die vuis sê Mandéla! Mandéla sê Máokeng!*' ['This fist says Mandela! Mandela says Maokeng!'] From there the poem takes on a life of its own. Mandela is among us. People are jumping: *Thaa! Tha-thaa!* Shouting: '*Die vuis sê Mandéla!*' The other poets take over, a mixture of Afrikaans and Sesotho. People are toyi-toying furiously, and now it turns into an angry, thumping dance where everyone aims imaginary AK-47s at the faces of the policemen, who, not to be outdone, brandish their own weapons over the fence.

But as if he has been doing it for years, the Chief Poet takes control. Subtly, he starts changing the rhythm of the slogans. He interjects more and more phrases in English, his tone gradually shifting from anger to lament. He draws the great crowd into a complete silence, during which a woman's voice cues in 'Nkosi Sikelel' iAfrika'.

✧

It is dark. Baleka sits with her hands pressed between her knees. Around her head a cloth of black and gold is knotted. She rocks gently while she sings. To and fro. Her eyes closed: 'Mandela, Mandela: show us the way to freedom! Freedom is in your hands.'

When some of the men join in softly with the bass notes, I get gooseflesh. Far away the Zambezi thunders as it tumbles over and over in a vast foaming cloak, smoking damply, at times bound with rainbows. The Zimbabwean waiters of the Makasa Hotel throng in the doorways to hear a song grow from lament to plea to indestructible dream. To see grown men singing and crying.

I was part of a group of Afrikaans writers who were invited to meet the exiled writers of the ANC at Victoria Falls during the spring of 1989. It would be the first time that most of us from apartheid South Africa stepped outside our country into Africa and were welcomed for it. On the other side of customs, Breyten Breytenbach awaited us –

visibly at home on the continent. The air fluttering with poetic voices and lowveld heat. Before I left home, Ghangha had brought me a fountain pen and a writing pad: 'Give this to Pallo Jordan. Tell him it is to write our freedom on – he who was born in Kroonstad.' 'The river? Is the river still there?' Pallo asked, pleasing me and my ancestors no end.

Over the days, the formal discussions on a variety of subjects kept spilling over into literature. The mobile voices of storytellers, the lamenting voices of poets seethed with languages and songs. As the nights passed, we splayed our country open like a carpet at our feet. We splashed a multicoloured covering. Our trampled country suddenly lay among us, tongued by the warp and woof of what our hearts were about. In front of our very ears the fabric of our country was being spoken into something totally new – an unmetallic story, a multicoloured song, sweet and sultry and tolerantly clear.

'I teach my children in London how to say "Schweizer-Reneke",' says Essop Pahad. Sankie Nkondo shows a photograph of her family, cheerful children, she herself rigid in the background: 'I live where politics never dies down.' 'I live in Lusaka, but my heart is in Cape Town,' says Jeremy Cronin. A mesmerizing Willie Kgositsile with his 'Change is Going to Come'. Albie Sachs gives me a T-shirt from Mozambique – 'Aluta Continua'. Barbara Masekela says, 'I want to go back. I want to be there on clear winter days.'

And so on the last night, the hotel bar is filled with unspeakable longing and desperate drinking. The yearning for home, for place that is also my place, becomes almost overwhelming. 'When you got off the bus here, you smelled so much of home that I felt as if my heart would burst from my throat,' says Rebecca Magaisa.

'When we watched you get off that plane,' somebody else says, 'we could tell: that one is a Boer, also that one, not that one. We recognize you, that obsession you have – like us – with the land: it shows, right here between the eyes.'

The night swirls up into this song about Mandela, sung by Baleka. Whoever he actually was after twenty-seven years in prison, wherever he found himself at that moment, whatever thoughts were on his mind, his name had become one searing sense of yearning, billowing across the continent.

That night an anguished dread tears at my throat. I am deeply upset by it all. By this immense longing around me – so thick that it can almost be touched. By the small shards of memory being held out to us. As if talking to us, embracing us, hearing us might transport them back to the country they have been driven from. But the gate to that country is locked, by my people. I can't sleep. I get up very early to go down to the waterfall, whose sound has been such a constant presence in everything we've said and listened to these past few days. It is our last morning. At the rails, a man is standing looking out into the mist. Spray gathering on his face and beard. I haven't seen him at the conference. We stand a long time next to each other, beholding the awesome spectacle. Then he says, as if talking to himself:

I do not have a voice like you, waterfall,
You speak and speak and speak never-endingly,
I sound like a fool when I try to explain in ink
All that you are: the damp skin of your face,
How noble and beautiful it is.

... you soothe every heart that limps forth in the dark,
That wanders with no place to lay down its sides.
As I sit looking at you, I find your word to rest in.

From under my umbrella, I gaze at him. He doesn't look right or left, but continues in a low voice with what I gather is a poem:

... your sound is the sound of honey.
It basks around your head
Like the hand of a woman suckling you.
She spreads her fingers along your eyebrows,
Her fingers lovingly trace the skin towards your hair,
They caress your hair to this side,
They caress it back to where it belongs.
However much you have wandered
You will be at peace here – beside these wings of foamm
Which fall and fall into waterfall – you who destroy the abyss between us.

I go closer, staring intently at him.
    'It is a poem from my country,' he says. 'B.W. Vilakazi.' Then he walks away.
    And I realize that he thinks I am not from South Africa.
    Something bursts in me. Inexplicably. And I cry. My whole inside gives way, flows out like foundation rubble, leaving me raw, empty, bereft, and yet so heavy I cannot seem to lift my head.
    After what feels like hours, I make my way back, dragging the corpse of white skin and Afrikaner tongue behind me.
    The bus leaves the hotel. From the window I look back at all of them – exiled. And somehow as lost as myself. Standing apart from each other, yet clumsily bunched together, their faces tautly expressionless – as if they dare not contemplate the fact that we on the bus may return to the country that is theirs by right. In my suitcase I have pebbles and a bracelet that I have to bury for Rebecca in South African soil when I arrive home, a poem about the longing for red grass and the Maluti by Marius Schoon.
    The word 'injustice' gapes like a precipice.

✧

I receive a phone call. 'Go and look at the hawker's stall on the pavement just behind Greg's Muti Shop.' The line goes dead.

And there they hang. T-shirts flapping cheerily in the spring breeze. Sporting the face of a man. He has a beard and a parting creased into his hair and his eyes seem ... sad. Above the face, these words: 'I have cherished the ideal of a democratic and free society.' And below: Cde Nelson Mandela.

I become aware of others beside me. A wall of black faces. We all stand and stare. Is it actually him? Is this what he looks like?

A woman stretches out her hand and touches the face. A young comrade bends forward and says, stressing each syllable clearly: *'Ha-laa-la!'*

On the back of the T-shirt, printed askew and almost illegibly underneath an ANC flag: 'I have dedicated myself to the struggle of the African people. I have fought against white domination, and I have fought against black domination. It is an ideal which I hope to live for, but if needs be, it is an ideal for which I am prepared to die.'

The eyes of the woman standing next to me are shining like two wet stones. The man who was just a name, a vehicle of dreams, has now acquired, for us on this dusty pavement, a face and a voice. This man who is still forbidden has come to show us his face openly and speak to us directly, here in Kroonstad.

Suddenly we recall where we are. And when we look around it feels as if the street is teeming with informers and policemen.

✧

The television is on at full volume. Mandela is to be released today. My house is filled with people. We sit on couches, lie on cushions, make buckets of popcorn, drink Coke, drink brandy. We wait and we wait. There is wors and pap and salad. Exquisite fish curry made by Mr Feris, Beatie's *frikkadelletjies*, Rutha's chicken. Someone asks for a towel, the Tituses' child has vomited all over the stoep – 'too much rich food, you know.'

I phone comrade George, who grew up in Kroonstad but is now working for a foreign television news agency in Cape Town. He tells me reporters have been waiting since the previous day at the gates of the Victor Verster prison. Winnie and several ANC leaders are with Mandela even as we speak, but they have no idea when the long-awaited release will happen. He tells me the latest rumours circulating at the gates. Apparently, one of the ANC leaders told Mandela the day before that hordes of cameras were waiting outside. 'Yes,' Mandela reportedly said, 'many more today than yesterday.' And how did he know that? It seems that initially F.W. de Klerk didn't let Mandela know exactly when he would be released. So for the past few days he has borrowed a pair of labourer's overalls from one of the groundsmen and walked over to the gates to study the media contingent. 'We went absolutely ballistic when we heard that. Nelson Mandela has been watching our reporters and photographers for days, when we would kill each other for a picture of him!'

George also relates how President De Klerk, with finely considered timing, released a photograph of himself and Mandela to the media the previous day. 'It was unbelievable,' George says. 'The journalists were all hysterical as they tried to be the first to get the photograph to their newspapers. It was as if the public image of Mandela was being coined before my eyes. The one would say: "A smiling Nelson Mandela ..." Then another one would chip in: "No, no! A smiling, charming-looking Nelson Mandela." Then another, shouting: "No man, the world wants to know whether he looks old or not. It should be: A smiling, young-looking Nelson Mandela." "Please," from the first, "people want to know whether he is a rowdy communist. We should rather say: A smiling, healthy-looking Nelson Mandela, dressed in an elegant suit, talks to the man who will release him tomorrow."'

'We see on the television that there are so many *iimbongi* present, George. The Chief Poet here in Kroonstad says that many *iimbongi* have silenced themselves for years, because the country wasn't free. Now, with the release of Mandela, they will burst forth and *bonga*. Can't you get your crew to interview one of them on TV?'

'Listen, I'm with the foreign media and they regard *iimbongi* purely as an African curiosity. They are only interested in having them bucking and gambolling in the background for their stand-ups. Besides, I'm definitely not going to translate praise songs *bonga-ed* in deep Xhosa for them, while I'm only getting paid as an editor of news footage!'

Ghangha is sitting with our dog on his lap. Sparky started barking furiously when he entered the house. 'Come here, doggy,' Ghangha said and picked him up, 'come sit with me and get used to a black man.' Since then Sparky has not moved from Ghangha's lap. No doubt it helps that he keeps feeding him pieces of meat.

'There!' someone shouts. 'Come! It's him!'

The camera zooms in on the man with his fist in the air. Winnie at his side. He is tall and handsome. The camera wobbles a bit, there is clearly a scramble for position, but before all of us can get a proper look, off they go.

What the hell. I phone George. But there is only an answering machine.

The television crosses to the Grand Parade in Cape Town, where thousands upon thousands of people are waiting for Mandela to address them. George phones back. Enraged. He stutters with anger, hisses as he looks for expression – the bloody Anglo-fucking-Saxon liberal shit of a journalist sent to get the story of the century forgot to switch off his bleeper. So just when the camera was full on Mandela, very close, the bleeper on his belt squirmed piercingly, with its red light flashing – immediately affecting the natural sound with a buzz, which means that the sound is useless and they now have to buy footage from the SABC to use in future bulletins. 'The most important moment of my career destroyed by a white arsehole.' I let the remark pass. This is not the time to split hairs. Thanks, bye. Besides, we are standing around, a bit flabbergasted. The big moment has finally happened, and yet ...

'And yet what?' asks Sheridan.

'Look at us, we are all still so much ourselves,' I say. 'We are the ... same, and yet something has fundamentally changed forever, for all of us.'

'Well, it's like taking away the cage from around an animal – we don't have a clue what to do, where to go, how to survive, the cage is all we know – nè, my doggy?' Ghangha looks quizzically at Sparky on his lap.

'Speak for yourself,' says Bongani, who has entered with a carton of mageu. 'I know exactly what to do with freedom. Here.' We all drink a bit of mageu, but my liberation, at least, will have to happen without it. Mamukwa fetches the clay pot of traditional beer which she stored in the fridge when she arrived and hands it carefully to Ghangha, who hands it on to Bongi. He sprinkles it on the ground in our yard. 'For the ancestors – to share in the day.' And when his eye falls on me, he adds hospitably, 'If they are white, they can also share. For today.'

We all take a break. I make crumpets. Somebody arrives from the township with vetkoek and *Slamse* koeksisters. We wait and we wait. It is almost dusk. Some people start leaving. I phone again. George is tired but recovered. And also waiting.

'What is the delay? The Paarl is just half an hour from Cape Town.'

He laughs. 'We hear that the driver went berserk when he saw all the people streaming towards the Parade. When he tried to turn around, he got caught in another huge crowd, who recognized them and swamped them so much that Mandela was almost torn from the car. When the driver finally got clear, he just raced off, and for a while nobody could find them. My girlfriend, who is part of the crew waiting for Mandela on the balcony of the City Hall, says they've just got word that he is on his way. Apparently Dullah Omar, just like the rest of the world, was sitting with his family in front of the television, when his doorbell rang. He gaped like a fish when he found Nelson Mandela on the doorstep. 'But shouldn't you be at the City Hall?' Omar asked. Whereupon Mandela apparently responded, 'Is that how you greet me after twenty-seven years?' Omar contacted Archbishop Tutu, who informed them that the crowd was getting restless because of the long delay, and now they say Mandela is on his way with a calmer driver.'

It is almost dark when Mandela appears on the balcony. We sit in complete silence as the camera pans across a crowd that seems to go on forever and ever. The sea of people is alive with flags and banners. Then his time is here. He raises his fist and shouts, *'Amandla!'* His voice. This is his voice. Strong, yet choked, his shoulders clenched. I feel shivers down my spine. This sound I will never forget. But everybody in the room is already on their feet, roaring so loudly that the windows rattle, *'Ngawethu!'* We yell with all our might towards this man, we sling our voices like cables, like streamers – to reach him, to touch him. The veins stand out on our throats. Our eyes are brimming as we take our first real sniff of freedom, as we stretch our arms. As if from our shoulders something loosens, something scooping fragments of air, something quite feathery.

What Mandela says, or the fact that he has to borrow Winnie's glasses to read his speech because he's left his own behind at the prison, doesn't filter through to us. We are suddenly so utterly aware, and linked as we have never been linked before. Each one with every one. He is of us. We could be the most beautiful colour of change the world has ever seen. The man is free and a new time has dawned.

✧

I make rice, put a chicken in the oven so that my family will have something to eat later in the day. Then I pick up everyone travelling with me. Ghangha, our Chief Poet, looks spectacular in a black, yellow and green sweater and a beautiful thickly-woven headband in the same colours, with plumes hanging to the back. We are on our way to the Free State's welcoming of Nelson Mandela in Bloemfontein. Ghangha fixes a little ANC flag to the aerial, which, to his great joy, causes several fleshy, white middle fingers to shoot out at us from cars passing us on the road. The turn-off to Bloemfontein is suddenly dotted with stalls manned by tough-looking Boer men in khaki clothes, selling little wooden ox wagons and Boer Republic flags.

The rally is at the Bloemfontein Stadium in the heart of the city. It will be the first time that so many thousands of black people have gathered here. All shops and cafés are securely shut. We find a parking place, and everywhere we bump into comrades from all over the Free State. At the gate a female guard stops me. Before she can catch herself, she says, 'Wait, *miesies*!' We stare at each other. She is surprised by what she just said, I am angry that I responded. Then she straightens herself up and says firmly, 'May I search you, comrade?' And I thank the heavens for a language and an ideology, however mangled, in which we can try to reach each other as equals.

Ghangha takes a seat on the field among the other poets and bands and speech-makers. The rest of us, together with thirty thousand others, file patiently into the stadium, row after row as directed by the marshals, and fill the stands. It is twelve o'clock. One. Two. We sit for hours and hours in the bloody sun. We sing 'Ntate Modise'. We sing 'Mandela, Mandela – Freedom is in your hands'. Over and over and over. On top of the tower block that houses the provincial administration I see something stirring like grass. I look again. Those are people! Hundreds of whites have come specially this Sunday to observe the proceedings from up there. It seems they are even braaiing there!

It is four o'clock. Quarter past.

And then he's standing there – completely ordinary, at the gate. Suddenly – just there. In flesh and blood. Before our eyes.

And we go crazy!

Physically, one could not have asked for a better symbol than the imposing figure of Nelson Mandela. In his biscuit-coloured suit and thin red tie, he towers head and shoulders above everybody else. He raises his fist into the air and the entire stadium is on their feet. He walks around the running track, past everybody. Deranged sounds tumble from our mouths.

Visibly, he becomes the collective of the dreams and yearnings of each of the thirty thousand of us. He walks past us. It is as if he notices me personally.

The Mandela freedom song bursts forth with a mighty sound over the stadium and you can hear it making a continuous echo over the city and drowsy Sunday white suburbs. When he takes his place on the podium, we sing 'Nkosi Sikelel' iAfrika'. It is as if years of harassment, resistance, aggression, fear, futility, despair, anger are cracking off in layers. Tears roll down our faces.

'This is the Free State, this,' says a moved Bongani. 'And a miracle of a man.'

Mandela's voice sounds young and strong: 'Bloemfontein is the Mother of the ANC. The ANC was born here. The ANC is strong because its cause is just. We bring together and we set free. We keep in our hearts the ideals of Bram Fischer and Moshoeshoe – known as "He-who-binds-people-together".'

Elated and ululating we drive back to Kroonstad, cassette tapes with freedom songs blaring; we fly ANC flags and my travelling companions give exuberant black-power salutes to white passers-by.

✦

Liewe Antjie,

Strange, wonderful times we are living in. Everything is suddenly possible. Bizarrely so. Over the weekend we celebrated my father's eightieth birthday and it was a real Groot Trek from all over the country to Wesselsbron – six children, nineteen grandchildren and eight great-grandchildren. I was a bit apprehensive because of my own children. To the best of my knowledge they are ordinary, like their mother (joking!!!) – even if Jaco has a cookie jar of dagga hidden in his cupboard. But it is my father and he is eighty and the family has not been together in a very long time, so we make the journey. The first to arrive. In dribs and drabs my brothers and sisters and their extended families turn up, professors and doctors, lecturers and dominees. My father sits in his favourite chair on the stoep, greeting his successful brood with pride. People arrive, greet him, then gather in the yard at the back for a spitbraai. Among the throng is my eldest sister's daughter Elmien. It turns out she is a lesbian, or a lesbyterian, as she jokingly says. She arrives with a tiny baby in a carrycot, accompanied by a rather butchy partner. They have adopted, she says radiantly. Pa swallows once, but greets them and even manages a playful touch to the baby's cheek. Then down the line comes my youngest brother's rebel daughter with the guy she is marrying in April. He happens to be black. Pa had to swallow twice, but managed a dignified 'Dumela Mongadi' in his best Sesotho. It turns out that Odirile is actually Xhosa and a big rugby fan, so the bonding with the rest of the family happens fast and fierce. Just when we think everybody is there, a flashy red cabriolet arrives – you could see the whole of Wesselsbron gazing after that car. And out climbs the family's crown prince. My eldest brother's eldest son, the one who carries the family name of the Steyns, the name of my father and his father: Rudolf Johannes Du Plessis Steyn. But Ruhan, it turns out, besides being an up-and-coming actuary, is also gay and has brought, guess what? – his very black lover.

We all simply stared. And I felt a bit sorry for my father. How much should a patriarch stand? He greeted them without batting an eyelid, but shortly afterwards he went to lie down 'because of the heat'.

But the day turned into one of the best family gatherings we've ever had, because for a change we didn't fight about politics, like in the old days. The bonus? My children have become my father's favourite grandchildren!

liefde,
Rina

CHAPTER TWO

AS A REPORTER FOR SABC RADIO at parliament in Cape Town, I am sent to cover Nelson Mandela's first speech to the United Nations in October 1995. I receive an American visa, a map of New York City and an entire kit that enables one to set up a mini edit suite in one's hotel room. Unlike SABC television, the radio division does not have enough money to put its journalist up in the same five-star hotel as Mandela. But there is this more reasonable hotel on Second Avenue, about ten minutes' walk or half a mile away, which is nothing in Manhattan. And while I'm there I must organize an interview with the head of the Anti-Apartheid Movement, as well as with the South African ambassador to the UN, Josiah Jele, and of course with South Africa's ambassador to the US, Franklin Sonn. Please also track down the lawyers involved in the case against Armscor. And while you're at it, what about a few interviews with African heads of state? Also, don't forget to file a couple of nice atmospheric stories on New York. These are my orders.

I arrive bleary-eyed and jet-lagged. On my bed is a note: Get accreditation NOW. I leave for the UN Building. But in order to get into the place where you receive proper accreditation, you already need some other sort of authorization. I try to explain to some policemen who understand neither English nor American. I ask. I plead. But I am dismissed in a version of English concealed in Spanish. I try to fight. Try to swear.

Try to cry. Eventually a South African journalist from SAPA sees me and indicates that I am part of his team. In at last. Before you receive accreditation to set foot in the UN Building, you are searched, prodded, sniffed and questioned, and all your equipment is taken apart to make sure that you are unarmed. This takes a day and a half. In the meantime, Mandela is meeting half the world and its mother.

Manhattan is full of Halloween ghosts and skeletons. I hear about the largest Garlic Festival in the world, where even garlic ice cream and garlic shampoo will be available, but I'm still queuing for countless hours in the hope of getting accreditation. I discover that the South African mission had to decline twenty-five requests by heads of state for bilateral discussions with Mandela, and that he has visited all sorts of interesting places – while the SABC's radio journalist is still queuing. When I get back to my hotel room late that night, my swipe card will not unlock my door. I hoist my bags and equipment again and stagger down to the lobby. What is wrong? The man behind the counter understands neither English nor American. He speaks only Money: he wants a deposit of $100. And he wants me to explain ... thees-a! slamming my editing kit down on the counter. The boss comes out of the office. People were too scared to clean the room, they had to get the police to come and check this out. Am I crazy? The place is swarming with heads of state! And do I know that I am not allowed to just change the sockets any way I like? That editing desk is going to cost me hundreds of extra dollars.

In the room a stack of hysterical faxes is waiting for me: where are your stories? You are costing the SABC thousands of rands while we have to use stories from other agencies. There are also faxes from Mandela's own efficient media staff, showing his entire New York itinerary together with times and addresses. Among them an invitation to be at his hotel at four the next morning to go and take a walk with him. This is exclusively for South African journalists.

Mandela is staying in one of New York's best hotels. His security team searched for days to find a hotel that provided rooms and conference facilities right next to an elevator, so that he would not have to walk very far. On the same floor, other rooms had to be available where a whole operation could be set up to keep in direct contact with South Africa, so that both the President and the Minister of Foreign Affairs will be able to carry on with their work as if they are still at home. The hotel is also next to Central Park, so that Mandela can take his early-morning walks there. Many Middle Eastern leaders are staying at the same hotel. You literally have to fight your way through just to get into the lobby.

I get dressed in my clothes for the next day and go to sleep in a chair. After years of travelling around as a journalist, there are two things I have never managed to master: the radios of hired cars and the alarm clocks in hotels. When I jerk awake it is already five o'clock. I grab my notebook and recording equipment and run. I dash across block after block. At the hotel door, the security guards assure me that Mandela and his entourage have already left. With burning chest and rasping breath, I jog into the park.

Eventually I spot a cluster of people up ahead. I take a short cut through the trees and start running flat out. Suddenly I find myself suspended in mid-air, a gun barrel pressed into my back. 'It's okay, she's with us.' One of the South African bodyguards recognizes me as 'the woman from the radio'. 'Are you out of your mind to run like this, in the dark, towards Mandela?'

I join the group. They say that if you want to talk to Mandela, you can walk up in front with him. I move up to the second rank where his personal guards, personal secretary and medical doctor are walking. They are all dressed in cheerful tracksuits. You can see that despite getting up every morning at five o'clock to exercise, a remnant of his prison routine, Mandela is finding it hard to walk very fast. My eyes stray to his hands – the way his fleshy palms bulge out, especially at the base of the thumb. Mandela has unique hands. Recently, when his eldest daughter from his first marriage appeared on television and gestured with her hands, one recognized them immediately: her father's hands with the fleshy palms.

So, here I am. If I walk forward, what do I ask him? In the back of my head is the hectic schedule that he completed the previous day, and the ones still ahead of him: discussions with African leaders, President Clinton, Fidel Castro – who has just received a hero's welcome in Harlem – Gaddafi, several European leaders, and then his official address today, which is already making headlines in the newspapers. And I think: what on God's earth should you ask him now, this saviour of South Africa, this man so many of us admire and love from afar, this man who has been described by poets as the one who does not laugh and does not cry, what do I ask him in this early-morning hour in Central Park?

What will you say to Clinton later? What is your view on the hero-worshipping of Castro in America? What pathetic questions. And should I walk next to him with my microphone in his face while he is strolling along? I realize that I rather want to take him by the arm and say, throw your shoulder blades to the morning breeze, don't talk to anybody. Just take it easy. Walk and see how the sky is lighting up. You don't owe anybody anything, least of all a journalist.

But I see another journalist working his way forward. He comes up beside Mandela and starts chatting to him jovially. It is Arrie Barnard, the American correspondent of one of the Afrikaans newspapers. Does Mandela know that the place where John Lennon was shot is nearby? he asks. Fuck it, I think to myself, John Lennon. Mandela was buried on Robben Island during the Beatle years, they weren't even allowed to read the newspapers. No, that he was not aware of, Mandela says, surprised, to my surprise. Arrie offers to go and show him. Mandela recalls how an English university once offered honorary doctorates to the two of them, to Lennon and himself. But because he would not be able to attend the ceremony, Lennon also decided not to accept the degree. 'I have always admired solidarity,' says Mandela. It seems, according to Arrie, that South Africa is one of the few countries that has never sent anything to be planted in the garden of remembrance for Lennon. Then and there, Mandela turns to his secretary and instructs her to see to it that some proteas are sent over.

My cheeks are burning from embarrassment. This is what a genuine journalist does. He uses a unique opportunity to create a story for his newspaper.

On the way back to the UN Building it becomes clear that the whole of Manhattan is one giant traffic jam. Apparently two cars have collided a few paces from the Waldorf Astoria, where twenty-two heads of state are staying. The reaction to the crash, according to a young boy on roller skates whom I quiz about it, was 'awesome'. Within seconds a dozen secret servicemen were running flat out to the scene and within minutes the two wrecked automobiles were surrounded by almost fifty police officers.

'The UN and New York had a love affair,' says Boutros Boutros-Ghali. 'Our love affair was celebrated by a marriage. But every marriage of fifty years needs work.'

The *New Yorker* points out that the United Nations remains one of New York's foremost tourist attractions, but that it has never been embraced by the city itself. 'The UN's financial contribution to New York is enormous. According to a study, the UN and its related agencies, missions and consulates channelled 3.3 billion dollars into the city in 1994, generating 16 700 direct job opportunities that led to 14 300 additional jobs, making the UN the city's third biggest NGO employer. But what really irks New Yorkers is the idea that the delegates are a bunch of wealthy deadbeats, ignoring parking tickets, rent agreements and other bills in the name of diplomatic immunity – the unpaid tickets added up to nearly 10 million dollars in 1994.'

'They want to move?' says Edward Koch, a former mayor. 'I say move! Where else would you guys get such cheap meals in such first-class restaurants?'

The UN is cordoned off. One's hard-won accreditation does not shield one from the protesters outside the complex. A group of Tibetans on a hunger strike, protesting against the violation of their human rights by China, are lying beneath a canvas lean-to. They are surrounded by women and children screaming hysterically. There are Kurds, Pakistanis, Tamils, Zaïreans and Taiwanese. On the East River pro- and anti-Castro flotillas drift past each other with angry fists waving.

The South African journalists are driven by minibus to where Mandela and Clinton will be meeting. We have to be there three hours earlier for the security clearance. We are ordered like schoolchildren to stand in a line and not make any noise. We will walk through this door and past the little stage where the two gentlemen are sitting. Just walk. No questions. The American President will not take questions from foreign media today. Only television cameras may roll, that is all, thank you. Next group. We troop past like a herd of sheep, my tape recorder running – maybe the stomach of the American President will make a noise?

'Oh, there you are!' It is Mandela. Not only does he recognize us, he also understands immediately that we are being treated like third-raters. So he starts talking. 'After so many years of being rejected by the world, South Africa has taken its place among nations. I am sure my friend here has something to add.' And not even Clinton can avoid saying something to us.

And so the lot of us get our special sound bites and footage.

The media hall of the UN is nothing if not terrifying. You can find a socket for any kind of plug on any kind of machine, for any kind of telephone, any kind of laptop. You can call up any filed footage on a computer system, isolate any sound bite, contact any place in the world at any time. While Mandela delivers his speech, I send the sound bites through to the news office in Johannesburg:

'What challenges us is to ensure that none should enjoy lesser rights; and none be tormented because they are born different, hold contrary political views or pray to God in a different manner.'

'... why should it be that poverty still pervades the greater part of the globe; that wars continue to rage; and that many in positions of power and privilege pursue cold-hearted philosophies which terrifyingly proclaim: "I am not my brother's keeper!"'

'For no one, in the North or the South, can escape the cold fact that we are a single humanity.'

There are many speeches, many leaders. After the opening speeches a photograph is taken. Clinton leads Mandela to the very front, but he is systematically worked backwards until he is standing somewhere higher up at the back, while the likes of Mugabe, Gaddafi, Nujoma and Chissano fill the front ranks.

The Anti-Apartheid Movement in New York is angry. 'South Africa has forgotten the people active in struggle,' says Dumisane Khumalo. 'The embassy did not issue a public schedule of the President's activities around which we could mobilize. Now all we see is the President hobnobbing with the rich people, the business people, not us. There is a feeling here that people who marched in the past no longer have any connection to South Africa. No, the New South Africa sits with the rich folks. Of course, it's good that people have finally discovered South Africa and who Mandela is. But we who protested in the cold and the snow see there is only space now for those in the cushy seats, those who did not even know how to pronounce "Mandela" a year ago. There is a saying among my people: "*Montsamaisa bosigo ke mo leboga bo sele.*" The one who walks me through the night is the one I remember in the morning. South Africa is denying how lost it was during the night.'

✦

In the week Mandela arrives home, I attend a lecture by Prof. S. Mayekiso which deals with one of the first poems written about Mandela, in 1954. According to the Professor, Mandela was an attorney in Johannesburg at this time and in the process of orchestrating the nationwide Defiance Campaign. This was also the year of his first restriction order, and the Treason Trial was just around the corner. In this period, an *imbongi* from Mandela's own Thembu clan, D.L.P. Yali-Manisi (1926–99), composed a prophetic praise song for the prince of his tribe. He called Mandela 'the Earthshaker', 'the Earthquake', and the first verse vibrates with 'z' sounds:

Ilizwe liyashukuma maLawundini!
Iintlambo zonke ziyaxokozela;
Iintaba zonke ziyadidizela;
Izizw'ezikhulu zimangalisiwe;
Kuba izizwana ziyagqushalaza.

The earth moves for the whites,
　　the uncultivated ones
The valleys heave green
All the mountains shudder
Mighty nations stand in awe
Because a tiny country is in turmoil

Like many people after him, *imbongi* Yali-Manisi was struck by Mandela's appearance. The poet called him 'the lively tawny-coloured son, the secretary bird who is so tall that he walks with his knees, the tough whiplash from the Xhosa leather thong'. With remarkable insight, Yali-Manisi described the effect that Mandela would still have on the world:

He shows up all over, he visits the ribs of the earth
He tries to change the world until it responds
He covers the earth like a blessed watersnake
He swims in the Orange River
He drinks from the Zambezi
He serves the nations of Africa

UMavelel'iimbombo zomhlaba;
Uzama-zam' ilizwe lizama-zame;
UMabhijel' ilizwe njengechanti.
Izilenz'elidada kwaweLigwa,
Liye ngokusela kwaweZambesi;
Umkhonzi wezizwe zeAfrika.

This handsome man, this entirely handsome man from the house of Mthikrakra
This man whom all garments fit
The prince's necklace as well as the duiker-skin loincloth
Yes, everything fits him

Yali-Manisi also described how whites would react to Mandela:

Because he was educated at university
He shakes the Boers so that they are worried
From anxiety they crawl on all fours
Wildly he sows fear among them
He stews them, he chafes them and moves them
The sun scorches the mean ones at last
Merciless it burns their bald heads

The words roll from Prof. Mayekiso's lips. The hall is alive with Xhosa sounds and ulu-lation. People cheer wildly when he recites: 'The one who pushes whites until they despair / One who shakes them till they falter.' (Umagxagxamis' amagxagx'axhalabe, / Umaphongomis' izizwe ziphonyoze.) As long ago as 1954, Yali-Manisi was urging the prince of his clan to speak out:

Speak then, son of Mandela! Speak out, my chief.
Speak without fear!
The sun emerges and burns those whose stomachs are red with cunning plans
These loafers try to escape because the sun scorches their heads
The indecent ones wander around without hope
The old ones see the nation burning

Laphum'ilanga latshis' ooTshinga-liya-tsha.
Baphutshuluk' ooBhakaqana ligqats'ezinkqayini;
Bagungquz' ooMgulukudu besoyik' imbuthu-mbutu;
Baphongom' ooRheme betshelwe sicheko
Zantantazel' iinyhwagi zibon' ukutsha kwelizwe.

Life so fittingly fits you
That you have become a sacrifice for our people.

People are on their feet. Dancing. I make an appointment with Prof. Mayekiso: I have to know more.

✧

Mandela opens a conference of the Commonwealth Parliamentary Association, involv-ing South Africa, Uganda, Botswana and Ghana. After achieving independence from Britain, each of these countries changed the institution of parliament to fit their particular needs. The first session puts the accommodation of traditional leadership within the Westminster system under the spotlight.

The Botswana parliament is a small one, Connie Mompei, the Clerk of their National Assembly, tells us. It has 44 members, of whom 16 – more than a third – are members of Cabinet and 13 members of the two opposition parties. This means that the Botswana parliament has just 15 ordinary MPs. They earn modest salaries, and apparently live in two-roomed flats!

'The problem with such a small parliament is that the government does not have a wide choice when picking its Ministers. Cabinet has to make do with the best brains from the back benches!'

The Botswana parliament is unicameral, with a single legislative body. The traditional leaders are accommodated in a second body, called the House of Chiefs, which acts only in an advisory capacity.

'People still believe in chiefs. So this House of Chiefs is really to ensure that our tradition is kept in place. Tribal and cultural matters are referred to them. Our biggest problem is the weak opposition, which breaks up into even smaller parties before every election.'

Ugandan president Yoweri Museveni is famous for his critique of opposition based on ethnicity. If traditional chiefs become the opposition, a country is in danger of fragmenting into ethnic groups. He himself will only allow opposition if it is based on principles accepted across ethnic lines. But Margaret Sekaggya is aware of the difficulties of developing an opposition in oppressive circumstances.

'When an African nation is oppressed, it yearns for the freedom of a multiparty system: but the advent of multiparty democracy has often led to clan warfare and dumped the country into chaos,' Ms Sekaggya suggests. 'When a country is trapped in the disorder of warring clans, it yearns for the discipline of a single-party state, for authorities who can rein in the fighting among self-destructive elites. The answer evidently lies in giving voters a wide variety of choices, but within a single-party system.'

'To me, Museveni makes a lot of sense,' I say. 'Why oppose a party simply because you are from another clan or race or group? Your loyalties should lie with those whose values you share, not your family!'

'Be careful that the values you share are not the elite ones in the end,' says Joseph Mareka, who is part of an NGO delegation from Botswana. 'It may be that the rich stick together across ethnic lines to protect their privileges.'

'No, what I mean is that it would make much more sense, say, to vote for a group within the ANC that upholds the communist or socialist or capitalist values you support, than to vote for an opposition party based on white or Zulu identity.'

Mareka assures me it is more complex than this. 'It is true that the Minister of Finance's views on financial matters are much closer to those of the DP than to those of the SACP. But it is also true that the real opposition to the ANC is *within* the ANC. So that is where the real debate takes place – within the party.'

'Yes, but if debate only takes place in caucus situations and never in public, citizens are deprived of the chance to participate in it, to listen, or to learn to formulate issues from a left-wing perspective. As things are now, the prominence of Tony Leon as the "voice of opposition" cons us into thinking that the real debate in this country lies between whites and blacks. And it does not. The real debate is between black people, between the powerful blacks and the powerless blacks; whites and coloureds and Indians have no real choice any more but to side with one of those two black groups.'

'Having said that,' says Joseph Mareka, 'it is still crucial to deal with the fears and aspirations tied up with questions of clan, ethnic group, religion or race, because these have caused the biggest problems in most African countries. Ethnicity is the plague of Africa. Many also believe that it forms the basis for endemic corruption. You favour people because they are your family, not because they have earned it through hard work or good planning or being the best.'

'How has the ANC avoided this?'

'As a liberation movement, the ANC was based on principle rather than colour or ethnicity. But now that it has come to power, it has grasped the essence of the modern political party: seizing the middle ground. The ANC is adapting its policies and changing its principles according to what the middle ground needs. A middle-ground party cannot be challenged successfully in terms of principles, because it encompasses all the principles and stands by none of them.'

'But aren't whites part of the middle ground? Why then do they all support the opposition parties, locked into fighting for their privileges?'

'I think you're mistaken. Most whites don't vote for the opposition. They don't vote for the ANC either – but they silently support it, because they still have all their privileges. They see the powerful middle ground protecting them.'

✧

I go to Prof. Mayekiso's office at the university. On his door is a picture of a man captioned: S.E.K. Mqhayi. He lets me in.

'Was your translation of the Yali-Manisi poem into English a literal translation?' I ask. I'm interested because I have since obtained a copy of the poem from Prof. Saule at Unisa, but when I worked on it with a translator there seemed to be divergences.

'Now how can you ask me that? Poetry translated literally dies on its feet. You have to use the original to find new feet for the poem in the new language. If Yali-Manisi is the best in Xhosa, I want him to sound like the best in English without losing his authenticity. It is difficult but doable, which may be why I prefer to work with poets when I do my translations. But that is not why you have come.'

The subject is neatly closed. 'No. I am here to find out from you what the "lynxes" and the "red stomachs" in that poem are about.'

He smiles. 'How much time do you have? You have just struck one of the most interesting chords in African poetry.'

His face glows with pure delight. 'This is the only way to learn about yourself in the world, by translating what others are saying. Xhosa and Zulu were among the first black languages that named whites in Southern Africa. The first thing that struck them about whites was their blue eyes and their hair. Therefore some of the earliest names for whites are "They-through-whose-eyes-the-wind-blows", "They-whose-hair-washes-down-from-their-heads".' He shifts to a more upright position, he's getting into his stride.

'After the Zulus had their first meetings with whites who were standing with their backs to the sun, they called whites "They-through-whose-ears-the-sun-shines", "the Pale-ears". The physical appearance of whites led to a wide variety of names. Other than "Lynxes" (red-cats), "Red-stomachs", "Stuffed-with-shady-plans" (Tshinga-liya-tsha), whites are also known as "They-whose-eyes-glitter-as-if-wild-rumours-had-been-whispered-into-them" (Mahlo a phadimile nke ba seetšwe) – I'm translating roughly so that you can get the drift. In the northern parts of the country, you are also called "They-whose-faces-crack-like-earthen-jugs", "Spiders", "They-whose-noses-cast-shadows-across-their-faces", "They-whose-beards-grow-like-feathers-but-are-suddenly-shed" – this comes from a poem about that Fynn guy, Henry Fynn, who served Shaka – "They-who-point-with-sticks-from-which-fire-and-lightning-burst". Thereafter the origins of whites started playing a role in their naming: "They-who-live-on-boats", "They-who-come-over-the-water-like-swallows", "They-who-live-where-it-is-always-wet". As we came into contact with a greater variety of white people, we started to differentiate between them. The English became known as "They-who-lisp" or "the Fish-eaters", the Dutch as "the Pig-eaters".'

I put in a new cassette. The man is an encyclopedia.

'In the black languages you are assessed and defined by your names. You get your first name at birth, then a new name at initiation into manhood, and right through your life you get praise names added, according to how you live or how you are judged to be living. Your names tell the story of your life.

'Gradually, the original inhabitants of Southern Africa started gauging the nature of white people. Whites were called "They-who-speak-to-others-as-if-they-are-bundles-of-washing", "A-language-spoken-with-a-sewn-mouth" (Polelo ya go bolelwa ke mašela, Polelo ya go bolelwa o rokile molomo), "They-who-just-speak-their-own-language", "They-whose-beards-are-rusting" (boTedukhulwana), "They-who-cut-the-glands-from-the-meat-because-they-think-it-affects-the-taste-but-do-not-realize-it-is-the-truth-that-lies-so-bitterly-on-their-tongues", "Latecomers-who-soil-the-water-as-they-grab-everything-for-themselves" (Nga mulandu wa nyeni dzo dzhavhulaho vhune ha danga / Dzi si fune tshisima tshi tshi vha tsha madilutshele).

'Do you know Mqhayi?' he asks suddenly.

I shake my head. Never heard of him before.

'Oh, oh, oh. That's a deficiency. A great deficiency. Samuel Edward Krune Mqhayi was the Shakespeare of Southern African languages. He wrote the words for "Nkosi Sikelel' iAfrika". He was the first poet recorded who took a firm stand on the selfish nature of whites, this man, in his immortal poem "A! Silimela!" "Silimela" is the Initiation star, the Harvest star, the Pleiades to you. This is the star by which a Xhosa counts the years of his manhood. Mqhayi often performed this poem, in which he distributes the stars among the nations of the world, when whites were present.' He goes to his shelf and pulls out a thin, threadbare book.

summon the nations, summon them here
let me mete out the stars
come, let me allot the stars on merit
you the Basotho
take the Dog Star, your harvest star before the winter
share it with the Tswana and the Chopi
and all of those who wear loincloths
you from Zululand
take the belt of Orion
and share it with the Swazi, the Chopi and the Shangaan
and with all the uncircumcised people
you whites
you-who-are-not-able-to-share-anything
the English, the Germans and the Boers
you can have Venus
and we?
we from the house of Phalo?
we will cling to the Pleiades
we will have the star
the only one which counts our years of manhood

CHAPTER THREE

UNDER MANDELA, SOUTH AFRICA HAS TO GLOBALIZE at breakneck speed. One of the first big international events hosted by the country is the twelfth summit of the Non-Aligned Movement. The planning starts a year before, as this is to be the largest gathering ever held in Africa. More than eighty heads of state with their Ministers of Foreign Affairs, spouses, ambassadors, security teams, advisors and media envoys will descend on the middle-class holiday resort of Durban in KwaZulu-Natal. The honour of the offspring of Shaka is at stake. No, comes the correction via a press release, the honour of *all* South Africans is at stake. It is time for us to put our money where our Third World mouths are.

And we do. More smoothly than a shopkeeper rubbing his palms together, the Old South Africa falls into step with the New. We work together. Yes, with pressing urgency, we work shoulder to shoulder without batting a racist eyelid. Expertise is needed, which makes the Old South Africa useful; black leadership and new ideas are needed, which makes the New South Africa essential.

Eighty heads of state are suddenly looking for presidential suites. Durban only has five. Government officials go pleading with one hotel owner after another to create larger suites with additional lounges and work spaces by breaking through into adjoining rooms. All this for four days, the hoteliers grumble, supposedly sulking, while they quickly quadruple their overnight rates. Some of them even reprint their laundry lists, so that for the price of two steaks, you can now have your socks washed. The largest hotel in Durban has been booked out completely by just two countries: the kitchen will be divided in two, so that the cook and the cook's mate can concoct to their heart's desire (or that of their bosses).

Did someone mention food?

No pork. Of course not. No alcohol. Of course not. No shellfish, mutton or beef. Whew! Okay. 'How can I prove my culinary talent with chicken!' one of the chefs for the gala dinner complains. No salt, no sugar. Heavens, wait a minute, let's simply dish out pills for the evening. Well, you've got a point there, because most politicians have got health problems, you know, high cholesterol, diabetes, hypertension. So for the whole duration of the summit, it will be nothing but fat-free breakfasts and alcohol-free dinners, tasteless food dressed in guineafowl feathers, porcupine quills and protea spikes. It appears that ice cream is about the only politically correct, religiously acceptable, culturally inoffensive dish – and even this has to be fat-free!

Traffic police are drafted from all over the country to make up escorts for the cavalcades from airport to hotel and from hotel to conference centre. No, they say confidently, there is nothing to fear. They managed the Rugby World Cup successfully.

186

The officials from Foreign Affairs break the news gently. The Rugby World Cup was nothing, but absolutely *nothing* in comparison with this NAM summit business. On that first morning, there will be 120 cavalcades on the highways and another 50 in the city itself – all on the way to the same place, at the same time, in order to be welcomed personally by the same man, President Mandela.

Two thirds of the heads of state preside over undemocratic systems, and so security is a complete nightmare. The gossip on the grapevine is that some leaders are even bringing their own journalists along – so that if a coup takes place while they're out of the country, there will be no one to report on it! 'Security islands' are created. The airspace above Durban is secured for four days, while cordons are thrown up around many hotels and the conference centre. Police reservists are bussed in from everywhere. A couple of buses are snowed in on their way from the Eastern Cape and have to wait for days in the high mountain passes for the snow to melt. By the time they finally arrive in Durban, the summit is already over.

The security islands demand safety precautions that look like madness to outsiders. The Hilton Hotel lies right next to the newly-completed conference centre. This means that every delivery to the hotel, from bed linen to shower caps to yoghurt, has to be searched with metal detectors and sniffer dogs. Big trucks are hoisted up and inspected, sharpshooters with rifles and binoculars can be seen on all the roofs. And though the hotel is one minute away from the conference centre, on the opening day the heads of state staying there will have to get into their cavalcades in the hotel basement and be driven on a fifteen-minute detour, just so that they can fall into a particular order and be dropped off at a specific time right in front of Mandela.

Of course, everybody has to *arrive*. For five days, aeroplanes descend on Durban in a round-the-clock sequence, drop off the dignitaries, and then fly on to other South African airports where they will be parked. Additional security measures have to be implemented at these airports to keep potential robbers and terrorists away from the waiting fleets of jets.

And Durban International does not have enough of anything. Not enough stairs for loading passengers, not enough vehicles to tow the aeroplanes, not enough baggage trolleys. Foreign Affairs makes a plan. Countries are asked to bring their own loading-stairs, and two hundred trolleys are borrowed from all over the country. Four hundred BMWs are imported to deal with any demand from the heads of state for additional transport. Four brass bands and troops of traditional dancers will relieve one another in shifts. Because it would have taken years for the bands to learn the anthems of so many countries, they will simply be playing marching music.

Rumour has it that a seasoned Foreign Affairs official is stationed permanently in the airport's control tower, just in case some head of state decides to fly in *now* – unannounced, discourteous enough to jump the queue. Or some plane finds itself with too little fuel to keep circling until the scheduled landing time. This official earns his keep with hours of the deepest diplomacy when both Robert Mugabe of Zimbabwe and Laurent Kabila of the DRC arrive unexpectedly.

✧

I am summoned home for an urgent family meeting. My father doesn't say what it's about, but it will take place on Saturday morning. When I arrive on Friday the house is fraught with tension. My mother and father speak for hours behind closed doors, my brothers are scarce, my sister is locked in her room. By eleven the next morning we are sitting around the long yellowwood table. Andries, my elder brother, leads the meeting. The debt on the farm has become too big to pay off. Lots of reasons why that is so, but this is not under discussion today. The problem is the debt, the meeting is to come up with a solution.

Why don't we sublet the farm?

We live too near the townships, nobody would be interested in farming where theft is such a constant factor. Besides, the rent wouldn't cover the payments and also provide something for my parents to live on.

Why don't we sublet the fields, but keep the sheep and veld for my parents to live from?

That is an option, but in winter months the sheep need to graze on harvested land.

Andries, who has been doing the books of the farm, says there is another option. He and Hendrik can form a company and rent the farm from my parents. They will then transform the farm into a business that has to provide a monthly cash flow. Put in irrigation from the spruit and dams, plant cabbage, spinach and pumpkin, mill our own mealies and sell them, take up the dairy and sell milk, enlarge the sheep farming, sell more and shear more ... but it means that one of them will have to come and live on the farm.

'Why are my daughters not included in this?' asks my mother. 'My father let all his children inherit equally.'

'Your father had four farms, so he could leave one to each child,' says my sister. 'You have only one.'

'Then subdivide the farm into four pieces, and rent your sisters' portions from them.'

'We have debt to pay. There is no way we can rent their pieces *and* pay off the debt *and* have something extra for you and Pa to live on. So forget that idea.'

But my mother soldiers on bravely. 'If a company is going to farm, my daughters must be part of it.'

'It is hard enough to farm, one cannot carry extra people,' says my father quietly.

'If you really want us all to inherit equally, then why don't we sell the farm?'

It's as if I have let a monster out on to the table. Everyone becomes visibly anxious or agitated.

'No wait,' says Hendrik, his hands in the air, 'we're not there yet ...'

188

But it is my mother who breaks through it all: 'I will never sell this farm. My father and my grandfather will talk to me from their graves. I inherited it. I will not sell it, I will hand it over to my children, just as I received it from my father. This is your birth-ground.'

Meanwhile, my father is looking at me as if he's seeing me for the first time in his life: 'I never thought that you would suggest such a thing ... you, of all people ...'

'I agree with her,' says Andries. 'It is archaic to cling to land. The whole basis of the economy has moved from land to knowledge. Land is no longer any guarantee of income. Now it's education, skill, knowledge. If we hold on to this farm, we will prevent the family member who farms here from ever having any mobility. He and his children will have to stick it out here in a redundant part of the economy. So I say: sell.'

'You don't understand, we are nothing without this farm.' My mother is putting up a desperate fight. 'Who will we be? Where will we be together? In some cramped little sitting room? In a city yard where your neighbours' dogs shit on your grass? Where you have no say in anything any more? Where you can be pushed around by any Tom, Dick and ... Thabo!'

I say: 'You would rather burden the family with debt payments to keep the freedom of a farm on which only one of us is living?'

'I know why you want us to sell. You're scared!' Hendrik is razor sharp. 'You think that the government is going to take our farm, you want to get rid of it because it has become politically sensitive to own farmland. I'm telling you, I and my family are not scared. I will farm here. But I want it to be written down somewhere that any of you who leave this country will not get a cent. Not from the farm, not from Pa and Ma's estate. This farm is for those who care about this land.'

Andries intervenes: 'Let us put it to the vote. If we don't sell, we'll form a company.'

Nobody says anything.

'Those in favour of selling the farm, raise their hands.'

I put up my hand. Andries puts up his. Outside a woodpecker has burst into crystal-clear sound. From the corner of my eye, I see my sister slowly raising her hand. My mother is as white as chalk. Her black eyes pieces of fury and betrayal. Then I become aware of my father. He's hunched over, staring down at the table, completely expressionless, while tears wash down his face. He doesn't make a move to get his handkerchief, the tears simply flow over on to his khaki shirt.

Three days later, Andries phones me: Pa has had a stroke. Nobody quite knows when, but he is lame in one hand and part of his throat. They are trying to get someone to rent the farm. He's going to have a chat with a guy called Joubert.

✧

Even before it starts, the media are writing off the NAM summit as nothing but hot air, a useless talk shop. All too soon, these notions are confirmed by events. On the giant television screens of the conference centre, we suddenly notice Kabila sauntering down the plush carpet, hands in pockets, shirt hanging out, chewing on a toothpick. Later we see him and Mugabe sneaking in through a side door so that they can avoid greeting their host, President Mandela. While Kofi Annan, in his opening speech, is saying, 'My brother African leaders, I appeal to you once again: we Africans must summon the will to resolve our problems by political and not military means ... For every day that we fail to do so, the innocent people of this continent pay a terrible price,' Kabila gets up noisily and starts talking loudly to someone at the back of the hall.

The summit starts against a backdrop of war in Burundi, Sierra Leone and the Sudan, a new conflict in Guinea-Bissau, the first interstate war between Ethiopia and Eritrea, civil war in the Democratic Republic of Congo, the Angolan peace process hanging by a thread. This is besides the bombings in Cape Town, and the bombings of the American embassies in Nairobi and Dar es Salaam.

Those of us who have just started to rub shoulders with the rest of the African continent find it incomprehensible that these countries simply continue with their conflicts, yet are so critical of South Africa. During press conferences, journalists from other countries revile South Africa as arrogant, the Yankees of Africa, and the media as one-sided. 'Even your black people behave as if they are white.'

'But we are all Africans,' a black South African journalist tries to intervene.

'What is all this "I am an African" nonsense? It is you who are new to the continent who are trying to stake out a legitimate claim. You will never hear us say, "There goes an African," or, "I am an African." We say, "I am a Nigerian," or, "There goes a Somalian," or, "He comes from West Africa." The better you know people, the more accurate your naming becomes. You here don't know us, that is why you like to wiggle yourself in under the so-called African blanket. There is no such thing.' The journalist has a Nigerian flag on his accreditation badge.

'Maybe there *should* be such a thing. Like Americans or Europeans, we should take ownership of our continent and be Africans, and maybe we would look after ourselves better then.'

'You see! Who's your example? America. As long as they are your point of reference, you stay their slave.'

'So you wear their Nikes and eat their burgers and claim they are not your reference point?'

'I eat their food and wear their clothes because they have achieved prosperity on the sweat of African slaves. I use their products just as they use mine in their art and their commerce. But I refuse to let them dictate to me how I should live on this continent.'

The tensions in Africa overshadow the entire summit. While officials behind closed doors spend up to sixteen hours a day hammering out the new NAM document, countless bilateral negotiations take place, especially to try to resolve the crisis in the DRC.

But this is also the moment of famous leaders. Tsonga-speaking political reporter Dumisane Nkwamba is at the airport when Fidel Castro arrives and passes by barely a metre away. Tsonga is one of the most neglected languages in South Africa. Apart from a single radio station, almost nowhere is Tsonga accepted or spoken officially. When the Cuban president lands, Nkwamba phones Radio Tsonga on his cellphone and they put him live on air. In detail, he describes the plane, the famous tall figure disembarking, his sparse beard, his alert eyes. 'His fingers, people, his fingers are as long as another person's entire hand!'

Until late that night, Tsonga-speakers from the most distant reaches of the country are phoning the SABC to say that their language has come into its own that day. The great Fidel Castro, who sent his soldiers to fight against the Old South Africa, who today is sending his doctors and teachers to help build the New South Africa, he spoke to them from the little transistor or the ghetto blaster. Fidel Castro has stepped on to South African soil in Tsonga. In other words: Tsonga has been globalized. The interview with Nkwamba is rebroadcast again and again on request, as one of the most popular items ever on Radio Tsonga.

It is the European observers who point out that South Africa is changing the NAM ethos for the better. For the first time, total secrecy has been abandoned and some of the discussions, such as those on economic policy, are open to the public. For the first time, the chairpersons of the European Union and the G8 have been invited to a NAM summit. South Africa insisted that in these times of globalization and liberalization, it is vital that the South start interacting with the North.

'Inasmuch as the slave cannot ask the slave master,' Deputy President Thabo Mbeki says during his opening speech, 'to provide the strategy and tactics for a successful uprising of slaves, so must we who are hungry and treated as minors in a world of adults, also take upon ourselves the task of defining the new world order of prosperity and development for all and equality among the nations of the world.'

The message is clear: if Africa cannot get her house in order, she may be lost forever.

'Any among us who is preoccupied with denying his or her people their democratic and human rights, who is fixated on waging wars against others, who is too busy looting the public coffers or who thinks that he or she must bow in supplication for charity to those whose wealth and assets set them aside as mighty, will not have time to participate in meeting this historic challenge.'

The final document drawn up by the summit sets as a goal the eradication of hunger in the twenty-first century. The non-aligned countries must stand together to fight poverty. Development can only take place if it goes hand in hand with democracy. 'Durban must mark the turning point where the formerly dispossessed, the majority, enter into their inheritance.'

But the gathering reeks of money and power and aftershave. It glitters with rings and silk ties and golden turbans. Journalists report that income at the most expensive malls in Durban has gone through the roof and that some of the leaders have had additional flights come in to take fridges, bar counters, carpets, sofas, even potted plants back home. The prostitutes are also experiencing an unheard-of demand and are impressed that so many of the foreign clients use condoms without much encouragement.

However, it is the war in the misnamed Democratic Republic of Congo that finally dominates the summit. In one way or another, the fighting there has drawn in all the countries of Southern Africa. Not only do nine countries border on the DRC, most countries have sent troops to support either Kabila or the rebels. To South Africa's horror, two of its neighbours – Sam Nujoma of Namibia and Robert Mugabe of Zimbabwe – have decided to back Kabila with armed forces. Rumour has it that Mandela has berated Nujoma, as South Africa has just written off millions of rands of Namibian debt.

But it is obvious that the two gentlemen, who have both altered the Constitutions of their countries in order to extend their terms of office, are highly irritated with the messianic proportions of Mandela's reputation. Nujoma, seemingly well informed about the tensions between South Africa and India, made sure that the Indian Prime Minister stopped over in Windhoek on his way to Durban. Nujoma later tells the media that he has promised his support for India's nuclear tests, as well as their request for a seat on the United Nations Security Council. A seat South Africa feels should go to an African country, evidently Egypt.

While Mandela, with the support of Kofi Annan, tries to convince other countries not to get involved in the DRC, Mugabe is believed to have told Mandela in so many words to keep his trap shut. If African leaders allow rebel forces to unseat governments, then nobody, not even Mandela, will be safe any longer. Mugabe's message to South Africa was clear: African leaders ought to support one another. 'Remember that the ANC only opened offices in Zimbabwe very late in the apartheid era, because Mugabe always supported the PAC,' somebody points out to me.

Almost every one of the eighty heads of state present wants to shake Mandela's hand and pose for the essential 'Mandela and Me' photograph. A logistical nightmare on the opening day. Although the cavalcades arrive at intervals of minutes, it takes Mandela and Graça Machel hours to work through the schedule. After an hour, Machel requests a chair for Mandela. She caresses his back and feeds him sweets or peppermints or medicine from her bag. It is strange to see him like this – almost vulnerably in the care of a woman.

However, Kabila is the news. Or rather the non-verbal news. The man epitomizes the unpredictability that comes with absolute power, he fascinates everybody. Moody as a despot, with the dress sense of a layabout, his expressionless face confirms every cliché about a certain type of African leader. Not the sly, spendthrift type, outwardly modelling their rule on British royalty, greedily chasing after money, no. But the thick-set, stupid type, swilling in blood, greedily lusting after power.

First, he let it be known that he would not be able to attend the summit. He was ill. But video footage from the international news channels showed a smiling Kabila, embracing all manner of leaders. His attitude towards the summit is blatantly disdainful. Yet when the SABC television cameras suddenly pick up his thick neck and sweaty head, an excited buzz sweeps through the media centre. Action! Somebody discovers that Nujoma and Mugabe have urged him to attend, because the summit is 'focusing too much on Mandela'. To this end, Nujoma even surrenders his speaking slot to Kabila.

We get news that Kabila is holding a press conference at nine. Not at the media centre, where everyone holds their press conferences, but at the Hilton Hotel, where room was hastily made available to him because *everybody* wants to speak to him. The Hilton has such elaborate security measures that it takes more than an hour to sniff and scan all the journalists. Tape recorders are switched on twice in case they contain bombs. Cameras are examined in specially sealed areas. Eventually, we find ourselves waiting in the corridor outside Kabila's suite. We sit in a line stretching back to the lifts. And we wait. Bodyguards walk up and down the corridor. Nobody may smoke. We wait and we wait.

At ten o'clock two waiters push a lavish trolley past us. The bodyguards carefully inspect the contents and we write in our notebooks: four whole roast chickens, potatoes, peas, salad, and a bottle of Chivas Regal on ice. Our mouths water. We wait. Just past eleven another trolley trundles by: again four roast chickens, with three buckets of chips, tomato sauce, and a bottle of Chivas Regal on ice. Meanwhile, the bathroom plumbing built into the wall behind me sings up and down. If nothing else, the sewage systems of the Hilton are being given a workout.

But how many people are inside there? It has been alleged that Kabila himself eats two whole chickens every morning, with a side order of pornographic videos. A journalist who speaks French starts buddying up to a bodyguard. It seems that Arafat is with Kabila. The one is speaking Arabic, the other French, but they are fast becoming brothers. Another trolley. Again four chickens, but this time accompanied by slices of corner-café bread and butter, a pot of apricot jam and a bowl of atjar. And a bottle of Chivas Regal, majestic as ever, on ice.

No, the thing is, says the guard, Kabila has fallen asleep on the sofa and everybody is too afraid to wake him up. We wait – high on exhaustion and low on nicotine. Suddenly the door opens. Innocently, Kabila comes strolling down the corridor towards the lifts, hands in his pockets as if he is completely alone. Everybody jumps up in confusion, you just hear cameras and recorders crashing and notebooks falling. Some of us shout out questions, a camera flashes. 'Will you be attending the peace talks with Kofi Annan this morning?' someone manages to shout in French. Kabila rolls his eyes up to the fake plaster ceiling, pouts his lips, sighs as if he is infinitely bored, and disappears mumbling into the lift being held for him by a bodyguard. The rest of the squad closes off the opening. Gone.

We are furious. It is way past midnight. We grab a Foreign Affairs official outside the hotel. Is this what we had to wait five hours for? He throws his arms up: 'What can I say? Welcome to Kabila!'

At the NAM summit, language is very important, or, more accurately, to take away the essence of language from language is very important. A specific NAM concoction of language is cooked up through the days and nights. The watchword is consensus. No term, no sentence may be included if there is not consensus on it. And the definition of consensus? There must be consensus on that too. Roughly, it means that a seemingly contradictory sentence is acceptable, as long as all the participants agree with part of it. Therefore, those who throw the bombs find themselves cosily in the same sentence as those being bombed. A mere semicolon separates militant labour unions from those who make children work in their factories. The feminist is in the same clause as the polygamist. There is a long hold-up over the phrase 'the equality of women'; eventually everyone agrees to abide by 'the development of women'.

On the last day, long past midnight, the NAM document is unveiled and accepted by the delegations. It has taken so long that some heads of state have already left, just so that everyone can be cleared away from Durban on schedule. Mandela is visibly ill. He is coughing, and during his speech his voice is hoarse and sometimes inaudible. We hear that Mrs Machel is very unhappy that, after being involved day and night for four days, facilitating bilateral conflict-resolution discussions, he insisted on being present at the closing ceremony, staying until all of the 127 pages have been adopted.

The Director-General for Home Affairs points out the smaller victories. The rights of women have been substantially extended, for the first time there is an admission of the possibility of violence within family and cultural contexts, and a recognition that this ought to be condemned. India has not declared itself as a nuclear power, nuclear testing in the East has been condemned, and the summit has committed itself to total disarmament. For the first time human rights have been made an integral part of labour relations and it has been accepted that the conduct of the North cannot be an excuse for violating the rights of one's own citizens.

A more mundane triumph: everyone is in agreement that this has been the best organized summit ever. There were four thousand delegates, one thousand media personnel, sixty-five private aeroplanes and ten additional scheduled flights per evening. The country has built up enormous capacity to host political events of this kind. Officials received several months of special training from the United Nations on systems for distributing documents quickly, on compiling consultative documents, on negotiating points of contention, and especially on building up a memory of the history of the particular event.

'Does such a summit, with the presence of someone like Mandela, not actually lend respectability and legitimacy to murderers and dictators?' a journalist asks one of the South African Ministers.

'I don't think so,' he answers. 'They feel the pressure and they see the writing on the wall. It becomes more and more difficult to defy the things so many people regard as important. Corruption and abuse may continue, but at least those behind them will know that they should be ashamed.'

'But people like Kabila and Mugabe, they say and do as they please and no one seems to repudiate them!'

A Foreign Affairs official smiles. 'Do you guys remember when Idi Amin decided that he was going to have tea with the Queen of England? And how difficult it was for them, because even after hundreds of years of running a palace, they hadn't developed a protocol for dealing with a despot who decides to pitch up on the doorstep for tea? It's a bit like that. Nobody knows how to ask why Mugabe isn't giving back his property in England and Europe, or why he doesn't close down his international bank accounts, and things like that. Summits by nature do not know how to deal with leaders like these. All they can do is put pressure on people to agree to certain wordings, which hopefully will be taken back by human rights activists to confront a government's behaviour. Then again, they say that America kills more people than any tyrant on this continent.'

We are walking along Durban's beachfront, eating pieces of the sweetest pineapple dipped in chilli. But we are irritated by the broad web of politics which seems to create comfortable space for unaccountable behaviour, lies, dreams of grandeur, atrocities, conceit, corruption.

'If you put a group of women, memory-less women, on an island, I wonder what kind of government we would come up with? How would we conceive of power, what would we give respect to? What kind of order would we establish? Less hierarchical, more inclusive, more respectful of nurturers and more disapproving of warmongers?'

'Let me relieve you of your feminist fantasies,' one of my colleagues says. 'You know what we should do with Africa? We South Africans should just climb in and start cleaning up. And the fact that I'm a Zulu has nothing to do with this,' he adds with a laugh. 'We put one of our people in power in every country for now, then we start building proper roads, put in telephones and water, send a couple of farmers to establish modern agriculture, get business people to open shops and things, and when such a country is on its feet, then we say, it is time to elect a leader.'

'What about corruption?' someone else asks. 'It is endemic. In my hotel room in Nigeria there was nothing. I had to bribe the staff for linen, a towel, some soap, and – most expensive of all – toilet paper. Then I said, "I don't use toilet paper for my own good, my brother. As far as I'm concerned, I could just wipe my arse on your walls and your mattresses. I use it to save you from extra work." But fuck it, eventually you have to buy it.'

A journalist from Zimbabwe joins us and suddenly we are all quiet, looking out over the neat waves of the Indian Ocean.

CHAPTER FOUR

IT IS HARD TO KEEP UP. We are all preoccupied with racial tensions, and now here comes a message that one of the reporters on the team for the NAM summit has been accused of sexual harassment. While the incident is being handled by the competent authorities as a 'misunderstanding' and a 'clash of cultures', it becomes clear that discussion will be needed on how we understand and react to one another's sexuality.

But it is tricky. We are a nation that consists of two genders, more than three colours, more than eight political groupings, fourteen ethnic groups, nine provinces, eleven languages, more than twenty cultural groupings, more than thirty different churches, and around forty-five million individuals, ranging from the dirt poor to the super rich. How on earth can we understand each other's sexual codes in a country where people have lived apart for so long?

A friend who works for a recently 'transformed' magazine is attending a workshop on sexual codes in the workplace. I go along as an observer, with the idea of perhaps organizing a similar event for the radio team. The programme is a mix of pseudo-psychological and academic topics – 'I'm OK, you're not OK', 'When does no mean no?', 'Changing the gender agenda', etc. The facilitators are boring: the woman sounds like a police sergeant, the man seems incapable of saying the word 'dickhead'. Everybody sits around bored and uncomfortable, until a coloured man puts up his hand and makes the following frank statement: 'The primary sexual stimulus in post-apartheid South Africa is skin colour. It is skin colour that lays the foundation for the hundreds of rumours we spread about one another's sexuality. All nonsense, these differences – basically, we are all the same.'

It's as if he has just tossed a lit match into a barrel of petrol. Some jump up, some start shouting from their seats. I write down what I hear. 'You sound like the farmer who said to his neighbour: no matter whether the topsoil is black or white, underneath they are all red.' 'The same? That's what you think! Since when are we the same? White women have always been the biggest taboo. Where were you back in the eighties when gangs of white men would storm into mining hostels to tear the posters of white glamour girls from the black miners' walls?' 'A white woman has always been first prize. That is why the rape of a white woman in front of her husband is seen even today as the ultimate revenge.'

The woman with the police-sergeant attitude cuts everyone short: 'Rumours? Rumours have nothing to do with the matter at hand. It is the abusive penis that is the root of all evil.'

'Speaking of cheroot, let's go take a smoke,' says the yawning man next to me.

Outside in the sun stand the smokers, the tobacco exiles, the intimidated addicts, puffing away. Among them is the man who has a thing about rumours. 'It is true! The rumours about our sexual abilities and inabilities flow thick and fast. Because why? Sort must shag sort. You have to keep to your skin colour.'

'Skin yes,' affirms his buddy, 'foreskin, foot-skin, all skin, same skin makes both the cunt and the prick.'

The group of us now enlarge upon (what else?) the penis. Dwelling not, as the police sergeant might have expected, on its knack for abuse, but on (what else?) its size and the frequency of its employment.

'Did you know that white women who only have sex with white men all their lives have the deepest sympathy of black people?' No, I didn't. 'Not only are white men less well-endowed, according to rumours of rumours, they are also much less virile.'

I remember some white women I knew in the eighties driving from the Free State to Johannesburg to see the political play *Asinamali* at the Market Theatre. Not because of the politics, but because during one scene the black actors are naked on stage for a few minutes while a 'mine doctor' inspects their genitals. 'And?' was the question on their return. Then the shoulders were shrugged, the lips pouted: 'Let me tell you … I've had bigger boerewors in my pan!' So the Boere could stand tall.

'The problem with white women is that they are too smooth inside, too wet, if you know what I mean. A man struggles to complete his … distance properly. Before you can help yourself, the point of no return has raised its head. Plus white women cannot gyrate their lower bodies like black women to help a man last longer … you know. We teach black girls these skills in our dances from a young age.'

A sister hisses at him in Sesotho and then continues in English, 'That may be so, but I can tell you this: if a black man has slept with a white woman once, he is damaged goods, he will never be of any use again. And why? Because of his own inferiority. He gets that feeling of victory, that realization that his bloody black plough has broken the most expensive, most protected ground of the white man … and for that a black woman has no remedy.'

I find myself among experts, that much is clear.

'She doesn't even need to be good in bed, if he can only put that black hand on that white tit, then he spills, with copyright!'

'All this black-ing and white-ing! Black women and white women are nothing, that I can guarantee you, compared with Griqua women. They are unsurpassable! Those in the know say that once you have slept with a Griqua woman, you have surrendered control over your prick forever. They say that inside the vagina of the Griqua woman there are these little suction cups, which shoot out of the labia when a prick comes near and suck it in. You can try to resist, but that thing slurps you up. And once inside, *oe, my broe*, it tingles and bleats and jols and nibbles – unknown, they tell me, on this earth.'

'Stop this Saartjie Baartman *kak*,' says a coloured woman and stubs out her cigarette.

I am amazed at the openness of the discussion outside, and also aware that the workshop will fail if myths such as these simply remain smokers' gossip, because the previous dispensation flourished on sexual myths. It needed them.

There was great concern in the apartheid years about *rondloper* husbands, men who 'walked around', who 'gallivanted' at night. This was the formal code for those more crudely known as '*meidenaaiers*' – 'kaffirgirl-fuckers'. White men, married, respected by society, who broke away some nights to sleep with black women. A *meidenaaier* was something entirely different to a *kafferboetie* – a 'kaffir brother'. The latter thought blacks were his equals, his brothers and sisters – it was a political choice. A *meidenaaier* was a pervert, someone who looked down on blacks by day, but couldn't get enough of them at night. Rural towns often had a group of men who went out to ambush the *meidenaaiers* at night and thrash them with whips – after slashing the tyres of the *kafferboeties* and 'punishing' the local *moffies* for the evening. Every policeman in a place like Kroonstad knew the licence numbers of those who picked up black prostitutes. The only time P.W. Botha wanted to take a writer to court was when Koos Prinsloo called him a *meidenaaier* in one of his short stories.

'What beats me is how white men can make out so endlessly before they go over to the deed. What a sentimental swooning. What a struggle. What a battle before they scrape together the courage to do it. I would already have had the woman four times in lust, while they are still crooning in her neck!'

'That's my point. If a black man does not have sex every day, his heart and kidneys become weak, his legs lose their power, his shadow disappears. That is why we need more than one woman. In the olden days, we had several wives to fulfil the quota, so we were faithful and prosperous, but it's these monochrome marriages that cause the problems ...'

Back inside, one of the Aids workers, also a smoker, sends me a note: This is, of course, the whole problem behind the Aids epidemic, the promiscuity of black men. And because government does not want to address promiscuity, they also prefer not to address Aids.

'Womanizing is part of African culture,' a prominent black academic confirms for me, albeit jokingly, some weeks later at a wedding. 'I am sorry to say this, but the amount of power equals the number of women.'

And so the rumours about rumours are translated into facts. But how important is it to put these kinds of myths on the table? Should one be aware of them or does that simply strengthen them?

I remember a former colleague, a black woman, who had an amazing pair of breasts. Whatever did not swell out in velvet and amber above, formed a downward curve beneath her see-through blouses that left you short of breath. Imagine my surprise when my black colleagues accused our white female colleague of sexual torture because she wore such short skirts. 'What is a thigh compared to a breast?' I asked. They informed me. In black culture, breasts are seen as maternal or nurturing, like hands, you can develop a fetish for them, but the killer blow comes from the thighs.

'Oh,' one of my colleagues moaned, 'those thighs are calling me. I can't even hear other people talking when I see thighs – the Zulu word we use for thighs means "loud-speakers", "amplifiers". A woman's sexual power, her shagability screams from her thighs. That is why nubile young women traditionally wear short skirts of grass or hide, but once they are married their thighs are covered with long skirts. That is why women are banned from wearing pants in Malawi. One simply cannot work when a woman's thighs are staring like that.'

Thighs versus breasts. What is personal, what cultural, and what racial? There is a Malian tale in which a griot teaches a man how to love a woman. You have to know the breast intimately – as if your own hand had formed it: there, where the breast attaches to the collarbone, you must know the slope of it; there, where the breast swells towards the armpit, you must know the soft swelling to the side of it; there, where the most ten-der side is, you must know the full weight of it, how it overflows the palm. The areola, you must know how it frowns in fear, expands in heat, and when you tumble her down, quickly, milk will spout from it. Tweak both her nipples, firmly, then go down on her. The Malian griot gives further advice: when a woman pounding wheat does not sweat finely between her breasts, then one should not marry her.

One of the only assets of the first *Big Brother* broadcast in South Africa was that it undermined black stereotypes. The black man and woman in the house were like a nun and a priest. They spoke no sex, they heard no sex, they saw no sex, but they had to endure the daily misconduct of their white housemates for three months. When the whites weren't swearing, they were binge-drinking; when they weren't binge-drinking, they were farting and shitting on the grass; they were always harassing one another in the shower or taking off their clothes in the jacuzzi; and then they would start fooling around, and feeling each other up aggressively, and in the evenings there would be des-perate jerking off underneath the sheets. The two black housemates only drank fruit juice, never swore, never set foot near the jacuzzi and only used their swimwear in the shower. Someone pointed out that in three long months, Vuyo never once masturbated or even had a wet dream. The black contestants were a model of unbelievable restraint, and were obviously horrified by the white decadence expressed so exuberantly around them. Not for nothing did Vuyo burst out at the end: 'I do not want to see a white dick ever again in my life!'

So what are black sexual morals and what are white ones? To what extent are we really the same? Or really different?

A recent newspaper report shows how dangerous it can be not to know the moral rules in force on one's playing field. A court in Zambia sentenced a German tourist to six years in prison for having oral sex with a Zambian woman. Wolfgang Seifarth (55) admitted to the charge of having oral sex with Pumulo Mbagweta (22), but said that he did not know it was illegal in Zambia. He was arrested one Sunday when passers-by informed the police about a deserted vehicle next to the road. When the police arrived, Seifarth and Mbagweta emerged from the bushes, and she admitted that they had had oral sex. Magistrate Aloysius Mapate, who sentenced the man to six years' hard labour, said that ignorance was no excuse.

CHAPTER FIVE

TRADITIONAL LEADERSHIP HAS LONG BEEN CONTROVERSIAL. After South Africa's first democratic election, several people pointed out to the ANC that they had lost in KwaZulu-Natal because of their antagonistic stance towards traditional leadership. At a conference on the subject, Prof. Thandabantu Nhlapo gives us a brief history lesson. He shows that ancestor worship was embodied in traditional leadership. The energy flows through hierarchies: the ancestors guide the chief, and the chief works through the heads of families in order to reach every individual in the household. The traditional leader's power lies locked up in two factors: birthright and the right to parcel out land. Colonialism affected both. When magistrates were appointed in each district, the continuity between the traditional leader and the ancestors was broken. Now the law no longer runs according to the will of the ancestors, but to that of the magistrate.

Thuli Madonsela of the Centre for Applied Legal Studies carefully asks whether it is possible for a woman to live out her fundamental human rights completely within a traditional context.

Some of the speakers argue for an evolving compatibility. Just as Roman law later became Roman-Dutch law, so Western and African legal systems can intermingle. Even if it means that African law must undergo a transformation to rid itself of discriminatory practices.

Other speakers disagree. They say that as soon as traditional leadership is drawn into a Western system of government, it becomes corrupt: the state now stands between the ancestors and the traditional leaders.

Does traditional leadership need to be sustained, rediscovered, adapted, scaled down or phased out? It is complicated. What does one do about the woman who would rather share a husband with four other women than battle open a single path in life? What does one do about the democratically elected leader who has more than one wife? The conference cannot answer such questions. Although the Constitution protects traditional systems, and traditional leaders themselves have come together in a single body (the Congress of Traditional Leaders of South Africa or Contralesa), there is clearly much discomfort. Should traditional leadership not be a central theme in the African Renaissance? And what about violations of human rights under the guise of traditional values?

Prof. Mahmood Mamdani, whom I interview afterwards, has strong opinions on the subject. 'Before any agreement can be reached, the concept of traditional leadership in an African context must be understood correctly. Before colonialism, those we refer to as "traditional leaders" were not the only source of authority. The entire social, economic and political life of Africans involved various traditional structures. There were structures at the marketplaces, within households, in local areas, during initiations and other rituals, so everyone had a place where their voices counted – women, children, men, the elderly, farmers, herders, chiefs, fathers, uncles, grandmothers. And everyone was accountable to society in general for their decisions. What colonialism did was to select a single structure, namely that of the headmen, and declare it the only traditional structure. What is more, this structure was no longer accountable to the people, but to the colonial authorities. It was therefore a complete perversion of what had existed before.'

'But wasn't that at least an attempt to accommodate something traditional, rather than destroying it completely as the missionaries did?'

'The colonial authorities realized, after a century and a half of warfare and rebellion, that they could not rule on their own. After 1910, they took a piece of tradition, removed its democratic fundamentals, and placed it under dictatorial authority. When I arrived here in your country, my first impressions, as an African, were of how different South Africa was from the rest of the continent. Your level of economic development and industrialization was closer to that of North America than to Equatorial Africa. But it also quickly became clear to what extent you were exactly like other African states. The whites belong to a race, the rest belong to ethnic groups; the whites are international, the blacks are indigenous; the whites have a history, the ethnic groups have traditional ways and habits; the whites are governed by civil laws adopted in a parliament which they themselves have chosen, the ethnic groups are governed by laws made by the colonialists and enforced by traditional leaders, who have no responsibility to their people; the whites have citizenship, the ethnic groups are subjects. This was a world I had come to know very well in Africa – it was colonialism, designed by the English and widely applied by the French, Belgians and Portuguese. But when I arrived here, lo and behold, I heard that they called it something else: apartheid.'

Mamdani is in his element. I do not even have to ask any questions. He knows all the arguments and counter-arguments. 'Liberation deracializes the state, but usually fails to deracialize society. The attack on racialized privilege in the state unites everybody. But the redistribution divides everybody, so the state now finds itself custodian of all the wealth which has been accumulated at the cost of its people. The big question is: how do you create structures of accountability overnight? How do you revive the structures that provided checks and balances in societies in the past?

'In Uganda, we turned the chiefs into civil servants with no executive or judicial or legislative power. They had to implement the by-laws passed by popularly elected councils and they had to ensure that the decisions arrived at by the independent judicial authorities were carried out. One notices that South Africa is going the route of the most conservative African regimes, which decided to reproduce the colonial heritage of chieftainship in order to ensure stability and control in the rural areas, at a huge cost in finances – and corruption.'

'The problem is perhaps more complex than mere colonial corruption of African traditions,' says a youthful Prof. Sipho Maseko in one of the next sessions. 'The complete lack of tradition in some countries at present sees them staggering between the tyranny of dictators and the anarchy of clans. Where Africa has tossed its traditions overboard and taken on the new from the West, the new, lacking organic roots, has never had any legitimacy. The result is large-scale corruption and chaos. It is like building the bodywork of an automobile around the chassis of a donkey cart. By the time the bodywork collapses, you realize that the donkeys have already died and you sit with nothing.

'This is the fertile field for corruption: a government that is experienced as illegitimate. It is not *your* government, these are not *your* people, so you can steal from them and undermine them as much as you like, and their failures will have nothing to do with you.'

As I'm making notes, I recall how many Afrikaners have been caught recently committing fraud. Is it because they feel estranged? Or because they come from a culture that made them feel entitled to privilege?

'Many of us are afraid that the South African Constitution will have similar consequences. Although a serious attempt was made to incorporate the views of ordinary people in the writing of the Constitution, some issues were simply not negotiable. Now we sit with a highly modern, internationally respected Constitution, while the people want to ban gays and hang criminals, and complain that the Constitution protects the prison inmate better than the law-abiding citizen. Our Constitution states that all people are equal, yet it makes room for a traditional system in which leadership is hereditary and women are treated like minors. One starts to wonder how deep the roots of this Constitution really are.

'But do we have a choice? We have to pace ourselves with the modern world. In order to ensure stability and the coherent passage of development, we have to get the donkeys to drag the home-made Mercedes for now. In the meantime – if I can follow my metaphor to an extreme conclusion – we must develop and install a proper engine and keep our fingers crossed that we will come upon a tarred road sooner or later, where everyone can choose the means of transport that suits them.'

✧

Some time before the second election, I find an envelope on my desk. On the finely tex-tured cardboard there is a blob of red wax with the emblem of a traditional hide shield and spear sunk into it. The card inside, printed in Celtic lettering, invites me to attend the Official Installation and Anointment of Sango Patekile Holomisa (*A! Dilizintaba*) as the *Inkosi* (Traditional Leader) of the AmaHegebe Tribe of the Thembu Kingdom, on Saturday 17 April at Lower Gqungqu Great Place, Mqanduli, Eastern Cape. Dress: Cultural. RSVP: Bantu Holomisa. On the front of the card, imposed on a leopard-skin pattern, is a photo of Patekile in traditional black-and-white royal attire, holding a staff covered in fine black-and-white beadwork. A woven string of beads is tied around his forehead.

Zola Ntutu, a colleague from Johannesburg, and I meet each other on Friday after-noon at the airport in East London and drive to our hotel in Umtata. Now it takes a while to get used to a town like Umtata. There is something neglected and used-up about the place, yet at the same time living at peace with itself. It has none of the over-whelming opulence that is part of South African cities, and none of the desperate squalor of the squatter camps. I am on the second floor of the Winchester Hotel. Does Zola want to stay on the first floor, where the boys will be having a bit of a party tonight, or would he rather also be on the second floor? As long as he can join the party, he would also prefer the second floor.

Before dinner we go for a walk. Zola forces me to say, 'Lower Gqungqu Great Place, Mqanduli,' until these names pop like jolly champagne corks from my mouth. 'If you slip up with the different placings of "q" and "x" and "c", your report will speak only to whites – you've lost the rest of us.'

Umtata is a town fully inhabited. Houses that look as if they were built in the fifties have been set up as spaza shops, dry-cleaners and tombstone-makers. The living-room window of one place has been broken out to make way for a pulley and other mechan-ical devices. Here and there a colonial building is peacefully decomposing behind what's left of the rambling roses and cannas. In between, stands a fearless apartheid building that looks as if it will last forever and ever. Amen. Everywhere little fires are burning and the smell of cooking is in the air. Taxis pass in a never-ending stream. Big, heavy, battered buses rumble desperately up the slightest incline. Well-rounded men are tucking into plates stacked sky-high with meat, rice, potatoes and gravy, genially laughing and chatting, filling up the dining room of the two-star hotel.

Robert Kinghorn, Radio 702's impressively named Eastern Cape correspondent, is also at the hotel. Have we heard? There is talk that the Thembu king, the very young Bulelekaya Dalindyebo, will not be attending tomorrow. He is apparently annoyed that Mandela has ordered him around. Yes, one can imagine the problems of hierarchy and status that arise in an ordinary rural kingdom when someone like Mandela shows up after an absence of half a lifetime.

Traditionally, Mandela's family were advisors to the Thembu king. When Mandela's father died, the regent took him into the royal household in order to raise him along-side the future king. Mandela was sent to Lovedale College and Fort Hare specifically to acquire an education that would enable him to assist the king in the modern world.

This led, of course, to clashes between Mandela, the fiery young activist, and his clan elders. They wanted him to devote himself to his people, the Thembu, and to King Dalindyebo, whereas he chose to claim all black South Africans as 'his people' and to become part of the larger struggle for freedom. There was at one time great bitterness between Mandela and his nephew Kaiser Matanzima, who accepted the apartheid government's proposals on traditional leadership and was appointed Paramount Chief of the Transkei. For years, Matanzima tried to visit Mandela on Robben Island, but Mandela refused, under pressure from his comrades. Such contact would have lent undeserved credibility to Matanzima and the whole concept of hereditary leadership.

When he finally returned to the Eastern Cape, which he'd left more than fifty years before, Mandela came endowed with the bloodline of a prince, the power of a president and the status of a messiah. Of course, as a master of diplomacy, he was aware that his sudden presence might destabilize things. Like any other local resident, he went to see the local traditional chief, in this case a woman, and humbly asked for a piece of land. She obliged, and over the following years got plenty in return: a ready supply of water and electricity, new schools, well-maintained roads and streams of tourists visiting Qunu. Mandela built subways under the roads for the use of schoolchildren and cattle herders, and every year he throws a gigantic Christmas bash for all the children in the area.

The young king now finds himself in a difficult position: traditionally, he is Mandela's boss, his superior in royal status, and Mandela is nothing more than one of his advisors. The king is a dedicated joller, says Robert Kinghorn, who apparently joins him on some of these sprees, and he's very irritated by Mandela's old-fashioned ideas about self-discipline, education and responsibility. Apparently, Mandela has had him unceremoniously enrolled in a private school, with instructions to pass his final exams before he thinks of making any further demands. It's also said that Mandela rapped him over the knuckles for not uniting the Thembu clan behind the ANC. So everybody is looking forward to tomorrow. Will King Dalindyebo really boycott the whole cere-mony? And what if he does? The king must be present to install a new chief, as a sign that the Thembu people at large accept his authority.

'But in parliament they say this inauguration is merely an election ploy on the part of the ANC aimed at knocking out Bantu Holomisa's new political party,' I say. 'The backbone of his support is the Thembu chiefs, whom the ANC is now trying to rally.'

'Everybody here knows that. They are laughing up their sleeves, because tradition demands that Bantu Holomisa act as the master of ceremonies. So he will be in the thick of things, like it or not. But that the event will become a display of traditional authority with the blessing of the ANC is not to be doubted. Do you know how many private planes are parked at the airfield in Umtata?

'The Xhosa nation consists of five clans.' Robert, a fluent Xhosa-speaker, is getting into lecture mode. 'Bomvana, Mpondo, Mpondomise, Xhosa and Thembu. This helps to explain why Marxist ideas about class don't quite work here in the Eastern Cape. You are first a Thembu, then a Xhosa, and then a member of the working class. It is very difficult for someone who belongs to the Thembu elite to be a prince at home and an ordinary member of COSATU in Johannesburg. That is why communism has never really been accepted in Africa. To be a good Marxist, you have to be completely Westernized.'

Robert shows me a quote in his notebook: 'Tribalism is a response of those who lose their bearings in a heterogeneous, changing society. They cling to natural or invented national group identities, which they relate to a past that is only partly real and largely mythological. One sees the invention of instant traditions, the adoption of new prac-tices designed to resemble ancient histories. People organize themselves around the ideology of inevitable conflict and see themselves as victims of those they are in fact victimizing.' He nods at me knowingly: 'This is the Chomskyan deep structure of it all.'

Early the next morning we drive out. The day breaks beautifully over the soft hills on the way to the Great Place at Lower Gqungqu. Zola adds another phrase for me to practise: King Xoliswa Sigcau will be at Lower Gqungqu Great Place, Mqanduli. Zola promises to point the king out to me, as he is seldom seen in public.

From afar, it is clear that big things are going to happen today. Hundreds of people are streaming along the footpaths that trail over the hills, others are arriving by taxi and bus. The whole area around the Great Place has been mown clean and an enormous marquee pitched.

May we conduct an interview with Nkosi Patekile? No, he is in church, where Archbishop Njongonkulu Ndungane is officiating. We find our way to the little white-washed church with broken windows, where Nkosi Patekile is sitting with his family. You cannot keep your eyes off his suit. Its dark wool has a kind of fine shimmer that folds almost like silk when he moves. The only sign that he is from Mqanduli is the shield-and-spear motif on his cufflinks. The handkerchief peeking from his pocket is in the traditional white with black stripes.

Patekile Holomisa, who is also an advocate, a Member of Parliament and Chairperson of Contralesa, is known as a man with impeccable taste in clothing. When he gets up to speak in parliament and reaches for the microphone, he sometimes dis-plays a very stylish set of designer bangles. He arrives for the opening of parliament in such subtle combinations of Western and African designs that only the sophisticated fashion eye picks up the allusions.

'The institution of kingship has been ordained by God from the beginning,' says Archbishop Ndungane, and blesses him.

After the service, we all walk across to the centre of activity. Zola raises his eyebrows: twelve gigantic soup pots bubbling on the fires, wheelbarrows and buckets filled with meat, enormous griddle-cakes laid out in rows on sheets, a mountain of pumpkins, a hill of onions. Among the rondavels three little generators, trailing rags of orange and purple smoke, are furiously pumping out electricity. The door of one rondavel stands ajar: inside you cannot move for cables and wires and adaptors charging hordes and hordes of cellphones. The floor is a tangled web of wiring.

But here, near the entrance to the marquee, lies the true test. This is what everybody wants to see, this is how the day will be judged: on the mown grass lie the fresh hides of seven cows and twenty-five sheep. We see some of the older men stopping to count them off with their canes, and then nodding approvingly to each other.

Suddenly, we are aware of a terrible racket. It is a military helicopter, landing on a marked-out spot. Cloths, blankets, scarves, hats go flying. A door in the side of the craft opens, steps are lowered and bodyguards jump down and run crouching to their positions. They are followed by several shaken but sprightly old men dressed in skins and bearing staffs, smiling from ear to ear and waving, while they are heartily teased by the women. It appears they are chiefs from Qunu, whom Mandela offered a lift this morning. And here is Mandela himself, with his grandson Mandla. Apparently he is accompanying Mandela more and more to traditional events – perhaps being groomed to take over his grandfather's responsibilities in the Thembu royal house, Robert explains.

Inside the marquee and around the entrance there is a throng of traditional leaders from across the whole of Southern Africa. Over there the Swazi royals, here the Botswana group. To the left are the traditional leaders from the Free State. Free State? Yes, they are from Qwa-Qwa. The Ndebele traditional leaders are accompanied by a praise singer, who sounds as if he's singing a full octave lower than what should be humanly possible. A bit like a didgeridoo, but more human. A whole group of women are moving with a slow and rhythmic grace towards the tent, pausing for a full three seconds between each step, the sunlight glancing from multicoloured ankle bracelets stacked all the way up to their knees. On the stage there are at least eight full leopard skins, heads and all. For the first time in my life, I wish I worked in television so that I could devote an entire programme to the different outfits, codes, traditions, colours. The place is buzzing with praise singers and songs, people dancing, traditional leaders walking with their staffs raised in the air.

Eventually Bantu Holomisa gets the whole ceremony going. Several speeches follow, interrupted frequently by *iimbongi*, who grab the microphone while their followers demand speaking turns. It becomes a warble of participation, watched from the stage by the smiling hierarchy of the highest traditional leaders.

'An *imbongi* does not let himself be guided by a time schedule or a programme,'

Prof. Sizwe Satyo of the Xhosa Department at the University of Cape Town explains to me later. 'He starts when he is ready. And he is ready when he has put himself into a kind of trance by making a range of evocative sounds, which allow him to reach the deepest levels of his consciousness and abilities, a communal pool of sorts, and turn what is there into language. The *iimbongi* themselves often do not know what they are about to say. To *bonga* is a higher state of consciousness. After a performance, the *imbongi* will walk up and down, cooling himself down again spiritually, as it were.'

In his book on Xhosa *iimbongi*, Jeff Opland writes that it is a mistake to translate the word *imbongi* as 'praise singer', because this suggests mere flattery. Literally, *imbongi* means 'the poet who walks in front of the leader', and his primary task is to act as a go-between between the leader and his people. He must praise the leader when he acts in the best interests of his people and criticize him when he neglects to do his duty.

Because the *imbongi* must be able to criticize a political leader to his face, the art has developed a wide spectrum of poetic and theatrical means, such as irony, sarcasm, sound mimicry, wordplay and metaphor. The oral nature of the praise songs means that nobody is ever sure exactly what was said, and days after the event the audience is still busy trying to extract the meaning of what they heard. Everything occurs spontaneously, and so you can also never return to a definitive text.

The *imbongi*'s function is to contextualize political events for the audience. He does this by interweaving historical and actual events with phrases and sounds that resonate with the listeners. In order to retain impartiality and credibility, the *imbongi* does not represent the leader but the community, and for this reason most of the *iimbongi* in the Eastern Cape are ordinary employees in magistrates' offices and schools.

Suddenly the low, throaty call of an *imbongi* resounds through the tent. The call is repeated, and then comes, '*Halaa-la Dilizintaba!*' Whoever was busy speaking takes his seat. Everybody knows: now is the time for the *imbongi* of the AmaHegebe. He is now ready to proceed.

But the AmaHegebe *imbongi* has a surprise in store for us. While he remains at the entrance, letting us hear his cries, a little boy of seven or eight, fully dressed as an *imbongi*, comes striding majestically down the aisle. The expression on his little face is furiously serious. When he finally comes to the space in front of the stage, he starts to *bonga*, with exactly the same accents, throaty sounds and gestures. Then he suddenly stops as if he is frozen, and the chief *imbongi* comes forward with the self-confidence and the intuitive connection with the audience that only a mature practitioner can have. It is an enchanting and colourful drama, in which the crowd participates with noisy cheers, calls and ululating. Only then do we see Nkosi Patekile. The designer suit and shiny leather shoes are gone. He stands barefoot in the dust. His hairless torso is clad in a waistcoat of beadwork, woven and linked into all kinds of shapes and patterns. Around his upper arm he wears a ring of ivory, around his narrow hips hangs a traditional black-and-white striped cloth.

Like Mandela, Nkosi Patekile is exceptionally tall, straight and light of skin. At one stage, the lightness of Mandela's skin was a big talking point among whites. That is why one can trust Mandela – he definitely has white blood in him, it was said. Oh please, with those high cheekbones, that is pure Khoi blood he has there. The Xhosa were the only people to welcome the Khoi. That is why there are so many tongue-clicking sounds in the Xhosa language and this lightness of skin occurs specifically among the Thembu people. And his height? If Mandela had Khoi blood, he would be short with a big backside. No, it must be the blood of shipwreck victims who washed up on the shores of the Eastern Cape and on whom the Xhosa took pity.

Unlike Mandela, Nkosi Patekile has piercing green eyes. 'That's not green, that's yellow,' somebody whispers. 'He looks at you with them as coolly as a lion.'

Nkosi Patekile and his equally attractive wife come and sit right in front on the stage. Everybody quietens down. It is Mandela's turn.

'Tradition can be a binding force. Here we are in this tent: people from different political persuasions, yet like a family we are one. Bantu Holomisa is my opposition in parliament, but here he is my brother. Tradition can make us care for each other. The past dispensation succeeded in separating the traditional leaders from their own people, but as part of a democratic order they should help to reconstruct rural societies shattered by apartheid. The challenge now is to marry our two traditions, traditional authority and electoral democracy, into one, so that we can better improve the lives of our people. Because it is true: democracy has brought a better life for traditional leaders. I will observe with interest how you as traditional leaders are taking our people into the next century.'

He calls Nkosi Patekile to the lectern. Everybody starts craning their necks. The day is almost over and King Bulelekaya Dalindyebo is quite clearly not intending to come. What to do now?

Mandela starts to talk, but nobody can hear. The microphone is dead. Bantu Holomisa runs this way and that. Finally everybody is asked to fetch their cellphones from the rondavel, as they are drawing too much power. Within a few moments, Mandela is audible again and his words catch most people off guard.

'Now I am speaking not as a president, but as a Thembu elder who knows our customs well. Nothing, no major issue, can be addressed in the Dalindyebo house without the Matanzimas, and nothing can be done of any significance in the Matanzima family without the Dalindyebos!'

'Yebo!' somebody shouts from the audience.

'In the absence of the King' – the audience shouts and laughs – 'I am now asking, I am instructing, as an elder, King Daliwonga Matanzima to install Chief Dilizintaba. A! Dilizintaba.' 'Dilizintaba' is the praise name of Patekile Holomisa, analogous to 'Madiba' in the case of Mandela.

From among the traditional leaders a man rises. You would scarcely recognize the familiar face used so often by the National Party in days gone by to lend credibility to their bantustan policies: see here, this chief from the Transkei, family of that communist rebel Nelson Mandela, agrees with us that the Xhosa do not want the country, do not want the right to vote, but prefer to rule themselves in their own territory. In *Long Walk to Freedom*, Mandela describes his dismay when he heard in 1980 that his nephew Matanzima, as the Chief Minister of Transkei, had deposed King Sabata Dalindyebo and, with the blessing of the white government, taken over the throne. Sabata had to flee the country because of his political persuasions and later died in exile (one of the first significant political gestures after 1990 was the return of his remains to the Transkei). Young activists from the Eastern Cape started arriving on Robben Island with the slogan: 'There are two paths in life: one is Mandela's path, the other is Matanzima's. Where do you walk?'

Today is the very first time since Mandela's release in 1990 that the two men will share a political stage. Matanzima has Parkinson's disease and can barely walk. He is carried forward by his helpers. With shaking hands, he drapes the leopard skin over Nkosi Patekile.

Zola rolls his eyes. What can one say? The man has let himself be used before, why not a second time? Or is he letting himself be used only because it is Mandela who has asked, and he wants so badly to make up with him? Should one question the wisdom of Mandela, who is using a discredited man, like the white government before him, for the sake of politics? Or is it for the sake of tradition? Is a Dalindyebo being stabbed in the back once again by a Matanzima? Or is it simply a matter of practicality: if the king isn't here to install the chief, then the king's cousin must do it. Does it really matter in the end?

The audience clearly has fewer problems. While choirs burst into song, we are invited to assemble for the meal. 'This is our tradition,' says Zola, 'you don't know who will come, but you provide food for everybody. Plates for everybody, cutlery, something to drink.'

While we're standing in line for the food, a voice on the PA system thanks several wineries, brandy distillers and breweries sincerely for their support. At a special stand, you can ask for something stronger. Zola shows me later: in a colleague's bag, snuggling up to his recorder, lies a bottle of good whisky.

We are still queuing for food when an enormous rainstorm breaks overhead.

'The ancestors are happy,' laughs Nkosi Nonkonyana. 'They like what is happening here.' So much for qualms about Matanzima.

I set up an interview with Nkosi Madoda Zibi of the AmaHlubi, part of the Xhosa clan. He is a professor at the University of Potchefstroom.

'What happened today is a turning point, I believe, in government policy on traditional leadership. Government is in trouble. Research has shown that little delivery is taking place in the rural areas. The incompetence and corruption of civil servants makes government more and more dependent on traditional leaders. We have access to everybody, and it is in our direct interest to see to it that the people living with us have housing and water and electricity. Government is realizing more and more that it needs us.

'It would be disingenuous to talk about an African Renaissance and then discard the very system that has evolved among Africans. But, like all institutions, we have to develop with the times. You will find that most traditional leaders are also qualified in a profession. I am a traditional leader in North West Province. When I am away at the university, I appoint people to take care of the daily traditional business. Over weekends and holidays I go back and try to sort out more important stuff like tensions or rituals. The central thing is that I have the contacts and knowledge to provide my people with water and electricity.

'One of the main strengths of traditional leadership is that it can transcend the divisions of Western politics. Because the leadership is hereditary, it is never threatened, and it should always rise above party politics. African leadership is also specific: one is a leader through one's people. *Kgosi ke kgosi ka setshaba.* The success and development of your people is your own development and success.'

I stop him. 'But unfortunately the opposite is also true: some leaders think that their starved and underdeveloped clansmen should be comforted by the fact that their leader drives a smart car, wears beautiful clothes and lives a life of luxury. Traditional leaders are being paid by the state, so where does their loyalty lie? Do you really believe that an occasion like this is not actively used to persuade traditional leaders that their people should vote for the ANC?'

'We have discussed this issue, but most of us feel that we should be above politics and make that very clear to government. We represent our people and we're trying to make the best deal for them.'

Nkosi Patekile Holomisa greets us. He stands with his soft bare feet in the mud, his sparkling white garments already spattered with brown, as he sees people off and they drive away through the puddles of water.

Robert Kinghorn, the Radio 702 reporter, is sitting dejectedly in his car. 'I couldn't get through, all these cellphones created massive congestion and I kept being cut off … And now they have the cheek to tell me that their listeners are not that interested in traditional matters anyway.'

Back in the car, we switch on our cellphones. An SMS message appears on the little screen: Halaa-la Dilizintaba!! – with a flashing reminder that one can also email Nkosi Sango Patekile Holomisa at dilizintaba@iafrica.com.

CHAPTER SIX

IT IS ONLY ME AND PEET and his son Jaco in the house. Rina is on a primary health-care course in Bloemfontein. A spectacular fire of thorn-tree wood is burning in the study. Rina left us some barley and meat soup, but my cousin and I are on wine and whisky, and talking in a way we have never talked before. I suspect our intense discussion was set off by his knowledge that I am taking a weekend break between two Truth Commission hearings in the Free State. Or by the computer game. Jaco was playing a new game I brought for them when Peet suddenly jumped up, shouting, 'Stop that! Stop that sound! Not in my house!' There was an uncharacteristic violence in his voice. Jaco and I looked at each other with raised eyebrows, and he turned down the volume.

Immediately, Peet looked embarrassed. 'Sorry, I cannot stand that sound ... it reminds me, you know ... of the border and things.' He turned the eight o'clock news a bit louder.

But it is past midnight now. Jaco has gone to bed. Most of the lights are off, only the fireplace is glowing and I am seeing a side of Peet I didn't know existed. He is distraught. Desperate.

'I loved that man. I worshipped the ground he walked on.' He is talking about Colonel Jan Groenewald, one of the trainers of the Recces. Two weeks ago, I broadcast a programme about the old security forces in which a psychologist suggested that the training programmes devised by men like Groenewald were aimed specifically at helping trainees to split their personalities. In other words, the training ensured that their actions took place in a realm cut off from their day-to-day personalities.

'You know what, that man worked some kind of magic on us. We would have done anything for him, any bloody thing, because he was so amazing. He had this voice, with a slightly rolling "r" in the back of his throat. Let me tell you, he could speak like a poet. And he loved us completely. I never felt so safe, so ... held in respect, as by that man. When we got back from a mission, it didn't matter what time, he would make them open the bar for us. It may sound like nothing to you, but when you have just returned from a mission and you are pumped up with adrenalin, and it is three o'clock in the morning and the soldier is not too keen to open up ... I remember one night how he walked in front of us into the camp, right up to that bar, and simply booted open the door.'

'But he sounds like a bit of a ... bully.' I am careful, because I see that Peet is trying to express things that do not come easily.

'It's not about the alcohol, it's about being respected for the fact that you've braved your life. And it's not the big tokens that matter, things like medals or promotion, but small things that he did for us, like he allowed us to wear our hair a bit longer than the others. So everybody recognized you immediately: *die manne van Groenewald*. He also relieved us of cleaning the camp. He used to say: my guys put their lives on the line, the rest of you will put the camp in line. And he was so brave himself, so utterly fucking fearless ... not in a stupid way, if you understand what I mean, but in the way that comes from facing your fear every day and breaking through it.

'There are two famous stories about him, the legends you heard from the others when you arrived at his training camps. The one was told to me by a fighter pilot, Renier. He was with Groenewald that day. They were flying in to bomb an ANC hide-out in Mozambique. In the air, Groenewald received a message that the enemy knew about the imminent bombing and had anti-aircraft guns in place. Renier said to me: you know, my body was already leaning to one side to swing the plane into a return curve, when Groenewald just gripped his knees a bit more tightly and said in a very quiet way, "Now we go in." At that moment, Renier says, your adrenalin just shot up. You crossed into another place, knowing you were going to be challenged like never before ...'

I say nothing.

'This adrenalin thing, it's unbelievable when it hits you, no drug can compare with it. As if your body has prepared itself for that injection. For weeks now you have prac-tised, you are so prepared you could do the whole job with your eyes closed.'

'Physically, you mean?'

'Ag, I'm not talking about physical training – that was a given. We were so bloody fit, you felt invincible. But say we were going to attack a base, then some of us scouted it out, we had it under surveillance for some time, we even moved in at night to take measurements. When we got back we could draw a plan of the whole camp, all the buildings, exactly how many metres apart, the position of the doors, which way they opened, the view from every window, how many people inside, their routines. Then this dummy base gets built, we work out a plan, and we practise it so many times you can do your part blindfolded. But they never tell you when you're going in. So you are on edge and you practise more and more. Then one night you hear, it's tomorrow early, and you eat well that night, not a lot, but your meal is part of your preparation. During the night you are loaded on to a plane and you wait to be parachuted in. And you are terrified, you are absolutely fucking terrified in that noisy plane, and then they start with that singing, until the whole plane is rocking with it, and that song pumps up the adrenalin, and by the time you jump you are so sharp you can see everything, you have bloody night vision, you see so clearly, hear and assess things before they happen, so acutely, you have become a machine. You land here, you run there, jump over there, kill here, run over to that building there, open the door, kill the man behind the door, and so on.

'One day, after completing a mission, a few of us were pulling out when we sud-denly found ourselves surrounded by a patrol from another camp. We were shooting, but it was clear that we were completely outnumbered. And then we just hear this noise above us, and among bullets and shattering glass and what have you, Groenewald jumps from the helicopter to join us. And we fucking well shot our way out of there. Out of those Swapos.'

'Is that the other story about Groenewald?'

'No, but I witnessed that one too. I was there.'

I leave Peet to determine his own sequence.

'We knew of a convoy of weapons on its way to an ANC base. So we waited along the road for days, we were dog-tired, I don't know if you know how hard it is to wait and watch without making a noise or movement because there are locals around. You are completely camouflaged, and at night you sleep an arm's length from one another so that if you hear something you just put out your hand in a particular way and the man next to you is fully awake. And then it is so heartbreakingly beautiful in Angola, you know, I saw bananas there as long as my forearm, it's an incredible country, and you see women picking up firewood, or even children looking after goats and things, snatches of ordinary life that devastate you with such longing, but you don't make a movement for a whole morning. It's a skill, you know, that Groenewald could teach you. Fuck, he was a great man.'

I see the whisky is now on the rocks. And imagine this human chain in the bush at night. Every link tested, every link surrendering his life into the hands of the links on either side. Believing that they will care. That they will be brave enough to care.

'And then we heard them and within minutes the first truck came into sight. There were three trucks and one other vehicle. So we had to wait for them to move deep enough into our ambush before we could attack. You pass into an incredible state, you could jump over a four-metre fence if you had to. And then without warning, without it being planned or discussed, Groenewald jumped from nowhere into the middle of the road, right in front of this big truck. But like ... elegantly, he just suddenly stood there, facing them, these big, thundering trucks full of soldiers and ammunition. As I watched him, I felt light as a feather. Then slowly, and I tell you slowly, as if the man had all the time in the world, he sort of gracefully knelt down on one knee, took aim at the first truck, and shot the guy in the passenger seat. There was this shattering foam of glass, and then all hell broke loose ... As long as I live, I'll never forget the sight of Groenewald, all alone, as if he was in no hurry, as if he trusted us unconditionally, and our skill to protect him ...'

'None of you died?'

He shakes his head. 'None of us, but most of them ... Some ran away.'

I get up and look at the display above Peet's desk. It is a row of test tubes mounted on wood. Beneath the floating pods and stems I read: Grasses of Southern Angola. Swampgrass, Herringbone grass, Black-footed grass, Hartjiesgras, Thimble grass, Knietjiesgras, Bloutwa– But Peet has covered his face with his hands. I go and sit next to him.

'Do you think about these things often?' I stroke his rough hand with its crusts and freckles, remembering the stiffened joint of his middle finger from a rugby accident. And whereas his hands always seemed rather stodgy and childish to me when we were younger, they have transformed their potential for cruelty into a clumsy vulnerability which catches my throat. He sighs, and it seems as if his shoulders have sunk into his torso, he looks not only depressed but defeated. I am not sure about the word: un-manned, perhaps?

'Rina helped me a lot. As a nurse, she sort of knew. She got me help in Bloem-fontein and I am actually fine, it is only that the Truth Commission is picking over all of this now. And these computer games all seem to have sounds that somehow come from there. I can't stand it.'

'And do you,' I hesitate, 'feel okay about what you did?'

'You see, that is actually the whole problem, a terrible problem that no psychologist can help you with.'

Peet's face is distorted; memory, and whisky, have turned this neat, punctual cousin of mine into a dishevelled, despondent heap. His voice wails nakedly as he pleads for understanding: 'These were the most important moments of my life, do you understand what I'm saying? I felt more alive, more proud, more brave, more real, than ever before in my life – or after. When I think of myself at my best, at my deep-est and most courageous, as pure and single-minded as a fucking flame, then these are the moments. Now, since the Commission and all the articles and discussions and things, now we learn, yes, the ANC hideout in Mozambique that we bombed was actually a jam factory, and the ANC had evacuated all their bases in the area anyway. We learn that a lot of the people who died at Kassinga were local women and children, and so on ... Now what the hell am I supposed to do with this? What does it make me? How do I live with this knowledge? Where do I hide this memory? How do I talk about it without destroying its integrity?'

He hides his face again, his body shivering feverishly. I hold him. He feels as if he's made only of sad, heavy flesh.

Indeed, what is he to make of it? The moment that defined him has now betrayed him. I rock him gently until I feel him sagging, breathing more evenly. He is asleep. I put some more wood on the fire, cover him with a sleeping bag and go to my bed, where the hot-water bottle he put there earlier has gone cold.

CHAPTER SEVEN

THE DATE FOR THE GENERAL ELECTION has been announced: 2 June 1999. It is in the middle of winter, but that cannot be helped, because the Independent Electoral Commission (IEC) needs more time than expected to prepare for this second democratic election. And as the process unfolds it becomes clear what a long way there still is to go on the way to a fully functional democracy.

In the first election, any South African could vote anywhere with any kind of identification. In the second election, you have to register as a voter at the place where you will actually be voting on polling day, and the process revolves around a voters' roll and a bar-coded identity book. This is seen as the most important difference between the two elections.

For those accustomed to established democracies and settled places of residence all this may sound like nothing. For South Africa in general it uncovers huge problems. On the one hand, a lot of whites refuse to queue for hours at the offices of Home Affairs to apply for the new bar-coded ID. On the other hand, it is found that some people's fingers are so work-callused that they cannot be fingerprinted effectively. It becomes clear how many people have never been in possession of a birth certificate: they have to bring a birth witness to the nearest office in order to obtain an ID. It also proves impossible to ascertain the actual number of eligible voters in South Africa, as the National Party, in forty years of rule, was never able to determine precisely how many people live in the country.

The 1991 census figures were sharply criticized because the bantustans and squatter camps had been counted by way of aerial photography. The 1996 census was conducted by one hundred thousand hastily trained census workers. Although the population was estimated then at 37.9 million, it was felt that the figure ought to be closer to 40 million. This indicated that there must be around 26.3 million voters. But four months before the election, Mandla Mchunu, chairperson of the IEC, declared that there were only 24.6 million voters; and he later deducted a further 2.2 million temporary residents, South Africans living abroad, people awaiting trail, people without ID documents and people with ID documents who do not exist. Do not exist? Yes, we are told, sometimes when a person dies the family keeps a finger in a bottle of formaldehyde, so that they can go on producing the fingerprint required for the collection of a pension.

Despite some cynicism about the numbers, it is a fact that an enormous administrative effort was made even in the most remote parts of the country. In the same areas where light aircraft were used in earlier days to count people like herds of animals, everyone now had to be registered at a location within walking distance of their home. With 22.8 million official voters, a remarkable voter registration figure of 80 per cent is achieved.

As the political parties start with their manifestos and campaigns, it soon becomes clear that the story of the election does not lie in what they have to say, but in the boundaries they have to cross in order to win support.

✧

But for better or worse, we as South Africans suddenly find ourselves being wooed from all sides by politicians. However we may differ from one another, however cynical and suspicious we may have become of politicians in general, they are putting on a vigorous display of democracy. And the parties are pulling out all the stops. With astonishing dedication leaders criss-cross the country, track down minorities, re-enchant deserters, reactivate the apathetic, resuscitate former alliances, get wet and ragged on lamp posts, pump endless advertisements into the electoral ears and eyes, and do their best to cut their coats according to our will.

Thabo Mbeki visits places no national politician has ever set foot in. He deliberately visits no-go areas and mosques. The election itself is being used to build up the personal image of Mandela's successor. Mbeki is no longer seen only in the plush surroundings of parliament or in air-conditioned international conference centres, but in the dusty streets of townships, where he has to shout speeches in indigenous languages over primitive PA systems to illiterate audiences, until his voice gives in.

Tony Leon of the Democratic Party is running a version of an American campaign, full of designer items and strategies never attempted before by an opposition leader. As the election approaches, his speeches become more and more complex. He uses the phrase 'white guilt' – a first for a white, English-speaking, liberal politician. He quotes Gramsci on the organic intellectual and places the word 'liberalism' centrally in his speeches. South Africa has always been a battlefield of contesting nationalities, he says, and this must change. Therefore the time has come for liberalism. But as the pressure builds up, he compromises. He starts actively addressing those Afrikaners who feel that the other parties are too 'soft' on the ANC. He delivers dedicated, audible, practised speeches in a tongue-twisting, anglicized Afrikaans on musty stages in the disintegrating little town halls of forgotten rural towns. One keeps on watching him for his breathtaking self-confidence. Without him, something would have disappeared long ago – the space to be your critical white self in good, clipped English.

Marthinus van Schalkwyk of the New National Party is often seen in black neighbourhoods, addressing people from the back of a bakkie, trying to convince them to vote for him. According to later polls, the NNP rates as the most multiracial party. Van Schalkwyk goes to lay a wreath in Sharpeville. When his predecessor F.W. de Klerk dared to set foot there, he was chased away in a shower of stones. Van Schalkwyk, however, is given the opportunity to make his case at leisure. But one simply feels sorry for him. His predecessors in the NP have dumped the entire mess of the past in his lap and are now sitting in their luxurious houses writing their memoirs. Like a good *boereseun*, one of a generation now reaping the bitter fruits sown by their greedy forefathers, he is mastering the art of survival.

Van Schalkwyk and Buthelezi make the biggest effort to broaden the base of their parties. In the end, both of them pay a price for it.

A new player in the political arena is the United Democratic Movement founded by Bantu Holomisa, a former leader of the Transkei who was expelled from the ANC for insubordination. Holomisa belongs to the same clan as Mandela and is also of royal descent. He is seen as a serious threat in the ANC heartland: he has influence over many traditional leaders who feel that the liberal and socialist tendencies in the ANC have always been unsympathetic towards traditional leaders and that it is merely a question of time before they scrap the whole system. Every time Holomisa touches down in the Transkei, Mandela himself is dispatched to appease the traditional leaders. During one of the first rallies in Umtata, Mandela is shouted down by Holomisa supporters.

The story of the election also lies in the uncomfortable body language of Freedom Front leader Constand Viljoen, the army general who suddenly has to sell himself on an election platform.

The fatal flaw of the election lies in the absence of a left-wing opposition and the lack of consensus that poverty is the country's biggest problem.

A month before the election the question arises: if the voters have indeed registered against all the odds, if the political parties have managed to pull off campaigns without violence, will the IEC be capable of delivering to South Africans the kind of election that is not only our due, but that will give credibility to the newly elected government? The miracle this time would be an administratively sophisticated election. Why a miracle? Because all kinds of people – people living in mansions, people living in the veld, people who burn witches, people who see UFOs, academics and illiterates – have selflessly hunted out election information for themselves and seen to it that they are ID-ed, bar-coded and voters'-rolled.

'May the IEC,' I say in a news report, 'by the grace of incompetents, thieves and instigators of violence, not leave us in the lurch.'

The 'Black Threat' of the first election is replaced during the second by the fear of the 'Two-Thirds Majority'. Some of the most important clauses in the Constitution can be changed with a two-thirds majority. Rumours abound that the ANC wants to change the clauses protecting private property and that the second chamber of parliament, the National Council of Provinces, is to be replaced by a House of Traditional Chiefs. Rumour has it that this rumour is being spread deliberately from ANC headquarters.

The NNP's use of the slogan 'Mugabe has a Two-Thirds Majority' has the Pan Africanist Congress up in arms. It is racist, they say. It implies that black leaders with a two-thirds majority cannot be trusted. But when white leaders like Milosevic do not even allow elections, nobody says a word.

The DP is also accused of racism over their slogan: 'Fight Back.' Against whom? Against blacks, of course. They are actually saying: 'Fight Black.'

'Do you trust Thabo Mbeki with a two-thirds majority?' Tony Leon asks from every stage. People speculate that the romance between the ANC and the IFP is simply there to ensure a two-thirds majority by way of coalition. The ANC denies that it is interested in a two-thirds majority and claims that it simply wants a strong mandate from the public – it is difficult to transform a country when the opposition continually puts a spoke in the wheel. In what wheel? asks the Freedom Front. The wheels of the country have fallen off long ago. Actually, counters the ANC, all the parties are looking for a two-thirds majority, except us. 'I don't know why they are struggling so much with this issue,' says Nelson Mandela. 'I'm telling you for certain, *I* want a two-thirds majority.'

The issue gets blown up into a panic. Just think how the markets will react to a two-thirds majority. The ANC would already have achieved such a majority in the previous election, but decided to cede some seats to the IFP in KwaZulu-Natal in order to allay international concerns and curb the panic about an all-powerful black government. Meanwhile, it seems that the IEC has discovered countless ballot boxes, still neatly sealed and never counted, left over from the first election.

The IEC takes various steps to deal with possible violence. At local level, small political liaison committees, representing all parties contesting the election in an area, are put together to resolve disputes. In the end, the diversity that is South Africa has forced politicians to think more broadly than their own self-interest. They now drive on our roads, share our food, embrace our children, shake our pensioners by the hand, and suddenly seem able to speak our languages.

CHAPTER EIGHT

'SOUTH AFRICA'S FIRST DEMOCRATICALLY ELECTED PARLIAMENT will be dissolved today, to be replaced by a newly elected team after the June elections,' says Arnie Theron on the seven o'clock news, followed by a voice report: 'Parliament will be addressed for the last time today by a man who has become one of the most revered symbols of the twentieth century. Mandela's stature has changed this country's status from polecat to crown prince, as he has led the way from apartheid to negotiation, reconciliation, and learning to live together. All the important leaders in the world simply had to meet him, as well as a host of pop stars, sports heroes, beauty queens and artists. But he is also a man of the ordinary people, breaking ranks to greet those who hoped only to see him from afar. The face which for twenty-seven years was known only to prison warders has since his release in 1990 become known to millions.'

But this story is hemmed in by reports on the NATO bombing of Serbian targets in Yugoslavia. And, as so often before, people clamour for Mandela to reach out what they see as his blessing hand and rescue the situation. The British MP Tony Benn urges Mandela to intervene in the Kosovo crisis, to call for an end to the NATO air strikes and organize a peace conference. 'If Mandela asks for the bombing to stop, the world will rally behind him as they have done in the past.'

The morning's economic news suggests that it will be to the shame of European Union leaders that they have broken their promises to Mandela. Not much has come of their initial undertakings to assist and strengthen the new South African democracy through trade and development.

Our parliamentary team has also compiled a report: 'President Mandela has tea with Mrs Verwoerd, he embraces Mr Clinton, he shakes hands with Colonel Gaddafi, he stands next to Michael Jackson – yet his moral status remains intact, has become in a way untaintable. Politics is the art of the possible – this is the dictum. But the politics of Nelson Mandela is the art of the impossible – to make the impossible possible. His legacy will lie in the brilliant way he used his moral authority to achieve the impossible.'

A CD has just been released with more than twenty songs about Mandela. A TV documentary shows how his name is being seen all over the African continent on shacks, sandals, rucksacks, shopfronts, T-shirts, business cards, tracksuits, in street names, schools, universities ... A black woman interviewed in London says: 'Nobody will understand how much that man has done here for us to lift up our heads about being black and being African. He measured whites according to their own so-called yardsticks and found them wanting. He has not only become the most moral black man, he has become the most moral human being. He has shown the world that it is possible for a political leader to live according to the highest moral convictions.' A man in Holland: 'Nelson Mandela shared his charm with millions. Where most political leaders have too many enemies to go unprotected, he often broke ranks to talk to ordinary people lining the streets to see him.'

We end our report like this: 'Nelson Mandela's biggest legacy to South Africans, however, is the dignity he has restored, not only to black South Africans, but also to white South Africans. He leaves us today – a worthy, dignified nation.'

That afternoon, Mandela is in his usual place in parliament. Dressed in a fancy grey suit and tie. As always, he looks up often to the presidential box, where Graça Machel and her daughter Josina are sitting. All the young journalists are in love with Josina. When she is in the house, the press box just next to the presidential box is suddenly much fuller.

✧

A few weeks earlier, an hour-long television interview with Graça Machel was broadcast. When her car arrived at the studios there was quite a commotion, because

Mandela had unexpectedly come along. No proper security clearance had been done beforehand and for a moment everybody sat frozen as his distinctive voice sounded down the passages.

'Do not mind me, ignore me, I have just come with her because she is a little nervous.' And there he sat in the control room with the editors and producers, on a hastily fetched chair, like an ordinary husband, waving animatedly every time she looked around.

Of course, the interviewer was even more tense and, it was said afterwards, hastily omitted some of the questions about her life with Samora Machel.

'But she was such a star,' said the producer afterwards. 'She answered everything very professionally and with wonderful humour. But it was so, in a way ... *cute* to see how every time Graça gave an unexpected answer, Mandela would slap his knee in admiration, looking around triumphantly: "See! See! This is why she is my hero."'

✧

The big farewell speech is vintage Mandela. In spite of the praise songs, poems, accolades, prizes – he is what he is because of others, black and white:

'To the extent to which I was able to achieve anything, I know this is because I am the product of the people of South Africa. I am the product of the rural masses who inspired in me the pride in our past and the spirit of resistance. I am the product of the workers of South Africa, who in the mines, factories, fields and offices of our country have pursued the principle that the interests of each are founded in the common interest of all. I am the product of the South African intelligentsia of every colour, who have laboured to give our society knowledge of itself and to fashion our people's aspirations into a reasonable dream.'

Then it is time for the rest of parliament to say goodbye. The afternoon often bursts into song. The galleries are packed, even some workers pop in to have a look. The Speaker of parliament, Frene Ginwala, reminds MPs of where it all started:

'Five years ago, four hundred South Africans came together in this chamber, from different backgrounds, rural and urban, women and men, academics, professionals, manual workers, soldiers, farmers, trade unionists, former political prisoners. We were a microcosm of South African society. And yet we managed to work together and can today be proud of what has been achieved.'

'The dramatic truth lies in our spectacular growth as MPs,' says IFP member Koos van der Merwe, amidst much hilarity, 'and today we have developed into an A Team.'

'No one will ever be able to take away from me the experience of having been part of the first democratic parliament of our country,' says Douglas Gibson of the DP. 'All of us, from all parties, have been singularly blessed and privileged in being part of history.'

In their farewell speeches, only a few politicians rise to the occasion of paying tribute to the greatest leader this parliament has seen.

'Because of Mandela, the threat of civil war has been averted forever,' Tony Leon says in a wonderfully articulate speech. 'This century has thrown up three remarkable categories of political leaders. The first is "The Great and the Bad", which probably includes Hitler and Stalin. The second is "The Great and the Good", with Winston Churchill and Franklin Roosevelt. And then there is a third category. Also of "The Great", but of leaders born with a special kind of grace, who seem to transcend the politics of their age. This is a very small category and, in fact, one can only think of two or three people in this century who fall into it. Probably the Mahatma Gandhi, the Dalai Lama, and certainly Nelson Mandela. Our respect and admiration for you are unconditional, sir. You have graced this house, you have graced this country, you have graced humanity.'

Marthinus van Schalkwyk: 'Mr President, you are leaving the world a richer place for having been in this parliament. *Hamba kahle*, Madiba.'

Mangosuthu Buthelezi: 'If we can have this election without fear and intimidation, it would be the best present for President Mandela.'

The PAC's Patricia de Lille: 'Will you please promise us that if the ANC comes to you and asks you to campaign on their behalf, you will chase them away ... You, Mr President, you have spoilt them, we are all going to miss you, we all love you, but the ANC will really miss you, you have done too much for them, you have worked overtime all your life for them. One can say without fear of contradiction: we will never have another parliament like this one.'

To everyone's surprise, the president-in-waiting, Thabo Mbeki, starts his speech with a praise song, delivered in the distinctive tones of an *imbongi*:

'Madíba!

'Dalibun*ga*!

'You answered the song that was called out. You have walked the road of heroes and heroines. You have borne the pain of those who have known fear and learnt to conquer it. You have marched in front when comfort was in the midst of the ranks. And now you leave this hallowed place to continue to march in front of a different detachment of the same army of the sun.

'But despite it all and because of it all, we are blessed.

'The accident of your birth should have condemned you to a village, but you have been where you should not have been.

'You have been where nobody should be asked to be.'

✧

While I'm filing the last sound bites of Mbeki's speech to Johannesburg, a friend of mine appears in the doorway. Conrad grew up with me in Kroonstad, where we both participated in the yearly Eisteddfod. Later he left for greener singing pastures in Belgium.

'I have come to inform you about the most significant change this country has seen,' he says solemnly.

'You, an opera singer, would know about the really important changes in South Africa?'

His face is beaming with excitement. 'Do you remember in the past how the entry of the choir was the most precarious moment in a South African opera? How insecure the sound was, how the top notes were carried by has-been sopranos and wobbling Pavarotti wannabes?'

'Ja , ja.' He knows that I know, because our parents took us regularly to the operas staged in Kroonstad and Welkom.

'That has changed forever!'

The next weekend, he schleps me to meet various people involved in opera in Cape Town.

'A seminar was held in New York about the disappearance of the Verdian tenor, the male operatic voice.' This is Angelo Gobbato, an opera director and head of the Cape Town Opera. 'I put up my hand and said, "Do not despair, my friends, come to Africa, where Verdian tenors are turning up on our doorsteps in droves. I can tell you, the Verdian voice is alive and well and streaming in from the Eastern Cape." They wanted to know why. I said it's because rural South Africans do not whisper into cellphones all day or talk only over the Internet! They may not be able to read music, they may not have heard opera, but they have fully developed opera voices.'

What does it mean, to have a fully developed opera voice?

'In Western cultures, singing is something apart from day-to-day life. One sings – and then one works, or parties, or relaxes. This means that Western singers take years to get their voices ... anchored, yes, *anchored* is the word I would use, as part of their bodies.' Diva Virginia Davids, who teaches the soloists at the Opera School in Cape Town, says, 'The singers arrive here from the townships with their voices fully anchored, developed, capable of moving professionally from the chest register to the top head register, with full use of natural resonance spaces.'

But the real story, Conrad insists, started with Michael Vanyaza and Vetta Wise.

'I saw this woman directing a choir,' says Michael Vanyaza. 'And she had something I recognized instantly: passion. More than that, she could ignite her passion in her choir.'

Michael is describing the day his path crossed with that of Vetta Wise, chorus master of the very first Opera Choral Training Programme. He is sitting opposite Conrad and me in a restaurant in Sea Point. He is a quiet man, except when he is talking about the love of his heart – opera.

'I have been singing all my life. Church choirs, school choirs. My life's always moved with music. While other boys played sport in the Cape Flats townships, I hung around houses and halls from which choir music spilled. I knew all the voice parts, all the songs sung in our area.'

When, at a very young age, he became choirmaster of the Seventh Day Adventist Church choir, which he'd joined as a youngster, he felt something was lacking. 'My choir won all the competitions, but I was not satisfied. It was as if something still needed to be ... unlocked.'

It was 1990. Nelson Mandela had just been freed, the ANC unbanned. Vanyaza decided the time was ripe to go to the white suburbs to look for a choir that would take a black baritone. He found one in Rondebosch. There, one day, he heard a choir led by Vetta Wise.

'I was enthralled. The way she directed – inspiring singers to bring forth an impassioned sound. She had everything I so desperately wanted."

The other half of the story goes like this, says Conrad. Well before the first democratic election in 1994, Angelo Gobbato called in Vetta Wise to help him change the racial composition of the chorus at the Cape Town Opera. With sponsorship from Sanlam, they established the Opera Choral Training Programme to train singers from the townships and introduce them to the opera milieu. At that stage Vetta already knew Michael Vanyaza in her choir and called him in to assist the project.

And the doors were unlocked.

Despite almost no advertising about the audition, the morning the doors of the State Theatre were pushed open, more than five hundred hopeful black singers were waiting outside. Word of mouth alone had brought them flocking in; without sheet music, with no knowledge of staff notation, scales or aural testing, they stood nervously next to their suitcases, blankets and food parcels.

Another audition was held in Port Elizabeth. 'I was hanging out in the township, playing ball, when a friend asked, "Why aren't you auditioning? The opera people from Cape Town are here."' Mthunzi Mbombela ran down the road, auditioned, and later received a call to come to Cape Town and study opera. 'My mother asked, "Hey, what is this *opera*?" and I said, "Opera is Pavarotti!" Pavarotti is all we knew, you see.'

Six of the first twenty singers were recruited from the Eastern Cape and they were soon on a bus to Cape Town to study opera for a year. Meanwhile, the Training Programme linked up with the Department of Labour in the Western Cape, which pays a subsidy of R1 500 per month per unemployed person for training. Opera training? Well ... training is training. The students were set up at the YMCA and provided with food, transport and extensive voice training.

It was hard work. They were taught how to move on stage in evening suits and ball gowns, how to clink glasses of champagne, feign conversation and silent laughter, how to embrace or sit or lie down, with diaphragm ready to keep on singing, how to carry the body as part of the voice instrument. Students learnt notation, how to read orchestral music scores, and how to pronounce German, Italian, Latin and French.

'The most important thing is to train the ear,' says one of the accompanists. 'Traditional African music does not work in the same way with the Western scale – half notes are treated in a different way. Just as Western music battles with the quarter notes of Eastern music. The ear must be trained to place the voice there. Plus, such a lot of singing is done a cappella in the townships, students are not used to pitching their voices to an orchestra. It is also hard to sing and act, while at the same time keeping an eye on a conductor whose movements don't all have to do with you directly. It is hours and hours of hard work. I sometimes spend a whole hour teaching a soloist five bars of music!'

Miranda Tini says: 'It is like you have been driving a car all your life and suddenly you are being taught the mechanical parts and the functioning of the gears and steering wheel. Now you have to adhere strictly to a specific code of driving. Where once it was free and easy, it now becomes hard concentration. In the beginning it completely exhausted me. Every note has to be thought about: where to place it, how to produce it, how soft to make it, how to support it. For women it is even harder, because in African traditional music we often produce our top notes in our throats. But the throat must be completely relaxed to allow the sound to float to the resonance spaces in your head.'

That evening, we see Miranda Tini in a production of *Lucia di Lammermoor*, with an imported Lucia singing her famous aria of derangement while making love to a table (or so it appeared to us). We notice Miranda moving forward slightly on stage to watch this Lucia with calculating eyes. To do it like her one day ... or to do it differently?

What's it like to be on stage for the first time? Michael Vanyaza smiles. 'When I walked on to that stage and started to sing, my heart wanted to burst. I just knew that my whole life, everything I was and had dreamed about, had led me to this specific moment.

'The other day in *Un Ballo in Maschera*, when Virginia Davids walked past me on stage and I heard her incredibly beautiful voice just soaring above the chorus, I wanted to cry, because we as the chorus were carrying her ... carrying her ...'

From the start of the Training Programme, Michael knew he did not have a solo voice. But he knew someone else who did. 'When Vetta and Prof. Gobbato came to me about recruiting black singers, I said I knew who should be first. I knew this man with the most remarkable voice, who was jobless and drifting through the streets. Whenever I saw him somewhere, desperate or exhausted or drunk, I thought: that body is housing one of the most wondrous voices of this country.'

This is how Fikile Mvinjelwa entered the Choral Training Programme. But when Gobbato heard him, he took him straight to the Opera School at the University of Cape Town to receive solo training. Since then Mvinjelwa has sung many major roles, among them the leads in *Rigoletto*, *Love and Green Onions*, *Porgy and Bess*, *Lucia di Lammermoor* and *Aida*.

'But why would you describe it as a significant change when black people do white people's things better than white people themselves?' I ask Conrad.

'Two reasons. Firstly, it's not that black singers are singing better than whites, it's that the influx of black singers has changed the face and sound of South African opera forever. The moment the chorus enters, the opera goes into a completely new dimension, it suddenly has a new energy – a unique energy. This energy is now shared with everybody. It no longer has to do with black or white, it's an opening up, an *enrichment* of something for the benefit of all of us, if you'll pardon the highfalutin term. And secondly, opera is generally loved for its famous solos, duets and quartets, but the sheer strength of the chorus now brings something different into opera: the "people's voice". While "the poor" have always been a presence in opera, they were usually linked to the hero or heroine, but through this unique energy, opera has gained a political relevancy never encountered before in the world, I would say. And I can't tell you how much I like that.'

The chorus master tells us that opera lovers from around the world come to Cape Town to hear with their own ears these operas performed by mainly jobless township recruits. The choir is on a par with that of the Metropolitan Opera in New York, is what the Met's chorus master said during his last visit. 'And you must remember that at the Met hundreds of singers come from all over the world to audition for a single position in the chorus,' says Conrad.

Although the opera house is very close to the Houses of Parliament, black MPs are not seen in the audience. Does it bother the singers that the audience is largely white?

'Not really,' says Michael Vanyaza. 'When I see them, I know what CDs they are listening to, and I know we are giving them better than they can get on most of those discs.' He grins.

But it does bother Mthunzi Mbombela. 'Only a black person will know exactly what it took for me to be there. I suspect people think we are just these natural-born talents, and we walk on stage and simply do our thing.'

Miranda Tini is too nervous to notice the audience, but she would like it if the reviews were sometimes written by a black person. However, family and friends are invited to dress rehearsals, packing out the theatre with an audience deeply involved in the plot, thanks to English surtitles. 'Don't think, when they boo, that they don't like the singing. They boo the bad guys and give wild cheers for the hero – whistles and comments when he embraces the heroine.

'I invite these people living in the flats next to us to the rehearsals,' says Miranda, who shares a flat with a soprano. 'They've heard us turn our opera CDs up to full volume and sing with the music. Now when they come for the real thing, they like it. They jump up from their seats, they shout, they go wild.'

The people who share a flat with Mthunzi do not understand why he doesn't smoke and drink. 'When your violin or piano breaks, you can buy another one. My body and vocal cords are all that I've got. Before a performance I'm very quiet, because I go through the whole opera in my head. The day afterwards I hardly talk because my voice must rest.'

Cape Town opera abounds with pavement-to-stage stories: the street-sweeper of Mowbray now studying at UCT, the trolley-pusher at Gardens Centre who joined the Choral Training Programme in January. Then there is Kaiser Nkosi, on his way to Munich with his unbelievable interpretation of Mozart; Abel Motsoadi at the Juilliard School; Maria Jooste, the tall white girl who sings like a black woman and is wanted in Bayreuth. There are also those as popular on overseas stages as here: Sidwell Hartman and Virginia Davids.

'I knew I was good, but I lacked the stability which only knowledge can bring. Vetta Wise and the others have filled those gaps for me.' Michael Vanyaza nods his head.

Miranda Tini walks along the backstage passages of the Artscape Theatre to rehearsal. Orchestral music rises from somewhere deep inside the building, we hear singers practising a duet. A group of dancers in the forthcoming production of *Cats* drifts by. Miranda turns around to us: 'Sometimes I get tears in my eyes, because I cannot believe ... my life is so beautiful.'

CHAPTER NINE

AND THEN, IN THE LAST WEEKS before the election, Thabo Mbeki and Tony Leon decide to visit the same town on the same day: Kroonstad. I plead with those in charge to take me off the Mandela election trail and please, please, please allow me to do the story for radio. The day before the visit, the television news bosses call me in. In the spirit of the Bi-media Project, would I please do the story for television? Radio has already agreed and appointed Joseph Mosia to report for the English and Sesotho services. The Great Bi-media Project, for those who don't know, requires that journalists double up on reporting for radio and television in the interests of stretching scarce resources.

My blood pressure leaps up a couple of points. But I know absolutely nothing about television! 'Yes, we realize that. But you know Kroonstad well, so do what you think is necessary and we'll prepare it here for television. Make sure you're here tomorrow at seven to pick up your cameraman.'

I do not sleep a wink. I am well aware of the impressive list of Kroonstad's famous and infamous sons and daughters. Many important politicians spent their childhood in Kroonstad – Ivy Matsepe-Casaburri, for instance, whose father, Dan Matsepe, was a famous educationist and had a street in the coloured neighbourhood named after him. Brigadier Oupa Gqozo of the Ciskei was born there. Also Alwyn Schlebusch, the Kroonstad MP who later became Minister of Justice and Deputy President. Mosiuoa 'Terror' Lekota, now Minister of Defence, and Ds Nico Smith, the first white dominee to go and live in a township, cut their adolescent teeth in Kroonstad. Clements Kadalie chose to make one of his political statements there, when he had his followers board the whites-only section of a train (they were thrown off at Rooiwal). The parents of Gill Marcus lived in Kroonstad once upon a time. So did some important journalists: Max du Preez, the famous *Sunday Times* editor Joel Mervis, Sello Thulo of SABC radio. Several writers made their home there, among them my mother Dot Serfontein; Chrissie Euvrard, who won the first Hertzog Prize; and the poet Peter Blum, who worked in the Kroonstad Library for a time. Pallo Jordan's famous father, the writer A.C. Jordan, was a teacher in Kroonstad, and saw to it that the girl who had caught his eye at Fort Hare University, the aristocratic Phyllis Ntantala, got the English post at the Bantu School in the town. In her book *A Life's Mosaic*, she dedicates an entire chapter to Kroonstad, describing the most important coloured and black families, the state of education and the overwhelming superstitiousness that existed among black and white alike, ensuring a stream of visitors to the sangomas in the township.

Mandela even talks about Kroonstad in *Long Walk to Freedom*. Just after he had passed his driver's test, he was asked to take valuable information to the ANC leader Dr J.S. Moroka: 'On my way down to Thaba 'Nchu I passed through Kroonstad, a conservative Free State town about 120 miles south of Johannesburg. I was driving up a hill and saw two white boys ahead of me on bicycles. My driving was still a bit unsteady, and I came too close to them, one of whom suddenly made a turn without signalling, and we collided. He was knocked off his bicycle and was groaning when I got out of the car to help him. He had his arms out, indicating that I should pick him up, but just as I was about to do so, a white truck-driver yelled for me not to touch the boy. The truck-driver scared the child, who then dropped his arms as though he did not want me to pick him up. The boy was not badly hurt, and the truck-driver took him to the police station, which was close by.

'The local police arrived a short time later, and the white sergeant took one look at me and said, *"Kaffer, jy sal kak vandag!"* ("Kaffir, you will shit today!") I was shaken by the accident and the violence of his words, but I told him in no uncertain terms that I would shit when I pleased, not when a policeman told me to. At this, the sergeant took out his notebook to record my particulars. Afrikaans policemen were surprised if a black man could speak English, much less answer back.'

All this mills through my head. During the Boer War, after the fall of Bloemfontein, Kroonstad became the capital of the Orange Free State when President Steyn temporarily made it his seat of power. It was at a meeting held at the old market that the Boers decided to implement their guerrilla-war strategy. How do I get all of this said?

The next morning, I arrive at the television news office just in time to hear various cameramen steadfastly refusing to go with 'a woman who knows nothing about television'. One of them says furiously, 'I am not here to teach amateurs their work,' and marches past me. I am ordered to go and wait outside at the SABC car. Joseph Mosia is already there. Jeez, all I wanted was to do a nice story on Kroonstad and now I sit with a whole television drama in my lap. A scowling young black woman comes storming out and introduces herself as Thandeka. Cameras, packs, tapes, tripods are loaded in and we are on our way. Mbeki will be in Kroonstad in the afternoon, and Leon in the evening. We could possibly use the time before to film some well-known places in the town, interview some long-time residents.

'I also just want to stop off at my mother's,' says Joseph. My day is made. Kroonstad will have *two* former residents to put its story in the news today. We are excited, we trade names and dates. Joseph grew up in the poorest section of the township, joined Umkhonto we Sizwe and went into exile in Lusaka.

Between Rooiwal and Kroonstad I pull over and ask Thandeka to film the white-frosted mealie fields, bleached grass and grain silos in the distance.

'Why?'

'Because this situates the story in the mealie plains of the northern Free State, one sees it is winter and it is cold.'

'This is a story dealing with two political leaders, and you want to ... *situate* it with nature shots?' She scratches her head irritatedly with long, manicured nails.

Now I may not know anything about television, but I know how to tell a story, and I will not let myself be told what to do by a youngster. 'Yes,' I say.

Very slowly she gets out, very slowly she stretches herself, very slowly she takes out the camera, peels the cellophane off a new tape without putting her nails in any danger whatsoever, very slowly she loads the cassette.

'If you could move from the silos towards the town and perhaps end with a shot of the thorn trees,' I say.

'I know my job. You stick to yours and I will do mine.'

I get back into the car. At the sandstone-coloured bridge that spans the green winter water like a great bow, we pull over again.

'I want the reeds, and this particular colour of water – it is the only river in the country with this colour. Also try to include the wintry poplars and willows on the other side.'

'Is this what you regard as the entrance to the town?' asks Joseph.

'Absolutely. When I cross this, my heart lifts. For you not?'

'No. That narrow, meandering tar road past Boitumelo Hospital tells me I'm home.'

Thandeka films everything with the resentment of someone who knows that her time is being cruelly wasted. She trains her camera on the sandstone *moederkerk*, which, the architectural guides tell us, is pinned to the big green island of the town centre like a golden jewel. She starts at the statue of Sarel Cilliers atop a cannon, his hand raised as he takes the Blood River Oath. She focuses at length on a group of black people sitting eating on the lawn and then pans over to the church with its copper roof. We drive up the main street, down through the subway underneath the railway line.

The subway closes off the town with a sandstone collar, behind which the township lies in the winter sun and icy breeze. Thandeka trains her camera on the plain of thorn trees, on the many-coloured rustling of plastic bags blown into the branches. Taxis crossing in between.

Joseph conducts radio interviews with the descendants of the well-known educationist, Dr Reginald Cingo, the very man who offered teaching posts to the Jordans so many years ago. Thandeka sleeps in the car.

✧

It is after lunch when the triumphant ANC cavalcade of Thabo Mbeki goes wailing through this town of words and politics to the Dinoheng informal settlement. Thousands are waiting. The police make space for him, get him on to the back of a 4x4, but he is clearly in for a tough time. He has to deliver his speech through a loudhailer. He has to speak English because he can't really speak Sesotho. Packed in with him on the bakkie are several arch-enemies: candidate for Free State premier, Winkie Direko; leading ANC member in the province, Ace Magashule; and white ANC member, Tony Khoury. Some bodyguards are up there too. Limpho Hani and Bridget Mabandla stand close by, as well as a man carrying a hockey stick and another one wearing a Basotho hat.

Mbeki tries his best, but apart from 'Amandla!' nothing really resonates. I am surprised at how unprepared political leaders are when they come to small rural towns, each with its own unique history and codes of honour. Thousands of people have lived their lives here over the centuries, their horizons carved by the northern Free State plains and sky, their dreams and sorrows wafted through by the smell of river and reed. How can Kroonstad be just another town on the list of the day, how can its people be no more than election fodder? Don't we deserve at least to be reminded that we are special, that we should feel proud of our town, not because the president-in-waiting is visiting us, but because he wants to visit us for who we are, who we have been and what we so desperately want to be.

Mbeki's next stop is the Delswa clothing factory, where scores of women sing and dance as he passes between the rows of workbenches: 'Holomisa is closing doors, Mbeki opens them.' I wonder whether Thandeka is getting the swaying bodies of the ululating women, framed by rails of ridiculously neat little twinsets. Some of them even draped in scarves and cheap pearls.

I run with Thandeka to Mbeki's car for a sound bite, but his bodyguards are immovable. He is to address a European Union delegation tonight before flying to Japan and he still has to do five other towns on the way back to Johannesburg. Mbeki waves smilingly at us from behind his bulletproof window.

Meanwhile at the other end of town the Democratic Party is preparing for the visit of Tony Leon later that evening. The old town hall has been opened up and dusted off.

This sandstone hall opposite the *moederkerk* nearly bankrupted the town council a hundred years ago. Architecturally it incorporates several styles and was one of the first buildings in the Free State to have a big, spouting fishpond with lamenting women rising from the water. Since the completion of the new civic centre complex with its modern chambers it has been hard to find any use for this stern building, which once hosted the annual Eisteddfods and endless church bazaars.

The DP hired the old town hall from the Witnesses of Christ. Various placards – 'Pastor Danny can heal you', 'God answers knee-mail' – christening troughs and pulpits have been removed and replaced by the DP's own paraphernalia. Tony Leon has a special vehicle, the 'Battle Bus', which drives ahead to the places he is to visit. The stage is set up in exactly the same way over and over again, following the special design of his campaign advisors. Leon is fairly short and a bit skinny. He is also rather pale. This is effectively countered by hanging an enormous, well-tanned image of him in the background. To make sure that he is not obscured by the lectern, the 'Battle Bus' carries with it a custom-made perspex lectern behind which he can stand fully embodied, as it were. No trust is placed in problematic local PA systems. The last time such crystal-clear and finely nuanced decibels passed through the space of this hall must have been during the special performance by soprano Erna Sack fifty years ago.

We arrive at the hall at the same time as an enormous truck filled to capacity with black people – clearly farm workers. 'Where do you come from?' I ask. 'From Baas André Botha's farm,' they say.

The Bothas, together with the Kleynhanses, Geldenhuyses and Serfonteins, are among the oldest white families in the area. A decade before the Great Trek, they settled along the Valsch River because the land as far as Winburg was directly under Moshoeshoe's jurisdiction. But the Bothas distinguished themselves early on as people with broader perspectives and more refined insights than the rambunctious and contrary inhabitants further upriver. When a teacher from Kroonstad was dismissed for claiming that the earth is round, the Bothas took him into service to tutor their children. When Kroonstad's transport riders called a bellicose meeting to try and prevent the new railway line from running through the town, the Bothas went and asked if the line could run past their property. When the Boer War was raging, and Kroonstad families found themselves in a concentration camp with one of the highest death rates, the Bothas were travelling from commando to commando trying to convince their countrymen of the absolute short-sightedness of fighting a war against the most powerful country in the world. The Bothas, one could say, have always been regarded as one step ahead of Kroonstad.

Inside, the hall is already packed. I recognize them: the butcher, the veterinarian, most of the attorneys, the doctors, and several young farmers. Thandeka says that she actually cannot film any more, because she didn't bring any lights with her. She was told that she would be back in Johannesburg by dark. With envy I watch Joseph moving around with his tape recorder, doing interviews and grabbing sound bites. How on earth can people work for television? How do two people put together one story?

Suddenly the great march from *Aida* explodes from the sound system and in comes Tony Leon, followed by a troop of young black people with banners and flags and balloons. Thandeka runs off to retrieve the camera from the boot of the car: the 'Battle Bus' has made provision for the fact that the (government-friendly) television crew will never have enough lights for the DP. The hall is aglow, as if bathed in sunlight, and the enthusiasm is deafening. Leon is a master of coinage, precise in articulation and in content. But apart from wrestling courageously through two paragraphs of Afrikaans, he also gives no indication that Kroonstad, like the twenty towns before and after, has its own unique history and inhabitants.

The young blacks in the audience give him a standing ovation. They are fed up with corruption and incompetence, they say after the event. The government is lazy and too comfortable in its power.

We drive back to Johannesburg. Thandeka passes me the tapes and wishes me a cordial good luck.

✧

That night I work out the text and decide what footage to use where. The next morning I am ready with my pages and my tapes, only to witness the latest row at the news offices. Doors slam, people storm out, are ordered back hysterically, and all that I can make out is that nobody has time to put together an amateur's patchwork. While this is carrying on, the news editor pats me soothingly on the arm. 'Don't let it get to you, it's always like this here. Each television journalist has his own editor, so it's difficult to work with anybody the first time.'

After an hour, a sobbing woman runs past me. A man who is white around the mouth hisses at me through his teeth, 'Come with me.' In the editing room he says, 'I have nothing against you, it is that bitch who can't organize anything.' He throws my tape in the machine and winds quickly through it, cutting out pieces here and there.

'Wait!' I say. 'Those parts are essential in order to situate Kroonstad.'

He keeps quiet for a few seconds. Then he bites his lower lip and says in measured tones, 'Give me your text.' He reads. Then he says, 'This paragraph here is too long, and this one. Cut it down to a single sentence. Meanwhile, I'll take out the usable footage.'

I creep away. It seems to me he wants to cut out everything meaningful and distinctive about Kroonstad. I take my substantially thinned and mediocre text back to him.

'Apart from the sound bites of Mbeki and Leon, none of the footage you brought back is useful.'

I try to explain about the church and the silos. He looks at his watch. 'It's lunchtime.'

I go off to record my voice-overs. After two he returns.

'I don't see your story on the broadcast schedule for tonight.'

I search through the endless maze of offices. Find the news editing office. No, the one who gave me the assignment is already off duty. The new one pouts his lips. 'Kroonstad? ... we've already done enough small-town stories.'

'Visited on the same day by two major political leaders?'

'So what?'

'So can I go back to radio and let this go?'

He nods.

Back in the radio office I hear Joseph's beautiful report, filled with sounds and songs and interviews. I start translating his story for the Afrikaans service. Somebody comes running in.

'Where's your Kroonstad story? Mrs Matsepe-Casaburri is from Kroonstad and she's very excited that you are doing it.'

Everything shifts into top gear. And completely out of my hands. Everybody helps. Now it seems that there is too little footage. Somebody rushes down to Archives to check what is available on Kroonstad. Why don't you bring in the prominent figures produced by Kroonstad? 'I did, but was told to cut it out.'

Just minutes before the eight o'clock news, the poor three-minute segment is finished and packaged and delivered, complete with subtitles.

My family calls: 'Heard you were in town yesterday. We are packed in front of the television.'

I watch the entire news bulletin. No Kroonstad story. The telephone on my desk rings: 'You know, unfortunately we had to can the story. The newsreader's interview with Constand Viljoen was too long. Maybe we'll use it tonight at eleven.'

After the bulletin at eleven I phone the news studio. 'Which Kroonstad story?' the man asks.

chapter ten

She is standing on the back of the bakkie. She holds on to the bars as if she is in the prow of a ship. The wind thrashes her face. She keeps her knees and hips slack to absorb the bumps. Her head and shoulders are dead still while she peers out over the plains, the flocks of sheep, the endless mealie fields fanning open into green troughs as the bakkie moves forward. She reigns over the earth and the sea and everything in it. When they pass the huts of the workers, her father slows down. Suddenly he stops. At Isak Mokokoane's hut, right in the front door, stands Hendrik, her younger brother.

But he is not simply standing, he is leaning against the frame of the door. In one hand he is holding a tin mug, with the other he waves calmly to all of them in the bakkie. On his face is a slight smile, as if they are strangers to him. Her father drives on towards the farmyard, but inside the cab she can see her parents fighting. When the bakkie stops again, she starts hearing.

'He looks at home. He is standing there as if it is his own home. He should be forbidden to go there.'

'You are overreacting,' says her father, 'the child is five years old. Isak's children are his friends. He plays with them.'

'Ja, and who else has family who've simply moved in with blacks?'

Have done *what*? She gets down from the back of the bakkie and goes up to the window.

'Go and fetch your brother,' says her father.

'But perhaps he is happy there,' she says sweetly.

'I am not asking you again. And if he is unhappy with us, then just maybe it is because he has an insufferable, big-mouthed elder sister picking on him all the time.'

Her school life passes in a haze. In class, she sits sunken behind her thick glasses and plaits, in her strange Harley Street shoes and heavy serge gymslip. Her head is swirling. She was invited to stay over last night at the house of the girl sitting next to her: Cathy Taylor. She didn't want to go, but her mother was so obviously delighted that she had a friend at last, that she went. Cathy's mother called them to run a bath. She was horrified. She had never bathed with anybody before. She had to take off her large cotton panties while Cathy simply kicked off a tiny nylon item. They were just settling in the bath when Cathy asked, 'Do you want to see bubbles?' and before she could answer, Cathy gave several powerful farts, hammering them out against the enamel, from where they shot up in distinct bubbles. When she came to her senses she was hanging suspended like a spider over the bath, her feet on the sides, her body flooded with repugnance, while Cathy burst out laughing. Now she cannot bear to look at Cathy. She gets up and timidly asks the teacher whether she can be moved forward in the classroom because she cannot see well on the blackboard.

She is moved next to a girl with the name of Rina.

Rina has strange, wonderful things in her school bag. A leotard and ballet shoes. Rina goes to ballet every afternoon and dances so long that her feet start bleeding. Every evening she has to put her feet in a bowl of spirits to harden her skin. She brings a special bottle of milk to school to strengthen her bones. Rina's parents live in a small town somewhere. During the week she stays with her grandfather and grandmother so that she can take ballet. Sometimes Rina turns up at school with blue bruises on her upper thighs. She never talks about it, she simply pulls her gymslip down over her legs.

Miss Erasmus sends her to take the register of the week to the office. As she's walking back to class, she hears the teacher's monotonous voice. She turns to go to the toilet. Opposite the toilets is a room with the door standing open. She sees it is empty and the floor is cool and clean. She goes in and closes the door. She takes off her shoes, spreads her toes and imagines herself dancing, floating.

The next day after break when the heat sets in, she tells Rina that the choir teacher wants to see the two of them. Miss Erasmus lets them go. She pulls Rina into the empty room. 'But you lied,' Rina's eyes are big. 'I want you to teach me ballet,' she says. Rina shows her how to place her feet, then how to hold her arm, slightly bent, with the wrist turned. Her fingers delicately inclining towards one another.

Under the guise of choir practice, they go twice a week, and then, as the Eisteddfod draws nearer, every day. She and Rina now dance several steps together. They take off their gymslips and dance barefoot in their shirts. Rina binds up their hair with pink Alice bands. They dance in vests and panties. Later they start to dance stories. They bring long, soft nighties from their mothers' cupboards, petticoats, muslin cloths, tea nets. Every day they develop their stories further, dying of love, celebrating victory, conquering enemies and wild men.

They do not hear the sound of high heels coming down the passage. It is only when she opens the door that they come to their senses, and find themselves facing Miss Erasmus's pale face and the red blotches spreading all over her neck. She tears the cloths from them and chases them back to class, where she ignores them for the rest of the day.

The next morning she and Rina are ordered to the principal's office. 'Explain to me!' he says sternly.

'Sir, it's like this,' she is surprised at her steady voice, 'we usually go to choir practice, it was only that yesterday the practice was cancelled, so we thought since it is nearly one o'clock ...'

'Stop lying to me!' he yells, and his face turns a purplish red. 'I can't believe my ears, you are ten years old and you lie through your teeth like this. Get out,' he roars, 'get out of my office!'

They go back to class. Neither says a word.

Her mother says nothing when she comes to pick her up. That evening she is called to the rondavel. 'You will go to the principal tomorrow and ask for pardon that (a) you bunked school and (b) you lied to him about it. Then you will ask the teacher for pardon that (a) you bunked school and (b) you lied to her about it. And finally you will go to the choir teacher and ask for pardon that you abused her in this way. Do I make myself clear?'

'Did you get a hiding?'

Rina whispers back, 'No, but my mother came from Wesselsbron yesterday and your mother came to see her.'

The next term, both she and Rina are transferred to the other school in Kroonstad and sent to live in the hostel. For weeks she paces the corner of the hostel grounds stretching towards the farm, bewildered by the crowding together of so many girls, the invasion of smells and sounds, the horror of sharing intimate space, the bluntness of mass-prepared food.

In the new school she has been separated from Rina and finds herself on a constant edge of naked fear. Her teacher, Miss Pels, displays flashes of uncontrolled behaviour that she is quite unaccustomed to.

'Esmeralda, please stand.'

Hesitantly, Esmeralda rises to her feet.

'You see class, Esmeralda will never have to pluck her eyebrows. Never. And that is a blessing from God.'

She notices that her other classmates seem equally dumbfounded. What exactly is 'eyebrow plucking'? And why would the rest of them have to do it?

Then Miss Pels pulls Cornelissen up from his desk. 'Look at him! Look at him, standing there with his mouth open, the spit dripping on his shirt, his mother is bedridden, his father in jail and now I,' she clutches her throat with both hands, 'yes *I* have to get him through Standard Three!' Then she spins around like a wounded person, wailing up to God to help her, for He is the only One who knows that she cannot continue by herself.

On another day she storms at Olaf Dreyer, a thin pale limping boy who had polio as a toddler, and pushes his head towards the floor, shouting, 'Look there, look there at the floor, what is it that you see there? Now stay there, because that is where you want to look all the time, instead of at the blackboard.' When Olaf comes up, blood is running from his torn ear.

She does her homework meticulously. She remembers Miss Pels's tricks for spelling *onmiddellik* and *interessant*, she learns to use pen and ink without ever blotting, she gets a hundred per cent for Maths and History. By the end of the term she is first in her class, and so is Rina in hers.

It is midnight. She slips the record from its Deutsche Grammophon cover. Something is hanging inside her, something unformulated, something like anguish, but bordering on a kind of excitement, a loose abundance surging with an immense yearning. She doesn't know what it is. She is longing for something to happen.

Her eyes are tired of reading. She has decided to put on one of her mother's records which she always sees lying around in the rondavel when she comes back from school. Along with the record, the libretto slips out. She reads the explanatory notes on the cover, then drops the needle on the last cut of Side 2. The piano starts, and she is plucked in by an intense frenzy. She follows the words on the page.

The first bars are astonishing, not only in their frantic movement but also in their spaciousness. She is no longer a mere listener, she is pulled in immediately, dramatically, as witness to an event. The first verse of *Der Erlkönig*, she sees, is in the present tense: who goes there?

Wer reitet so spät durch Nacht und Wind?
Es ist der Vater mit seinem Kind;
Er hat den Knaben wohl in dem Arm
Er fasst ihn sicher, er hält ihn warm.

Who's riding so late where winds blow wild?
It is the father grasping his child;
He holds the boy embraced in his arm
He clasps him snugly, he keeps him warm.

She hears the question. She sees the father. She notes that the word 'father' and the word 'arm' are on either side of the 'child': the father holds the child warm and secure in his arms. The protection is complete. She plunges with them through a moving landscape to the rhythm of beating hoofs and anxious hearts. With them, she is brushed by branches, she catches glimpses of uncertain things passing. The pace and pulse are feverish.

But the child is restless. The father picks it up. Why do you move in my arms as if you are scared? He asks: '*Mein Sohn, was birgst du so bang dein Gesicht?*' My son, why do you hide your face so fearfully? The explanatory notes say that the poet Goethe is describing the possessiveness, the uncontested claim of a father/son relationship, the celebration of reason and unquestionable authority, in these two words: 'My son.'

She hears the frightened voice of the child: '*Siehst, Vater, du den Erlkönig nicht? / Den Erlenkönig mit Kron und Schweif?*' Schweif? She sees the translation says 'tail'. The Elf King with crown and tail. What is this ... king, this thing with a tail? But the father assures her in Dietrich Fischer-Dieskau's comforting voice that it is nothing but a streak of mist: '*Mein Sohn, es ist ein Nebelstreif.*'

And they are into the third verse. She picks up yet another tone produced by Fischer-Dieskau. He has been the narrator, the father, the son, but now he is the Erlkönig himself: 'Child, come and play on the beach with me. My mother has a lot of clothes.' The voice takes on a kind of falsetto, an extra lilt in the vowels, an extra lure in the 'l': '*Du liebes Kind, komm, geh mit mir! / Gar schöne Spiele spiel ich mit dir.*'

'The child sees an enticing, magical, powerful world along the road, but the father not,' the notes say. 'He proclaims confidently that it's merely a patch of mist. Things exist only insofar as they form part of the Father's frame of reference. The father is authority, he is reason and intellect. He is stern and sober, warm and comforting.'

She sits up very straight on the carpet of sewn-together springbok skins. She feels her whole body growing taller, as if she's shooting up from her hips. She is experiencing all of this by herself. She recognizes the authoritarian tone, the seduction. Her breathing becomes shallow as she rests her ear against the radiogram. The son is in a panic. She knows it more by the piercing minor ninths of the piano at 'Mein Vater, Mein Vater,' than by the words themselves. My father, do you not hear what the Erlkönig is promising me?

'The child sings in a light voice, trembling with insecurity. The father hears only the child. The child, in contrast, hears the father as well as the Erlkönig. But the father is in control. The father knows everything. The father deals with everything. What the child sees as menacing, enticing, strange, is a mere rustle of dry leaves.'

She breaks out in goosebumps. She hears the father singing, 'In dürren Blättern säuselt der Wind.' The wind is rustling in the dry leaves. The piano accompanies him with such suddenly formal traditional harmonies that she knows instinctively it is a lie. The notes say: 'The father is trying to bring the other voice, the unknown voice, under his control. He uses the traditional to establish his control over the "other conversation". Very little is left by now of the minor key in which the composition started, and the different voices pull everybody through a variety of keys in flailing attempts to arrive back at the original key.'

The Erlkönig speaks. He no longer uses 'dear child', but 'fine boy'. Her heart beats faster. This Erlkönig simply transgresses everything she is and was: this sleeping farmyard, this stone house, her life here in the middle of the night. The Erlkönig has no gender, no border, no age, no place, no weather, no physicality ... The son shrieks and points to a dark place filled with figures. But the father puts his foot down: 'Mein Sohn, mein Sohn,' it is the grey glow of old willow trees.

The father explains everything but sees nothing, acknowledges everything but understands nothing, promises everything but guarantees nothing.

The Erlkönig is undeterred. He throws his cards on the table. Forget the nice terms like 'child' or 'boy', he openly states: 'Ich liebe dich, mich reizt deine schöne Gestalt,' I love you, I breathlessly yearn for your beautiful body. I am in a kind of ecstasy about how beautiful you are, and if you do not submit willingly, I will use violence – and Fischer-Dieskau's voice on the word 'Gewalt' (violence), rhyming with 'Gestalt' (body), is heavy with desire and evil.

In panic-stricken chords, the son calls to the father to hold him tight.

The final blow: 'Erlkönig hat mir ein Leid's getan!' He has done me grief. It is already too late. The demands of the outside world have brought an end.

'The piano lunges passionately towards other keys in tones of desperate grief, it hangs on to a major key in one final effort of hope against hope, before it falls back to the original key. Fischer-Dieskau's voice on the word "grauset's" (gripped by fear) indicates that the father is realizing for the first time that he is up against something beyond his control. He holds in his arms the "ächzende Kind" (the delirious child).'

But when he arrives at the house, in his arms the child is ... (and she waits for

Fischer-Dieskau to sing the last word without any vibration in his voice, clean and void of emotion) ... dead.

She bends forward on her knees. Dead. Oh, how she is dying for that death.

She puts the needle back at the beginning and turns up the volume. She listens like someone possessed. On the record cover she reads: 'Goethe wrote his famous ballad *Erlkönig* after visiting friends on a farm. During a stormy night, he heard a horse's hoofs passing the house. His friends told him in the morning that it was a father rushing off to find help for his ailing child.

'Franz Schubert was barely seventeen years old when he composed the music for *Erlkönig*. He published the song as his Opus One, and it is still regarded as the most remarkable first work in musical history – this piece of scare-mongering, which, over centuries, has retained the power to chill the blood.'

She plays it again – this time with the volume at full blast. And again. Again. Suddenly everything goes dark. The lights have gone out. It is quiet. She sits motionless. She is not scared. She waits. Nothing happens.

Someone must have switched off the mains to stop the sound. Outside the rondavel are crickets; far-off, a commando bird. She puts everything away and goes to bed. Her feet feathered.

Saturday afternoon. The Peugeot is the only car on the endless road. It feels as if the whole world is sleeping or playing tennis in slow, lazy strokes. Behind the wheel is Isak Mokokoane. The two of them are making their way over the vast plains of veld for an hour's violin lesson in Odendaalsrus, a nearby mining town. Isak sings to himself, low and monotonous. He sings a song with long intervals between verses:

O ya kae Monyankwane
O ya kae Monyankwane
O nkile kojwana tsa hao le dieta

Mampa-tona le Rampa-tona tafoleng
Mampa-tona le Rampa-tona tafoleng

She doesn't know what it means. 'I learnt it from my elder brother, Abel Jonkman,' he answered evasively when she asked him once. 'Your father and I used to sing it when the red whirlwinds came out over the dry veld.'

'Blow!' her mother says.

She cannot believe what she's hearing. She stares at her mother. They are standing beside a sweet-thorn tree in the veld, in the stem of which her mother has just carved a deep cut with her biltong knife. At eye level.

'How do you mean, blow?'

'Block one nostril with your finger and blow with the other one into the cut.'

'Let me get this straight,' she says in disbelief, 'you want me to blow snot into that cut?'

'Yes,' says her mother, 'the woman in Potchefstroom, who heals people by merely laying her hands on them, said that she knew of no one who was not healed from hay fever after performing this ritual.'

She looks at her mother as if she has seen a ghost. It was a bit strange, this invitation to go for a walk, and her mother putting her knife in her apron pocket. And when she asked, thinking she was being funny, is this now the feminine version of Abraham and Isaac, her mother even smiled slightly.

'And then what?'

'Then you do the same with the other nostril, and I bandage the cut with one of your vests, and then you will never have hay fever in your life again.'

'You're not really serious?' But her mother's face indicates that she is more than that, she is determined.

'Come, let us get it over with.'

She sniffs, turns on her heel and walks away. Her mother catches her from behind and drags her towards the tree. They are shouting at each other. She pulls loose and runs away across the veld, her mother shouting, 'So scared, so scared you are to set foot outside your tiny bloody brain!'

CHAPTER ELEVEN

AT THE SABC, radio and television live in two separate buildings. The entrance halls of the buildings differ like night and day. At radio, bedraggled figures sit among important works of art drinking endless cups of coffee. Only when somebody talks or laughs in passing does one recognize the famous voice and think in amazement: is this the man who reads the news every morning with such authority, this little fellow with the pampered moustache and civil-service hair? Is this the woman who sounds so young and sexy in the evenings, this blimp rowing past like that with her mighty upper arms?

Just as radio is for the voice, television is for the face. The lobby of the television building focuses on *arrival* – whether ascending (from the parking garage below) or descending (from the studios above). Wherever you enter from, you have to move from escalator to escalator against a backdrop of giant banners sporting well-known television faces. As you ride upwards, one of the gorgeous continuity announcers on Channel 2 will be descending on the opposite escalator, with such smiling magnificence that you find yourself looking back to check whether you have missed the crowds that are surely waving at her downstairs. Although she is sharing the lobby only with your face-for-radio presence, she feels the eyes of millions on her. On the upper level at reception, you see the Beautiful People, the ones with sunglasses in their hair, sipping green tea and mineral water.

At both television and radio, however, only parts of the building are used. You can wander around for hours past studios, halls, bathrooms, training booths, conference centres, news rooms that stand dark and deserted, or locked up and musty, left over from the days when the apartheid powers, staggering under illusions of grandeur, embodied their wildest dreams in cement, panelling, equipment and propaganda.

These two buildings are linked by a kind of underground maze. It is through these tunnels that I am scurrying on my way to television current affairs, where I am 'wanted'. Phil Molefe will be conducting the last-ever interview with Mandela as President. It will take place in Qunu – the President is inviting the nation into his home for an hour, as it were – and he has asked that I be Phil's co-interviewer.

Initially, I was not surprised, because radio news had put in several requests to interview Mandela, without receiving a reply from his office. By inviting me along with the television reporter, he would be killing two birds with one stone. But when I started hearing rumours that the news anchors were very resentful, that there had even been attempts to get the decision overturned, I realized the sheer luck of being chosen.

The production secretary and political editor for television will give me special assistance as a radio person. The production secretary takes me by the arm: 'Get your hair sorted out, shorter, maybe a little colour to liven it up. And get an outfit, something with a collar that makes you look professional, but can be unbuttoned for a little informality, as the setting is Madiba's house. Maybe a scarf or something to add colour.'

'But please, not white!' says someone with a trolley full of tapes.

'Yes, and also not blue – blue has been so overused. And nothing, absolutely nothing that is striped or checked. It irritates the viewer's eyes without them realizing it.' Here comes the friendly heart-to-heart. 'It has often happened with Minister Bengu, who has a fondness for checked suits and restlessly striped ties. The viewer becomes incredibly irritated with the Minister, when in fact his jacket is the culprit. You don't have to worry about the questions: Govan, our current affairs editor, will work them all out. Phil will ask the hard-hitting political questions and you must cater for the human interest and the personal. We have a special flight to Umtata tomorrow morning at six so that we can check things out and set everything up, and then the broadcast will be live tomorrow evening.'

Human interest? Personal? I am busy formulating: Am I wrong or is that sexist? – but there is no real opportunity to object to anything. The focus is on appearance. They give me the names of hair-dressing salons and boutiques.

The next morning we get on the tiny little aeroplane bound for Umtata. Govan sits

next to Phil to go through the questions with him. 'May I come up with my own questions?' I ask. Well, you could, but it is really not necessary, because the broader scope
has already been determined by the other programmes in the series, and there has to
be a coherent link between them all.

The women sleep in the two-star hotel, the men in the four-star. 'It is better like
that,' says the production secretary in a tone of voice that indicates: don't ask questions.

Crisis. Phil's shoes and his aftershave have been stolen from his suitcase. All top-
quality, duty-free acquisitions. Crisis overcome, we meet next to the swimming pool of
the four-star hotel to discuss the whole programme. It appears that Winnie
Madikizela-Mandela is also staying in the hotel. She has been sent by the ANC to
garner the support of the AmaPondo for the elections. The AmaPondo, the clan
Winnie belongs to, are grumbling that the ANC is doing everything for the Thembu
and other clans but nothing for them. Two other politicians have been sent along to
keep Winnie on the straight and narrow, but she thinks it is too cold to go outside and
has been sitting in the hotel for two days.

An icy wind scatters dead leaves across the deserted patios. Govan has a whole set
of questions. The aim is to show Mandela as both the statesman and the ordinary man.
More important, we must get at least one answer from Mandela that will lead to a good
follow-up news story. Phil will ask Mandela's opinion about specific political matters
and I will ask about his memories. Phil will also do the welcome and introduction. Phil
gets his questions and starts practising. Everyone orders water. 'Could I ask something
about the Truth Commission?' 'Certainly,' says Govan, 'but first we must get Phil's segment sorted out. Tell you what: we are leaving for Qunu at three. We can go through
your questions one by one there on the set itself.'

It is more than half an hour's drive to Qunu. The further one gets from Umtata, the
more peaceful and round and regular the hills become. Every now and then you see a
group of huts painted in the distinctive green or pink of the Eastern Cape. The hills are
dotted with cattle and aloes, and linked by the spidery lines of well-worn footpaths.

The road to Qunu is wonderfully tarred. When Mandela was still a poor attorney
in Johannesburg, he bought himself a plot in the Transkei, because he believes that a
man must have a place to live close to where he was born. However, the poverty into
which his political activities dumped him and Winnie forced him to sell the plot eventually. When he was released from prison, he acquired a plot from the female chief of
the Qunu area and built a house there on the same design as the prison warder's house
in which he had lived for the last years of his imprisonment at Victor Verster. The mind
boggles. Why would he want to do that? Why make his prison part of his freedom?
Mandela's own explanation is that this was the first house in which he had lived for so
many years, and he knows the space so well he can find his way around comfortably at
night. Here among the round huts, the yellow face-brick house is a bit out of place, yet
in a sense also humble. The outbuildings are an odd collection of huts, rooms and

garages. A wall with barbed wire, satellite dishes and a guard tower had to be added after Mandela became president – so the whole set-up is as incongruous as the man himself.

When we pull up at the house, a bulldozer and earth-movers are thundering around, and a little group of men are talking next to some cars. They introduce themselves as an architect, an engineer and a quantity surveyor from Port Elizabeth. The three-bedroomed house is totally inadequate to accommodate Mandela's children, grandchildren and great-grandchildren, who all gather here in Qunu every year, at his insistence, to spend Christmas with him. Now Mrs Machel's family has also been added. She has given instructions for the addition of an entire wing with bedrooms, in the style of the house.

Two gigantic SABC trucks have moved in next to the house so that the broadcasting infrastructure can be set up. Thousands and thousands it is costing, says the sound engineer, to bring these trucks over the bad roads from PE to Qunu. And we have to decide as soon as possible in which room the interview will take place, because they have been chased out of the house.

Frowning, Phil and the production secretary walk over to the front door, where they are met by Priscilla Naidoo, one of Mandela's assistants. She is very firm. Mandela is overworked, he is enslaving himself to the election, he is wiped out when he gets home. She will not allow the whole house to be taken over by television crews. If he wants to take a nap before the programme starts, or go to the bathroom, he will have to squeeze past a bunch of strange people. No, absolutely not. We can set up in one of the rondavels or other spaces.

There is a rondavel that is used for special meetings with traditional leaders. The floor is covered with carpets. But it is too small. The other rondavels are bedrooms and ablutions. Now what about the little hall? At the bottom of the property, Mandela has built a hall of brick and corrugated iron, with a cement floor, where he hosts his yearly Christmas party for schoolchildren. It is large and spacious, but the acoustics are terrible. It sounds as if you are talking inside a corrugated-iron shed. It looks like that too. This cannot be, says Phil. The advertising for the programme says that Mandela will be receiving the nation in his home – and now he receives them in the shed outside? Priscilla is made of steel: 'I will not allow it. My priorities are the peace and convenience of the President.' And she walks off.

Now the cellphones are pulled out and people start making calls. Editor phones Supervisor. Supervisor phones Boss. I go for a walk. Outside at a little table a woman is cutting offal into a pot: scrubbed pink trotters, head with jawbone and snot-pale eyes, stomach with the seams scrubbed so white and clean that it drapes into the pot like off-white mink. Coarse salt. 'For Madiba,' she says. 'Especially in the winter when he is so tired, then he likes this very much.' From behind Mandela's house you can see quite a distance. There are little patches of cabbage and greens, there are drinking troughs for cattle. The garden looks as if it too was imported from Victor Verster – roses frosted to death next to bleached kikuyu grass.

I must come and help. Priscilla has agreed that we can remove carpets and furniture from the house in order to create a kind of imitation living room inside the shed, so that the viewer does not get the idea that Mandela actually lives with a plastic table and chairs, on this cold grey cement floor. That would be a scandal.

It becomes almost barbaric. Everything is examined and touched. Is this quintessential Mandela? Is it African enough? What can we hang against these terrible walls? How do we prevent the whole business from appearing like a tourist stall at a rural festival? Are the things in the house really Mandela's? Or are they presents he had no room for in his other houses or things his family couldn't endure?

I stand at the sitting-room window and cannot help but think of Mandela, standing precisely here, looking out like this in the Victor Verster prison. And I marvel at the kind of man he is. The kind of man who would want to take the same construct, the very same structure of imprisonment, pick it up and put it down in the veld, in Qunu, in freedom. This yellow-brick clot of hostility he transforms into a place of homecoming and care. It may look alien, uncomfortable, but on his insistence, with his example, his personality, his ability to change perceptions, he makes this house his house, filled with the future. He doesn't simply rush for the new, he transforms the old, he forces it to adapt; even if it bursts here and there at the seams, or cracks around the edges, it has made space for the new. The structures of captivity have been transformed into the structures of freedom. It can be done. He has done it.

While the plundering and pondering of the Mandela interior continues, a notebook next to the telephone catches my eye. It is a shopping list: carrots, onions, feather duster, Yeltsin phoned, will call again at four, flour, sugar ... 'Yeltsin' is spelt correctly after three attempts.

Everyone helps to carry, throw down carpets, hang paintings, place staffs and calabashes, select three chairs with white upholstery, check that they do not make all sorts of noises when you sit on them, yes, add a few books, magazines. Then the technical team moves in to do the lighting, cabling and sound checks. It still sounds too hollow. People carry in anything they can lay their hands on to make the hall sound less like a hangar. Garden furniture, luggage, boxes ... There is only an hour left before the set has to be ready. The questions! Yes, I will ask what he intends to do when he retires. Will he garden? Will he visit Qunu more often? I must ask him why he likes strong women – there was Winnie, now it is Graça, what is it about strong women that attracts him? What is his most pleasant memory from his term of office? His most unpleasant memory? What would he still have liked to achieve? What does he see as his greatest triumph? Oh, and if you must, then the TRC question. Meanwhile, Phil practises: 'Good evening. You are here tonight with us in the house of President Nelson Mandela ...' Hm, should he not rather say 'Madiba', because it is a kind of informal discussion?

No, says Govan, stick to the formal, the audience do not know where you are yet and they may think that you are too much at home.

We get dressed. Darkness has fallen and it is bitterly cold. Teeth-chatteringly cold. Mandela, who left here at five this morning, is finally on his way back, having spent the whole day drumming up support from voters. Somebody wonders if he ran into Winnie somewhere. Even without his favourite aftershave and his imported shoes, Phil is dressed to the nines. Someone adjusts his silver tie and I wonder if the checks were a good idea. They remove the last shiny spots from his forehead.

My turn. The black make-up artist complains that she hasn't brought make-up for whites. And so the wheel turns. In the not so distant past, it was the white make-up department at the SABC who made the discovery that different skin tones need different products. A full study was made and a special kit of 'black make-up' assembled. The next thing there were complaints of racism: the whites and the blacks are being made up from different kits.

When she is finished, she holds up her mirror. A snow-white ghost looks back at me, with blood-red lips.

'Am I not too white?' My question sounds like the centuries-old plea of whites in this country. Uninterested, she shakes her head. 'It will be okay on TV.'

While they are still struggling to fix the little earphone behind my ear, Mandela suddenly appears. He is wearing a thick, thick coat and a scarf, and is visibly exhausted. He greets Phil and looks frowningly at me. I am introduced as 'the Person who will do the interview with Phil'. His frown deepens. 'I thought it was only to be you, Phil,' he says and sits down. Phil explains the structure of the interview and more or less what kinds of questions he will be asking.

In my earphone, I can only hear orders being shouted, someone yelling. Govan runs outside to the monitors in the truck, and after a while I hear his voice in my ear: 'Relax, drop your shoulders!'

Someone takes off Mandela's heavy coat, and here we go!

'Good evening ...'

We are sitting in this glowing little spot of light in a frozen hall through which the wind cuts like a knife. Everywhere, technical crew, camera and sound personnel are moving around, and it seems like utter chaos to me. Mandela's face looks like granite. Grey and chiselled. His eyes look dead, and lowered with exhaustion and something like anger. When he begins to answer Phil's first question, he has no voice for a second, and then this hoarse, whispering voice comes forth. Short sentences. I hear in my ear: 'When Madiba has finished answering the next question, it is your turn.' God! I realize for the first time that I do not know what to call him. I will not be able to bring the word 'Madiba' out of my mouth, it sounds so utterly phoney to me when a white person says it. President? Sir? Mr President? ... but then I am on. I sit on the edge of my chair.

'Mr President, you are seen as someone who has made the impossible possible. What would you regard as the biggest success of your term in office? The thing you thought was most impossible but that has happened?' I smile, professionally I hope.

Mandela turns to me. 'It is not helpful if you want to participate in the building of a country to talk about the impossible. We as the ANC deal with the possible. The question you ask me is therefore not relevant at all, because we try to do what is possible.' And his mouth shuts like stone.

My ears chime like two bells. Red bells. I try again, but the more I formulate, the more pathetic and inadequate it becomes: 'Is there anything you regret about your term in office, anything you always hoped to achieve but could not?'

'I don't think it is correct to personalize issues. We are a collective. We are a team. We in the ANC do things as a team. I would find it much more relevant if you ask what the ANC still has to do. This government has done an excellent job. During the past 250 years no government has ever delivered what this government has delivered. Our performance is beyond reproach.' He turns his whole body towards Phil.

In my earphone I hear the voices from the control room: 'What is going on with the Old Man? Antjie, take it easy, calm down. Don't look upset. It's nothing.' Meanwhile, Phil here next to me has also taken a bit of a fright at Mandela's aggressive correcting of questions. He stumbles through the next one: what will Mandela do when he has retired? Mandela laughs, albeit curtly: 'Perhaps you have seen the poor little vegetable patches here behind the house ... I want to talk to children ...'

'Ask the question about the strong women,' says Govan. I shake my head vigorously. 'Don't!' he screams in my ear. 'Don't shake your head – you're on camera!'

But the only thing I can think of is that the President of the country has thoroughly thrashed me. I may be white and television-dumb, but I am not stupid. Would I really ask him about strong bloody women so that he can cut me down to size again? I draw my coral-red lips and white face together.

'You are emphasizing over and over the fact that you are not an individual but part of a collective. How difficult was it then for you to receive the TRC's final report from Archbishop Desmond Tutu, while the ANC was trying to get an interdict to stop the handing over?'

'The task of the President sometimes differs from that of his position in the political party that he is a member of.'

I feel tears leaping behind my eyes. It is silent in the earphone. You can tell that the operational room has also run out of strategies. Mandela speaks extensively to Phil about this, that and the other thing. He answers the political questions as well as the personal ones. Here and there I still try to chip in my two cents' worth, but the blow has been dealt.

Afterwards Phil looks at me. 'What happened? Why was the Old Man so angry with you?' I don't know, but one thing is clear: Mandela could not personally have *asked* for me to form part of this interview. Maybe when he arrived on the set he saw me as some unknown white missus, put in to make sure that Phil doesn't give him an easy ride? Or something to that effect. I really don't know, but I feel devastated. And pathetic that I feel that way. Everyone's cellphones are buzzing.

We drive back to Umtata. I wish I could disappear to my room, but we have been invited for dinner by an elated Phil. Before we sit down, there is a sudden hush. Into the dining room march twenty-three men, some with Palestinian scarves around their necks and guns openly displayed on their hips. 'En route from Durban to Cape Town,' the waiter tells us, without moving his lips. We all become more subdued.

I see Mandela's personal secretary at one of the tables. She admits that she's never known him to be quite as severe as this. 'But you have to understand, Mr Mandela is dog-tired. He is giving all of himself to the ANC for this election, campaigning cease-lessly, and he's not that young any more.'

Of course not. And it is his good right not to like a journalist. Or to ridicule the questions. But it feels a bit like finding out that *God* doesn't like you.

'You can console yourself with this,' says my husband over the phone, 'nobody would have recognized you. Every time you appeared on the screen with that spooky white face, we laughed so much we couldn't hear a word you were saying.'

CHAPTER TWELVE

A FEW DAYS BEFORE South Africa's second democratic election there is a huge influx of journalists to the newly completed IEC building at the Pretoria show-grounds. What was once an empty hangar has been converted into the operational nerve centre for the election. It involved the installation of 2 400 square metres of raised flooring to accommodate about 40 kilometres of cabling, 1 000 telephone lines, 12 radio studios, 5 television studios and a media hall for 500 journalists. On voting day, operators on 350 personal computers will have to handle 45 000 telephone calls from presiding officers and 15 000 calls from polling stations when counting gets under way.

SABC radio has deployed journalists with cellphones and recording equipment all around the country. We are the only medium able to involve so many people, and we will therefore be the only body, apart perhaps from the ANC itself, which could mon-itor the activities of the IEC.

The media will have direct access to the computer system for news on voter turnouts, problems and election results. The IEC's head of planning, Howard Sackstein: 'The media said they wanted one location where they could access polit-icians, the IEC, as well as the results. The politicians said they needed a location where they could access results and problems as well as the media. While we, the IEC, on the other hand, need the media to verify and enhance the legitimacy of the results.'

The IEC has set up an elaborate system for cross-checking results. Initially, the result will be phoned through. For the sake of transparency, the presiding officer will make an official announcement and stick the result on the door of the polling station. Security measures and codes have been established to verify the results coming in via phone calls. The result will only be declared legitimate once the officer has faxed through that same result. This official result will then be entered on a wide-area satellite network. In the end, the data from these different sources will be compared by the computers at IEC headquarters.

The journalists are sceptical. During the previous election, there were places that could only be reached by helicopter or four-wheel drive vehicles. Who will be taking the ballots there this time? Who will ensure that there is no intimidation? Where will they get fax machines? Are there cellphone connections in these desolate areas?

Sackstein expects three kinds of problems: 'Firstly, results may not come in from far-flung polling stations, but our staff are being trained to chase those results. Secondly, results may not match because of incorrect data-processing or garbled phone messages. And thirdly, there could be legal challenges in the specially created electoral court. But whatever is humanly possible, we have done. That is why we invented the VD and the Zip-zip.'

What?

'In case you all thought that VD means "venereal disease" and Zip-zip is the title of a steamy pornographic film, let me put you straight. VD means "voting district" and the Zip-zip is the Electoral Commission's secret weapon against administrative problems.'

It seems that bottlenecks occur in the electoral process especially when officials cannot find someone's name on the voters' roll. 'We cannot depend on the patient goodwill of South Africans again,' says a spokesperson. 'We have become an irritable bunch. So speed and short queues are crucial.' To speed up the administrative process, the IEC has developed this device called a Zip-zip. The person controlling the queue at the polling station will use the Zip-zip to scan the bar code in your ID book and print out a strip with a serial number on it. This number will allow the official controlling the voters' roll to find you immediately. The Zip-zip can also indicate how many people actually voted and identify those whose names do not appear on the voters' roll.

After your name has been marked on the voters' roll, you will receive two ballots – provincial and national. How will an illiterate person tell the two ballots apart? The IEC cannot say with any certainty. Furthermore, the ballots will simply show photos of the political leaders and their party logos. How will an illiterate person, without access to television or newspapers, recognize the party they want to vote for? The IEC feels that this question should be directed to the political parties. Rev. Kenneth Meshoe of the African Christian Democratic Party appears first on the ballot, since his party won the draw – which just shows that God is on their side, Meshoe said jubilantly. Will voters be able to distinguish Mbeki from Meshoe, or Van Schalkwyk from Luyt? If you are one of those people to whom all blacks or all whites look the same, you have an even bigger problem. Meanwhile, voter educators report that many people still indicate that they will be voting for Nelson Mandela.

✧

On 26 May 1999, the IEC holds a briefing in its enormous media hall. All voting stations except the mobile ones will be open for a few hours one week before voting day to process applications for special votes. Special votes are for those who can prove that they are too old, too disabled or too pregnant to get to the voting station on election day. Such people will be given a form, and then visited within the next two days by two voting officers so that they can cast their vote.

We listen in disbelief. If one is too old to get to the voting station on election day, how on earth will one get there at any other time? Why aren't the mobile units going out? Are old or disabled people in the rural areas really expected to walk further to apply for a special vote than they would otherwise have to go on election day itself to a mobile unit? If you send someone on your behalf, will they be able to fetch the form, bring it back for you to sign, and then return it before closing time? The presiding officer must approve your application. Who is this presiding officer? How many of us know who our presiding officer is?

The IEC spokesperson clips his files together and leaves the conference room, while these questions remain floating in the air.

And this is more or less the style right through the election. The big things work. But many smaller concerns are not dealt with, cannot be responded to, are never answered or explained.

On election day, the rural areas produce their share of stories. Like the one about the polling station in Thohoyandou. When the electoral officers arrive, a long queue of high-school kids is already waiting for someone to open the door: this is the venue for the annual beauty pageant. At another station, an old woman turns up wanting to vote for the man with the gap between his teeth. She cannot remember the name of the candidate or the party. They drive her down the main street of the town to look at the posters. Suddenly, she points her finger, there he is: it's Thabo Mbeki, who has a chipped front tooth.

There are no violent incidents, no shortages. People queue. A lot of people. It seems that South Africans are not as blasé about democracy as some have predicted. There is so little news that reporters have to focus on where the politicians themselves voted and what they had to say.

Then comes the counting. For two days there is a constant flow of results, but by Thursday afternoon the Big Freeze sets in. The numbers stay the same, with no change in the proportion of voting districts that have already responded. We all wait. The IEC's spokespersons are vague or unavailable: it looks like thirty per cent of the votes are still missing, but no problems have been reported and no one seems to have hacked into the system (as they did the last time around). When the weekend arrives most of the reporters pack it in. On Sunday evening, the election is declared free and fair, with the results more or less unchanged from previous days. A huge fuss is made of the fact that the ANC did not get a two-thirds majority. The ACDP has increased its support substantially, while the NNP and the IFP have lost much of their former power. The DP under Tony Leon becomes the official opposition in parliament.

One of the older commentators, a veteran of elections in Lesotho and Zimbabwe, says: 'In an election in a Third World country, there always comes a point where you have to close your eyes and muddle through, because enough of the important things have gone right.'

CHAPTER THIRTEEN

THE END OF THE ELECTION is the beginning of her vacation. She has taken two months' leave, one of them paid and one of them unpaid, to see what remains inside her of the being of a poet. After so many years of recording voices and transcribing them, after so many years of testimony at the Truth Commission and political rhetoric in parliament, she does not have a clue whether she can still write even a line of poetry. Does she still have the voice coming from somewhere inside her or has it taken leave of her long ago? Or has she been turned into a second-rate reporter with poetic aspirations? Does she still have anything like her own voice or have the years of reporting and repeating reduced her to a mere mouthpiece? What will she hear inside herself when everything is completely silent around her? Nothing? Will anything ever come drifting towards her from afar if she sends her ears out into the nothingness.

More urgently: will she still be able to work in her mother tongue? Has she been so affected by constantly working in English on the radio that she can no longer experience all those nuances that can stir the inner pool of being only via the mother tongue? Her literary output seems to be divided in two. All her life, her poetry has been Afrikaans. Her professional journalism has been English. Her greatest literary achievement has been in English prose, and the money she earned from that has now allowed her to take unpaid leave to see if she can still write an Afrikaans poem. Split by languages into genre and theme.

Over the years it has become ever clearer to her that it is impossible to keep a full-time profession as well as a full-time family life going, while truly making a qualitative impact as a poet – unless the full-time work involves lecturing at a university, where you at least have a few holidays a year and perhaps a day to yourself each week. The poets she knows have followed a variety of options: some make desperate attempts to survive financially on translations and articles; some publish very little and very seldom; and a few get by on alimony. For a long time, she was the only female poet in Afrikaans with a husband and children and a job.

And why is poetry so different from prose? Poetry sells less. But more crucial is that a poem does not come like an invited guest. It doesn't care about your whereabouts. It checks in at strange times. It strikes you like the urge to take a dump. And when you say, not now, not this morning, wait until tonight when everybody is in bed, then I'll see what you have to say, you end up with nothing more than constipated little pebbles. A poet cannot say: I will write a poem every evening or on Saturday mornings or only on Sundays. If it comes, it is there, and you have to be available. And your paper has to be ready with the right kind of HB pencil and your eraser within reach. And you must be able to cleave your ears into that place, that pulsating entrance, that thin membrane where you can hear the stirring.

That is why one cannot take off six months or whatever like a novelist with the intention of writing a book. One cannot sit like the writers of prose, every day behind one's desk, writing so many thousands of words. Prose writers create and oversee a landscape, poets mine a vein of sound.

Why is she not a prose writer? Why does she mistrust anything that starts with a capital letter and ends with a full stop? Why does she lose her way in a line that can be broken anywhere to fit the size of the paper? Why does a structured sentence obliterate her into a single dimension?

'Thank God you are no prose writer,' a friend, who is a writer himself, quotes from the *Michigan Quarterly Review*. 'Their souls are heavy and managerial. Writers of fiction are by nature a sullen bunch. The strain of inventing one plausible event after another in a coherent chain of narrative tends to show on them. As Nietzsche remarked about Christians, you can tell from their faces that they don't enjoy what they do.'

No please, give me a better reason, she asks.

'Fiction writers cluster in the unlit corners of the room,' writes her friend, 'silently observing everybody, including the poets, who are usually having a fine time in the spotlight, making a spectacle of themselves as they eat the popcorn and drink the beer and gossip about other poets ... The prose writers notice everything about you, and sooner or later they start editorializing about you ... while the poets get the party going and dance the longest. Unfortunately, they don't know how to work the stereo and therefore have to wait for the prose writers to show them where the on/off switch is. In general, come to think of it, poets do not know where the on/off switch is anywhere in life.'

As a postscript he writes: 'Remember and be kind: When a poet loses a poem, a beloved is lost. When a novelist loses a novel, a country is lost.'

Can she write an entire volume of poetry in two months? Of course not. But if she writes only one single poem, her cup will run over. Just to know that she hasn't lost it all.

She gets on a plane to Upington. She is going with photographer Paul Weinberg and his girlfriend Heleen to the Richtersveld. He to take photos, Heleen to paint, she herself to breathe in the mountainous desert – the most silent place on earth. So Heleen says.

They travel far. And it is hot. At Brandkaros and Bloeddrif suddenly the landscape stumbles into stone. She sits in the back of the jeep, but what she sees is so ugly and hard and rough that she closes her eyes to cut out the ugliness. But the landscape does not let itself be told. The landscape lets her have it in the face. 'See me, you!' it seems to say, 'I'm stone. Nothing but stone in its ugliest, stoniest stone.'

She opens a bottle of muscadel. No majestic formations or dramatic colouring – just a harsh mess of stone. Untidy stone. She realizes she has only one word for stone, and that is stone. One needs language for this place, she thinks, and takes a deep gulp. While the photographer waits for the best light to capture the landscape and the artist makes notes on mixtures of colours, she sits dumbly in the jeep. It won't help to get out, she thinks, 'I have no language for what I see.'

And then there is the heat. Dry, clear, fierce heat in the day, but cold at night. She simply sits next to the jeep. Mostly with her head on her knees. At night her body is the throat of many voices. But as the days fall away in blurs of heat and stone, she feels the scales of tension and exhaustion and ageing and politics slowly melting in her veins. They sleep at the place where the goatherd stays.

'The thing here is the river,' says Oom Jacobus de Wet, and although he has been talking for days, she hears him for the first time. 'We don't call him "the Gariep", we don't call him "the Orange", for us here, he is "the River".'

'The thing is not the River,' says Dawid Links, 'the main thing is the mist. He whom we, as Namas, call "Huries". This mist wells up from the cold troughs of the Benguela sea, is blown on land by the wind, then limps across the veld where the koppies intercept it. When you see the mist you know: bushes, stones – they all drink dew. Too much Huries, the old people said, makes the veld blue. But we can live here because of the dew.'

Dawid Links is speaking a poem. She feels the knots in her stomach loosening. If it ever comes to her again, it is here that it will come.

'Once the River has had you and held you, you never get away from it,' says Antonie Visser that evening in the bar. 'It never lets you go. You can move wherever in the world, whether you are sitting in church or in a car, one day you get up and you know you have to go back. Especially if you hear the River is in flood. Then you must be here. I know of big businessmen who are millionaires today, when they hear the River is in flood, then they get into their private jets and they come. Because you have to swim him. You must feel him again, that force. That first force you measured yourself against.'

She hears from him that there is a geologist on the mines who can explain stone to her.

It is Sunday in Kuboes. The whitewashed church stands clear against the quartzite sky. 'O God, blow and bleed your love on to us,' prays Oom Adam. The congregation sings: 'Djiesus is a rock in a thirsty land, a thirrr-sty land.'

Not the fountain, not the water, but the rock.

'Thou art like vapour on me ... Djiesus, Djie-ie-ie-sus,' they sing.

It clearly takes a lot of God to hang on here.

'Grandpapa Mandela, I voted for him,' says Maria Domroch. 'Why is it that to be a Nama today means something? Why do you people come all the way to Kuboes? Why am I on television? Because we are somebody now. Under the old government we were without name. Over the years we have been driven out to the most barren of places. Coloured Reserves. We were nothing. But today we are something. And it is him, that Old Man Mandela, it's him. No, Mandela-*goed* got my vote.'

'I am very close to cattle,' says Mrs Farmer of Eksteenfontein. 'A house to me is nothing; the open veld is my house. I have length in the open veld; in a round house-let. When we arrived here many years ago, chased out to here, it was raining and the daisies were so high that when I squatted I was under a floor of flowers. From that day I adopted this place and I've loved it until now. For its disposition. For the veld.'

The people of the stone desert speak and her ears gulp. Such language. Such inflection. Such secure grip. Healing her mother tongue.

'Around Jerusalem are mountains,' says Oom Jacobus de Wet. 'Here, alone with the goats in the veld, are also mountains, but all around is God. The whole evening now I've felt Him coming from this side of Akkediskloof.' They are sitting around the chattering fire among the sand dunes close to Oom Jacobus's *staning*. Oom Jacobus has a cup of sweet wine. He is tired, because today he slaughtered an almighty buck by himself, spread out the kidney-fat on the shrubs, scraped out the intestines and the stomach-stuff, roasted the liver with onion and tomato that we brought, salted the ribs, rump and hindquarters, and strung them up.

'Day and night I am alone here at the post with Christ. We talk. I can lie back and look at Him with clear eyes. I only have to look to see Him, because spirit is always aware of spirit. My grandchild, Benjamin, does the herding nowadays. I heard this from his own lips this morning. He said he wanted to be a goatherd. And I was so deeply satisfied. God put into everybody his own talent. At night at the camp we needn't talk, we know where grazing took place and where it should take place. Herding is a good life to give to a child, because every child has his honour. Let me say it to you: it is tasty to be with a grandchild. He makes me laugh. He lets me say untoward things. Yes, it is good to be with Benjamin.'

Her one-man tent is pitched on the bank of the River. The whole night it flows past her, silent and broad as blood.

By the light of a torch she tries to find other words for stone: washing stone, grinding stone. Her memory of the ugliness of the stone rejects any poetic stone phrases. It is thing. It disintegrates brutally from barren slants into stone dandruff, into slovenly stone flakes. No cute stonewords to be bled from it. No cropping of beautiful stone phrases. 'I prance past you,' the stone seems to shout to her in her tent. 'I vomit from your lines about molten stone, leaking stone, lashing stone. I taunt the stonelovingness of your attempts at stroke stone, the turdsoft usefulness of grinding stone, brey stone, washing stone. I am my own thing. I am unforgeable, insoluble, inaccessible.'

The next day she goes to the mine to find the geologist. He takes her to what seems like nothing more than a quarry of dead grey shards of stone. 'You are standing now in the most beautiful place in the Richtersveld,' he says in a voice that takes the shoes from her feet. He shows her plumes of magma, of elephantskin-weathering on dolomite. He helps her trace dolorite squirting like dark toothpaste through the crust of earth. He points out lighter granite peeling off in regular layers. He breathes fault-line and matrices of mud. He teaches her three basic kinds of stone: those that coagulated like ironstone and granite; those that were sedimented like sandstone, shale and mudstone; and those that were transformed like marble and quartzite.

'I cannot live without the language of stone,' he says before dropping her off at her tent, where a whole flock of tiny birds burst away like tassels over the River. That evening, for the first time, the obtuse hills ladle light past the halfmens tree.

The next morning the heat settles early. Before breakfast the stones are bleached into blue and the shade becomes thin. She walks behind Benjamin Cloete as he takes his goats to the veld. Light-footed, flight-footed he crosses the dunes. *Haii-haii*, whistles his whip. Noisy and flat-footed in her Adidas and jeans, she trudges behind him. The goats sink into the overgrown riverbanks. They munch themselves into silence. Benjamin filters himself softly into river-willow shade.

'And now?' she asks.

'Ma'am can catch a slumberling,' he says.

'How do you know nothing is going to happen to the goats?'

'Because I know their bleating. I know which one is bleating and for what.'

She stares at him. He lifts his fingers one after the other: 'There is the big bleat, the flat bleat, the forlorn bleat, the gay bleat, moan bleat, spoilt bleat, vexed bleat and I-am-boss bleat.'

She walks away on to the stones. Fragile lies the River, like an open artery in the heat. This landscape is unthinkable without this broad, fragrant, brown-green scar, indestructibly older than the oldest human breath.

'It feeds the goats of dreams and the goats of dying,' says Oom Jacobus. 'Of nothing too many, of nothing too utterly few.'

She's been here a week. The mountain on the other side of the River looks as if it's leaking into the midday hour. It slakes in blue, strains away from its tainted bronze.

The vygies on the banks hiss in cyanide pink. She looks at her watch. It is twenty minutes past two and it means nothing, absolutely nothing. She lies down on the sand-bank and drowses between shade and grazing and heat.

Then she hears it. Faintly. She sits upright. It steps softly into her blood: *'Ek is hier ... ek's by jou ... ek het gekom in laventel blou.'* Again please, she pleads. 'I am here. I'm with you. I have come in lavender blue.'

She has no pencil, no paper, but she lies back. She breathes through her ear, over-come with loose-limbed happiness.

how do I follow this fault-line towards you

as late light knells along the stones
when Tattasberg is the very beginning of me

how do I grow you here?

The phrases simply drift across her mind and waft away into the heat. Like faint blessings. Benjamin's whip calls her. The sun has tilted. The goats are on their way home. In short woollen waterfalls some of them plunge from the trees, flicking piss and droppings. At the post, the kids are struggling to escape from their tethers to have the first suckle. And she realizes that nothing is as soft,
nothing as snouty
as delicately mouthed
defencelessly eyed as lambkin of goat
in the evening when dusk sets in.

On the way back they stop at Paradysdraai and for the first time in ten days there is warm water and flushing toilets, and they buy cheap red wine and steak. 'I can see your auras turning more aggressive as you gobble up that red meat,' says Heleen, who is a vegetarian.

She phones home from the public phone booth. 'Thank God you've called. You have just won a prize,' says her husband. 'The fax arrived here three days ago already. A big prize worth thousands of rands from Sweden.' She sinks down on to her heels.

'We can fix the roof now,' he says. 'And buy you a computer.'

✧

While I'm working my notice at the radio, I get a call from one of Mandela's close friends. She picks me up in her car. In the back sits her teenage son, decked out in designer-label clothes and oily dreadlocks, noticeably sullen, bored and angry. She takes us to a restaurant in Bloubergstrand. Her son refuses to get out, leans into the front and turns the radio on full blast.

'If you want to stay here and put the music so loud, you must close the windows,' she says to him. As we walk towards the restaurant, he winds up the windows, turning the car into a thudding popcorn machine.

We have a table at the window, looking out on the profound cliché of Table Mountain across the bay. As we sit down, she sighs: 'That child has been so disrupted. Then in London, then in Lusaka, then back to Europe, then Johannesburg, and, after the election, Cape Town. He doesn't know what he is. He wants to go back to London, but when he visits there, he phones all the time to come back here.'

The waiter brings the menu.

'I brought you here for two reasons: the first one is the menu. Read it carefully.' She smiles mischievously.

I start reading, and ah! how well she knows me, my mouth starts to water. With the kind of classy decisiveness that only the exiles sometimes display, she asks for the chef to be brought to the table, to talk about the menu.

'As a chef, I know that the gourmet's tongue is as sensitive to sound as to taste.' His accent is French, his register flattery. 'Therefore the exquisiteness of the taste must be mirrored by the exquisiteness of the word. The tongue should taste what the eye reads.'

'But how does one put together such a poetic menu?' she asks.

He pouts. 'The art lies in the freshness of the verb and the colour of the adjective. So, for starters, I present a slice of turkey marinated in Thelema white. Lasagne laid out with pastrami and little silver onions.' His voice lifts with the last syllable of every sentence as if to say: the world is *open*, the choice is *yours*.

We giggle, and I notice the shiny wetness of her big eyes. And remember how I couldn't look away from those eyes when I met her the first time at the Victoria Falls, in the days when we were still regarded as 'budding poets'. We were so serious then, so earnest about our dreams.

The chef glows as he gesticulates us into the main courses. 'The very best: veal perfumed with rosemary and paprika chutney. Or beef fillet reclining on a foothill of tongue and oysters.'

We order. She asks for mineral water, I ask for a glass of Diemersdal merlot. We drink a toast. 'To the eye of language,' I say. She laughs, 'To the language of the eye.'

'The menu is a spectacular enough reason to bring me here,' I say. 'Still, I'm curious about the second reason.'

But her eyes have fastened somewhere behind me. It is her son. He is standing in the doorway looking very agitated and jittery, throwing a ball from one hand to the other. She gets up. I see them talking, she tries to lead him out, he pulls away. She comes back and takes her handbag. 'I'll be back just now.' They leave.

I look towards the mountain. The southeaster had been lashing the Cape for days on end, but this morning, when I woke up, it was absolutely quiet, the kind of quietness that you sense even before you open your eyes.

What do I know of this woman whom I care so much about? She has the same rights as I have, she has more power and more money. Yet the past is like an undertow all around her.

When she comes back there is a tiredness in her neck that was not there earlier.

'I'm sorry about this. I've called a driver to fetch him. The child is on ... something. He has been sent away so many times. Every so often I think I simply want to make peace with the fact that there will always be ... debris after change, you know, things discarded, because, through no fault of their own, they become unusable, waste material. But most of the time I do take complete responsibility for trying to change his life.' She shrugs and opens her napkin on her lap.

The first course arrives, but we have lost our appetites. I call the waiter and ask him to keep our orders back, we want to go for a walk on the beach. We cross the street, take off our shoes and walk slowly in the cool draught of blue and foam.

'Do you remember when the "inside" of the ANC met you exiles in Paris that December before De Klerk made his speech?' I ask.

'Yes, I remember well. Trevor was released specially for the meeting, and he fell so sick on the plane, eating all that rich Air France food, having just come out of jail.'

'Every morning, I shared the breakfast table with two female comrades from the Western Cape. And every morning we had these hard French rolls lying on the tablecloth next to our knives and forks. No little side plates, nothing. So we left them there. Every morning we left them there, wondering why they kept on putting them on the cloth, so uncivilized. Then one morning Breyten Breytenbach joined us and started eating his bun, but on the table, as if the cloth was a plate, and when I looked around I saw, indeed, that was how the people ate them, there on the table. But when Breyten left, one of these comrades got up with her big white serviette, bent over the table and energetically whipped off the crumbs into her cupped hand, saying, "Now who is supposed to clean this mess after him?"'

'I remember how we were warned that De Klerk was going to unban us, but we just laughed. Impossible. Ridiculous.'

We walk fast. Our eyes feast on the bay and the far-off mountain, on our feet in the sand. I see her face slowly softening, her hair becoming untidy, the bottoms of her silky pantaloons wet. Her eyes getting that brightblack back.

'How is Mandela?' I ask.

She smiles. 'He's well, I think. But I had an interesting experience yesterday. Someone who had visited him asked me afterwards why he repeats some of his stories, word for word, just as they've been written down in *Long Walk to Freedom*. Could it be old age? So I discussed it with Mandela's right-hand man, and he says Mandela does it only with certain stories. It has nothing to do with age, it's very deliberate. Mandela is doing it intentionally, he believes, to undermine what he calls the whole postmodernist notion of ever-changing texts or something. As if Mandela wants to say that there are certain truths which should always exist as truths, and that these important truths should continue to exist in precisely the same way if people want to find one another.'

'Maybe he's right. The time when we needed ever-changing truths in order to survive each other is hopefully over in this country. For people to be able to live together, to start singing from the same fold of skin, as it were, there is a need for unchangeable truths. We need common ground to grow a common humanity.'

God! I think to myself as she sidesteps a rush of foam. This is perhaps what I appreciate most about this new country – this interaction. This kind of opening up of perspectives. How impoverished my life would have been without it.

'The other day I saw a television programme on literature and one of the critics was irritated by the word "humanity" – *medemenslikheid* – in a poem. "What a cliché. The word has no meaning whatsoever!" And I was wondering what is happening to a world or a language in which this word is no longer usable or meaningful?'

'Mandela uses the word often in his book and his speeches. Maybe that's another reason why he insists on relating particular stories in exactly the same way. In the stubbornly unalterable framework he creates, he opens up safe spaces in which words like "humanity", "human dignity" can be resuscitated. Get breath, as it were, and some colour in their cheeks ...'

Barefoot we walk into the restaurant. At the table, we tuck in with relish.

'Now for the second reason you brought me here.'

'Oh yes. I watched the interview you and Phil Molefe did with Madiba and saw exactly what went wrong.'

'A million things went wrong, that I do know.'

'No, that's not what I'm talking about. When I heard your first question, I knew what was going to happen. There are certain things you have to understand about Mandela if you ever want to make real sense of him. And it's not all these phrases you hear bandied about. If Madiba says that he is part of a collective, then he is not simply using a political charm, or an eccentric trademark, or wearing an old-fashioned coat. It is really the quintessence of what he believes.'

'Oh, come on, Rebecca. It is the kind of hackneyed phrase he is expected to use. The humble position for a man of his stature. It is not me, it is them. But it is *his* face, not that of the ANC, that has become the best-known face in the world. It is *his* name, not the name of the ANC, that is familiar to millions of people who don't even know where South Africa is or who is governing here. As much as I respect the stance, even admire it, you cannot expect me to take it seriously as the essence of the man.'

She turns her dessert spoon over and over on the white cloth. I see that she still bites her nails.

'While Mandela was on the Island in 1980, the ANC in exile decided that the liberation struggle needed a face. And it could have been anyone, but they chose Mandela, for a variety of reasons ... But the point I want to make is that it was in a way an arbitrary choice. People did not vote for it. He'd been inside for so long that no one was even sure whether he would be able to command from a new generation the same kind of mass support he'd enjoyed before he went to prison.'

'I know all that. But he was in many ways a born leader. The prison authorities regarded him as the obvious leader, so did his comrades. The ANC in exile also had to liaise with him. He might have been the chosen face, but he was very much the leader as well.'

'That I don't deny, but what I'm trying to say to you is that nobody knows better than Mandela how crucial the collective is to hold a leader on the right road. In prison, before he held talks with the white government, he consulted Walter, Kathy, Raymond – all of them.'

'Wait right there. Mandela himself admits that he initiated the talks without consulting anybody. In his biography he says: "I chose to tell no one what I was about to do ... There are times when a leader must move out ahead of the flock, go off in a new direction, confident that he is leading his people in the right way."'

'Ja, but you're omitting the most important point he also makes there: "The ANC is a collective, but government, by locking me up alone, had made collectivity in this case impossible" – or something to that effect.'

'Okay. So the collective holds a leader on the right path?'

'Yes. It holds a leader accountable. He has people he has to consult, structures he has to obey. If they disagree with him, he has to convince or argue with them. Dictators are always isolated and never accountable. They ignore their party structures and only take lackeys into their inner chambers. Also, collectivity always undermines the cult of the leader, prevents the sense of power from going to his head. A leader can only step down from his position if he really believes that the collective rules. On this continent, in this country, the collective nature of political leadership is essential and Madiba, through instinct and through reason, feels deeply that it should be respected. So if people ask questions about his personal triumphs and regrets, his role in making the impossible possible, he *will* get angry.'

'I don't know. To me it felt as if he was angry just seeing me there.'

'But he might have been irritated that he was working in the Eastern Cape, ignored by the cameras, unacknowledged by his party leadership, canvassing like an ordinary foot soldier, while somebody like Winnie feels it is too cold to go outside, as you told me.'

'Talk about a cult figure!'

'You see, that is what he abhors, because he knows so intimately what destruction it can bring. But there is a second layer to his insistence on a collective approach. He has reached out to whites in reconciliation, he has bent over backwards to forgive – and what does he get? People only accept *him*, only regard *him*, while still dismissing his people. Mandela wants to impress on the world that he is not an exception: I am of my people, I am like them. If you are impressed by me, you have to be impressed by them. If I am remarkable, so are they. But whites constantly sing the praises of Mandela, while continuing to treat black people as they did before. That is why, whenever he receives recognition, he keeps on repeating like a robot, it is for all my people. I am accepting it on behalf of all my people.'

I sit quietly for a long time. Not so much embarrassed as deeply aware of the extent to which my perception of being in this world is constantly informed by this African-ness. Black-ness or African-ness, I don't really know, but it is a way of looking at the world that neither I, nor the culture I grew up in, nor the books I have read are able to come up with. I seem to find it only when I sit opposite a black face.

'Okay. I hear you. But what do I do with the feeling that he was irritated just seeing me there. I mean, here is this man who typifies reconciliation and he is angry at the sight of a white person? Have I misread the situation? Am I overreacting? And listen here, I'm not disputing his right to dislike me, it's just that he seemed to reject me because of my colour.'

'You read him as an individual, he resisted that. He read you as part of a collective. You can resist or accept that.'

'Surely I should resist it?'

'Why? Why don't you allow him that reading? Why are you unwilling to grant him a nuanced space in which he can reach out and reprimand because he knows and believes all people are equal, while at the same time feeling free to let his frustration surface at times, and be accepted for it? The space of sainthood is not really a space – besides, one cannot learn from a saint how to live in this world.'

And he is teaching us a way of regarding the world, this miracle of a man, of being at grace with people, of being human in benign spaces, of preferring the skein of humanity to the fanatic purity of principle. To have that kind of human-ness infuse every single muscle of memory in oneself. 'I think therefore I am' *versus* 'I am because I am with you'? No. Much more than that.

I look at the woman opposite me. Her eyes are soft and kind. And I know she needn't have done this, and I have nothing to give her in return. I take her hand with its bitten nails – this white hand clasping this black hand. A cliché like the mountain across the bay, but because of that no less real.

'Why would you care?' I can hardly hear myself.

'Because I know one takes a lifetime to reach this colour.'

She bites her lip. Then continues: 'Because you are part of my collective. Madiba has taught me that. And because the price we have paid for it is so much greater than we ever thought possible.' She pauses. 'The personal price. The only way we survived our pain in the past was to generalize our humanity. I need to live in a world now where intolerance and revenge are being discarded as part of the debris of transformation which we talked about earlier, while at the same time making space for all the different shades pain takes on.'

Back in my office, I find that my thoughts have laid themselves down peacefully. Nothing is as simple as skin.

✧

From a cramped little butchery up in Kloof Street, I phone my mother. 'If one cannot find Swartkopsrivier salt, how much ordinary salt should one use for boerewors?'

'Why are you making your own wors *there*?' She is surprised.

'I want to give someone a very special gift.'

She hesitates slightly.

'Where did you get the coriander from?'

'From Atlas trading store in the Bo-Kaap, but I scorched it and put it in my blender.'

'The thyme?'

'Pick 'n Pay.'

'Have you got grape vinegar rather than spirit vinegar?'

'Yes.'

'Okay. Because you are not using Afrikaner beef, keep the amount of salt as it is, even if it is not Swartkopsrivier, but the rest should be one and a half times the amount.'

I leave at Rebecca's gate: one kilogram of boerewors and my last jar of *nastergal* – found in Harrismith and sent to me specially by Rina.

*O*n a spring morning, the bushwillows with their silver-green leaves might have felt Joseph Orpen riding in among them. Pausing on the highest point of the riverbank, amid the sound of babbler, fisher-bird and snake-bird, wild goose and duck, he perhaps pointed to the lush, grassy plain with its thorn trees, enclosed by a horseshoe of river, and said: 'There! The new town will be there.' And so the people came, and you came with them.

You were a weeping willow, a fingertip tree. You were brought here as a cutting by Mr and Mrs Hill and planted among the local bushwillows. Once you had taken root, you gave yourself over to the earth with all your sap, you blazed up and pushed out, blossoming and drooping down in the most tender, needle-thin green over a large pool cupped in solid sandstone. In summer, you witnessed the spilling of cascades over the lip into foaming hollows beneath. The shore was lush with ferns, horse-grass, wild irises and blood lilies. Your toenails wound in a thousand red sprouts in and out of the stone layers, your ankles were slimed by snail and worm, your shins gnawed away into crab-tunnels, your armpits adopted by otters and finches. Your thighs tugged the water. Then a timber tea house was slung around your waist, and on Sundays men in suits and ladies wearing straw hats rowed across the river to take high tea on the wooden balcony. Once, a boy came to live high up in your collar-bones. After the school bell rang in the mornings, he crept down the bank, took off his school uniform and hid the bundle with his satchel among the reeds. Then, in his underpants and bare feet, he slid up your trunk and for the whole day he inhabited you like a prince, dangling on ropes from bough to bough, imitating the sounds of birds. With a pocket knife he carved his name into your bark from right to left. When the people built the first weir, the waterfall flattened out into a quiet, full river. Now you became familiar with the regular sounds of regatta-rowers on the still waters over weekends. The islet further upriver was blasted away so that the first puffing river boat could have a mooring. Rumours of dams and irrigation schemes came downstream. The first bubbling of townships. A narrow suspension bridge of Scottish cast iron crocheted in fine lacy patterns was spanned beside you. On the long summer evenings lovers walked slowly amidst the willows across the swaying bridge. One day the foundations were laid for the enormous harp-shaped bridge that linked the main road directly to the heart of the town. At Christmas time the riverbanks were transformed into a festival of light, and the long strings of coloured lights strung across the river ribbed the water with floating reflections. People camped out in tents or stayed over in rondavels, children rode in tumble-wheels and swung against the streaks of light, young men dived from the bridges, while the carols played by the Salvation Army's brass band drifted from the open-air chapel across the water. You noticed that the man mooring the boats never smiled. The man emptying the rubbish bins never looked up. Those who strung up the lights never looked back to see how lovely they were.

It was winter. Your bare branches hung in the water like whips. On the frost-white grass they sat. Two men. The one kept saying how grateful he was that the pamphlets had been printed for free, and the other simply answered, 'Clements, in this case I am on your side.' Next to him lay the Kroonstad Times. You could not see the headline: 'Wife of American singer Paul Robeson attacks Kroonstad.' You were unaware of her words: 'Before our tour through the country, everybody warned us against Kroonstad, a cracker town en route to Johannesburg. Africans hate and fear this town. And there right in the middle of the main street one of the elegant balloon tyres blew out. Pauli and I strolled through the town in search of the Post Office. We were stared at all the way by pork-pie-faced Boers with their small eyes set close together in mean faces. The sight of the undernourished little African nurse girls carrying those overstuffed Boer children on their backs sickened me.' You knew nothing of this either: 'Inhabitants to be moved from Location A have been advised not to pay their taxes by Clements Kadalie, head of the Industrial and Commercial Workers' Union of Africa. Kadalie promised to take the case to the high court.' You would have stood more peacefully among the reeds had you been able to read the column headlined 'Jonathan writes': 'Last year I was with a large number of tiny tots waiting for Father Christmas to arrive on the river boat. I stood talking to B. de Wet Erlank, the big, friendly principal of the school. We were near the boathouse. Suddenly Erlank broke off in the middle of a sentence and gazed into the distance. "Look at that view. Look at the willows and the clouds and the reflections in the water. Dear God, it is a beautiful place this." Erlank spoke these words quietly and with feeling. I looked at the riverbanks and there was such beauty in them. If you are weary, my friend, go down to the river and contemplate that scene awhile.'

Of these things you knew nothing. You did not notice the young man with the brittle moustache who kept watch from a distance on the two men with the newspaper. And so you did not recognize him when he returned, this same man, many years later. He seemed to be in charge now, he was ordering policemen and soldiers to build walls of sandbags as protection against the raging river. You had been standing on these banks for more than a hundred years and you had seen many floods. You had been confronted, tested – knee-high, thigh-high, breast-high – but always you had managed to stand firm. To keep your place. Hold your space. And afterwards, when the flood had spent itself, subsiding into a timid, muddy vein, your wide, furry branches still winged the breeze and you shook your crooks clean of debris. Your chest young and firm again. But this time it was different. You were digging in when you felt the water rising. You braced yourself, but when it came, it came with fury. Like hatred. It pitted itself against you in a sweep of sudden waves and ferocious pull. You strained, you curbed, you braked. You heard the sound of lightning. Of wet wood tearing. Then, with a blinding pain, you snapped. Ripped from mud, from gravel, from soil, torn from stone, from underwater crevices, from earth you were hurled as if you had always been nothing but rubbish. Excess. Around your body your branches snapped like the teeth of a comb. And in this tumbling disregard, you saw your immense roots for the first time, as they churned, and you saw how bleak they were, how clumsily knotted and vulnerable, malformed by the decades of living in, giving to, bearing up and holding on. Your autumn foliage wrapped around you in the foamy mantle of the maelstrom. Your enormous rump hit the delicate footbridge like a battering ram. It hit and hit and hit until the bridge snapped with a dreadful howl and rushed with you in mangled iron-wrought lumps down the river.

When the flood waters dropped after three days, the sandstone bank where you had stood bled like a torn gum. And the delicate bridge from bank to bank was gone.

PART FOUR

A Translation

... translation is an intentional interaction intending to change an existing state of affairs.

Christiane Nord

... for the notion of translation we would have to substitute the notion of transformation: a regulated transformation of one language by another, of one text by another.

Jacques Derrida

Until I am free to write bilingually and to switch codes without having always to be translated ... my tongue will be illegitimate.

Gloria Anzaldúa

Having been borne across the world, we are translated men. It is normally supposed that something always gets lost in translation; I cling obstinately to the notion that something can also be gained.

Salman Rushdie

I use the personal when I am applying a mask to my face.

Anne Sexton

Vivlia Publishers have asked her to translate Nelson Mandela's *Long Walk to Freedom* into Afrikaans. She finds herself in Mandela's sitting room in Houghton, Johannesburg, along with the designated translators of three other editions, waiting to discuss the work that lies ahead. Prof. Bheki Ntuli will be doing the Zulu version, Prof. Maje Serudu the Sepedi, and Prof. Peter Mtuze the Xhosa.

It is a relaxed Mandela who walks into the room. He embraces them warmly and teases Prof. Ntuli about the fact that he does not yet have a grey hair on his head. 'Muti,' says the professor, 'great muti we have in KwaZulu to keep an old man young!'

Prof. Mtuze indicates that he will be translating the work into classical Xhosa. This is the story of a Xhosa prince, so to speak, and Xhosa royalty should not speak street Xhosa peppered with a lot of English words. His problem is the exact relationship between Mandela and Kaiser Matanzima. The English book simply uses 'nephew', but in Xhosa there are particular words for every kind of relation, specifically denoting age and hierarchy. Mandela and Matanzima had several clashes over the years and, depending on the specific way in which they are related, a Xhosa reader would be able to draw conclusions about whether Mandela treated Matanzima with unbecoming disrespect. It takes them almost a quarter of an hour to work it out.

Professor Ntuli says that he wants every Zulu to be able to read the book with ease and enjoyment, to absorb it as part of his own life, to make it a text he can live by. His translation will veer more towards everyday Zulu, which means that he may use words like 'i-democracy' and 'i-gallery'. But of course he will employ a different register when it comes to the political speeches and praise songs. He would really like to translate Mandela's Rivonia Trial speech in a kind of lofty, praise-song style.

Mtuze will not be using words like 'i-democracy'. Alternatives do exist in Xhosa, he says, and now is the perfect time to dust them off and have them take their rightful place in the language.

She and Prof. Serudu ask why Mandela wants the book translated into all South Africa's languages. Research has surely shown him that people with an interest in the book have probably already read it in English, and that, with the exception of Afrikaans, books sell particularly badly in the other tongues. They cannot think of a single bookshop that keeps books in any of the African languages.

'This book has been translated into practically all the languages of the world. I can go to any place on earth and my story can be found there in that language. Except here. Here I exist only in English. I want to be part of all the languages of my country.'

'You wrote a poem about me in which you named all the ancestors on my mother's side,' Mandela says to her as they are walking out. 'How did you know that?'

'I translated the praise poems delivered at your inauguration as president. The first poet used your mother's ancestry and this was pointed out to me as most unusual.'

'One's language should never be a dead end,' he says, as he takes his place among them for the usual photograph. 'That is why I believe in translation: for us to be able to live together.'

While they are posing, she asks, 'You have always married strong women, Sir. What is it about them that attracts you?'

He laughs. 'It is not I who chose them, it is they who chose me.'

✧

Dear children,

I am staying in a bed-and-breakfast joint. It has a toilet with a ledge in the bowl – so that you can study the evacuation, says the owner. I wonder about a people who want to *see* their evacuation daily, to study it, smell it, prod the texture before flushing it away.

But enough of that. Since my arrival in Flanders I've had some eerie experiences with my Serfontein forefathers.

Driving through the town of Peruwelz, suddenly before me was the signpost: Rue de Cerfontaine, as if I had been guided there. I found myself looking around with a proprietor's eye. Was it well looked after? Clean? Needless to say, it was. At the end of the street was a restaurant, the Moulin de Cerfontaine, and when I got out there, the first sound I heard was the rustling of poplars. I pushed open the wooden gate and then I got goose pimples all over. Because next to the mill is a dam. And in the middle of the dam is an island with grass and a small tree. As I stood there, a wild duck came down the slope and glided into the water. I remembered how my cousin, who built a dam for us on the farm, asked me: 'Now where should I put the island? Because whenever I make a dam for a Serfontein, he wants an island in the middle.' How is it possible, my children? Is blood that strong? The owner of the restaurant said there were no Serfonteins left in the town. But they had been there once. That I knew.

Then I stopped at the church in Soumange. While strolling around in the church-yard, I came across a slate headstone with the inscription: 'Biertrant Cherfontaine. Ici repose un honnête homme. Trespassa 18 Decembre 1644.' Here rests an honourable man. Precisely a hundred years before the name 'Serfontein' first appears on official records at the Cape of Good Hope! That was when a Christina Abrahamse had her son Willem Serventyn baptized. She came alone to the ceremony. Her child was inscribed under the heading 'slavenkinderen' and the Nederlandsch Oost-Indische Compagnie signed as a witness.

Now, I may be just another indifferent Serfontein, but I stood there in the church-yard with my heart burning in my throat. Who was this man? Did he have the kind of reserve that made you notice him in a group? Would he say only two words and ges-ticulate the rest? Did he have the same penetrating blue eyes as my father? Then it was as if I could see him in front of me. On the other side of the world, across three cen-turies, he spoke to me, this man under the gravestone. However far-fetched it sounds, he knew that I had come to look for him. In the deepest kernels of our souls, Biertrant Cherfontaine and I still gave out the same vibrations, we knew and translated one another – in the same way that posterity will look for me one day in a headstone and find me among poplars and the gurgling of sparrows.

Please tell your father that men just like him, his age and build and everything, are wearing aprons and carrying trays in the restaurants at Schiphol.

Your mother

✧

On the plane home, she thinks about the whole notion of translation. Perhaps transla-tion is one of the most accurate barometers of the power of a language. It seems to her that works are usually translated from weaker into mightier languages. The more a language is threatened, the stronger the urge becomes to translate *from* that language. The mightier a language, the stronger the urge to be translated *into* that language. England or America could not be bothered how many of their major works are trans-lated into other languages, whereas Holland, Sweden, Germany, France not only ensure that books by J.M. Coetzee, John Updike, John le Carré, Chinua Achebe are translated into their languages, but also that the important works in their own tongues are translated into English.

She reads an interview with the Dutch poet Gerrit Komrij about translation. 'Translation creates space in a language. It lets the osmosis of human knowledge take place between cultures. Translation is like gymnastics for one's language, an exercise in language that not only makes literature accessible, but ensures that all kinds of concepts are brought in for which you have to discover equivalents. To me, translation seems essential for the depth and suppleness of a language.

'Clinging exclusively to your own language creates anxiety and narrow-mindedness. I realize that it is incredibly expensive and a luxury, but to have the literature of the entire world available in Dutch keeps the language fit and strong. We have just completed a fourth translation of Shakespeare's works – a complete, fresh, modern, adjusted Shakespeare. Classical works often receive a new coat so that they can breathe new life and richness into the language. The translation of works from other cultures makes for a more open-minded society.'

In South African literature, English is the language in which writers reach each other, meet each other, get into conversation or debate. And, in the way of a mighty language, English does not care two hoots whether there are brilliant writers in Afrikaans or Xhosa or Sepedi; if the writer does not write in English, he or she does not really exist.

She realizes that translation is therefore one of the key strategies for survival – not only for writers and publishers, but especially for a language itself. If it does not develop a strong translating tradition, it can shut up shop, because some of its best writers will leave. If power shifts turn English into the language where people meet, then writers in the smaller languages should demand the right not only to write in their own language, but to be translated in order to form part of all the voices of their country.

'Translation is empowering, because in my mother tongue I have access to the entire pipe organ and all its registers; in my acquired language I try to express myself on a toy piano,' she thinks aloud.

'Be careful,' warns Christina, a Swedish expert on translation, as the two of them chat on a balcony in De Waterkant. 'People who prefer not to write in their mother tongues often enrich a language precisely because they are not cluttered with tradition or intimidated by the great writers of that language. But the right to be translated should exist in all languages.'

'I feel at times embarrassed that I want to be read in English, like I have sold out, betrayed something, or revealed a shameful desire ... and I am not clear how much of it has to do with a resistance to colonization, giving in to power, being owned, accepted by the colonizer's hand – because English has become the door to the Father, if you know what I mean.'

'Why are you interested in the Father?'

'That is my problem: I am not. I think I simply want to be read by people whom I care for, and some of them happen not to understand Afrikaans. I know full well that I can never play a role in English literature as I do in Afrikaans, because I do not have T.S. Eliot or Philip Larkin in my bones. I have somebody else. I actually think you can only *revolutionize* a language if you have grown up in it, in that house; coming from somewhere else, you can only bring interesting versions of living. The changes you have brought to your own living spaces will get lost in an English house.'

Christina smiles as if all of this is amusing. Then she begins to talk about how the act of translation works.

'Some things are easy to translate. Other things more difficult. But with a little effort the difference from one language to another can be bridged. At times, however, things will come up that strike you because of their difficulty, their complexity, the way they resist the resources you yourself use, in your own language and culture, to make sense of the world. These things – from lexical items, through speech acts, to fundamental notions of how the world works – are called "rich points". And a translator has to be very aware of the rich points relevant to a particular translation task, aimed at opening communication between the groups or subgroups on either side of the language barrier.'

'Are you saying then that translation is a cultural exchange?'

'More than that. It is a comparing of cultures. Translators interpret source-culture phenomena in the light of their own culture-specific knowledge of that culture.'

'Give me an example.'

'Take the word "forefather". Or would you use the word "ancestor"? Does it carry the same content? A foreign culture can only be perceived by means of comparison with one's own culture, the culture of primary enculturation. There can be no neutral standpoint for comparison. Everything we observe as being different from our own culture is, for us, specific to the other culture. The concepts of our own culture will thus be the touchstones for the perception of otherness.'

Christina can see that she does not understand. 'Translation is essential if we are to learn to live together on this planet. We have to begin to translate one another.'

'I am not quite sure how these ideas apply to Mandela's book. He wants to be translated from one of the mightiest languages in the world into a few powerless ones.'

She takes off her blouse. 'Forgive me, but I cannot resist this sun. I come every year from Sweden to soak it up.' She adjusts her bikini top and fastens her hair with a tortoiseshell clasp. 'The best example to look at is the Bible, which was translated during the nineteenth century, with great dedication and eagerness, into several languages of the South. As you know, not only were these languages powerless, but their speakers were also illiterate, with no written tradition. Although perhaps intended otherwise, these Bible translations are seen today as a form of colonization in the guise of conversion and civilization. It was how Western values gained access to closed communities, in order to destroy what were regarded as primitive traditions. In writing them down, the missionaries adapted the languages, sometimes with scandalous distortions, in order to convey the Christian message. This process trapped languages in structures that can at best be described as hybrid: on the one hand, the language as people use it is oral and flexible and "pagan"; on the other hand, it is written down, and inflexible, and the carrier of the "highest and best of Western values".

It was only after she started translating *Long Walk to Freedom* that she realized to what extent Mandela's story is a case of 'the Convert Writes Back'.

✧

We are sitting in a fake piazza in one of the most obscenely expensive shopping malls in the country. Behind the mall is the conference centre where the South African Conference on Racism is taking place, a precursor to the international conference planned for the following year. I was invited to speak at the event.

'Who the fuck shops here?' asks Mamukwa, taking off her shoes.

'Look at the price of a beer,' wails Ghangha.

Staggered by the opulence inside, we have drifted out one by one to these umbrellas in the late-afternoon sun. I haven't seen them for a long time. After the first election, our lives took different paths away from the town we all come from: they went on to positions in the municipal and provincial government of the Free State, I went as a journalist to the Cape. When I bumped into them a couple of days ago in the foyer of the hotel, I rushed up to them enthusiastically. Although they were glad to see me, they were clearly uncomfortable too. As the conference has progressed, I've realized that white friends have become an embarrassment of sorts because they speak of desperate times. So I was glad to find them under the umbrellas, much more like I remember them.

It appears Ghangha now lives in Bloemfontein in a formerly white suburb. 'It is fine, really. We had some problems in the beginning, but it's okay now.'

'What kind of problems?'

'Eish. The usual. I was to be held accountable for every single thing a black person did. If a black man rapes a child or steals a million, the neighbours or my colleagues want me to explain. And if I want to know why it is I never ask *them* to explain when a white farmer shoots a black baby – is it perhaps because I know them well enough? – then they're quick with this ubuntu thing: blacks stick together because of ubuntu, you know? And I can tell you, nothing pisses me off more than whites pretending to understand or even care about African concepts like ubuntu.'

'Why has race become the only debate?' I ask. 'Nobody talks about class, or human rights, accountability, how to prevent future abuses, how much of the past is already part of the present, collective guilt, moral choices, the definition of "perpetrators" – the only thing we hear is race, race, race. As if my only identity is "white", and I'm not allowed to be more than that!'

Mamukwa refuses a cigarette. 'You stopped smoking!'

She nods gravely, and says, 'Well, just look at the standing ovation Mbeki received during his address here when he said: "We know whites did not fight apartheid, because when we were in the trenches we didn't see them there."'

'My God,' I say, 'that is such populist bullshit!'

'It's true!' they shout simultaneously. I could always rely on these two comrades for a lively discussion.

'Oh please! How come, then, that when one of the best-known struggle songs was sung during the break this morning, many blacks around me didn't know a single bloody word? They could do the jive, all right, but they'd never heard the words. And why? Because they were never in the trenches either. Now they are in the forefront of entitlement. And there were no struggle songs about that. If you ask me, the people around me grew up with the capitalist theme song, "I want it all ... and I want it now!" Do you think these blacks walking past us with their designer labels, their tiny cell-phones and their enormous shopping bags, care a fuck about justice or the poor? Let me tell you why we only hear about race. The new black elite hates it when the debate turns from race to class. They will keep the race issue spinning, so that their greedy hands can grab more and more, until they have it all. They need whites as a serviceable Other. As long as a few whites are still living on a farm or two, no matter how modestly, no matter how strongly they identify with Africa and all that shit, the black elite will cry race, they'll send in the poor to do the dirty work and afterwards they'll throw them to the wolves.' I am surprised at my anger.

'The second thing I hate is when whites pretend they care about the poor,' says Ghangha. 'Meantime they use the black elite to defend their own privileged positions. You can jump this way or that, but whites are in complete denial. Not for nothing did Malcolm X say that racism was like a Cadillac – there's a new model every year. The latest model is the denial of whites.'

We order beer from a waiter who says he comes from Serbia. He seems alarmed by our fiery talk – he certainly brings the drinks in a hurry.

'Let me tell you a story, Ghangha. I went to see the play *Zulu* by Mbongeni Ngema. It was blatantly anti-white. At interval, I didn't want to go out into the foyer. I said to my friend Prabhakara, "I feel uncomfortable, I am the only white person here and all I've heard for the past hour is how horrible and stupid and ridiculous we whites have been." He scoffed at me, and in the end we did go out. And you know what? The black people there, mainly young people, they didn't even *see* me. When I walked past them, they looked right through me. As if I didn't exist. So I was relieved. But Prabhakara said, "Ja, they look through you the same way whites once looked through blacks – and what was the outcome of all that? I'd rather you stay a factor and I stay a factor to inter-act with, because the more secluded, the more deluded and self-indulgent a group can become."'

Ghangha laughs curtly. 'Arthur Ashe once said it was easier for him to cope with having Aids than it was to cope with being black. Whites can never know what it is to be black.'

'That's why you of all people should know that race is a trap! Race is the only thing about yourself you cannot change. I can change my perspective, my words, my thinking, my body language, but not my skin. So if you have a problem with me because I'm white, I'm trapped. There is no room for change. Race moves the debate from moral questions – how are you acting? – to narrow, nationalist ones – what colour are you? what group do you belong to?'

Ghangha orders us some exotic-looking cider served with lemon and ice. I bum cigarettes from the neighbouring table for Mamukwa and me.

'I'm not just talking about skin: "white" is a mindset, an outlook. Whiteness is pervasive: it's not only in the way you walk and gesticulate, in your words and thoughts, it also has to do with confidence, with where you start from. With exclusion. With the assumption that your way of running a country is the best, that your definition of a town, what you need to be happy in a town, to call it your town, is the only one.'

'Ghangha, I am trying to find a way into your definitions of "African" and "South African", I am trying to access those categories that you closed off so quickly with skin. I think it was Prof. Mamdani who said that whites have to learn to see themselves as African, to accept the African roof. But to me this commitment feels like only half the story. I still have to be accepted by those who proclaim themselves the guardians of African-ness. The Jews in Germany felt themselves to be German, yet when push came to shove, they were regarded as the very antithesis of German-ness. I can say a thousand times that I am an African. And when you dispute it, I can say, fuck you, this is also my continent and country, whether you say so or not. But who would want to live the life of an unaccepted African?'

'And if you were just unacceptable rather than unaccepted,' smiles Mamukwa, 'would you also have problems with that?'

I'm a bit stuck. 'As long as you accept that we can share a variety of identities and don't keep narrowing it down to colour. Because as we sit here, the three of us, we *do* have a few things in common, a home town, several political rallies, a party or two, a march, we have this personal identity that we share. And I have a problem when you two refuse to acknowledge it, when you force everything into the category of race and leave all three of us with our lives impoverished in some way.'

'The moment you learn to live the black life of risk, you will become one of us.'

'Bullshit,' Mamukwa says sharply to Ghangha. 'She can never become black. She will always be a ... what did they call Max du Preez the other day? – a kangaroo! Her people have been living here for generations, surviving, but when we see her, we know she is a kangaroo from elsewhere. Still, we like her and we live with her. And she, for some reason, likes us and prefers to live with us.'

I am stunned. Of all things! A bloody kangaroo, hopping around in the Free State. I would have preferred something like ... well, like a eucalyptus tree. From elsewhere, granted. But impossible to imagine the South African landscape without it. Small towns, farmyards, railway lines, forests, windbreaks. The eucalyptus towers over so many memories. It's used in mines, in pole fences, furniture. It is a handy tree. Tenacious. *'n Windskerm*. It's true that nothing will grow under it, that it consumes more water than other trees, but it has turtle doves in its leaves and sheep in its shade. And where it is desolate, there it grows. And it gives great honey.

'The point is,' says Ghangha, 'we do not have to be hugging one another all the time, as long as we live together amicably and caringly.'

'But I want to ...'

'Belong' is the word I want to say, but do not say, because another couple has joined us and the conversation turns light and jovial. I get up. Mamukwa decides to come with me. We walk slowly back to the hotel, window-shopping. The future already unfolding in different ways between us.

✧

Somebody bumps into her on the street and says, 'Hey, I hear you're translating "Outa in die Lang Pad" into Afrikaans.'

What?

So she discovers that the title of *Long Walk to Freedom* has already been satirized in Afrikaans as *Outa in die Lang Pad*. The reference is to a cheerful little ditty, in which an old black man, an *'outa'*, takes the long road to Mebosspruit, playing his tin guitar along the way. *'Outa'* is a folksy, rather derogatory term. What to do now? The obvious translation of *Long Walk to Freedom* is *Lang Pad na Vryheid* – but how can she use the phrase *'Lang Pad'* without evoking the word *'Outa'*? She considers various alternatives, but they all have their own weaknesses. Eventually she decides it might be time the *'Outa'* echo was taken on and challenged by a worthy opponent. The book will be called *Lang Pad na Vryheid*.

The most consistent thread in Mandela's autobiography is the notion of being an ordinary man in extraordinary circumstances. The life of the world's most famous political prisoner, the most respected statesman of the twentieth century, is also that of an ordinary man, with his loves and fears. Throughout the book Mandela stresses that it is respect for the ordinary that helps you to hold on to your humanity, and also enables you to take extraordinary action. The fact that you are interwoven with your community, and not your lonely singularity, finally determines your greatness.

This view of the 'great man' runs counter to every mainstream assumption. Look at the work of the most important poet in Afrikaans, N.P. van Wyk Louw. He focused in his poetry on the role of the 'lonely individual', the man who 'goes where higher, colder paths' lead, who carries the 'ark of civilization' on his shoulders safely through the milling masses. If he is crushed, then the animalistic and barbaric overwhelm the nation. The ultimate is beauty. And beauty is loneliness. Mandela provides a totally new account of leadership within the nation, and in so doing opens up space for an interesting debate in Afrikaans.

The book is dotted with little cameos that speak of more than good storytelling technique. Nowhere does Mandela allow for the traditional separation between the public and the private. When the book first appeared, the *Mail & Guardian* reviewer complained that in this text the man had become the mask; but a more careful reading suggests that Mandela saw to it, in the most thoroughgoing way, that the private always remained part of the public, the individual part of the collective. Take this example:

I raised my fist to the crowd, and the crowd responded with an enormous cheer. Those cheers fired me anew with the spirit of the struggle. *'Amandla!'* I called out. *'Ngawethu!'* they responded. *'iAfrika!'* I yelled; *'Mayibuye!'* they answered. Finally, when the crowd had started to settle down, I took out my speech and then reached into my breast pocket for my glasses. They were not there; I had left them at Victor Verster. I knew Winnie's glasses had a similar prescription, and I borrowed hers.

What does this have to do with translation?

'You have to make up your mind what the main thrust of the book is,' says the translator with the sunburnt shoulders, 'what it is that Mandela ultimately wants to say, and what he wants to say to Afrikaans-speakers. All of this should inform your decisions on style and language.'

Afrikaans is and always has been a highly politicized language. Formal Afrikaans, academic Afrikaans, standard Afrikaans, higher Afrikaans, friendly Afrikaans, alternative Afrikaans, loose Afrikaans, mixed Afrikaans, slang Afrikaans, kitchen Afrikaans – they each imply a background or an unspoken political point of view. Your Afrikaans says who you are, where you come from and who you sided with in the past.

✧

'I am not very hungry,' says her father, listlessly prodding the food on his plate. 'Besides, the food is really ... dull.' She also puts her knife and fork down. Thank goodness. She hates offal and cabbage.

Her mother goes to the kitchen and returns with a few small Moirs bottles. 'All the food you put in your mouth has been grown on this farm. The fruit you hand out to your friends has been dried or preserved by me. The soap that washes your clothes has been boiled up by me. If you want more colourful food, I can transform it.'

Then she empties the bottles of colouring into the food on their plates: one in the offal, one in the cabbage and one in the mash. She stirs the offal into a purplish sod, the potatoes she churns to emerald green, the cabbage steams a canary yellow. Her father leaves the table. Her mother goes on eating, putting the garish food in her mouth like a queen.

⟡

Long Walk to Freedom was not written in flowery or academic English. The style is sober, and the vocabulary professional but accessible. Yet the tone is complex, a mixture of the intimate and the formal – something one might call 'friendly dignity'. The Afrikaans used in the translation should be able to accommodate different ranges: the sharp critique of the intellectual, the sloganeering of the activist, the formal and stately tone of the advocate and international statesman, without ever giving up the warm accessibility of the failed husband and grieving father.

The choice makes itself. Already on the first page, where a decision has to be made about the word 'clan', the book demands to be translated into a more formal and correct Afrikaans. It's as if such a 'subversive' story actually needs to be translated into the kind of Afrikaans in which apartheid took its first steps, so that, over the hundreds of pages, precisely that kind of Afrikaans can be undermined. Given a different sound. Mandela's resistance and criticism are not expressed in alternative or struggle or even friendly Afrikaans, but lie embedded in what could be seen as formal Afrikaans, but now with a new or rediscovered tone of grace and warmth.

In some Afrikaans history notes she sees that 'Defiance Campaign' is translated as '*Uittartingsveldtog*' – Provocation Campaign. My word! There is surely an important difference between defiance and provocation? She contacts the people in charge of the Afrikaans dictionary in Stellenbosch. They must help her. And they do. They debate, they test out words on each other. And so they decide to go with '*Uitdaag-kampanje*' – Challenge Campaign, Defy Campaign.

However, the biggest decision that has to be made concerns the word 'African'. Who and what is an African? Mandela uses 'African' quite often in his book, but in a rather haphazard way: at the beginning 'African' means only the Thembu, then it means the Xhosa, and later on it refers to everybody black. She enquires about Mandela's use of the word, and is sent the following answer by his office: he means blacks and coloureds – the Indians and the whites are from other continents, the blacks and coloureds not.

This may be Mandela's logical explanation, but during the Treason Trial he used 'African' for everyone who wasn't white, and on Robben Island he told one of the Afrikaner warders that he was also an African.

The most important question must therefore be answered first: should she follow Mandela's judgement on the meaning of 'African', or should she interpret his use of the word in context, to say that now he means 'black in general', and now he means 'not white', and now he means 'only black and not coloured or Indian'? Although interpretation is part of a translator's work, this would perhaps be stretching it too far. In any case, Mandela's own emotional enlargement of the concept of 'African' is an important motif throughout the story itself.

Then for the second obstacle. If she does retain Mandela's use of the word 'African' as it occurs, what shape should the word take in Afrikaans? Again, if the tone of the book was struggle Afrikaans, it would be easy just to keep the word in English: *die deur van 'n* African *huis staan oop.* But the tone is formal. She phones the dictionary man: 'Maybe it is time that Afrikaans eyes and ears become used to the word "*Afrikaan*" in all its grammatical forms, instead of it always seeming strange, like an imported construct?'

Of course, the word '*Afrikaan*' is used in Afrikaans, but as an adjective it causes real problems. A man from America is an '*Amerikaanse man*' or an '*Amerikaner*'. A man from Africa ought to be an '*Afrikaanse man*' or an '*Afrikaner*', but white Afrikaans-speakers awarded themselves these titles centuries ago. As a result, Mandela cannot now be the Afrikaans equivalent of an '*Afrikaansche man*' or '*afrikanische Mann*', which one would find in the Dutch and German translations – unless a serious broadening of the term is on the cards! The alternative is to use '*Afrikaan man*' and '*Afrikaan*', but because this sounds so incorrect grammatically, most speakers simply use the word '*Afrika*', as in '*Afrika man*' or '*man van Afrika*', which in turn leads to further confusion of meaning. '*Afrikaan nasionalisme*' and '*Afrika nasionalisme*' are surely two different concepts. If she uses this 'new' word, then Fort Hare will be an '*Afrikaan*' university but Stellenbosch an '*Afrika*' university.

Writers like Frantz Fanon and Es'kia Mphahlele have insisted that it is important after liberation to rethink society and rename it imaginatively, so as to ensure that old concepts and ideologies do not continue in the guise of the new. So for her it is very moving to see how the word '*Afrikaan*' for the first time finds its balance in a paragraph and rigs its sails to the winds of change: *''n Afrikaan kind word gebore in 'n Afrikaan hospitaal, huis toe geneem in 'n Afrikaan bus, leef in 'n Afrikaan woonbuurt en woon 'n Afrikaan skool by ...*' ['An African child will be born in an African hospital, will go home in an African bus, will grow up in an African township and attend an African school ...']

✧

'They wanted to see blood and tears. They didn't like the rage they reaped, and they squeezed and drugged me. At last came the convulsions and my exhausted memory got stuck. Then they knew wherever I'd be, I'd sit out my sentence, in the single cell of my mind. And they let me go in the mist.

'We finally kissed my children, you and I, but I'd been too far. I seek a man to kiss, but I've been too far. I seek my friends, old and new, but there is always the mist. And so I walk on, alone.'

(Helene Pastoors, after her release from Kroonstad Women's Prison for political prisoners)

✧

And so the four translators live with Mandela for many months. They phone each other to say: Oh, but is it not funny how he taught Winnie to drive? Is it not moving when he puts her on the train to her first anti-pass law demonstration: 'I embraced her before she boarded the train. Winnie was nervous yet resolute as she waved to me from the window, and I felt as though she were setting out on a long and perilous journey, the end of which neither of us could know.'

There is a wide variety of Afrikaners in the book. She translates the passage about the two female warders, Afrikaner women, who visited Winnie after her release from prison, boarding the blacks-only train to Soweto to join the Mandelas for Sunday lunch. Who were they? They lost their jobs because of this outing, having been reported by the police. What happened to them? Where are they today?

For weeks they struggle through the bleak, disconsolate years on Robben Island. The time Mandela refused to run on the double and was grabbed by an Afrikaner warder. How he removed the warder's hand from his collar and said: If you touch me, I will sue you in the highest court in the land. The warder was so shocked, and Mandela himself realized that he was shaking with fear at what he had just done. The time Mandela received word that his mother had died, and then his son too – how he lay on his bed for days, how Walter Sisulu took the telegram from his fingers and tightly held his hand. The terrible feelings of guilt that his mother had died exhausted and poor; that he was failing his children, his wife, his family.

Mandela's request that Afrikaans be one of the first South African languages into which his book is translated is filled with irony, she realizes. He is using this request, with his usual instinct for power relationships, to force Afrikaans to make room for all the people of the continent. He is forcing Afrikaners to go back to the roots of the word they took so exclusively for themselves, to share it with others, to transform the language of apartheid into a language of coming together, to rid it of the vocabulary of power and retribution.

How strange it is, she thinks, to translate this in a world that so respects anger, celebrates revenge and admires the purity of hatred. But this Mandela man, she has come to see, represents the best, most human face of this country, its courageous spine, its most caring ear. Indeed, this Binder-together, in many ways already the ancestor of the world, has translated her language.

✧

The translations are launched at a formal event at Gallagher Estate. Tables laid out, speeches, music, politicians ... Later she sees the stacks and stacks of books in the publisher's offices and wonders: who on God's earth will buy them all?

*Y*ou draw a constellation of water from the dark. Along fault-line and follow-rift you rise upwards. Your soft, large, lidless eye surges to the surface – slightly embarrassed by the light, slightly breathless to be unearthed from that intimacy which has given you breath, content, being. You are here now. You seep up, you well up mildly, unwillingly contained, and then – flow out. Lightly and comfortably you spill over. From eye to trough to gully to crag to valley. Your lower lip finds bed. Your flanks brush riverbank. Your vertebrae hobble in the sun. You flow. You deepen. Into your easy flux come brooks and fountains, streams of friendly brown waters filled with insects and frogs, retreating crabs, catfish with blinded, muddy eyes and slimy whiskers. A stone shelf embraces you in rock, then lets you loose to tumble downwards, unwilling yet light, in carefree spray and exuberant purls. A pool opens itself up and ah! escapes from you. A valley of water slips so silently into you that you melt together into lake or delta. And then another river runs you through! And so you flow. For millions of years. Wearing many cloaks of time and season, enchanting many species, conjuring many dreams, destroying the late ambitions of bridge and dam and irrigation scheme. You are indestructibly in your place, fed from the deepest hollows of the earth's crust.

When exactly you first became aware of it, you are not sure. Was it a piece of flotsam that itched at you, or a sudden discharge, or even an erosion during a flood? Maybe it started with that first weir, you cannot remember. You just know that one day you were tired. Exhausted. Worn down to the deepest myths of your being. The clear cool water feeding you from subterranean veins suddenly felt lukewarm and thick. The air bubbling from stone shelves came to lie warily in the back of your head. Your body bleary, the underground water lumpy with dregs, without clarity. As if it remembered nothing, as if it was filled with a sediment of hopeless fatigue. Or sadness. Now even the water from mountains, from cliffs seems ashamed to be water. There is no new confluence of colour, no sparkle of joy. Your body has become the catchment for an entire landscape of despondency. You are too tired to play, too heavy to turn, too sluggish to stream, too silted up to ever dream yourself out of it all.

I cannot bear the earth without you, and so I do not keep quiet. I talk to you. And a 'you' always calls forth an 'I'.

'I am here,' you say. 'Where are you?'

I shift myself into your shores. You tug at my body – yes, two thirds of me is also water. Your lips move. 'Down to my last leavings, I am tired,' you say, 'tired of trying, accommodating, holding out, being worsted. Despair seeps from the stone, and the dregs of the town's weariness well up in me. I am carrying a town within me that has no future, no vision, no hope. A place that finds nothing in itself pleasurable, that no one listens to any more, that is passed over by the afternoon clouds. A place that no longer claims itself, that cares for nothing, that simply sits and stares across the water, waiting to die.'

How can I talk to you? You with your surface as warm as skin and your icy undertones? Do I need a special language? A new tongue? How?

You should imagine yourself through me and I myself through you. But you lie like speechless vocal cords between your shores. Listless and weary. I see you drifting past me, your smell billowing among the willows.

On the wall of the toilets across the river somebody has written in spray-paint: Kroonstad suck ckokc.

PART FIVE

A Journey

prologue

'Dakar requests certificate of immunization,' reads the telegram.

She goes to the British Airways special office for African travel in Cape Town. When the doctor sees the word 'Mali', he whistles through his teeth, shakes his head, blinks his eyes in pity and scorn. He opens a drawer and puts a bottle on the table, then another and another and another. It becomes a pile: yellow fever, meningitis, Hepatitis B, Hepatitis A (there are two kinds? Many kinds, he says), rabies, diphtheria, typhoid, tetanus, polio.

She leaves with two injections in her left arm, one in the right, one in her bum; a mosquito net, insect repellents, tablets for diarrhoea and malaria, antibiotics and horror stories. About black moths that prefer the throat and the thin skin over the collarbones. The moment they touch the skin, these moths collapse into big black blisters. About moths that lay eggs in your panties and socks, where you've left them to dry next to the basin. From these eggs come maggots, which burrow into flesh. You will only notice them the day your flesh starts falling in.

No salad, absolutely no salad. No water. No buying from locals, all food must be 'piping hot'. And of course no sex, the doctor shudders, no exchange of fluids (does she get his drift?), and he throws in a special vaginal cream for thrush. 'You should actually also take a litre of blood along, you know ...'

She remembers that most of the second-hand accounts of journeys to Timbuktu she was able to get hold of ended with variations on the following line: *He arrived on the west coast of Africa in May 1811* or thereabouts *and was never heard of again.* But to travel in Africa with a bag of your own blood in your suitcase is perhaps the place to draw the line.

Faint of heart, she leaves South Africa.

The shadow of the aeroplane drifts meagrely across the Namib, then out across the sea as they bypass Angola. Then it brushes against the western cheek of Africa. Abidjan is water and lakes and massive islands sprouting ragged thickets of trees. The airport consists of a single moist, overpopulated terminal in which hundreds of people await the announcement of their flights clutching variously coloured boarding passes. The announcements are in French. Suddenly doors to the tarmac are thrown open and someone holds a brown placard up in the air. Everyone with a brown boarding pass rushes to the plane. She among them. People trample one another up the boarding stairs, scramble for seats. First come, first seated, with your luggage on your lap, between your feet, underneath your seat, next to you in the aisle.

She remembers Thackeray's lines:

In Africa (a quarter of the world)
Men's skins are black, their hair is crisp and curled;

And somewhere there, unknown to public view,
A mighty city lies, called Timbuctoo.

As she disembarks in Dakar, a little van comes driving up, makes a dashing turn and stops on the tarmac next to the stairs. In a minute she is being led past customs and border guards into the air-conditioned Ambassador's Lounge, where some of the other poets are already waiting with the Minister of Culture of Mali, a woman with the poetic name of Aminata Dramane Traoré. Everyone is cleared without any red tape and taken to the harbour. It is already after midnight. In a special white speedboat, they are whisked across the dark water to where Gorée Island lies asleep. Kofi, a poet who lives in Brussels and is involved with an NGO that deals with Southern Africa, awaits them on the quay and accompanies them to Soros House for bottled water. Their luggage is brought through the sandy streets in two small pushcarts. People have to be roused from their colourful mats and neckrests to let the carts pass, and then they lie down mumbling to continue their sleep.

day one

She awakes on a large white bed in a bright white room with white floors and white linen drapes that stir gently in the breeze of a fan. But it is as if the heat is already loosening her wrists. She pushes open the sea-green shutters on to a whirl of salmon-pink walls and little terracotta roofs. Somebody clip-clips at a bougainvillea, a broom scrapes across the sand. Behind this all sleeps the ocean.

Breakfast in a cool courtyard of leaf and sculpture and colour. Aromas of coffee and croissant.

A workshop is held, where all ten poets are brought together and the origins of 'La Caravane de la Poésie' are explained to them.

'The concept of the caravan goes back to ancient African traders. These primarily commercial trips always had a cultural aspect as well. Along the trade routes of West Africa, not only people, but also their tales, songs, dances, myths and legends travelled. Trade as negotiation between people also included the celebration of the word as the core of human interaction. The idea of a Poetry Caravan to Timbuktu has been wandering since 1992 in the mind of Breyten Breytenbach, poet, painter and member of the Board of Trustees of the Gorée Institute. The idea has been conveyed to other poets and kept alive over several years, and now it is finally being realized before the start of the new millennium.'

But for the sake of transparency, everyone should be aware that some problems have arisen: there is not really enough funding to complete the journey. Nobody is therefore quite sure of anything. Except that they will be accompanied by a medical doctor, a photographer and a television crew.

As the workshop proceeds, tensions surface. Every now and then the Tuareg poet makes insinuating comments to the Minister from Mali about her government's treatment of his people. The organizers try to calm him down, since she is footing the bill for everyone's stay in her capital Bamako and in Timbuktu itself. The Institute's accountant and the organizers of the journey as well as certain Board members are locked in argument behind closed doors. Accusations are thrown in all directions.

One of the Zimbabwean poets is fighting for translation. Such a journey will be senseless without translation along the way. Will someone be tasked with this or must they rely on other people's goodwill? The latter, it seems. The travellers quickly separate into language factions: she finds herself in the English camp with the two Zimbabweans; the poets from Senegal, Mali, Cameroon, Tunisia and the desert Tuareg make up the French camp; while the Egyptian poet, the Belgian poet and the organizers speak both French and English, and several other languages between them.

She sits at one of the countless cafés on the beach underneath a lean-to roof of palm fronds and works through the pamphlets and the books. It soon becomes clear that for centuries all journeys to Timbuktu have started in the same way: argument, and a lack of resources, underpinned by total excitement. Because Timbuktu, or Tombouctou, has always been a place that fired the imagination – burdened by legend, covered in myth, enmeshed in memory.

Timbuktu was (and still is) a dream-feeder. It is caught up in two dreams: the Western one and the African one. The foreign one is older. It is a yearning to plunder the purling splendour of a city whose wealth has always been described in tender detail by Western adventurers. From the fourteenth century onwards, 'Timbuctoo' was the word by which avaricious dreams were charted. People talked to each other of roofs glittering with gold from afar in the desert, of clear rivers in which herds of hippopotami could be seen trampling open veins of gold on the riverbed. Their mouths grew moist at the telling of how the desert wind would scour open footpaths of gold in front of your very eyes.

In 1324, a caravan of Mansa Musa, the Emperor of Mali, the man who had liberated Timbuctoo from the Tuareg at the city's own invitation, stopped in Cairo on its way to Mecca. It was a caravan unequalled by anything seen in Egypt before. Traders from other parts of the world gasped at the display of wealth in the size of the caravan, the spectacular clothes and jewellery, the harnesses of the camels and cattle, and of course the gold. This all, they believed, came from Timbuctoo.

'Timbuctoo' became a magical word, expressing something beyond the limits of experience. Dreams rising into fulfilment. Distance and isolation. The city was cosseted like a jewel. On one side lay the Sahara, from which few returned unharmed. The most merciless, most feared expanse of sand in the world, a place where thousands of camels disappeared into sandstorms, where the skeletons of animals and people indicated the direction of the next oasis. On the other side lay a protective tropical belt of damp, steaming jungle filled with deadly insects, snakes, fungi, and incurable diseases.

Then there is the newer dream, the African one. This dream holds that Timbuktu is a place of miracle and wisdom, the origin of all knowledge and civilization. It holds that a fruitful exchange between the different African, Moorish and Arabic cultures over three centuries led to the spread of philosophies and scientific knowledge from ancient times. The fact that there are still traces of the medical heritage of Hippocrates and Avicenna in the traditional healing methods found in Africa fuels the desire to locate the origins of all civilization in Africa. To have all things come from Africa. From Timbuktu.

With surprise, she suddenly remembers a saying from her childhood, something one said when all other sources of knowledge had failed: 'I will find someone from Timbuktu who knows.'

That evening, all the rows smouldering at the Institute erupt. She depends on translation to keep abreast. The Tuareg desert poet, Eraf Hawad, is refusing to depart the next day. He says they will murder him in Mali, they are already murdering his people in the desert. The Malian government held a cultural festival, but his people were not invited – instead the government is penning them in so that they will die out, their nomadic lifestyle is being murdered.

This is not true, the Minister from Mali replies. But of course she understands why he makes such claims: he has refugee status in France, but if he can enter Mali unhindered in this Poetry Caravan, then his arguments to the French government will evaporate, and he will lose the money they pay him. In any case, the Tuareg in Mali must acquire permanent residence, as human rights dictate that their children go to school and attend clinics. The Malian government is under pressure to see to it that the Tuareg access their rights.

Why has he waited until he is here on Gorée before making this announcement, Mariame Sonko, the manager of the project, wants to know. Now he is in breach of contract.

Hawad explodes. Amal Matur, one of the Board members, translates: 'I hate the word "caravan". What nonsense is this to call it a caravan? Caravans are nothing more than a commercial gimmick for the benefit of Western tourists!' Then he changes tack. 'Nomadism is a way of being. God is nothing other than a nomadic sound. God goes everywhere. God can only resound where there is space. The nomads are the roots of all life. The nomads are the trees of life. The dunes. One can only be a human being when one migrates, one only becomes true desert when one is always moving on. The more you intermingle, the more you become from here.'

Nobody quite understands what he is saying, but the arguments continue.

The budget for the journey has already been overspent by several millions. Too many friends of friends are going along, rumours abound that the Malian government has appropriated some of it. The head of the Institute lets them know that the entire journey is to be cancelled. Amal Matur and Mariame Sonko cut the journey in half, the desert part gets dropped, a third of the stops are cancelled, perhaps the Malian government will not be paid for anything. Bitterness is high. It is because the Institute is not entirely in the hands of West Africans. The Board members feel nothing for culture and also have no clue how things are done in these parts. Of course, there is more than enough money, and it is all here in the bank in Dakar. But okay, let everyone reduce their luggage.

day two

Crows, crows, crows. They drift past the palms out over the ocean. Between the crack of dawn and the call of the muezzin, she sees somebody tip away into sleep. Memory unfolds its lukewarm palms. She waits next to her luggage on the quay for the *chaloupe* to the mainland. She feels unfinished and strange with anticipation. Her tongue nudges no language, but lies loosened in saliva. Her ears feather the heat.

Back to the port of Dakar. In a bus with the luggage bound staggeringly high on the roof, it takes a while to leave the city behind. Entire neighbourhoods are under water after recent rains, goats totter on the roofs of houses, bleating, people wade peacefully to the market and back. The bus honks. There is a crunching sound under the wheels. A duck. '*Le sacrifice!*' yells the Senegalese poet elatedly, 'now the gods will look after us.'

Were Were Liking sits in front with her wooden staff imperiously planted – a female figure with hard, angry breasts and horns piercing the plastic roof of the bus. It is cool inside. Outside it is sweltering. When they stop, two poets, the photographer, the doctor, the sound man and the accountant kneel towards Mecca. Accountant? Yes, he has unexpectedly been sent along to oversee the finances. The little case he is kneeling next to is full of money. The other case next to the doctor is full of emergency medicine.

Just past two o'clock they arrive in Kaolack, where a whole entourage sits waiting in the horrific heat. Here a special symbolic stop is being made to ask the blessing of the local poets for the journey ahead. This town has a female griot. In the blinding sunlight she throws back her body like a sabre, her shoe flicks into the air and she cries out above the sound of the drums.

The Senegalese poet Thierno Sall stands next to her. He spreads his arms: we started at the door through which no one returned. The slave portal of Gorée. We stood at that door. There we took the words in our hands. We took the words back over that threshold from which no one returned. We now carry those words into the continent. We track the trail of those who could not choose, whose bodies were turned in one direction and their longing in another. We return to find the balance between the direction of the body and the direction of the longing. That is the point at which the body can begin to dance again.

They eat at a local tavern run by a soft-spoken Lebanese man and his grim, sweating sister. After waiting in a queue for the toilet, she finds she has started to menstruate. No headache, no PMS, she simply bleeds peacefully and powerfully. All her accessories are in her suitcase on top of the bus. She walks into the teeming street, finds a small shop like a spaza with a very old robed and bearded man. He doesn't speak English. Nobody speaks English. She points to her pubes, and draws a pad and tampon on the counter, but he stares at her in total incomprehension. She assumes that all kinds of lewd possibilities are flashing through his mind, but she forges ahead. She goes in behind the counter and points to a packet of cotton wool. One of the other customers shouts something. The shopkeeper glares at her in a sudden fury. From underneath some bolts of cloth he whips out a box of Kotex in packaging she remembers from her forgotten youth and proceeds to wrap it up in so much newsprint you would think she had just bought two pairs of boots. With the package in her hands she once again joins the queue for the genderless toilets. The pads are so old that the cotton wool has bulged out of the sides in yellowed chunks. She tears a couple open and cobbles together a kind of coherent hammock. The rest she leaves behind in the paperless toilet cubicle.

She asks the Lebanese man behind the till: 'Why do you stay here?'

'I was born here. I grew up here. It is peaceful here and, in their own way, people are happy here.'

'Why don't you leave?'

He looks at her through his thick lenses as if focusing on something obscure. 'Where to? This is the only place that will have me ... have us, Lebanese.'

That evening after eight they stop in front of the hotel in Tambacounda. In the lobby she squashes three cockroaches with her heel. She gets a room. The air-conditioning equipment looks as if it was salvaged from a ship wrecked in World War II. A thin stream of water leaks from it. She rolls up the mat to stop the water from running underneath her bed.

Outside the town a makeshift stage covered with orange tarpaulins stands in the sand. The moon slips into full. People throng together in different phases and genres of celebration. A terribly fat man stands on the stage, wobbling independent layers of fat to cries of joy from the audience. Drums are heated next to fires and tuned every now and then, and whenever one reaches the correct pitch it simply joins in. The poets are being introduced one by one amid loud applause, the sound system seemingly carrying feedback from the whole of Africa.

'Since the white man brought plates of corrugated iron to Africa, it has suddenly become very hot here,' says the man from the Institute, Amal Matur. 'Since he brought the microphone, everyone has suddenly become deaf.'

A group of men appear on stage wearing elephant trunks made of sisal. They carry hats and swords and shiny breastplates reminiscent of the crusaders. Now a group of women approach. In tight-fitting black skirts they dance forward centimetre by centimetre, black staffs held upright in one hand, cow's tails in the other. The music is simultaneously familiar and unearthly.

She looks on nervously. She is not performing this evening, but how does a poet function here? The elderly Malian poet Albecaye Ousmane Kounta with his billowing robe whispers into the microphone: the griot is the double shadow of the people, it is the word and the journey of the word. We are but birds from all over Africa to see the word passing, to eat the word, to transform sword into word, to forge the collective word to take us to Tombouctou.

Were Were Liking in colourful skirts and headscarves, with beads and musical instruments. She sings, she swings her body. It is not only the word, but the journey of the word. The trace of the word. The colour of that trace. It is also the journey towards that word and travelling with open eyes.

Those not reciting, dance; those not dancing, sing. It becomes a festival of colour and sound. She sees Nhamo Khadani, the Zimbabwean poet, moving from one person to the other, his ears attuned to snatches of translation. She joins him and in this way they establish a kind of procedure: those who can speak both French and English will start translating the moment an ear tilts towards their mouths.

She thinks of the handful of poems she has brought with her. How will they ever work here? *What* will work here? Does poetry have three tiers then: an elitist poetry, a kind of First World poetry, enjoyed by the well-known and the well-heeled, the poetic aristocracy as it were; a middle-class poetry protecting its middle-class grievances of love, lineage and lime tree; and finally an oral, working-class poetry about struggle and liberation? Can the one talk to the other? But such questions are immaterial here, and that is the real nightmare. Whatever she has to say will be inaudible, because her language does not exist here. Only her body and her colour. She could talk utter nonsense, she could recite other people's poetry, and no one would be any the wiser. There is no one to translate her.

That evening, Amal Matur and Eraf Hawad return to Gorée. Matur to keep an appointment at the Institute, Hawad in fear of the Malian government.

day three

Endless road through the sand. Sometimes tarred.

See thorn tree and flower.

Everything shimmers in a haze of heat as they stop at the border post. No, the man says, he will not accept these passports and visas.

'But what about the Minister –'

'The Minister carries no authority here,' he interrupts. Besides, the chief border guard has gone home for lunch.

They give him two T-shirts sporting the 'La Caravane de la Poésie' logo, but he does not bat an eyelid. It appears that he would consider taking money. But the accountant remains immovable in the bus. He bribes nobody, he says. Bribery is the curse of Africa and he will not be party to it. In any case, the Caravan does not have enough money to start bribing people. Here are the passports, here are the visas, issued by the Malian embassy in Dakar, everything has already been paid for there, here is the receipt, so what is the man's problem?

They stand around sweating. The venerable Albecaye Kounta is sent to track down the chief border guard. He finds him just in time to join in the prayers towards Mecca.

In the meantime, they walk around among the market stalls. 'Market' is actually an exaggeration. The place is packed with people but there is hardly anything to buy. Just here and there a counter with sweets, boxes of Marlboro cigarettes and Nescafé sachets. She has this desire to go to the border guard and ask him: why do you have such a problem allowing us to enter what seems to be the absolute heart of fuck all?

Everyone sits around in the heat. Not sitting fanning themselves, nor sitting reading, nor sitting talking, nor sitting listening to a radio, nor sitting working. Simply sitting, with such clear, clean eyes one can walk through them. She buys a piece of bread from under a cloth of uncertain colour. After a while, someone underneath a tree chops some meat and starts grilling it on a piece of corrugated iron. Just when she's decided to buy a piece, her eye falls on a dead rat with one of its thighs already pinkly decomposing beneath a blanket of maggots, flies rising sluggishly when somebody passes. In the empty office the guard who wants the bribe is sleeping at his desk with his head on his arms. The thing seems to be to outwait one another. Beer? Muslim country, ma'am, says the photographer. This heat, this desperation, and absolutely nothing to help you get through the days but religion? As she walks across the sandy plain, she realizes that she has never walked so slowly. She rocks slightly at every step, her feet are swollen in the heat. Zein el-Abedin Fouad, the Egyptian poet, quotes from God's Bits of Wood: 'We are used to the sun. The sun of Africa is a native.'

Suddenly they can go. The accountant is still sitting in the bus. Everybody scrambles in. It was the praying towards Mecca that did the trick.

At Kayes the group is split in two. One lot will be sleeping at a hotel built of stone, the others are taken to a cluster of bungalows on the banks of the River Senegal, where both the air conditioning and the lighting have broken down.

Before the performance, each poet receives a mouthful of milk from a flat earthenware dish, and a large rose-coloured nut, for inspiration and potency. God knows, she can do with both – her stomach is in a knot. She notices that the men buy lots of these nuts afterwards and stuff them into the folds of their robes.

The evening is dominated by the unique voices of female griots, among whom the main personality is Amy Diarra, a woman in a wheelchair. Dressed like a queen – microphone in one hand, the other skilfully manipulating one wheel of her rolling-chair – she skittles with astonishing speed all over the cement circle, her long silky tones trailing in silver threads behind her. To one side, just off the circle, stands a very tall, very skinny woman, her face impassive, indestructible as volcanic rock. In a long green cloak she stands, bringing forth sounds: the ancient, angry cries of the Malian Empire, more than six centuries old. Nobody stirs. It is a sound human in fibre, but other-worldly in tone. Something seems to shudder through the audience. None of them breathe.

Then Were Were Liking rises slowly, plants her staff majestically in the ground and cries an answer. An answer of here, of now. They fall into an enchanting dialogue. As if drawn and chosen by an unreadable code, the poets move up one by one in order to recite in the background. From the mouth of Zein el-Abedin Fouad fall classical Arabic rhythms; the poet from Zimbabwe, Nhamo Khadani, shuffles in small steps as he calls out in a mixture of Shona and English: 'I migrate to follow the word.' Thierno Sall skips into the circle on one leg, flapping his arms like wings: the imagination breathes. The imagination breathes.

She sits crumpled up, unable to make any judgement, any analysis, any sounding that would allow her to put together a contribution. Since she cannot get a grip on the context, she is unable to decide what to do. Initially, she felt that she had dressed inappropriately, that she was using the wrong language, that she was caught up in the wrong genre – she is accustomed to writing, not performing. But now her estrangement is so complete that she sees no bridge. The three sheets of poems lie uselessly in her lap. Race no longer matters. As far as she can tell, nobody cares what colour she is or who she identifies with. Nobody has a problem with the fact that the person representing South Africa is white and speaks Afrikaans. She cannot even figure out whether she is expected to go into the circle now, whether it even matters at all. Maybe she should just babble along as the spirits lead her. Spirits? What spirits? Should she sing? But what is her equivalent of what is being sung here? 'Shosholoza'? 'Sarie Marais'? Mimi Coertse's 'Heimwee'? 'Nkosi Sikelel' iAfrika'? A waltz? If she must bring 'her own culture', then what exactly in her history of fabricated and reconciled identities is her own? Should she try to fit in as best she can? Knowing full well how embarrassing it looks when a whitey tries to out-Africa Africa. Should she just stay out of it all?

A dancing black woman suddenly appears in front of her and stretches out her hand. She rises, the sheets in her fingers, her body stiff in the rhythmically moving group. The rolling-chair darts forward and the microphone is held out to her. As if dreaming, she takes it, lifts her papers and reads: '*nie die intimiteit van jou voorkop mooi soos reën nie / nog die geweld van jou liggaam agter lakens terughoudend nie ...*'

She is unable to hear herself. No, that's not exactly true, she realizes. Between the calls and the countervoices, the word and the rewording, she hears snatches of Afrikaans. She hears it, but in the tumult of colour and sound and light she feels clumsy, uncomfortably gnarled. She knows that there is a little of everything in these different interactions. People are reacting in voice and dance and song to one another – taking the lead, making space, being with ... she will have to learn this change of tongue.

Back at the bungalows a few people are drinking in the beer garden. Some of them are white and from South Africa. They have contracts on the goldfields of Mali, that is why this area has tarred roads and electricity, there is an exclusive neighbourhood and school here for South Africans. Food is flown in regularly, as well as newspapers. And one can easily tune in to M-Net via satellite.

Later that night she is woken by a noisy brawl in the beer garden. The sound of fist against flesh, cries of *'Fokken moer!'* and *'Fokken poes!'* – a rowdy exchange in comforting, exclusive Afrikaans.

day four

The others emerge dazed from the stone hotel. There was no water, no electricity. Everybody walks over to the station and the waiting train, accompanied by swarms of children carrying bags and begging for ballpoint pens. Half a coach has been reserved for the Poetry Caravan. The coach is open at the back like a delivery truck. The yellow upholstery on the large benches is cracked and split. Below the windows, which can no longer be opened or closed, she reads *'öffnen'* with a little directional arrow, and *'schliessen'* with a little directional arrow. The upholstery is so cracked that she has to throw a jacket around her shoulders to protect her from scratches. Mariame Sonko comes around: it has been decided that everybody on the train must write a poem today. Later it will become part of a book.

Her stomach turns. Yet another thing she is not good at: writing to order.

The train stops at every village, and people rush up to the coaches with baskets of food: apples, guavas, custard apples, a kind of melon, peanuts. At a larger village they all get down and everyone can eat wherever they choose. The entire village square is filled with cooking. Enormous cast-iron pots full of orange rice, drums of river fish, chicken and sweet potatoes. Over open fires the meat is being grilled. When a piece is ready, the griller bangs a panga against a drum and everyone with money rushes over. The meat is chopped up with the panga on a metal sheet and you grab the pieces you fancy. Or you can ask for it to be wrapped in brown paper.

Around her everyone seems to be eating heartily. The revulsion lies so thickly in her throat that she knows she could die from it, absolutely die, if she eats anything. The guava is full of worms, the apple sour and crawling with mites. She becomes aware of someone else tightly squeezed into a corner of the coach. It is Amina Saïd, the Tunisian poet who lives in Paris. She just shakes her head urgently when food is offered to her.

Sometimes the train moves through wooded areas, sometimes through grassland. Endless deserted stretches of land. Sometimes you spot cattle, emaciated beasts with their hip bones sticking out. The nearer to a village, the more struggling little fields there are.

Zein writes a poem in ten minutes. Reciting from memory after a while, he delivers a whole long poem in Arabic. 'How do you manage it?' she asks.

'In Arabic poetry there are specific patterns that you have to keep to. For example, certain forms demand that the first line contain the vowels, say ... a, a, e, a, i, and the second line must have e, e, i, e, a, or something like that. Therefore you look for words that fit into these systems of sounds. As a poet your ear is finely attuned to words that contain these vowels, so it obviously becomes quite easy to remember any Arabic poem.'

The part that he translates for her has an immediate, surreal edge. 'It is because the words were chosen firstly for their sound value, and only after that for their meaning. That is why it is so difficult to translate the Qur'an. You must be familiar with the Arabic literary traditions before you can translate or interpret anything.'

'Then you *do* link up with the oral traditions of Africa,' says Chenjerai Hove, Zimbabwe's best-known poet.

'Yes, but there is an important difference. In Egypt we have had a written poetic tradition from time immemorial. So it is not because we cannot write that we are orally inclined.'

'One could say then that you are not within the true African tradition. You function in an Arabic context that has nothing to do with the African one.'

This Zein does not like. 'My ancestors lived on the banks of the Nile before any other kingdom ever arose in Africa. And, like most Africans, my mother tongue has also been taken away from me and I now operate in the language of the conqueror, but that does not make me less of an African. Would you say that the fact that you write in English makes you less of an African?'

The train stops at Kita, where the mayor and a whole variety of orchestras await them. In a boisterous procession, clothed in a stifling blanket of dust, they all walk through the streets to the hotel.

They wait in the courtyard for rooms to be assigned to them. Suddenly a furious argument erupts between the Senegalese poet and the television editor. Mariame Sonko, the doctor and the photographer intervene, but it is obvious that everybody is exhausted.

That evening, Albecaye Kounta is asked to talk about his work. He starts by telling them that he lives in Bamako, the capital of Mali, although he was born in a distant village. He was born into the intellectual caste, whose task it is to advise political and traditional leaders. When he was twelve years old, he wrote, without the knowledge of his family, to the senior political leader in Mali and asked to be given an education so that he could fulfil his role as advisor. Although he was surprised, the leader agreed to the request, fully aware that the child lived thousands of kilometres away and could not bother him. But before he knew it, Albecaye Kounta was standing before him, come to receive the promised education. He was sent to Russia, where he spent a few months learning the language before starting to study accountancy. Homesickness led him to write poetry. One of his poems is translated piecemeal:

soon the peaceful caravans, the slumbering caravans
will meander through the desert towards Arouane
they will pass again and again
in the ochre shadows of evenings
with their lullaby of silk

this is the hour when the mistress leans on the window sill
her arm tired of lifting the teapot
invoking the night which is swallowing the flamboyant sunset
or the unveiled glow of moon
this is the hour of the muezzin
slamming down the noise and agony of the day
this is the hour of prayer and silence lowering its veil
on Tombouctou of the days of glory
on Tombouctou of the ancient days
...
Tombouctou of the full moons, the milky sand
Tombouctou of the violent winds, the ephemeral oases
Tombouctou of the shimmering, of the mysteries
Tombouctou of bare feet, of burning noons
Tombouctou of languishing dusks, of slow daybreaks
Tombouctou of drums, of humour
Tombouctou of praises, of verdicts
Tombouctou of faded rhythms
...
Wake up, city of the ancestors
let the dew return
over the forgotten oases

There is no air conditioning in the hotel. She falls asleep fully dressed.

day five

It rained during the night and the roof leaked neatly into her suitcase. She doesn't care in the slightest. She walks through the streets of Kita. There is a lot of activity, but nothing seems structured. People are sitting around, a few of them talking, some women are cooking or washing clothes, a lot of the men sit with sticks in their hands scratching in the dust. After a while she realizes two things: she is lost and she is being followed by a phalanx of small children. She has forgotten the name of the hotel.

'L'hôtel?' she asks the children. They gesture and, it seems to her, lead her even deeper into the town. In between houses, down alleyways, across squares. Eventually she comes across a group of men sitting around a table playing dominoes.

'L'hôtel?' she asks again. 'Deux hôtels,' says one. Damn! It would be just like her to get lost in a town with two hotels. She shrugs.

He indicates something to the children and they lead her further. She walks and walks. It could go on like this forever. Sweat streams down her body. It seems to her that she is walking through the whole of Africa's misery and it will take her all of her life. The ever-present hunger, the vacancy of despair, the immobility of poverty, the meagreness of ignorance, the blight of sores and flies on millions of faces. It feels as if she will carry on walking like this because poverty and misery have no horizons. She has gone way beyond tears. She speaks no one's language. She will never again see any-one she can talk to. Anyone she knows. She will never again eat anything delightful. The children stop. It takes her a couple of seconds to recognize the building in front of her as the hotel. She bursts into tears. She takes a handful of notes from her bag and hands them to the children, who run screaming down the road.

'Are you out of your mind?' says Nhamo, who is standing in the entrance of the hotel. 'You have just given them enough money to pay a whole family's school fees for a year.'

She sinks into a chair smoothed down by ages of sitting and is overwhelmed by such a wonderful peacefulness. She feels the exhaustion flowing from her. It's the chair, she thinks. This chair evidently has a deep understanding of the human spine. She feels her skeleton growing fragrant. From here she will never rise again. Here she will sit for all eternity.

'Did you know that the Swahili word for "whites" is "They-who-surround-you-with-questions"?'

'How true it is.' Kofi, the Belgian poet, has joined them in the lobby. 'During the expansionist period of the European empires, people were specifically trained to ask the right questions. You had to work out very quickly whether the natives confronting you were hostile, who their enemies were, whether there was gold or diamonds or ivory around, whether there were natural boundaries, illnesses, water sources, and so on. In order to make a strategic value assessment, you need to be able to ask the right questions.'

The whole group visits the house of the well-known Malian writer Mansa Makan Diabate. Then they pay a courtesy visit to the mayor of Kita. And finally they arrive at La Maison de Parole – the House of the Word, the place of the griots. A building they have occupied since the fifteenth century. Everyone removes their shoes and sits down on mats against the wall. Across the room, about thirty male griots are sitting, mainly very old men, with here and there a more youthful one of seventy. They nod: the Caravan may ask questions.

They ask: What is the role of a griot in society? How is a griot trained?

The griots deliberate among themselves and then appoint one to speak on their behalf. 'We eat the daily word. We live by the daily bread of the word.'

But the more he explains, the more it seems that griots simply resolve arguments in the community. Zein translates in her ear. 'Griots are a caste. You are born into it. You are taught by your father and your family. The griots have tasks they have to perform during festive occasions, births, weddings, funerals. It is the griot's task to establish the place of a newborn in the community. He reminds the family of its bloodline, of the history from which it comes, and he places the individual within that context. The griot must be able to use his language skills to transform points of contention and conflict into enriching insight and ultimate peace.'

How do they transform conflict? Why are there no women?

'No women may enter La Maison de Parole, although we have graciously made an exception today. It is so because it has been so for centuries. But we have decided recently that women may now stand in the doorway to listen if we are discussing a matter concerning them. We do this because it is we who have the burden of protecting women in times of war.'

'Women have always been able to kill just as well as men,' says Were Were Liking in a demure voice. 'Women have also been able to produce poetry just as well as men. I myself come from a part of Cameroon where women have been griots for centuries, and we find that where female griots operate, there is no war, no famine and no despair.'

The men, including those in the Caravan, start stirring uneasily as her voice becomes more and more assertive. 'Here is also Amina from Tunisia. For generations, the male members of her family have been the chief griots of Tunisia. But today she is one of the most important poets in France. What does this tell us?' Were Were Liking suddenly looks straight at them. 'The word is used here to abuse, not to transform. And we know that the moment the word is abused, it abandons the abuser. You may not know it, but the poetry dies from your lips.' Somebody quickly rises and brings proceedings to an end.

That afternoon, only a few people turn up for the event. It is because the griots were insulted. One does not insult another in his own front room, the women of the Caravan are scolded. There are right ways to take on tradition and there are wrong ways. What happened this morning was wrong.

Were Were sits quietly braiding her hair and does not say a word. But others take up the discussion. Wasn't the whole point to have interaction and share ideas? Of course. Look, a white woman could have said all that, because people realize that they do not know any better, their remarks come from ignorance; but when a black woman speaks like that, it goes against so many cultural grains that you cannot address the real issue in the end, you just have to put out fires of anger. If you want to fight for women's rights, go into politics. When you are busy with literature, you lift yourself above politics. It would have made much more of an impression had Were Were delivered poetry of such a high standard that the men could not ignore her.

'It is good that you as a white person did not enter into the talk about the absence of women this afternoon,' Nhamo says to her afterwards, 'certain kinds of criticism, to be really effective, should only come from blacks.'

'So why didn't you speak out about their absence?'

'People should be granted the dignity to fight for their rights.'

That evening, Were Were Liking will have an opportunity to speak about her work. In the late afternoon she disappears into the town to make preparations. Much later they are called to a special room in the hotel, where she has gathered every available carpet, chair and plant. She greets them, breathtakingly dressed in multicoloured cloths, dramatic jewellery, hundreds of decorated braids. From large pots, which she collected in the town, she serves a special milk drink with a wooden ladle. On a little round table, her laptop stands flipped open, with the evening's programme displayed on the screen.

> we are the carpenters of memory
> we plane words
>
> the grain of the word is the culture of mercy
> there is the dignity of the word
> the nobility of the word
> the place of the word in a room
> in towns of sand
> in towns of wind
> the word moves from one being to another
> until all words are together
>
> we are the masters – not of creation
> but of the transmission of the soul
> the route is the journey
> the wings are the language
> to see the world pass
> to see the word pass in the foyer of language
> with breath in its ribs

Liking uncovers all the pots. Then she starts turning. Silently. Round and round, faster and faster, until she stabilizes in a certain rhythm, and for almost seven minutes she spins around soundlessly in one place, a blur of colour. A myriad fragrances of herbs and spices stir up from the pots. Everyone sits breathless and mesmerized.

day six

At half past three the next morning they are woken up to catch the five o'clock train to Bamako. On the train, they learn that a couple of the poets have been robbed. Zein's camera was stolen from under a chair while Were Were was performing the previous evening. Now Kofi also discovers that his camera has been stolen from his shoulder as he was getting on to the train this morning at Kita. He bursts into heart-rending sobs. That camera was his life. His friend. They were together for years. His wife left him, his children fled, but the camera stuck with him through thick and thin.

She sees some of the other poets engaging in ever more urgent discussions with the doctor, from which they return with little packets of medicine. Two have upset stomachs and have been unable to sleep for many nights. Another's eyes are red and swollen.

Bamako is enormous. The city stretches as far as the eye can see. The poets are taken in a little bus across the kilometre-wide Niger to the University, where they will each have a room in one of the hostels. Her room has an air conditioner. She switches it on and it begins to recycle hot air, crying insistently in A flat. She stays in her room. She lies on her bed. She feels estranged from everybody. She feels overcome by the exhaustion of not belonging. Not understanding. Not being understood. Being cast as a stereotype. In the streets, black children run after her with outstretched hands, crying, 'Dollar, s'il vous plaît, l'Américaine! Dollar!' Whereas the Belgian writer is accepted as an African, because he is black. Her whole body pains from it. Is loneliness a kind of desperate non-belonging? An absence of voices to root you? She wants to go back. She wants to go to where he is sitting in front of the television or making food in their kitchen and spill like blood against his chest. But as she lies against him in her mind, she finds him more vulnerable, more uncertain, more burdened and bungled, so much whiter than herself. Another white person cannot rescue you from this, she knows, this deep precipice of not belonging.

The hostel has a dining room and a bar. She sinks into one of the chairs and orders a brandy and Coke, and a beer. The only other people in the bar are the two poets from Zimbabwe – peaceful, already into their second round of whisky. Wordlessly the three of them sit, thrown together by cultures that tolerate alcohol and use English as a common language.

Now they are in the bus again. They pass through incredible vistas of poverty and rubbish, a tumult of smell and colour, along seemingly impassable roads where 4x4s nod through gigantic potholes in low gear, past overflowing sewers, gigantic canals dug into the river, choking with garbage. The bus stops in front of a high wall with a door set into it. Although it is already dusk, it is still unbelievably hot. When the door is opened, she is struck by the coolness of dripping water and plants, of smooth cement floors, thick, roughly plastered walls with niches, the smell of spices and the enchantment of well-designed lighting. In the background a griot sings softly to the music of a stringed instrument. Aminata Dramane Traoré, Minister of Culture for Mali, awaits them like a queen, in a beautiful cloak of ochre and copper. This is her shop and restaurant, and people may buy if they so wish. Here are the best and most beautiful products from Mali. She personally tours the country, places orders, makes suggestions for improving design and manufacture; she also has her own team of young designers making new products based on old Malian designs, patterns and materials.

The furniture and garments are of breathtaking beauty. Chairs covered in dyed leather quilts, tables the wood of which is embroidered with brightly coloured twine bound with golden thread, a dining-room table and chairs based on the Tuareg camel-saddle. On a small podium stands a chair with an abstract half-moon for a backrest. A special area is hung with beautiful dresses, cloaks, shawls, belts and handbags dramatically covered in ancient patterns.

Have the poets noticed how many people wear gold and silver jewellery in spite of their poverty? Have they seen women coming out of hovels in the most colourful, flowery garments? It is because the gold and silver and cloth families of Mali protected their secrets through the centuries, the art of making things inexpensively enough so that ordinary people can afford them. Here gold is not only for the rich, a poor woman can own a pair of dazzling golden earrings. 'Good taste is in the blood of every citizen of Mali,' says the Minister. They each get a present. She receives a long, tasselled shawl in rust and white and copper. The Minister folds it twice around her shoulders so that it cups charmingly at her throat, while the tassels lap-lap at her feet. She looks at herself in the mirror for a long time: the shawl has transformed her from a pale, insecure, T-shirt-and-jeans white person into a tall, worthy, graceful woman of unknown origin.

From heavy earthenware dishes they eat couscous with all manner of vegetables and meats, for pudding cool pieces of pawpaw flavoured with nuts and soft-boiled cardamom. Small cups of sweet tea.

Her hostel room carries the glow of the shawl as she drapes it over the open cupboard door. She finds that her ankles have been bitten raw by mosquitoes.

day seven

Early the next morning everyone goes to the artisans' market in Bamako. Apparently such markets exist in every town in Mali – a building where the craftsmen of the district can practise their craft in comfortable surroundings and where buyers can find them all under one roof. There is a hubbub of sound and colour and aroma. Here goatskin and camel-skin is tanned, and leather-workers sit easily making shoes, sandals, handbags, belts. Next door, the silversmiths are busy applying the finest patterns to teaspoons, bracelets, rings. Goldsmiths, wood-carvers, weavers, tailors, the head spins. Right outside the building food and muti are sold: baboon is big, it seems, snakes, crocodile snouts, vulture heads, musk-cat claws, CDs, videos. She sits underneath a tree and waits for the others to finish. The man sitting next to her asks: La Caravane de la Poésie? She nods, it's written on her T-shirt. They arrived yesterday from Kita? She nods again. Yes, he heard everything on the radio. He is following the progress of the whole journey because he heard that there is a poet from South Africa in the group. He just returned from South Africa. And he wants to ask this poet why South Africans equate poverty with ugliness. If you are poor you must have nothing that is beautiful. You can go anywhere in Mali, he says, and nowhere will it be as ugly as the townships of Soweto or Alexandra. 'The worst is, then they think they are better than us. People who live without beauty always react in a cruel and crude way.'

She remembers that she once interviewed some people who had moved from the farms to the township of Maokeng and lived there in the most precarious conditions. She happened to know the farm that one particular family had come from. Did they miss it? No. Did they miss the river? No. Was it not beautiful on the farm? No. She read an article afterwards that stated that a consciousness of beauty is only developed once the basic requirements like hunger, thirst, shelter, safety have been satisfied. Is the lot of a squatter living within sight of Table Mountain better than the lot of a squatter living next to the highway in Ventersburg? No, said the article.

The man shakes his head. You are talking about a Western notion of beauty – one that can only result from money. First you make money, then you buy something beautiful. For us beauty is an essential part of being human. Being creative with your body and your surroundings is a basic necessity.

The people at the border crossing did not seem too concerned with beauty, in fact they were dreary and dirty. It is the bribery at the border post, the man says. The people are there for one reason only: money. As soon as money becomes the most important factor, creative interaction with beauty falls away.

That evening's performance starts at nine o'clock in the municipal building. An excellent sound system has been erected beneath wide banners proclaiming: *Hommage aux poètes et griots dans les jardins de la mémoire.* Several bands perform, the Bamako elite arrive in gorgeous outfits. French summaries of the poems of the non-francophone poets are read out. Poets from the Caravan alternate with young poets from Bamako. Tall young women perform with total control of the dynamics of dramatic microphone technique and the power of repetition.

Were Were Liking sets up her laptop, decorates it with spectacular silken cloths, stretches out her arms and rattles a collection of seed pods like little castanets. Her lips are green, her eyes golden. Her voice grows from a vulnerable whispering to the boom of a war goddess flinging battleaxes. The entire Bamako clan of Albecaye Kounta arrives. Softly and peacefully, he reads his poem about the dunes of Sankore. His large white robe hangs still. Nhamo Khadani starts to yell *Yes! Yes!* And then *Oui! Oui!* The audience follows him, echoing his cries. He leads them through all kinds of Yeses. Aggressive *Yes! Yes!*; uncertain *Yes? Yes?*; impatient *Yes! Yes!*; reluctant *Yes! Yes!*; innocent *Yes! Yes!* His head shakes a teary, negative *Yes! Yes!*; ecstatic *Yes! Yes!*; orgasmic *Yes! Yes!*; furious *Yes! Yes!*; murderous *Yes! Yes!*; caressing *Yes! Yes!*; encouraging *Yes? Yes?* The audience gets so worked up that they leap to their feet, the youths jump down from their perches against the walls, the poor people listening outside come storming in. And from the centre, the tiny figure from Zimbabwe controls a crowd of people whom he indeed has no language to communicate with.

Wiping the sweat from his face, he slips into the chair next to her. 'I was so frustrated by being from this continent but having to scratch at its edges because I cannot speak French. I said to myself: real poets always find the heart of human beings, from whatever language or culture.'

On the way back to the hostel, everybody is famished. They stop at a spaza shop and buy bleached chocolates, cheese wedges and crushed cream crackers. At the hostel they sit outside against the pillars, eating and drinking whisky, Coke and water. Somebody has managed to buy a few beers during the day. The last of a tube of Tabard is scraped clean with fingernails and smeared on the ankles. Around them frogs with open mouths and red eyes are leaping like part of the biblical plague. The empty, crumbling swimming pool is filled with frogs. In the corners they clamber on top of each other in silently palpitating agglomerations as they try to jump out and escape. Others dangle open-legged on the edges, about to fall in. On the way to her room they plop away from her feet in dark splashes into the night.

All night the roar of a croaking chorus fills the courtyard.

day eight

She gets up early to phone home from a roadside telephone *cabine*. Her son sounds unwilling to talk. Her daughter says they nap every afternoon until their father comes home from work. Are they smoking dagga at school, she wonders when she puts the phone down. It is hard for her to explain to them where she is and what is happening. Her life has become completely unreachable.

During the day she washes her clothes and takes a hard look at the poems she brought along with her. She writes a new piece, and it doesn't trouble her that it contains so much of her favourite Afrikaans poems: it's as if she finds herself in a pool of poetic awareness. She carefully works out sound possibilities for the existing poems, how to use various parts and levels of her voice, rhythms and intonations, and she rewrites them accordingly. The concerns of some of the poems are too distant from where she is now to even contemplate alternatives. She translates a few into English, seeking some affinity with the Zimbabwean poets at least.

During the afternoon hours a lively discussion about African writers takes place on the veranda. Starting with the fact that most of them live in Europe or America. 'It can't be any other way, this continent is hard on its artists and intellectuals. And there are now so many exiles that a writer actually has his own exile market and need no longer be too concerned with his country, its language and its illiterate people.'

'But should exiled writers be writing about their countries and their people at all? Countries change, and then writers have to get by on second-hand information. Why are they writing? Aren't they just feeding the illusions of exiles? Helping to undermine their own countries in the West? If your country does not read your work, then who are you writing for?'

No one says: I write for myself. Or: I make art for art's sake.

'The smells and the textures of your youth you never forget,' says Amina Saïd. 'It doesn't matter where I write, it seeps into my work like sand from the desert.'

'The educated citizens of African countries do read. As soon as a new book is published, hectic debates start among the academics. Take the *Abyssinian Chronicles* by Moses Isegawa. It led to fascinating discussions in Uganda.'

'I am disgusted by the lack of vision of the well-known writers of this continent.' Everybody looks up in surprise. It is the accountant speaking. The entire past week he has not opened his mouth, except to bark financial instructions at Mariame Sonko. 'Okri, Isegawa, Marechera, even Soyinka – it is such a hopeless vision, there is no balance. Everything is either corrupt and lost and beyond help – or it is wonderfully African in its underdeveloped and sexist way. All the blame must be heaped on colonialism – or the only hope is some primeval African wisdom, which is just a lot of bullshit. I mean, what are you writers actually trying to say? You write about countries that no longer exist, for people you no longer know, in languages that neither you nor the suckers like us who stayed behind speak any more. All I hear is complaints that the West does not treat African writers well, that the publishers are unwilling to publish books by Africans, that the awards always go to whites. When actually you are trying to catch the spotlight in a world you pretend to loathe!'

A proverbial spark in the powder keg. The argument explodes in many tongues, but he still manages to shout: 'I wish the Europeans and the Americans would be like Mugabe and deport everybody who is black – force them to come home. Writing literature in exile is a bloody cheek, you should be coming back to fight and endure the injustice and foolishness here!'

Chenjerai Hove takes the reins. Who is he talking about? All the poets on this Caravan live and work on the continent. Some might lecture elsewhere, but they are completely in tune with their communities. Perhaps the accountant wishes to be enlightened on the exact functions of a poet in a society?

'No, all I'm saying is that perhaps these griots you've been working with over the past week play a much more important role in helping oppressed, hungry and dying communities than you could ever do.'

'Oh bullshit,' says Were Were, 'the griots help to sustain the oppression. They are used by despots to keep everybody subservient. They escape into the abstraction of language. The word "word" becomes a metaphor, the word "hunger" an image.'

'I have just read a book by one of my favourite writers, I'm talking about *Disgrace*,' says Nhamo, 'and I was sort of confused. The man has given voice to so many people – old people, frail people, women, coloureds – but never blacks. It's as if he is prepared to give voice to anyone but a black person. And I was wondering why that is.'

'I know the work of Coetzee' – the accountant pronounces it *Coutzier* – 'and I give him full credit for acknowledging that a white man cannot simply produce a voice for a black man. He realizes the fundamental difference. Unlike these other books where blacks and whites all sound the same.'

'Well, I'm furious that a writer regarded as one of Africa's best manages to say that if you want to become part of the continent, you must be prepared to be raped.'

The Belgian has barely finished when the accountant jumps in: 'Oh shut up, you. What do you know about this continent? Don't ever try to write as if you are one of us, living there where the responsibility for failure is always that of the whites. Come and live here. Come and carry the weight of stupidity and corruption with us.'

Disrupted by translation and background argument, the discussion goes nowhere.

That evening they are invited for dinner at the home of Albecaye Kounta. He and his sons greet the guests on the front veranda. He introduces them to his first wife, a worthy-looking, oldish woman. Inside, a toddler is running around. It is Albecaye's child with his second wife, who is quite a lot younger. She is sent in to talk to the guests while the first wife serves the food and drink. Everybody takes off their shoes and sits comfortably on the carpets. She finds a place with Nhamo and Chenjerai where they can lean against a cupboard – their backs and hips cannot endure this sitting on the floor all the time. They eat fried banana chips and marrow-soft venison kebabs, followed by slices of watermelon and mango. The meal is rounded off with citronella tea.

As they're driving back in the bus, Mariame Sonko addresses them. They have reached the exact midpoint of the journey. Until now things have been easy. The worst lies ahead. They must do what they can to lay their hands on toilet paper, soap and mosquito repellent. In the next week the wheat will be separated from the chaff, the mettle of every poet will be tested. They all stare grimly in front of them. How many kinds of tests are there for poets in Africa?

day nine

Early the next morning they depart by bus and drive over flat, grassy plains. This is the

Sahel, they are told. Gradually the architecture becomes more Arabic in style. There are fewer and fewer decrepit Western ruins and more and more adobe constructions with harmonious lines and shapes. Tallish adobe buildings are constructed by inserting sticks horizontally into the walls to support further construction, layer after layer, until the desired height is reached. When everything is dry, most of the sticks are pulled out, but a few are left to serve as ladders when external maintenance work must be done.

The bus drives into Segou. The poetry reading starts at five o'clock in the town square. It surprises her that all these rural events start so punctually and she asks someone about it.

'The day is divided into parts by the five evenly spaced Muslim prayers. This is one of the unbending laws of Islam, it is unforgivable to delay the prayers. As a result there is a great sensitivity towards time in these parts of Africa, and has been for centuries.'

The griots are the first to perform. They use the microphones in a way that shows a remarkable grasp of the sound system; in fact, feedback is one of the modern griot's most important performance skills. A poet will shout into the microphone to cause distortion, then swing the instrument down in a swanky curl to change the distortion into a howl. Sometimes he will bring the microphone sharply down to the floor in quick successive movements, releasing piercing squeals into the air. Or he will roar into the microphone, first softly, then more and more loudly, then mingling his voice with the distortion as it sets in, letting it die out with the applause from the crowd. From the front seats, through all the dancing and performing and dust, she looks away and spots a Berber and his horse on the fringes of the crowd. It is like a mirage. The blue of the Berber's robes, desert blue they call it, his white turban, his black hands on the reins, the sparkling white horse with henna dots in its mane and tail, prancing, arching its neck. If she wrote about this, she thinks, it would seem like magical realism. Her soundchecks on reality are shifting.

While Zein is reading, a herd of goats comes grazing peacefully through the crowd. The poem becomes the sound of Arabic and bleating. While she's reading her new poem, she sees, from the corner of her eye, a small motorcycle stuttering past the back of the crowd. The woman's cloak billows happily, the tassels of her bound headdress slightly askew. Without thinking she works it into the poem, as part of the reading. The motorbike and the goats and Afrikaans. She feels an unexpected glow of pleasure and embarrassment sifting over her. Surrendering? Pandering? Exploring?

She is back in her seat, for the first time feeling less ... lost. The master of ceremonies speaks for a long time. At one point she hears 'L'Afrique du Sud'. One bit of French she understands. Then the master of ceremonies walks over and holds out a gallant hand to her, the people open up a passage and the band comes closer to her. What in the world is happening here?

'They want you to show Segou the South African Dance,' whispers the accountant.

God, dear Father. Jesus in heaven. The South African *Dance*! Christ and the Holy

Grail! What is that supposed to mean? *Is* there such a thing as the South African fuck-ing dance? Two-step? Toyi-toyi? Tiekiedraai? Or is it something she will have to *invent*? The *toyikiedraai*? Sweat bursts from her scalp. Her eyes bulge with adrenalin. This must surely rate as the most awful pressure ever put on a South African poet! To *dance* on behalf of a country that is still making up its mind whether it considers you an African. And rightly so, it is clear, because on this continent of singers and dancers, she *cannot* bloody well dance! The band has become deafening, and now she hears the crowd chanting, 'Mandela! Mandela!' Oh my God! On behalf of Mandela too! The cultural activists at home would shit themselves if they knew she was dancing on behalf of the country in the name of Mandela.

Nhamo nudges her forward. Dear Lord, what should she swing? What should she shake? What should she do with her big feet in their size eight Adidas? Sweat pours from under her arms as if from two shower-heads. She lifts them up. A blackout occurs in part of her brain. She starts shaking her tits, and surprises herself by managing it quite well. She looks down, yes, they are indeed shaking. The drums sink into a merciless rhythm. Her feet gradually retrieve the memory of toyi-toyi, her arms now swinging loosely at her sides, while she stamps out: *Thaa! Tha-thaa!* Then Nhamo jumps up and joins her, his white teeth flashing comfort, his exuberance urging on a free-for-all. They all dance and are swept as a group into the streets, a bundling, danc-ing, music-blaring cloud of dust, which eventually halts in front of a modest little house bearing the inscription: 'La Maison de Mandela.' Inside there is a wall painting of a man: the hair has the side-parting that Mandela wore during the Treason Trial, the face is that of any black man from Africa. She gets a free cooldrink and has to scribble her name on the wall.

Afterwards, they go to a restaurant for dinner. Everyone orders chicken. A few minutes later she sees a swarm of children chasing after a chicken in the yard, she hears the stifling sounds of a beheading, and in half an hour the roasted chunks are served with rice.

That evening, the air conditioner in her hotel room manages to lose its head com-pletely: the little fan pops out on to the floor and whirrs there for a while. A waiter comes to remove the fan and shut the hole with two tea trays.

She asks the Lebanese proprietor of the hotel how he keeps it going. The trade routes through Africa have been known in Arabia and Asia for centuries, he says, and fifteen years ago he came out to investigate them, to look at the possibilities. Eventually he decided on Segou. He had a hotel built here, because of the availability of very good artisans who knew the building techniques of the area. Then he had his one brother qualify as a plumber and the other as an electrician. All of them now live here with their families. The one maintains the sanitation and water supply, and the other looks after the electricity. The wives have an enormous vegetable garden and an orchard, and they raise poultry. Once a month he charters an aeroplane to Dakar where he buys stock, and once a year one of them goes to France to buy spare parts for the engines, air conditioners, and so forth. The children are first tutored by their mothers here in Segou, then they go to Dakar to attend the embassy school. He bought a house there next to the school, where his unmarried sister lives, and she sees the children through high school.

'It is the secret of surviving in Africa,' he says, 'to be completely unreliant on any government or civil service. If I want a telephone signal, I don't apply for it or bribe somebody for it, I negotiate directly with an overseas company and they install a mast for me here on my property, from which I operate cellphones, faxes, computers and everything. The community doesn't have a problem with this either, because apart from the fact that more tourists come here now that there is a proper hotel, we also have a little medical installation, the smartest children come to study here with ours at home, some I send to Dakar, we sell vegetables and meat to the people – so in general it is an ideal life.'

day ten

They sit for hours in the sun on the bank of the river. The ferry that has to transport the bus across to Djenne is out of order. People beg the poets to buy from them: everything on offer in Bamako, but a thousand times cheaper. Everybody is desperate.

'African Muslims here look so colourful, African Christians back home look so dour. Why?'

They, the southerners, are sitting in a small piece of shade.

'In my home town lives this retired professor, Gabriel Setiloane,' she ventures, 'and he wanted to understand why African ancestral ritual plays such a significant role in how black people practise Christianity. As a fourth-generation Methodist, his mother, for example, would dish out food for the ancestors at night after evening prayers. After going to church they would also visit a sangoma. He was curious why neither he nor his parents, devout Christians that they were, experienced any contradiction or betrayal.'

Somebody calls. The ferry has been fixed and they are going across. The water is so still that it forms a perfect reflection. On the other side, the bus trudges on towards Djenne and she goes on with her story.

'Anyway, when Gabriel Setiloane became a minister, his white colleagues pressured him to purify himself of these heathen practices. It was then that he realized, he said to me, that in his mind and heart the two religions did not exist separately from each other. For him, Christianity formed a compartment inside the traditional African religion, and not the other way round. The religion of his ancestors was so spacious that Christ fitted comfortably into it as a main Ancestor.'

'But I'm sure I've heard about this,' Kofi insists. 'Isn't he the guy who looked into what the missionaries wrote about the religious practices of the blacks?'

'Could be. He discovered that the missionaries often admitted to their superiors in Europe that they could not classify the blacks of Southern Africa as heathens, because it was clear that they did believe in *something*. They had no idols, no totems, and whatever the missionaries told them fitted in with their notion of a Higher Being. It was quite a spanner in the works of missionary training. If these people were not heathens, then what were they? And how could you convince them that what you were bringing had no links with their own beliefs?'

'He published something in Holland,' says Kofi. 'Or it could be somebody else. But I remember it was about a new sort of African Christian hierarchy. Christ is in the same realm as the ancestors, the intermediaries, and He interacts with God, who is the ultimate Ancestor of everybody and everything. Our ancestors, among them Jesus, connect us to God, and God connects us to the world – its people, its animals, its landscapes.'

'You see, this is what I mean,' says Nhamo. 'It's as if the West decided that Africa could not see properly and needed a pair of spectacles. So Africa put on this pair for short-sightedness – the same prescription as the West, you know – and indeed it could not see a thing. And the more Africa peers and gropes, the more it stumbles and breaks things. Africa should just throw away the spectacles, and it will find out that it can actually see quite well.'

When she picked up her air ticket at the travel agency before the start of the journey, there was a poster on the wall hailing Djenne as the 'twin sister' of Timbuktu. 'Timbuktu the mysterious! Djenne the mystical.' Djenne is a place of mud. In the middle of the town is the famously beautiful three-storey mosque built out of mud. Women are not admitted. Neither are men who are not Muslim.

The hotel in Djenne is full. One of the local griots makes his house available. It is built around a courtyard with a well in it. She shares a room with Amina on the second floor, next to the bathroom and toilet. There is a bucket of water next to the toilet for flushing it out. This is the first time that they have had to share rooms. She cannot make out whether she or Amina feels more uncomfortable. She has started menstruating again, out of all pace and rhythm. She lies on her mattress and listens to Amina rolling around.

Someone takes a heartfelt dump in the toilet next door, you can hear him neighing slightly between volleys, like someone whose last drop of blood is being tapped. The stench belches into their room. They do not hear the dumper using the bucket. Later they hear another person going in and calling out in shock. He fills three buckets and flushes the toilet. Then he throws up. Then he takes a dump. Somebody starts banging urgently on the door. It sounds as if he is allowed to pee in the bath. The smells become unbearable. She rises silently and creeps up to the roof, where people are lying peacefully asleep. As the cocks crow, the sun peels like an apricot through the haze of the river and she can hear donkeys braying and goats blaring.

She tries to go for a walk, but the streets are full of large holes filled with dead water in which mosquitoes and gigantic gnats gather. She hears a noise above her and stands aside just in time to avoid a slag of excrement that comes splattering down into the street from a kind of gutter overhead. How is it possible that people can produce such sophisticated architecture, such beautiful lines, let such colours bloom beneath their hands, yet are unable to deal effectively with their own excreta? And all of it beside one of the largest rivers in the world. In Bamako, the sewers from the colonial era are even still there, somebody, for God's sake, just has to lift a sluice gate to wash away the rubbish and the sewage; but no, everything is left in the streets, the streets along which the most beautifully decorated women are passing, sparkling with loveliness, calmly raising the hems of their robes and carefully stepping in their golden sandals around piles of human pellets. And if you do step in something, it isn't really a problem, because you take your shoes off anyway before going indoors.

What does this tell her? She does not know. Is the clearing away of shit important to her because she is white? Cannot be. She remembers reading in a biography of Shaka about the strict sanitation rules he imposed. Is dealing with excrement a matter of culture then? Is an abhorrence of shit a suppressed shame at normal bodily functions? Is she abnormally absorbed in shit? She does not know. She does not even ask. After all, who is to explain the lack of a sewage system on behalf of the whole of West Africa?

She has switched over to survival mode. She eats nothing, but grabs like an addict at sachets of Nescafé instant coffee, which she mixes with spoonfuls of Nan milk powder for babies. It is that or goat's milk. Which has run out anyway. Nobody bats an eyelid. She wipes away with her tongue the sand that stays behind in her teeth.

She sits with a bowed head and waits for them to depart. Back across the river to Mopti. Here rows and rows of trucks are waiting for dusk before driving into the desert. They travel in convoy for safety's sake. Apparently after heavy sandstorms they sometimes find the remains of old trucks with the skeletons of drivers still behind the wheel, uncovered after decades in the dunes.

The hotel in Mopti is beautiful, but she has lost track of the passage of time. It is just as well that she is not due to perform here, because she is dizzy with hunger. In the bar she comes across her southern countrymen. Beer. She gulps it down like a swimmer doing the butterfly. To his consternation, Chenjerai's foot has started bleeding and swelling from high blood pressure. The doctor, who can be seen running around in every town trying to replenish his supplies, has given him some medicine which is not to be taken with alcohol. 'That will fall on deaf ears,' says Chenjerai drily. She buys more beer to keep in her suitcase. She drinks until she is full.

Later that night everyone sits in the courtyard to hear more of Amina Saïd's poetry. She says that silence regulates her poems.

I write on the back of death
I write against time   that makes us   unmakes us
creates   recreates itself

I write because I have learned to read sand and water
shadows   clouds   and the flights of birds

I write to catch myself on the edge of the world
to get my breath   pause   behold   listen

I write because it is my way of being free.

'You speak a lot about loneliness. You speak about silence. You use the word "I" a lot in your poems. Are these not un-African concepts? In African communities a thing like silence does not exist. Therefore there is also never loneliness. Being alone is a European notion founded on a selfish, individualist philosophy. Or am I wrong? Do you feel that you connect with what would pass as African poetry?' This is Chenjerai.

Amina just stares ahead of her and says that she is not prepared to discuss her work. She will read some more, but she has nothing to say about it.

'You cannot invite people to your home, and then slam the door in their faces just before they come in,' says Were Were. 'We all learn from each other. I know that your family used to be the great griots of Tunisia. I want to know how you tie into this tradition or break away from it. A poet is not just her voice. There is the *body* that moulds the texture of the voice. There is the *space* around the body in which the voice resounds, which scorches the body into bringing forth the voice. Pretending that you consist of your voice only, or that others may access that voice and nothing else, is problematic. Other people have demands made on every part of their lives, all their comings and goings, but the poet feels no, only my voice. Why should the poet be an exception? Meanwhile, giving voice is your duty, because you have a voice solely through your community – whether it is language they give you, or ancestral stirrings, or food, it doesn't matter.'

'The emphasis on loneliness in Amina's work links with the Arabic Muslim tradition,' says Zein. 'One of the very first poems written down in Arabic reads:

the moon
the dune
the sound of my horse

by this I live

'It is a poem about the peace found in silence and loneliness.'

'I never feel lonely,' says Chenjerai. 'Even if I am alone, the grass talks to me, the trees, the ancestors, history. My mother was a famous storyteller. We inhabited our world by way of stories. When I go to visit her in the country, I tell her my stories and then she laughs, because I have made some of her tales mine and so they live on. Whatever you wish to say calls up a whole community of poets with it. How can you feel alone? Through your voice many other voices speak. And the creative process is fundamentally a healing one. I simply do not understand the focus on loneliness and misery.'

Amina sits quietly for a long time before she closes the discussion with the following reading:

Words create
other light

we work with light

That evening she stands for a long time with the telephone in her hand, and then puts it down again slowly. If she were to call home now, she would not know what to say.

day eleven

The bus rumbles onwards in the dust, nods jarringly through the potholes, while kora music crackles over the speakers. Around the bend, suddenly, the river. And on the mirror surface, two narrow wooden boats – pinnaces, they call them – with intricate patterns carved into their bows, divided into booths, laid out with grass mats, ribs of timber holding up a roof of reed matting. In the stern is a grass-mat partition where you simply do your business through a hole in the deck into the water. Every boat has a metal plate for cooking, upon which a slip of a girl already has the fires going.

As in a dream she gets into the pinnace. They all recline on the grass mats. The poets in the one boat, the rest in the other. The boats move forward with softly clicking engines.

Suddenly it is as if oxygen explodes through her system. The enormous river broadens all at once into a lake, then contracts after a few hours into visible shores. At times the water is eggshell. Then pewter. Later it becomes a dark-green, rippling grate.

She sees Zein taking out pencil and paper. Amina sits fidgeting with her handbag. Were Were and Thierno are already busy writing. It has always irked her to see people writing in public. Writing is such an intensely private act, something you do aside, in secret. Underground. It is so phoney to sit and write where everyone can see what you are doing.

Along the side of the pinnace is a plank catwalk. She sits there, her feet in a wild sparkling glare of water, a collar of radiance. She lies on the matting roof, she splays herself open and feels her every fingertip unfold.

How can she hold on to this? This plunge of air. How to let it breathe forever in her blood without scarring it into language? How to?

She takes out a pencil and a notebook. It skates on to the page soundlessly light:

oewer van riet
oewer van slik
oewer van duin en stilte en sloep

shore of reed
shore of silt
shore of dune and silence and creek

over the still shoulders of water
    one by one slip
ochre scarves of sand

Fragrant rice and river fish. Watermelon. Some tumble into slumbering. Others drag their hands through the water. Somebody hums. Somebody rinses bowls out over the side.

Zein speaks about the river. The Niger takes its name from the Tuareg expression 'N'ger-n-gereo', which means 'river of rivers'. The Niger is also known as 'the Nile of the Negroes'. For more than two thousand years, the source and the mouth of the river remained a mystery. Although it is the tenth largest river in the world, nobody could determine whether it was flowing east or west, or whether it was a tributary of the Nile or the Congo, or whether it flowed into the Atlantic, or into some lake in the interior, or went underground beneath the Sahara to the Mediterranean. The confusion was rooted in the course of the river: there is no logical geographical connection between its origin and its discharge, over three thousand kilometres away.

The Niger sprouts from granite hills just a few kilometres from the Atlantic. It pushes north for all it's worth, away from the ocean, collects some tributaries and then arrows due east towards the desert. For five hundred kilometres it forms the boundary of the Sahara desert. Then it heads abruptly south, through a belt of sub-tropical forest, and empties out into a gigantic continental delta on the underside of the hump of Africa.

From the shore somebody waves and holds a kora up in the air. Albecaye instructs the boatman to pick him up. He is a river griot, the new passenger says, and he also sells desert sandals (which he proceeds to take from his bag and display neatly on a table).

Then he sings in Bambara and Albecaye translates:

'The Niger is unlike any other river. The Niger makes possible other ways of being river. The Niger hides nothing. It flows openly along its course. It hides neither its beginning nor its end. But those who say they can read are unable to read the Niger. The Niger does not allow ownership. The greedy tried to conquer it, but the Niger does not allow conquest. The rulers tried to travel and control it, but the Niger turned its back on them. The Niger knows no boundaries. It always touches all sides. The Niger destroys the one who tries to find a single voice. The Niger has many tongues. The Niger gives oxygen. The Niger dissolves all boundaries along its flanks. The Niger is a slit of promise: not of being, but of becoming.'

They buy sandals on which the camel hair is still visible. At the next cluster of houses the griot is dropped off. The pinnace drifts like a reflection in glass. As if in a dream she takes out her notebook again. Pencil. She writes words as they drift into the space all around and inside her. Old words she has forgotten about, words filled with l's and o's: languid, loam, warble, doze, the boat drowses along in a scoop of bliss and water and trepidation. The river becomes beloved.

The sun draws water in shades of amber. When the hot disc of the sun touches the water, Nhamo says, 'Sssss!' And they look at one another as if experiencing a miracle. Then, in an instant, it is dark. The two pinnaces scratch out on to the sand. People are waiting for them with electric torches and they all struggle over the dunes with their luggage. Everything is swathed in darkness – the whole of Niafounke is without power. By torchlight, names are ticked off and keys are handed out in the lobby of the hotel. In the passages people stumble into one another as they search for their rooms. Once again she shares a room with Amina.

Outside on the lawn they are invited to dish up their own dinner. Ribs and paws, scorched black, protrude from buckets. It smells of intestine and horn. She takes couscous, and when she bends for what appears by torchlight to be vegetables, she gets a whiff of grass-dung in her nostrils. It is offal. She goes to her room to fetch her last beers. In the light of the torches and fires, a man in camel-coloured trousers and white shoes dances the dance of the camels. For almost an hour the audience, its numbers swollen by people from the darkened town, watches a camel walk, run, drink, sleep, roll over, flee, court, laugh ...

Most of the torches have run out of power. In the darkness they find their rooms and fumble for their beds. She and Amina lie sweating, trying not to keep one another awake. Amina has taken sleeping tablets, but they don't seem to be working. It is difficult to sleep in a room with someone you don't know. The breathing is strange. The sounds are strange. What if you snore? What if you cough just when she's about to fall asleep?

day twelve

At five o'clock, Mariame Sonko knocks on the door. The breakfast bread is fingered grey and rock hard. She stirs the contents of her Nescafé sachet into water boiled on the open fire. But it is with a song in her heart that she walks down to the boats, and sits there waiting long before the others arrive. She has lost track of which day it is. Her brain has lost its capacity to discriminate. She observes everything, but she forms no opinion. That some arrive late, that somebody steps on her suitcase, that the boat tilts dangerously and takes on water, none of this causes a reaction in her. She finds herself in a kind of stupor of well-being.

She writes: between sky and silver I mirror light into language.

She dozes through the day with words pluming the air. Across from her sits the accountant. The briefcase that he has kept clasped to his chest all this time, as if somebody could tear it away from him at any moment, stands between his bare feet. He is wearing a beautiful blue robe. Immeasurably blue. She asks about it.

The blue? There is only one woman in a small town outside Dakar who makes this specific blue. It is impossible to counterfeit. It took a long time to track her down. In Bamako, in the streets around the Reserve Bank, he saw several attempts to copy the colour, but an expert would know immediately that it is not the right blue. Albecaye, sitting forward in the pinnace, has a lighter blue robe. It is the colour of the main clan of the Tuareg and is called desert blue.

She hasn't noticed that Albecaye's suitcase or the accountant's is larger than the others, so why do their clothes seem so freshly ironed? The accountant arches his brows. The ironing of Muslim robes is a valuable art practised only by some families. A household will search far and wide and pay well when they find somebody who can wash and iron these robes. The greatest skill lies in folding it so that it will fit into a suitcase without creasing.

'West Africa works in castes. And there is one for the minders of robes. But I actually reject the entire notion of caste and I'll tell you why. My father was a fisherman. I come from the fishing caste, which is one of the most humble. That I qualified in America as an accountant makes no difference to anybody here. No woman from the political or goldsmithing castes would be allowed to marry me, her family would forbid it and reject the children. That is why you find that so many West African men fetch themselves white women overseas who do not care for this whole caste business. Technically, my robes ought to indicate my status. And although I do not bother myself with it, you can be sure that everybody on these pinnaces knows exactly that I should be dressing like the son of a fisherman.'

She thinks about how difficult it is for her to wear dresses. A dress changes your personality. You feel vulnerable. Child or man or even wind can lift your dress against your will and leave your thighs exposed. She has also come to realize that as soon as she wears a dress to work, the men find it harder to carry out her instructions. They patronize her, flatter her, and she feels too dressy or skirty to stand her ground. As soon as she wears pants, she is another person. She speaks more authoritatively, she gestures more forcefully. And her instructions are not queried – especially when she wears a jacket and tie. The accountant left Dakar in a suit. By the time they got to Kita he was already in jeans, in Bamako he started wearing soft robes of dark green and ochre, and now this morning he pops up in this smart robe of blue damask.

Does he feel different in a robe compared to a suit? He frowns. 'No.' After a while he says, 'Yes, I feel holier. When we go to mosque on Friday afternoons after work and I arrive in my suit, I feel wrong, tied down. When I arrive in my robe, I feel cooler, lighter, more done with the worldly, almost free. But I will never wear robes to work. It places me in a category of tradition and religion that still does not quite run smoothly with monetary practice.'

'Allah is the God of the nomad,' says Thierno. 'Unlike your God, who has to be worshipped in a temple in a fixed place, Allah is everywhere.'

'Maybe so, but why have you fallen into fundamentalism? Is it just coincidence that so many conflicts around the world involve Muslims?'

The accountant sits up annoyed. 'Your prejudice glares from the word "fundament-alism" – as if the foundations of Islam are rotten. The correct word is "extremism": there are Muslim extremists, just as there are Christian ones.'

'One of the main causes of Muslim extremism is translation, or rather a lack of translation,' says Kofi, who is Muslim, black and Belgian. 'Arabic is a language that centres around imagery on various levels, and this makes it almost impossible to do justice to all the complexities of a text in the act of translation. This is why Muslims around the world know the Qur'an mainly in its original language. If they do not speak Arabic, they only know a couple of beloved passages. And so things are often taken out of context, passages are read together that do not belong together, a single text is allowed to undermine the larger message. Because so few people have mastered the whole Qur'an, misinterpretation can seldom be countered effectively. Incidentally, did you know that in French the word for "translate" sounds a lot like the word "betray"?'

Lunch arrives: spaghetti and coffee and big pieces of watermelon.

'But what about the intolerance? In the city where I live, many liberal, educated Muslims have been so threatened and terrorized that they've left for America, of all places. The country so zealously preached against has become a safe haven for Muslim intellectuals. And the intolerance is not only against new ideas or ways of thinking, it is also against women.'

'It is important to remember that Islam is the religion of the oppressed,' the accountant insists. 'The most powerless people in the world are Muslim. And it is pre-cisely because they are powerless to bring about change that they often turn on each other. Just as women turn on each other because men are entrenched in power. For me, we must think first about the liberation of Muslims around the world, before the injustices inside the religion are addressed.'

The discussion goes nowhere. She moves over to Chenjerai and Nhamo. With undisguised pleasure, Nhamo is busy going through a gigantic haul of CDs and cassettes that he bought in Dakar and Bamako. He tracked down artists he thought existed only as legends. Chenjerai has lost the plug for his rhino-horn snuffbox. He is leisurely carving himself a new one from a small piece of wood.

The sky changes to the colour of baked quinces. On the shore the ruins of adobe houses stand like scraps of lace. Albecaye watches birds through a pair of binoculars and makes notes in a little book. Thierno sits in the stern with an unending flood of words streaming from his mouth. He composes long poems for each of them, bowing deeply afterwards and laughing abundantly. Amina smokes lazily and stares with hooded eyes across the water. Kofi drums his fingers against the side of the pinnace. Were Were is busy applying fine beadwork to two marionettes that she bought in Mopti. It took her a whole day to track them down. These dolls from Mali are world famous, she says. Made of sacking and wire and wood and string, they are manipulated with one's entire body.

They go ashore again, and four brand-new 4x4s carry them the fifty kilometres to Goundam, the place of the Tuareg. Although it is late afternoon, lakes of mirages shimmer everywhere. Goundam is no more than a scattering of houses and what appears to be an abandoned hostel. In the courtyard, a few chairs and an iron table. On the floor of the room she and Amina will share, two worn mattresses. It is unbearably hot. There is neither water nor electricity, but they will try to have everything up and running by the time the poets get back from the reading.

The 4x4s take them down to a sandy hollow where the whole of Goundam seems to be waiting. The colourful severity of the scene takes her breath away. A whole row of people sit in front with their faces covered by cloths of cobalt blue, muslin white, deep purple or bottle green. On their chests hang finely-crafted copper amulets on camel-hair strings. 'Why are some of the women's faces covered and some not?' she asks. No, the women's faces are open, it is the men who cover theirs. The ones with the fine long noses and large brown eyes are *men*? Indeed. The women with cowrie shells woven into their hair seem to have whitened tongues that rattle and patter at great speed in high-pitched ululating. Little drums are clasped under the arm and played with both hands. Little guitars emit woeful sounds, whereupon the men sitting on the ground make slow movements with their wrists and shoulders.

Two men among them stand up, hitch the windings of their turbans higher up on their noses and lift their sabres against the darkening sky. Everything looks so different, everything sounds so different to what has gone before. There is something specifically *not* African about it, she thinks, yet these people are the rulers of the largest desert in

Africa. They have adapted completely, they are more comfortable in this part of Africa than anyone in the Caravan. Light-footed, they dance across the sand, interacting so graciously with one another. Bony wrists, elegant thin ankles, hard shin bones, and they all have these eyes. Eyes without mouths and noses. Enormous brown eyes peering from deeply coloured silk cloths. A trace remains of the stifling feeling she always gets when people cover their faces and their hair like this, as if they want to remain unknown, as if they do not want their essential human features to be read.

Both English and French now have little value. Nobody seems to understand anything. Meanwhile it has turned pitch dark. The vehicles are drawn up in a line and their lights switched on. And so by the grace of the Pajero the poetry of those who have to read off paper can continue. Zein reads the Timbuktu poem of Albecaye, which he has translated into Arabic. The people sit silently and listen, as if in wonderment. She reads her poem about the stone in the desert of the Richtersveld, and the Afrikaans sounds hard and strange and angry in the moonless night. She notices that the Caravan poets all sound strangely secure in their differences.

The poetry of the desert griots has a completely different sound, everything is performed at a higher pitch, with a great deal of rustling that sounds to her like wind and flapping tents, like the soft feet of camels in the sand, like goat and blue and oasis. The Berber language that they use is speckled with Arabic words, to which Zein listens with incredulity. Even for him it is all strange. For her, there is something completely abstruse about the performance of the nomads and their poets, something estranging even about their cracked, work-worn hands and fabulous jewellery. No implicit brotherhood or sisterhood asserts itself between the Caravan and the Tuareg, yet there is an apparent pleasure in and surrender to each other's enchanting sounds and habits.

'That was a very strange evening,' she says as they walk back to the 4x4s.

'We are crossing over to the northern reaches of the continent,' says Zein. 'Central Africans would like to pretend that Africa is only black, but Central Africa is also Muslim and that links them with the North. The history of slavery also complicates perceptions. It is true that many slave traders were Arabic, but we must remember that many more were black. Who are we to say that the Tuareg are not African? They are not black, they do not speak French or English, but they survive in the most feared parts of Africa.'

Back at the sleeping quarters, only the water flow has been restored, but someone has run a cable from the nearest power source fifty metres away and a naked bulb now shines mercilessly on the evening meal. A large bowl full of chopped-up bones with lumps of meat attached. The bones bear the scars of many failed chopping attempts. As she bends to dish up for herself, she smells the bitter core of hardship meat. The bread seems to have been chopped up with an axe. She puts down her empty plate and buys two beers from the owner of the hostel.

Suddenly the power is flowing. Which is definitely a hyperbole. Four light bulbs start glimmering weakly in different parts of the building. With a cry of joy, Amina jumps up with her towel and hurries to Albecaye Kounta's room, for he has kindly given her permission to use the shower there despite the irregular water flow. After a minute or so one of the bulbs blows up and everything is cast back into darkness. She begins to wonder if Amina is all right, and shuffles off through the dark to check. As she opens the door, she hears suppressed cries. 'Help me! I am going mad. The soap has fallen, I have dropped my towel in the water, I can't find my clothes. There is no more water, and I am full of soap.' Laughing hysterically, they sort out the invisible textures.

They borrow the accountant's large torch to go and prepare for bed. Mariame Sonko has placed a sheet on each mattress. They cover their mattresses, and she wraps her Adidas in a towel to make a pillow. She considers drinking her second beer, but then she may have to use the communal bathroom later, and according to reports it is in bad shape. Amina takes a sleeping tablet. They are both already hysterical. 'Heavens, but you have a large collection of medicines!' It is because of the doctor in Paris, Amina explains. When he heard that she was on her way to Africa, he supplied her with a small clinic of medicine. She has already passed on her stomach pills, eye drops, anti-allergenics and several types of antibiotic to the doctor. 'This is the best!' She takes out an enormous wad of material attached to a wheel. It is an authentic mosquito net. They laugh like two hyenas in the torchlight. 'This end is supposed to be tied to the roof and this goes over your bed.' They look at the two worn little mattresses and know that mosquito bites are the very least that could happen to them tonight.

She lies down. She has not brushed her teeth. She has not taken her malaria pills. She has stopped eating. She has stopped talking. She is nauseous. She wants to stop processing. She wants to stop existing. Become bowelmovementless. Through the frameless window she hears people arriving from the desert with bleating goats and neighing camels. There are greetings and flickering fires. What day is it? She rolls around. A relentless rhythm starts up somewhere. Not a drum, not a marimba, but a peculiar loud thumping that goes on and on. The tam-tam, she thinks, that's what Albecaye called it in his poem. She is feverish. She hears thousands of mosquitoes swarming around her. It is too dry for mosquitoes, but she hears them in their furious gathering. They suck and suck and then pump her full of germs and viruses.

Like the cannibals during the Mfecane, the mosquitoes know this already: once you have tasted white people's flesh, you want nothing else. The spices and herbs and sugars they consume make their flesh a delicacy. Poems about flesh-eaters tumble through her head: the cunning son of Magaguba, his mouth red with blood, he harvests men like sorghum, he mows men down like wildlife. In a swoon she remembers a report detailing how the Ndebele beheaded whites, sliced open their hands and baked them with fat in clay pots. How bunches of penises hung in the trees, and the cooked limbs of children were found in grain baskets. 'Are you as brave as your grandfather? The one whose name you carry?' Yes, it is a praise song, it shimmers through the sweltering dark. 'Will you chop off the Boer's head with your axe? Will you walk into the palace, like your grandfather before you, and hold the head by the chin?'

She sweats. She rolls around. She is freaking out.

And eventually she has to. The thing she has feared. The thing she hoped to postpone until the boat the next day. This night, now, she has to go to the toilet. With the accountant's torch she goes into the communal bathroom. There were three toilets once, but only one remains. It is leaning to one side and brimming with excrement. Dried, gracefully curled turds lie exhibited on the porcelain rim. The other stalls are packed full of broken pipes and washbasins.

With the sound of clashing stainless steel she shuts her arsehole. Tightly forever and ever. Amen. She goes outside. So many people are sleeping in the sandy street that she cannot consider it as an option for what she feels building up inside her. She sits on the steps and tries to think of other things. But it cannot be postponed. It must be done now.

She goes, breathing desperately through her mouth, to the bathroom. She scrums into the stench. She squats. And by the light of the torch she shits a shiny and solitarily massive turd in the shower.

When she wipes her arse with her right hand, she knows that she has broken through something forever. Her startled fingers she rinses at a leaking pipe in a basin with broken taps.

Outside she breathes like someone who has just come back from a run. She sits for the rest of the night with staring eyes. The burning torch in her passive left hand.

'My sister,' Chenjerai greets her cheerily the next morning, 'you look terrorized!'

She shakes a packet of instant Nescafé granules on to her tongue. It has to be conceded, she thinks, Nescafé has cracked the coffee market all the way to Timbuktu. Everywhere, on the edges of the outermost wilderness, no matter how meagre the spaza, how dusty and deserted the house, how primitive the shelf, somewhere in the back, neatly stacked, there it is: fucking Nescafé. It has become the only constant on this journey.

day thirteen

Everybody seems to be sick. Amina has a fever, Were Were is throwing up, Zein spent the night fighting stomach cramps. Nobody looks up as they stumble from their rooms. Everybody looks slightly dismayed, but nobody says a word. It is our continent. Ours. And we take what it dishes up for us.

In utter joy she sinks on to the grass mats in the waiting pinnace. They leave Goundam behind in a cool breeze of water. The river looks like a mirror. Restfully, Albecaye starts telling a story, and without being asked the accountant starts translating. Between the light and the water their words flow:

'Among the Fulani people were a man and a woman. They gave birth to twins. The one was a boy, the other a snake. The human-brother looked after his snake-brother very well. He milked the cows for him. He created a special drinking place for him, one for milk and one for water. Each day he washed the bowls and refilled them with fresh water and fresh milk.

'The snake-brother looked after his human-brother very well. "The sky is blue," said the snake-brother, "but not a blue of the earth, a blue of the imagination. You must know that the sky is not blue and quiet, the sky moves like waves, restlessly, and I can hear all of it. I can hear everything everybody is saying. Even the birds, even the smallest little bird, I hear them and I tell you about them."

'One day the human-brother returned ill from the desert. He looked as if he was dying. "I cannot breathe any more," he said, and his body contracted until it was only bone. He coughed. And unexpectedly from his mouth he belched forth seven wet, slimy lumps. The snake-brother recognized a mist of sky, a word of giraffe, a burning moon, a weeping tree, a clump of water, a railroad track and a feathered wing.

'"I don't know what it means," said the human-brother.

'"I will teach you to become them, to see what they mean," explained the snake-brother, "and live with grace on the earth."'

The other pinnace scrapes against them. 'There is the island,' calls Mariame Sonko, 'the island before Timbuktu!' They crane their necks. It looks like an advertisement: golden sand and palm trees. A few of them tumble into the water and swim out as the boats scuffle on to the sand.

They look at one another, a bit dazed. They are here! They have made it! Against the dune, Albecaye, the accountant, the cameraman and the photographer kneel towards Mecca, their robes billowing like colourful shavings in the breeze. When they rise, they each bear on their foreheads a golden blaze of sand.

It is a magical moment. She has a deep need to perform some meaningful act, to carry out a ritual that acknowledges the marvel of the moment, but her tradition has left her only with memories of crosses planted, cannons fired and flags raised.

Unconsciously, the southerners gather together. They share her last beer and Nhamo's last cigarette. After photographs and embraces, they take the boats into the harbour where the 4x4s are already waiting.

She recognizes the drivers. Yes, it's the same four who were in Goundam. They came here overland and will be part of the team on the last leg of the journey. Everyone is introduced to Mohamed Halice Ahassane, the tour guide with the most beautiful business card in the whole of the Sahara. It shows a camel caravan crossing the foot of a perfectly stylized sand dune, while his telephone number floats up above in the blue sky. 'With Halice on your side, the world may throw anything your way,' says Mariame Sonko. They leave for the state hotel where Minister Aminata Dramane Traoré is waiting to welcome them.

She is given a room. She switches on the air conditioner, but it makes a sound as if a kitchen knife has been lost inside it. A waiter comes to check and she is given another room. She switches on the air conditioner, but a stream of water pours from it. The waiter comes back and she is given yet another room. This time the air conditioner simply stirs the air in its immediate vicinity. She showers and washes her hair, unpacks her suitcase and falls into a deep sleep.

It is practically dark when she awakes. Downstairs in the courtyard she walks into a proper argument. The fight proceeds mainly in French, but everything is being translated at breakneck speed for Chenjerai's benefit (he is involved somehow in the management of the project). It is about money. The accountant is accusing the organizers of having failed to budget properly for Timbuktu, with the result that he is now expected to find thousands from somewhere. Thousands? Yes, nothing has been budgeted for Timbuktu. And Were Were Liking only agreed to come on the journey if she could return to Dakar the day after their planned arrival here, in order to fulfil a previous engagement. Now there is no aeroplane, because the harmattan has come up and it might not blow over for another five days. There is a private flight, but the pilot needs to be bribed. They must read his lips, says the accountant, he will not offer a bribe. He will pay for a legitimate ticket and that's all. Corruption and bribery will be the end of Africa. He will not allow the continent to drag him down. There is more than enough money in that suitcase, Chenjerai counters. He collected it himself with Mariame Sonko. The only reason there is suddenly not enough is that they still want to deduct expenses for the Institute. The accountant is furious. He draws himself up to his full height of Tuareg blue and hisses something to Mariame Sonko so venomous that she crumples before their eyes. They all get out of the way.

She walks out into the heat. Timbuktu lies in a haze of dust. Deserted, as if already claimed by the desert. As if already given up. Given away.

She recalls the words of René Caillié, one of the first whites to arrive in Timbuktu, in 1828: 'Everything was enveloped in a great sadness. I was amazed by the lack of energy, by the inertia that hung over the town ... a jumble of badly built houses ... ruled over by a heavy silence.'

According to her West Africa guidebook, when Bob Geldof came here, he asked, 'Is that it?'

In front of the hotel a row of hawkers are sitting in the dust, their faces muffled in turbans. Her jeans and T-shirt feel heavy and lumpy on her body, her Adidas are like two clumsy jeeps on her feet. She buys two Malian robes and a turban, which they show her how to wrap around her head. If you tie it correctly, they say, you form the name of Allah in Arabic script. With the cloth around her head, her breath suddenly comes back. In the lobby she finds Amina, who already has a cloth across her nose and mouth. This is the only thing that keeps out the sand, she says. It seeps in everywhere.

She phones home. 'I am in Timbuktu.' How many generations have laboured just so that she can say these words?

'What does it look like? The buildings?' asks her husband, the architect.

She sees immediately that, like so many whites before her, she is caught between the myth of Timbuktu and the reality. Acknowledge one and you betray the other. Just like Kroonstad, she wants to say, but built of mud and stone. Yet she realizes that she does not even have the language to describe Timbuktu within a South African context. 'Different ...'

'Different how?'

'Just ... different,' she says unwillingly.

'Damn it, woman! All your children are standing around me here like meerkats to find out what it looks like, and the best you can come up with is "different"?'

'Well, I'm standing *here* in a Muslim robe and a Pagad headscarf with camel-skin sandals on my feet. A waiter in a white jacket just put a Castle beer down in front of me for which he wants a shitload of money. When I got out of the Pajero in front of the hotel, I stepped in a pile of camel dung. I have seen nothing of Timbuktu because the place is hidden by a dust storm, just like Ventersburg in August. Does that help you at all?'

'Very much,' he laughs. Oh, their car was stolen last night, he says. This morning when he went outside, it was just gone. A neat empty space among the other parked cars in the street. But one is thankful that there was no violence involved. Yes, one is.

Their first meeting with the local griots takes place at a long table in the back court of a restaurant. Among the Timbuktu griots there is actually a woman, but this is clearly a group without any young and upcoming poets.

Timbuktu begins: 'We are the memory of the Sahel. We are the source of memory. All you have is the voice of the memory and the imagery thereof. Memory comes to you only in hearing. If we write the memory, we burn the memory.'

The woman continues: 'Timbuktu ties new relationships. Timbuktu is the great amalgamator, the collector of north and south, of salt and gold, desert and water, nomad and farmer, buyer and seller, Tuareg and Bambara. Timbuktu brings together many differences, many ethnicities, many religions, many languages. Timbuktu is the oasis of the many, of varieties that feed and revitalize one another, comfort and enrich one another, strengthen and enjoy one another. The myth comes from there, the facts come from here. The starting point.'

Another griot adds: 'Timbuktu the oasis. Timbuktu the well of the Tuareg in the eleventh century. Timbuktu of the Malian empire of Mansa Musa in 1313. Timbuktu of the Tuareg in 1400. Timbuktu of the Shongai empire in 1500. Timbuktu of education and trade. Timbuktu of the invasion of guns. Timbuktu where scientists and learned men lie shot down in the squares. Timbuktu of the Andalusian murderer, Djouder Pasha, and the Moroccan soldiers. Timbuktu of the heavy, closed, metal-studded timber doors. Timbuktu that draws into itself. Timbuktu that survives. Timbuktu that makes up for everything.'

This is why La Caravane de la Poésie is welcome here.

'We thank you for welcoming us,' says Albecaye, but he has something to share with them. They should not take it the wrong way, they should recall that it is a tradition of the age-old caravans not only to trade poetry, but also ideas and thoughts. He just wants to express his bitter disappointment over the sad state of Timbuktu. He is probably the only poet who has written several poems about the city, but of all that he wrote about, nothing has remained. He went for a walk this afternoon and was shocked at the dilapidated buildings, the impassable streets, the unhygienic conditions, in short, the misery that he saw everywhere.

What is going on here, asks Thierno Sall. Why are they doing nothing? What does it help to preserve a memory, if it is betrayed every day?

Now everyone wants to talk at the same time. A poet from Timbuktu says that the condition of the city has nothing to do with the griots, it is the responsibility of the city council and the Minister of Culture, who is staying so grandly there in the state hotel. Zein wants to know whether this kind of criticism from the Caravan is not just an echo of the West's mythology. Timbuktu is supposed to be made of gold, but failing that, it should at least be postcard pretty. Timbuktu carries the scars of time, of worn-out myth. It is a place that has always just tried to be itself, but has always been weighed down and taxed by the dreams and expectations of others. Nhamo says he thinks it is unnecessary for strangers to take their hosts to task like this. Because reality has not lived up to poetry! What kind of criterion is that? And what became of the idea of not criticizing a person in his own place?

The female griot says that women have always been accepted as griots in African tradition, it is only since the coming of Islam that they have struggled for recognition. Then a dramatic discussion erupts in the local language. The accountant translates for her Albecaye's conclusion: 'Islam has always been more tolerant of African traditions than Christianity.'

day fourteen

It is the day of the builder caste. Every year, at the end of the rainy season, it is their task to repair the famous Djinguereber Mosque, which was built in 1327 by the Andalusian architect who brought adobe brick as a construction method to Timbuktu. It is a festive occasion. The whole city comes to help and the builders give direction. They conduct the process. Mud cakes are mixed a distance away from the mosque: real earth, the correct amount of water, no stones or gravel. Then young boys carry the mud in grass mats to specific places around the mosque, from where it is handed up to someone beside the wall, then thrown to someone halfway up, standing on the protruding sticks, and from there to the upper storey, where the builders use it to seal holes and finally plaster over repairs. Meanwhile, a great deal of cooking is going on and the griots are busy singing and rhyming the work in progress. It is an honour to be part of this. The accountant stuffs his briefcase full of money in her hands and joins the queue in his billowing robes, setting the muddy grass mats on his head and carrying mud cakes until he is dull with dust and caked with mud. On the far side, the worthy Albecaye has also joined a queue, and so has Zein – all with a kind of rapture on their faces.

Later, they visit the pride of Timbuktu: the library of valuable writings. On the way there, they are shown a statue of the city's great protector: he is depicted on horseback, a white figure against a blue-green background, with his cloak billowing behind him (it all looks suspiciously like the Mobil logo). He is El Mansour, according to the post-card; Al Farouk, according to the local guide. The saint who rides through the streets at night protecting the sleeping. 'Al Farouk' means 'one who makes a difference between right and wrong'. He prevents people from doing evil at night. Really? Yes, people with bad intentions have come across him on his white horse, with his fiery cloak flapping. He is one of the 333 saints of Timbuktu, where every street is protected by a holy one.

They drive past the place where the learned men were shot dead, past the mosque built by a marabout. The marabout had a revelation that a holy one would one day come to Timbuktu and that there should be a mosque waiting for him. Forty years after the mosque was completed, a man arrived out of the desert and asked for the keys. It was Sherif Sidi Yahya, imam and holy man.

Suddenly they stop. The lead vehicle can go no further, the road is too bad. Too bad for a 4x4? Well, actually someone is building on to his house, and he is using the street to store materials and make bricks. Just opposite, another man has pitched his tent and is brewing tea, while his goats amble around him. They cannot pass. The construction industry in Timbuktu is entirely indigenous. Every structure is an expression of what the people who live there want. Nowhere do you get the feeling that people are living in structures they did not create, do not understand and do not know how to maintain. Nowhere do you think: someone was here before, these people are living in someone else's failed endeavours.

Finally they get to the library, the Centre de Recherches Historiques Ahmed Baba, where they are joined by the others. Were Were Liking is on the aeroplane, they hear. Did the accountant pay the bribe? The plane was already on the runway, they are informed with a wink, the pilot had been cleared for take-off, with an empty seat behind him, but he refused to open the doors before he received the money. Were Were started crying hysterically. It was only when the accountant waved a fistful of notes in the air that the pilot opened the door, counted everything out carefully, and let her on board. The accountant seems unperturbed. It's as if a great burden has finally been lifted from his shoulders: the moral salvation of Africa no longer depends on him.

The library, a modest modern building, is part of a residential complex for accommodating researchers. Two chubby American girls are currently in residence. They learnt Arabic at university, and then received postgraduate scholarships to search for references to America in the scriptures housed here. Have they found anything? They start giggling. It was only when they arrived that they realized their knowledge of handwritten, historical Arabic was insufficient to do the research properly. They will be flying out just as soon as the harmattan dies down.

A curator shows them around. Under glass lie displayed some of the library's two and a half thousand documents, one of the largest and most important collections of Islamic scriptures in the world, testimony to the mathematical, scientific, judicial and social knowledge present in Timbuktu, in Mali, and in Muslim Africa. (Centuries before 1652, she thinks.) Because Islam forbade the glorification of the human or animal form, Arabic calligraphy took decoration to astounding extremes. This intense decorativeness later spread to Arabic architecture, clothing and other aspects of everyday life.

Some of the manuscripts, difficult to protect from the ravages of dust and insects, were donated to the library by well-known families of the region. The curator unlocks a cabinet and removes a manuscript, which he shows to Albecaye. The old man shakes his head and looks around to see whether anyone realizes the significance of the moment. This is a manuscript from his own family, his direct ancestors in the intellectual caste of Mali. It is two centuries old.

Outside the library a little girl is playing near the 4x4s. She waves at them. She has stiff little plaits and a dapper stem of a neck, and her shoulder blades fold like butterfly wings under a T-shirt bearing the face of Lady Di.

They are invited to lunch with the local imam. A cool breeze drifts through the upper storey of his clay and stone house, where they sit in groups on the mats. Three men come around with a kettle and a bowl so that the guests can wash their hands. She sees that most people wash one hand only, but the three southerners wash both. Small bowls of dried melon seeds are sent around, and then bowls with thin strips of cheese. The cheese appears to be dusted with cinnamon, but actually it is fine grains of sand. It is so delicious that the sand does not bother her.

After that the men come in with bowls which they place in the midst of each group: a kind of round-grain rice, with peas, finely chopped egg and mayonnaise. They eat with their hands. Someone shows her how to scrape the mixture together with the top two joints of the fingers, work it into a controllable ball with the thumb, bring it up to the mouth and pop it between the lips. She struggles. If the food was just not so delicious. So delicious that the fine grains of sand are indeed no bother.

While she manages to get something in here and there, she sees how the others are emptying the bowl with systematic dedication. When the bowl is removed, she wonders what to do with her food-encrusted hand. The others leave their hands lying gracefully in their laps. Hers, however, is so mucked up that she has to keep it up in the air. Then a large bowl of couscous with shredded chicken in a delectable chilli and tomato sauce arrives. She shifts nearer. If she sits cross-legged in her new gown, she is too far away from the bowl for her amateur eating-with-the-hand style. She folds her legs in one direction so that her shoulder is pointing towards the bowl. Her back hurts from sitting on the floor, her stomach feels as if it's bulging out from under her robe. The sauce drips down her chin, which she has to keep wiping with the back of her other hand.

When she glances up after a while, she becomes aware that her comrades of the bowl are sitting in varying degrees of dismay. They are watching her. From the corners of their eyes. She knows they are thinking: My God, when will this barbarian turn our way and devour us? She wants to call out: People, after weeks of torture my taste buds are bursting with pleasure. I would gladly spare you my eating manners, but bloody hell, I am crazy with hunger for this fragrant, sense-enchanting food. She smiles apologetically and keeps her clean hand cupped beneath her spooning hand, which has turned into a sort of dripping red mechanical shovel. She stops eating. It was unpronounceably delicious. So delicious that she did not notice the fine grains of sand at all any more.

When they come to fetch the bowls, she has to keep both her hands up in the air. She sees the imam instructing one man to bring the kettle and the bowl to her. Now she cleans her chin, wipes her neck and washes her arms up to the elbows.

Everyone receives a large, flat bread. A dish of meat is brought which is so fragrant she almost dips her entire bread in it. She tears a hole in the bread and stuffs it full of meat and onions. But as she's busy, she starts to recognize the ingredients: liver, tripe, chopped-up chicken feet, brains. And there she sits with a fistful of meat that she has always found repugnant. But the hunger that has built up over the past two weeks now grows to convulsive proportions. Her stomach lurches like a bloodthirsty flanker near the goal line, her throat lets it be known that if nothing more comes his way, he is going to drag her tongue down in desperate hunger. Her brain keeps warning her not to do it. You hate liver. Offal makes you retch. She leans forward and devours the bread like a wolf, and the brown stains join the red stains on her robe. She sits back sweating with pleasure. The men come around with the kettle and the bowl.

Everyone goes back to the hotel to rest before the evening's performance. She looks over the poems she brought along with her and feels miles away from them. As if somebody else wrote them. As if nothing that she is remains in them. Paging through her diary of the journey, she sees that the early pages are filled with practicalities and horrors, in the middle there are new insights and viewpoints, while the later pages contain some of the most beautiful poems she has ever written. She will use those, unfinished as they are.

She puts on a sparkly white shirt, a pair of wide desert pantaloons that she bought at the artisans' market in Timbuktu, a dark jacket and dark boots, and she knots a gold and orange tie made of soft silk around her neck. Of the ten poets who set out from Gorée, seven are left. Each of them has translated Albecaye Kounta's poem about Timbuktu into their mother tongues. This is the night!

When they arrive, the square in front of the Djinguereber Mosque is packed with people. The Minister is ecstatic: more than two thousand people, practically the whole city is here! The griots bring in various groups: a troupe of men dressed in street rubbish, plastic bags, empty bottles and tins, one man adorned with the empty boxes of the only brand of cigarettes available in Timbuktu – a necklace of Marlboro. Then a group arrives leading donkeys laden with sacks of salt, then a group of men with shovels. She deduces, from an explanation given to her in very broken English, that these are all the functions of the city council of Timbuktu. A city council? Municipal services? She knew that every 'foreigner' had to report to the police station when they arrived in Timbuktu, but a municipal set-up?

One woman after another goes forward to dance. Like lovely multicoloured birds, they strike the earth with their feet, their arms flapping like wings. And each one continues until her headdress flutters to the ground like a nest. Smartly she picks it up and runs from the circle, while another jumps into her place. Griots dance and recite, poets from the Caravan dance and recite and read. The audience bubbles with enthusiasm and support. She is aware of how far she has come – no longer feeling threatened or exposed by the activities, nor indulging in them like a tourist, but simply part of it all.

When Zein finishes reading his work, a group of men sitting right in front get up with tears streaming down their cheeks. It appears that they are Berber teachers from the desert, who teach Arabic to the Tuareg. When they heard that a poet would come from Egypt to Timbuktu and present his work in truly classical Arabic, they combined their resources and journeyed for days through the desert to be here tonight. Now they throw their hands up in wonder and beat their chests with emotion, while kissing his hands over and over. They have also brought a whole list of grammatical questions that they would please like to clear up with him.

Albecaye's poem is presented in all the languages and the air is awash with the sounds of the continent. Each poem gets a louder cheer than the one before it. In between, the griots snatch phrases from the different languages and build up new structures on them.

She reads in Afrikaans:

the boat buttons water to the sky
the boat drifts down the delicate cincture of sand
the boat drenched in blue is heavy with heart

my ears feather from peace and heat

not of being
but of becoming
many becomings
past lost and drifting spaces
   many many becomings

And as her first words tumble across the darkening square, something in her body gives. Here the language resounds that gave her soul its existence: scarred and contaminated by so much shame and humiliation at having lost its compassion, at ruling without mercy. But in its effort to find a new rhythm in a new land, the language, as in the years of its origin, has become vulnerable and fragile on the tongues of its speakers.

die boot knoop die water aan die lug
die boot sny langs die smal seintuur van sand
die boot deurdrenk met blou dra swaar aan hart

my ore veer van vrede en hitte

nie van wees nie
maar van word
baie worde
verby verlore en ontheemde ruimtes
   baie baie worde

As she's reading, she looks up and sees a young boy standing across from her among the others, his head loosened from its turban like a flower from its calyx. His hair like slender, troubled flames. He ought to understand nothing of her Afrikaans, but his mouth is half open, a delicate frown between his brows as if he can comprehend this soft filtering into some new sound.

When she finishes reading, an ovation erupts over the square. She is incredulous. Women ululating. She does not know why. And it does not matter. One of many mouths, many tongues. Accepted as, part of, sharing in. The air fair with tolerance. The frame of the earth is green. A forest breathes in her chest.

When she returns to her seat, Nhamo gets up and hugs her. 'I'm so proud of you!'

Part of her wants to ask why, the other part simply wheels.

That night she sleeps lightly and without dreaming. Her hands smelling of food, her body at peace.

day fifteen

It is the last day. She goes for breakfast.

'Why is your coffee and your beer three times more expensive than elsewhere in Timbuktu?' she asks the waiter.

'The tourists fly in, walk around a little and then sit in the foyer waiting for a flight out,' the waiter says cheerfully. 'By the time they realize they are paying too much here, they are already leaving.'

'Strange people, these,' says the man at the next table. She's seen him in the lounge of the hotel for the past two days. He is also waiting for a flight out. It seems that nearly everyone here is waiting for a flight out. The first plane should be arriving the next day for the Minister and the Caravan. He will have to take his chances after that. He is a despondent French citizen, he says. Sent here by a European NGO to set up solar-powered wells in the desert: water is brought to the surface by sun-driven equipment. The NGO will sponsor the drilling of the wells, and organize and fund the construction and maintenance, but in return it wants a small amount of money to assist with the upkeep. So he has spent a month in Timbuktu, meeting endless delegations of Tuareg from the remotest parts of the desert. Nobody understands why they should pay. They all want more wells, yes, they all want stable and easier access to water, yes, but why should they pay? He sighs. 'I explained that they could plant vegetables and sell them. At the word "vegetables" they stared at me as if I'd mentioned foie gras. Vegetables? "We eat meat and milk, perhaps dates, sometimes watermelon. Who will buy vegetables from us? It takes us days to reach Timbuktu, so who will buy all this wilted produce from us?" Well, you could sell water to the caravans passing by. But this was an even bigger mistake. One of the absolute rules of the desert is apparently that you never, ever refuse someone water.' He opens a sachet of Nescafé. 'My wife wouldn't believe I've come to this,' he says with a shudder, as he pours water into his cup.

'What is the matter with this continent?' asks the accountant.

For some reason they have all ended up in the courtyard with a few of the locals who speak reasonable English. Everybody looks at him questioningly. 'Africa is bleeding,' he says dramatically. 'African kills African. African is making African go hungry. African robs African. And those calling the loudest for their rights are the corrupt and fat ones. The rulers who think like medieval despots. What I see is one big facade. A facade of roads, cellphones, fax machines, money, 4x4s, universities. In reality, these things function on a plane of their own, or in pockets of wealth and power, while most Africans gather as silent beggars on the outskirts, without access to money or resources, and with their own skills and knowledge dying off. Look at ...,' he throws his hand in the air, glancing around, 'air conditioners! Africa is filthy with air conditioners. But nobody really seems to understand why, or if they are necessary, or how they work. Especially that. Roads, sewage, you name it.'

It is silent in the courtyard.

'Achebe says it is the wrath of the ancestors,' says Nhamo. 'They are angry. They are furious. Our ancestors are punishing Africa by making sure that nothing works. They are destroying us. Because we have turned our backs on them. In our shame about being African we have run after the West and Islam, and now we are left behind in dilapidated ruins, with rusting railways, exhausted mines, crumbling roads, being exploited by the very same monsters we have created: African leaders devoid of humanity. Westernized dictators moving in bulletproof cavalcades, who could destroy entire countries with their weapons, but are unable to do a stitch of work, produce an administrative plan or plant a mealie.'

'Oh nonsense,' says the accountant. 'Ancestors my foot! Every African must take responsibility for the corruption.'

'And colonialism is simply a myth?' somebody else retorts.

The accountant moans from deep inside his body. 'Africa is the first continent, so to speak. Colonialism was with us for no more than a hundred years. For God's sake, do not insult us by implying that we have only one history, which is colonialism. Each and every one of us must take the blame for the corruption, the inhumanity and the moral bankruptcy that Africa is experiencing.' The bribery of the pilot clearly still fresh in his mind.

'If the West and Islam are responsible for the destruction of the moral fibre in Africa, what then should be the source of the so-called new morality? Or do you want us to accept that Africans before colonialism lived in complete peace and charitableness?'

As nobody ventures an answer, the Frenchman says, 'In some places people ate one another! Burning witches, killing twins, fearing lightning ... oh man!' He sounds quite emotional.

'You see, that is my problem.' Nhamo wipes the sweat from his face with his colourful shirt. 'In Europe and America, they not only eat one another, they also eat the rest of the world. But that is okay.'

'Stop blaming the West!' shouts the accountant. 'Stop treating us like children. I have a brain and a soul and an intellect and a history. I organize my own life and take responsibility for it. Of course a lot of things influence me, but I refuse to become corrupt or kill my brother or exploit my neighbour because of something the West has supposedly done to me. I am better than them! I am more than them.'

'Then stop cradling that suitcase,' Nhamo interrupts drily.

'I agree with you, my brother.' Zein has been quiet up to now, drinking one glass of tea after another, all made for him by one of the locals right there in the courtyard, on a special little stove. 'We are better than them. We can show the world how a life should be lived.' He hands the tiny glass back to the man crouching at the stove. 'We believe in the continuity of things. We respect that. We call it the ancestors or spirits. For my Egyptian forefathers there was no separation between life and death, you simply moved from one house to another. In most indigenous African cultures, tangible reality and the spiritual realm are one and the same thing. A tree has a soul, a river has a soul, and the spiritual world is always present. If the ancestors and the living are interdependent, the ancestors will be present in each moment that is important to the living. When we performed last night, our ancestors were there.'

She tries to imagine her grandfather there on the poetry square last night, with his undemonstrative nature and fierce impatience. She cannot. Would he be with her in Holland, this man of the veld, of red grass and Afrikaner cattle? Even less. Is this a problem in Africa – the absence of ancestors? Can one make one's own ancestors or adopt them?

But Nhamo is speaking. 'It is of no use "us" showing "them". We cannot do without them and vice versa. The completeness of my being human depends on the completeness of their being human. It is therefore my duty to see to it that they reach their full humanity. If they have plundered, enslaved or killed me, I have to assist them, for my own sake, in repairing their defective humanity. It is only when they realize that it is wrong to plunder, enslave or kill me, that they can become completely human, and I can come at last into my own humanity. Contrary to its claims, the West has never been sufficient unto itself, it has always needed Africa and the East. So too Africa needs East and West.'

'The West needed you to become rich and prosperous,' says the Frenchman. 'Now you need them to become human? Seems a bit ridiculous to me.'

'That doesn't bother us,' Zein is quite calm.

'Dog eats dog, but here in Africa, dog has nothing to eat,' the Frenchman says, quoting Ali Mazrui, as the waiter comes to announce that their transport is outside.

The last afternoon in Timbuktu has been set aside for tea in the desert with the Tuareg. The invitation came from the mayor of the small town of Arouane. They leave the sultry state hotel in 4x4s under the vigilant eye of Halice. It is far. After a while the young drivers start racing one another with cheerful recklessness through the dunes. The poets hang on as best they can while the drivers goad one another through the open windows.

In reeling circles of sand, they draw up below a dune. The poets settle their shaken bodies and get out.

They step into another reality. Spread over the sand are large, colourful carpets with tassels of intricate knots, edged by low, stuffed couches. The sun is setting like a red moon over the lip of the dune. The Tuareg serve them small glasses of sweet tea. They drink. The afternoon thickens into dark and with the dusk comes poetry.

Arabic poetry. 'Oh, the woman with the whitest eyes,' says the mayor of Arouane. 'She folded a cloth around her breasts. Whether she said, "Be greeted" or "Come in," I cannot remember. I was lost. May Allah grant that she becomes mine or I will lose my mind completely.' The nomads cheer and slap their colleague on the shoulder.

Darkness implodes on them. Dunes glow, she observes. Silence feeds the sidelines to the evening star.

She recites from the San poetry of her country:

the stars take your heart and feed you a star's heart
and you will never be hungry again
because the stars say: tsau! they say: tsau!-tsau!
listening to the stars in summer saying tsau!

Ikĭ hã. Hé tíkẹn ē, hi lné ta, ikụattẹn sse á hi á Ikụattẹn ( ) lĭ, hí ssiṅ ‖Ɪkụã Ɏaʹuki ttaṅ.

Ikụãlkụáttẹn ‖kụaṅ kã kã: "Tsa̰ü! Tsa̰ü!" hé tíkẹn ē Iχam-ka-ḷk'é tã kã, ikụãlkụátta ‖Ɪkao á hi wái ( ) tsãχáitẹn; ikụãlkụátta ka: "Tsa̰ü!" hi ta: "Tsa̰ü! Tsa̰ü!"

The Tuareg chieftain raises himself. He pushes his thin-boned fist in among the heavy stars. 'Even if they break my pen, my words will take fire; even if they destroy my horses and camels, my teeth will hang from their wrists; even if they take my last breath, I will scorch their palms. I am the revolution! I am the desert! The dunes have set me free.'

Zein recites: 'You sleep in the tent, not a single rose, but your opened heart and the vows. I bend over to cover you with fragrance, and find him there between us in his black cape. He shares our pillow. I see him at the edge of our sleeping carpet. He has toes.'

ضحكْ في كُمُّه
يوم ما اتبادلنا الدّبَلُ
مَيَّل علَيّ وقال لي على اسمه
ختم بكفه – قبل أصحابي – أوراق الجواز
شُفته في أول ليله
بيعّد القُبَل
واقف، ما بين الشيش، وبين القزاز .

جَتّ نابلس المسهوره
وقِفت تحت شبابيكى
بتغنى ليّه، وايكى
غنوة فَرَح
جاب الغُنا الناعم
قمر نايم
فى بستان طرح

She fights down the word 'privilege', but it comes to rest in her mouth like the clean line of some silent sky. Enchanted by colour and language, the smell of sand, the taste of tea, she knows that she wants to be nowhere else but here, wants to be from nowhere else but here, this continent that fills her so with anguish and love – this black, battered but lovely heart.

'I don't think, I sing. I am the poet of silence,' the accountant translates into her ear. The language now is French.

Then Arabic. The Egyptian poet translates: 'I am the vagabond of the word, the nomad, I swindle the silence of words, because I live in them. They are my tent and my waterhole. I belong to the word.'

Bambara: 'Poetry is always busy with light. Poetry glows from the inside. Poetry is the ritual of draping sound over light. So that you can live opened.'

French: 'With the scar of our tongues, we write the land beneath our feet. We write a landscape of breath. Our word smells human, our tongue tastes African. To write is to belong.'

When she packs her bags that night, she feels light-footed and loose-limbed, sorted out and rooted. She has no soul other than the one breathing in the enormous shade of this continent.

*Y*ou walk with your mother. You have been walking like this for a long time. You do not look up, you only see the navy shoes you know so well. They are walking differently now. The rhythm of the shoes is different, as if somebody else is walking in them. Your mother has not spoken since the previous day. Then she sat beside the baby, and looked into nothingness, until the crying stopped. When you woke this morning she was still sitting like that, as if she hadn't blinked her eyes at all during the whole night. You saw her getting up, mutely, putting the baby on her back and shoving her feet into the cracked shoes. When you ran up to her, she took your hand without knowing it. And now you are walking. Along an endless road. The place among the thorn trees just a shimmer in your childhood thoughts. You have been walking the streets of the city for many months. You can do without food, but you want water. You do not ask though, because your mother is walking next to you as if locked in stone. The gravel under your feet, the smell of rust, and your mother suddenly sits down in a space that is nowhere. She takes the baby from her back, holding it in one arm. With the other she pulls you kindly on to her lap. You sit together in the blinding sun, the three of you, as if cast from one flesh. One shadow. In front of you the brilliant cut of rails. Now you hear something approaching, feel the ground shivering. When you look over your mother's shoulder to find out what is howling like a hooter, you see a monstrous maroon thing tearing down on you. You pull yourself loose but your mother grabs you, you yell and cry and pull away, for a brief moment looking back at her face like a dark button against a crushing horizon. She yanks you with surprising strength back on to her lap and folds her body over you and the baby. Everything rushes to black.

PART SIX

AN END

CHAPTER ONE

'THE ORDER COMES: EYES FRONT, FIRE! Now I see that Colonel Grové and Jacobs and Joubert are lying next to each other, then a couple of other guys, then me. I can see this Colonel Grové. He takes out a case filled with his bullets. Ours are just lying on our boxes. Not his, his are in a neat little case and he dips them carefully in a little bottle before he slips them into his magazine. Now I lie and I watch him, how he neatly wipes everything down with an oil rag.'

It is the early-morning flight to East London. In the smallish aeroplane, we sit squashed in on either side of the central aisle. My travelling companion is in the military. He's telling me what it's like for a former MK member in the newly integrated defence force. This story, which he tells with gusto, is about how he made life difficult for his white colleagues at shooting practice.

'Now he lies down, this Grové, with these yellow glasses on. In the target pit sits a guy with a triangular sign on a long pole. He's supposed to check out the target and show you how close you are. When you shoot a bull, he points with the sign to the top left of the target. When you miss completely, he just waves the triangle in the air. Now Grové takes aim. But just before he pulls the trigger, I shoot a wild shot towards his target. Now the guy there in the pit waves the triangle, saying it missed completely. I see Grové frowns.

'Then Jacobs wants to shoot, but just before he shoots, I fire into the ground in front of his target, you just see a cloud of dust, then the guy waves his triangle. Now I hear Jacobs say, "You know, there are guys working in that pit who don't know what they're doing." Then I see Grové is going again. I wait and just before him I shoot past into the corner. The guy in the pit waves his triangle. A miss. I hear Grové saying to the lieutenant who is in touch with the pit, "Listen, please have a word with the men there at A3 and A4," and he is very nice and calm. He knows we are now integrating, and he is determined that *they* will set the example of professionalism and standards and protocol and respect for discipline and orders. "There seem to be men at the targets who don't understand the system. Just tell the officer there in the pit he must please check things out for us. Please man."'

The flight attendant brings our meal. She addresses my travelling companion respectfully as Colonel Mentoor, but he dismisses her formality with a friendly smile. He is on his way to Umtata to attend a funeral.

'Now they *talk* on the radios. But just when Grové shoots again, I put a shot to the side. There the guy waves his triangle again. Then Grové says, much more terse this time, "Ask those men what is going on there?" The lieutenant says, "Sir, they say there in the pit that you shot to the side, *far* off the bull." Then Grové says, and he's now very uptight, "But I didn't *fire* yet!" Then the radios talk *warra-warra* back and forth, then the lieutenant says, "Colonel, they say you *did* shoot!"'

Colonel Mentoor is getting louder and louder. A few people in front of us turn their heads to catch some of his animated talk.

'Now I let them be for a while. I see Grové is shooting bullseye, bull, bull, bull. Then I shoot again. Just into the dust there between the targets, and both guys wave their triangles. One shot, but both wave. Now Grové thunders down the line, "Give me that radio! Target pit come in. Target pit come in. There are guys fucking around at A3 and A4. Get other bloody people in there!"

'Now you can hear them shouting and ordering over there. Then Grové lies down again. He adjusts his yellow glasses, uses his oil rag. I wait. My comrades are finished with their rounds and they're standing at the back killing themselves laughing. They can see my rifle is completely skew. Just before Grové shoots, I shoot. The triangle waves. Grové grabs the radio, but the guy on the other side says, "Colonel, what do you want me to do, you're shooting into the bloody ground!" Grové is beside himself: "Lieutenant, I DID not FIRE yet!"'

Just as I'm about to ask what he hoped to achieve by all this, he says, 'When we had our meeting that evening, to discuss the integration of the top structures, they didn't quite have the same legs to stand on that they'd had a few hours before. I can tell you that!'

We fasten our seat belts for the landing.

✧

We turn off the N2 at Eagle's Nek. The minibus crawls along a near-impassable road until it simply can go no further. There are five of us in the party: the executive director of the Institute for Justice and Reconciliation, a project manager, a media manager, a church minister, and me, as a member of the Institute's Board. We get out of the bus and walk the remaining few kilometres to the huts. Hairy piglets trot past us. We have been invited by Bantu Holomisa, the leader of the United Democratic Movement, to undertake a fact-finding mission on poverty in the Eastern Cape.

It is a Monday morning. The hut is full of young men aged eighteen to twenty-five. They have no work. Their clothes are scant in the rainy cold and they are all scraggly thin. In the next hut, a woman with the limbs of a gnarled old vine is making food. She supports nine children and grandchildren on a pension of R620. In the hut after that, two women are watching over a mentally handicapped boy; the child, who is covered in sores, is crawling happily across the hard-baked dung floor, drooling. These two women look after sixteen grandchildren, four jobless teenagers and two retrenched children, all on a single old-age pension and a disability grant.

Why don't they plant something, like cabbage or spinach or potatoes? Everything you plant here is eaten by the pigs and the goats, a bag of seed potatoes costs R25, nobody has that much to part with. As we move further away from the main road, the poverty intensifies and we hear the word 'gulumente' more and more. Government should fence in grazing areas, government should fence in homesteads, should build roads, should give seed and tractors and diesel. Government should lay in a water supply, provide electricity, build schools, make transport available to the nearest hospital. Government should fix the IDs. Government should build clinics, increase pensions. It soon becomes clear that the elderly are supporting practically the entire Eastern Cape population and the stress on them has become unbearable. Loads of grandchildren and great-grandchildren are growing up without any discipline because the grandmothers struggle all day long to produce a meal from handfuls of mealie meal and beans and samp. The children discipline each other!

We go back to the minibus. On the road again, we pass several women who are identified as teachers. It is already twelve o'clock on a Monday morning, yet they are still not with their classes. Some have babies on their backs. It is a problem, a head-master tells us later. Nobody wants to come and teach in these areas because transport is irregular or non-existent. Teachers prefer to live where there are better work opportunities for their spouses and better schools for their own children. After the floods the previous week, these teachers now have to walk from the highway, as everybody is doing. In every school we visit, however miserable, there are at least plenty of books.

And this becomes the chorus. Everyone wants seed and tractors and fences. Everyone wants roads, clinics and proper schools. And the correct IDs.

Late that afternoon we drive into Butterworth. It is jammed with taxis and covered with litter. Plastic bags flutter on every fence and tree. Butterworth recently achieved the distinction of being declared the dirtiest town in the country, the media manager tells us. Hoards of people live in the rubbish dumps. Up to ninety-five per cent of the people here are unemployed. Forty-five factories and businesses have closed down since 1994, as the new government did away with the tax concessions of the old bantustan authorities. We stop at the hotel just off the main street, and wait for an hour in the lounge, which is filled with fat black men in expensive suits, drinking large bottles of Coke and Fanta and watching *Big Brother II* on the television, before we are led into the conference room. Here we are awaited by Eastern Cape Premier, Makhenkesi Stofile, the MEC for Education, Stone Sizani, and a Director-General in the Health Department, who hardly seems to be out of his twenties. It is already dark outside. In the yellowish hotel light, they look tired and depressed.

'We fenced several properties, but a lot of the fences were broken down, taken away and sold. Then we delivered the wire and the poles at various points and asked people to fence their own properties. And what happened? They asked who would pay them for putting up their fences. When we said there was no payment, they simply left everything. The stuff is still lying there, rusting away. We gave tractors. Those are standing broken or they've run out of diesel.'

The roads?

'Should we build a road costing millions upon millions to some far-off hilltop where there are eighteen huts inhabited by the poorest of the poor? These people don't have cars, but a road would enable a teacher and a clinic sister to work among them. Should we build it? Or should we rather spend the money on building new roads linking main towns and maintaining the existing roads and infrastructure?'

Right across Africa people are fighting over land. In the neighbouring states, black people are violently demanding the return of their land. Here there are endless hectares of highly fertile soil that sustained farming in earlier years. What is going on? The land exists, it belongs to the people, but nobody plants so much as a head of cabbage. And this while thousands of young men are sitting around jobless and aimless in the huts.

'People have lost all their initiative. Most of the roads can be repaired with a spade and some stones and gravel. Nobody is prepared to do it. Because they have no cars, they say. The people with the cars must fix the roads. If everyone built a thorn enclosure next to their huts like in the old days and planted their vegetables inside it, the malnourishment would end. But nobody does anything.'

Schools?

'In the coming year we will build more than two hundred schools. But take a closer look, and you will see kids matriculating who can't speak a word of English. Or going on to do a BCom at the University of Transkei where Accounting is not part of the course because they can't find anyone to teach it. People are getting qualifications that are meaningless.'

Clinics?

'Built hundreds of clinics. Many of them standing empty, because the roads are so bad that nurses and medical supplies cannot get through.'

Governing the Eastern Cape is obviously no easy ride, and one picks up a kind of despair when some of the enormous problems are related. Mr Maye, who facilitated the discussion with the politicians, gives us some insight into the situation. 'For decades, the Eastern Cape has provided the entire country with leaders. Generations of leadership. And it is still doing so today. Top Xhosa people are regularly headhunted by other provinces, which means this region has been sucked dry. This has created two problems. Firstly, local communities are without leadership. And secondly, there's a culture of entitlement: our people are governing over there and they must make good to us. Wherever you go in the Eastern Cape, people will tell you, "Everybody is waiting for Madiba," because they know that Mandela personally canvassed for millions of rands to be pumped into the area of his youth. This is why people say so easily that things were better under apartheid. Then you could blame the white government. Now it is difficult to blame yourself or accept that what is wrong is within your power to change.'

✧

The next day, Bantu Holomisa takes us to Gengqe, Bacela, Futye, Gogozayo, Upper Ngqungqu and Khotyana. The General – as he is still widely known – comes with us in the minibus so that we can ask him questions, while his own driver goes ahead in a blue bakkie. Holomisa was the head of the Transkei defence force when, in 1987, he unseated Stella Sigcau in a bloodless coup d'état and took over the government. Having displaced the corrupt bantustan government controlled by Pretoria, he was hugely popular in the Transkei, especially when he pushed up the salaries of traditional leaders and repealed the tax on cattle. After testifying at the Truth Commission about the corruption of Ms Sigcau, then a Minister in the new democratic Cabinet, he was removed from his post as Deputy Minister of Water Affairs and expelled from the ANC. Holomisa then founded his own party, the United Democratic Movement, and in the previous election acquired control over the heartland of the Transkei.

He is already busy organizing for the next election, he says, because he wants to become the official opposition. He pays his fines for being absent from parliament in advance, because he refuses to wait three weeks for the dismal three minutes of speaking time he gets in the House, during which he is shouted down by the ANC in any case. He operates outside among the people, he says. If he can take over the Eastern Cape and one or two other provinces, then his chances of supplanting the waning Democratic Party will not be that bad. Anyway, South Africa ought to have a black opposition.

But what is his opposition based on? On ethnicity or principle? 'You will never hear me say that I am in opposition to the ANC, because I am not. I only represent an alternative. We agree on fundamentals, but I will do things in a different way. Less corruption, more cooperation between traditional leaders and the government, delivery to the poor.'

Won't he simply be dismissed as a front for white interests, like the Movement for Democratic Change in Zimbabwe?

'With the NNP joining the ANC, we now have equal proportions of whites in our parties, and that is how it should be. We must be able to criticize each other without being called ethnic or racist.'

The road is nearly impassable. Big pools of water splash in chocolate-brown waves up the sides of the minibus. We drag through a marsh, we ooze through a soggy mush, and suddenly the bus skids forward, turns sideways in the road and sinks up to its axles into the mud.

'We may as well walk back, we will never get this minibus out,' says the project manager.

'Should my driver take over?' asks the General with a faint smile. 'I always feel very safe with this man behind the wheel.'

We scurry out of the open door and wade through the mud to the grass banks on the sides. The General sits tight. The General's driver, Michael Ngqondo, shifts in behind the wheel in his khaki coat. The man is built like a rugby forward, his neck and smallish head bulging out from enormous shoulders.

Michael puts the minibus in reverse. And it is a masterpiece to behold. Now this gear, then that one, the wheel like this, then like that. Then the back wheels spin and the front wheels are dead still. Then the bus roars, then it smokes, then it moans, then it howls, then it neighs like a foal, then it hiccups, then it chatters like a chainsaw, then it growls like a lion. And suddenly it begins to scrabble along the road sideways. Neither backwards, nor forwards, but *sideways* the bus shoulders through the mud and out the other side. In my entire life, I have never seen a car driven sideways before. Meanwhile, people from the surrounding village have gathered around the spectacle to call out encouragement to the driver. But when the mud-encrusted door slides open and the General sticks out his moody head, applause breaks like waves from the crowd. Women throw down the bundles from their heads and come running up. From afar, across the hills, you can see children running elatedly towards us. Holomisa is received as a hero and praised and sung.

Can he see? the people say. They want roads. Does he know that he is the only politician ever to come here?

'Here we are, struggling to get from one village to another, and meanwhile people are landing on the moon!' mumbles the project manager.

We stop at a mud-brick school. A little table has been set out, with a tablecloth fluttering in the icy breeze. Behind the table are five chairs. Across from the table the chiefs and headmen are sitting on a log. The veld is drenched and our chairs sink into the mud. The people are skinny. An ancient fellow coughs as if his insides are made of shards of glass. The old women sit with unblinking eyes. Behind them a whole group of young men is standing, observing the proceedings sceptically.

They want roads and work and IDs. Why do the people in the cities get R20 000 to build a house, when they already have roads and schools and clinics, but the people in the rural areas get nothing? Could they not each get R20 000 just to buy seed? Work? Look at these young people, their parents have seen to it that they are educated, even in their great poverty, but here they are standing around, some have university qualifications and they sit without work.

We move further into the hills, where unbelievable vistas unfold of untamed veld, soft grassy swells, bunches of huts painted in green and pink hues. If you did not know better, it would appear idyllic. Large, solid huts with small windows and thick walls, clay floors that keep out the cold and the heat, enough land, enough veld.

'Where have all the trees gone?' asks the General, who, in his capacity as Deputy Minister of Water Affairs, was once involved with the 'greening' of the rural areas.

'We have always chopped out the wattle for firewood,' says the chief. 'Then the new *gulumente* came and said that it was alien vegetation, so they removed it all and planted indigenous trees. Those trees are already four years old, but they are just *ncinci-ncinci-ncinci*,' with his fingertips pressed together barely at hip height.

We drive past the Bacela pension payment point. Thousands of people are waiting on the grassy plains. Somebody recognizes the General through the rear window. People jump up and run in front of the minibus. 'Stop!' says the General, and Michael skids to a halt. When he gets out he is swamped by raging pensioners.

'The people here with me want to know what your biggest problem is.'

'IDs! IDs!'

'What is this thing with the IDs?' he asks.

It appears that many people do not have IDs because they have never had birth certificates. If you do not have a birth certificate, someone who witnessed your birth has to give a statement to that effect to the police. Many people living in remote places, whose births went off without notable mishap, or whose mother was never ill enough or rich enough to visit a clinic, now have nobody to testify to their birth date. They might have been told that they were born during the Great Influenza or the Great Typhoid, but nobody recalls actually being present at the birth. Without an ID, they cannot get a grant or a loan or a pension. Some complain that they were born in 1938 or 1927, but the dates in their IDs have been scrambled and show that they were born in 1983 or 1972. If these dates are followed, they are obviously far too young to be eligible for a pension. In their lifetimes, they will never grow old enough to qualify. Some old people are using their pensions not just to support retrenched children and unemployed grandchildren, but also siblings or spouses stuck with these defective IDs. Some believe the confusion was created on purpose, in order to reduce the enormous amounts being paid out in pensions.

'I am fifty,' says the advisor to the local chief. 'I cannot find work because I am too old, but I am too young to receive a pension. As a man, I will only get a pension at sixty-five, but my wife already receives hers at sixty. Where is the equality of the sexes now? I have to beg my wife for money for at least five years.'

A young man who has brought his grandmother to the payment point says: 'It humiliates us to beg money from our grandparents. There is no work or training to give you pride in yourself, so that you can lift your head in your community as someone who makes a meaningful contribution to things.'

Amidst enthusiastic ululating, Michael drives carefully from the crowd. Our welcome at the next village is even more impressive. A team of drum majorettes, each one wearing a different remnant of white clothing and clutching a stick, marches ahead while somebody beats out a rhythm on a drum. Michael drives behind at a steady pace over stones and grassy clumps, through ditches and puddles, to the school where the meeting is taking place.

'We are hungry,' say two scrawny women, rubbing their stomachs. In the meantime, plump, well-dressed teachers are setting out bowls of cheese curls, prunes, peanuts and sweets in front of us. Each of us gets a glass of Coke or Stoney ginger beer. Right in front sit rows and rows of little children, whose saucer eyes follow every movement of a snack to our mouths. We stop eating.

'These are the first whites we see here,' says the chief. 'Mandela told us that we must solve the problems of the country with talking and forgiving, not fighting. But we see no water, no roads, no electricity. The rainbow has brought us only hunger and neglect.'

'To get a tractor to come and plough a field costs R350, a bag of fertilizer R100. If I pay it from my pension, there is no money left for the twelve souls I have in my care.'

In earlier years, people sent money from the mines so that the ploughing could take place and stock could be bought in large numbers. Those retrenched from the mines now sit around here, and no more money comes into the rural areas.

We are invited to stay for a meal. In one of the classrooms there are pots of *umngqusho*, rice, macaroni, potatoes and chicken pieces. Everybody gets a glass of *umqombothi*. But there are villagers standing against the walls, staring at the food with visible hunger. Shouldn't they eat instead? 'No,' orders the General, 'you will insult the people by not eating their food. They have scraped together this meal with great effort and sacrifice, and if you don't eat, or if you just distribute it to others, you will hurt them tremendously.' We dish up for ourselves, but the food thickens on our palates when a man in a torn jersey covered in grass and patches of cow dung swoops on the table outside and grabs a handful of snacks, before being chased away. The headmaster tells us that there is not a single facility for the mentally disabled in the entire Transkei.

Just as the choir at the next school finishes singing, we hear the low sounds of an *imbongi*. Siphiwo Maphongwane of Mqanduli is from the same area as Bantu and Patekile Holomisa. He is in Standard Eight, and dressed in a red and black tracksuit. To the great joy of the audience, he delivers a praise poem in honour of Holomisa. The community asks for more classrooms, roads, a functioning clinic.

We drop the General off at home, where his mother is expecting him. Dusk is well advanced when we arrive at the hostel of the King Sabata Dalindyebo Technikon in Umtata. Some young men are playing soccer in the parking area, and one of them is asked to show us his room. The lobby is pitch dark and smells overwhelmingly of urine. We have to hold one another's hands as we're led up the stairs to the first floor. In the glow of a street light we can see naked wires sticking out of the walls where light fittings have been torn out. On the first floor we step through a lake of water drifting from the toilets. Apparently, only one of the toilets is working; the copper fittings of the others have been ripped out and sold. The student sleeps in a kind of dormitory decorated with posters of black soccer, rugby and cricket stars. At his bedside he keeps a Bible, a mirror and a comb. The room across from him is completely ruined. The ceilings have been torn out and you can see the sky through the roof sheeting. The floor and the iron bedsteads are scorched, the window frames have been stolen.

Wordlessly, we all get back into the minibus. It is properly dark when we arrive in Malungeni. Where one can sleep in utter silence and be woken in the morning by the crowing of cocks, the hissing of geese and the clatter of goats tottering past. This is ostensibly why so many old people return to the Eastern Cape, you can live better here, more comfortably. But the medical services? A trip to the nearest doctor costs R80 by taxi, the doctor wants R150 for the consultation. And mealie meal costs more in Umtata than in East London. It is expensive to be poor.

✧

The next morning we drive through Ngqeleni, a pretty town hidden in wild valleys, shaded by gigantic chestnut trees. A luscious paradise within sight of the ocean. The Ngqeleni Hotel, which is right next to Hollywood Coffins, hires out its dining room to two women who prepare the afternoon meal of chicken and pap for the guests. A room for the night would be R70, explains the hotel manager, as she digs devotedly in her ear with a paper clip. In the backyard, the hotel's water supply is hoisted from the bottom of a well.

A Greek by the name of George owns the Sondelani Supermarket, which sells everything from condoms to coffins, ploughshares and nails, cheese curls, flour and candles. The entire Eastern Cape is running on pension payments, he confirms. He cashes their cheques. The priorities have changed totally in recent times, he adds. And the hunger has increased. People buy Lotto tickets, then cellphone time, and then the cheapest mealie meal. Whereas people used to buy dried and canned goods, they have stopped completely now. Yes, he has been robbed, three times. Shot. His children are studying at universities in Greece, and he and his wife sometimes socialize with the broader Greek community in Umtata.

Cellphone time?

'You must remember that black people are very sociable,' says the *mfundisi*. 'And here you can see how people struggle to get from one place to the other. Add to this the fact that half the people are away, trying to find work in the Western Cape or elsewhere in the country. With cellphones you can stay in touch. My mother in Malungeni can phone me where I am in Gugulethu and tell me that she has run out of mealie meal. I can then phone the taxi in Umtata and ask them to drop a bag at my mother's on their next trip in her direction. There where they stop on the road they can call my mother to tell her that the mealie meal has arrived. People are also desperately looking for work. And if somebody hears about a job they can immediately call a family member and say, come! People are now in contact with their families, children with their parents, and so it is more and more difficult to just disappear and escape from your responsibilities in the rural areas.'

We meet up with the General at his house in Fort Gale, Umtata. He informs us that he has to catch the four o'clock flight that afternoon, and so we should try not to waste any time. We drive north-east towards Mount Frere, and the Eastern Cape falls open before us in all its beauty. The soft, lively brown fur of grass ridges curves away, uninterrupted by fence, road, erosion or plantation. Unspoilt pastures. For hours we drive on a good gravel road, with stone and sand heaped on the verges. The Kokstad road to KwaZulu-Natal is being tarred. In soft pleats, the valleys of the Mtata, the Mzimvubu and the Msikaba rivers descend.

Michael is behind the wheel again, and has to be admonished often in Xhosa to slow down. Why is nobody talking about Aids, we want to know from the General. People won't do it, he says. To say you have Aids is to admit to promiscuity, which is very difficult in a region so overwhelmingly Christian in outlook and norms. But the fact that people complain so much about the lack of treatment at the clinics is an indication of how great the need is.

Manka in Tsolo. As on every previous occasion, our reception is enthusiastic and heartfelt, and the General explains that he is not from the *gulumente*, that we are not from the *gulumente*, but that we are observing everything and will be reporting back to the *gulumente*. At Qumbu, we sit on a slope facing a crowd composed of nothing but young men, as far as the eye can see. Clean open faces. One comes forward to speak. He has been looking for work for five years. When he hears of opportunities, he goes, but he has never found anything. 'I am twenty-three years old. I have matric and I am strong and healthy. Every day I must get food from my grandmother and beg money from her to buy simple things like soap. If the chance should befall me to steal something,' he says, as if thinking aloud, 'then I will steal. Every day that passes when I have to ride on an old person's back makes me less human.'

'How far is Mdabukweni?' asks the General. Just over the mountain, says the man in the tweed jacket, who was responsible for organizing the meeting points today. So we drive on. At each village we pick people up and drop others off. The General's blue bakkie is full of passengers.

Why is the country not embarking on a large-scale socialist programme to mobilize young people, in order to build roads and schools, and plant fields? 'Forget it,' says the media manager. 'The government dare not be seen as socialists, or the West will crap in its pants.'

'I am actually sick of being held to ransom by the West,' grumbles the *mfundisi*. 'Do this, do that. What has all this free-market stuff brought us? They don't give up a thing, not tariffs, not lifestyle, yet we have to be more capitalist than Wall Street.'

'The government is clearly doing something,' says the project manager. 'Everywhere we go, we see schools, all the schools have books and desks, we've seen several new police stations and a magistrate's court or two, some good roads. But it is obviously not nearly enough. You need more than a good policy, you need an enormous budget and a change of heart. Can it be so difficult?'

In the minibus, the discussion turns to rugby. The General lists his choices for the national team. The others make suggestions, Springbok coaches are compared, the new rules debated, everyone has an opinion on the spectator who tackled the referee during the game against the All Blacks in Durban. Suddenly, without any warning, like the crack of a whip, a voice comes from the back of the bus: 'Stop!' And, as if there are no other conversations in progress, Michael stops. There and then. Dead halt. We look at the General in surprise.

'Open the door. I must turn back now or I'll miss the plane.'

No furtive scanning of the watch, no weighing of pros and cons, no consulting about how far we still have to go. Nothing. Just immediate, decisive action. He picks up his coat, gets out, and goes over to the blue bakkie, which has come reversing back quickly to see what's happening. The General jerks open the door: 'Why did you lie to me? You said the place is just across the mountain. You lied. Get out!' The man in the tweed jacket scrambles out. In a flash, the General and his driver are back in the bakkie, it is swinging into a U-turn before the doors are properly closed, and off they go. Our own project manager still inside and Michael miraculously behind the wheel. The whole thing has taken no more than three minutes and we've hardly had time to close our mouths. The man in the tweed jacket gets sheepishly into the bus and we drive on to Mdabukweni.

Traditional dancers, *iimbongi*, choirs and crowds of ordinary villagers form a guard of honour as we make our way up the mountain to the dilapidated school. The crumbling mud walls are kept upright with poles. When the wind starts blowing fiercely, the entire class has to go outside in case the gable collapses. If a child falls ill at school, somebody has to piggyback him down to the village in the valley. One day a teacher fell ill, and she had to remain lying in her classroom for days until she was well enough to walk back home by herself.

Some unemployed young women perform traditional dances, while the fiery teacher, Miss Jola, conducts her choir. Cheese curls, peanuts and sweets are put in front of us, glasses of Coke and Stoney. The children cough all around us in the cold air, on the stoep an old man is seized by an asthma attack, women sit staring out dazedly in front of them.

Back in the minibus we get an anguished phone call from the project manager. 'I have just given my soul to the Lord anew. We stopped in front of the plane just as they were closing the door. But the General got on and the rest of us stumbled back into the bakkie suffering from jet lag. That Michael simply put his foot down and drove like the devil on these terrible scarred and donga-ed roads – not a car in sight. The only concession he made was to lean on his hooter when we saw animals.'

It is dusk when the man in the tweed jacket has us turn down yet another impossible track. We protest, it is not in the schedule. He just sighs: I promised them. We shake our heads and hang on. The minibus groans and scrapes. We come, quite literally, to the end of the road. And then suddenly schoolchildren start streaming into the glare of the headlights. We stop. Little children come jittering down the hill, shivering in their thin shirts and tunics. One of them is wearing a cap that says 'New York'. We climb out into the icy wind.

Gungqwana Junior Secondary School consists of two little mud buildings containing five classrooms, so small that only a single long school bench can fit into each one.
More than eighty children go to school here. In the glare of the minibus's headlights we
see that the door frames have been rained loose and are now held in place by poles. The
blackboards in the classrooms are so washed out that several layers of faded lettering
shine through to the surface.

The children go on singing in the darkness. The media manager is standing next to
me. 'Do you know what they are singing?' I shake my head. He translates for me:
'Blessed, today we are truly blessed. Our voices have been heard. We are blessed.'

'We thank you for coming here,' says the principal, 'tonight is the first time for us
to see the rainbow nation.'

A new school was supposed to have been built here, but the lorry bringing the
building materials got lost on the bad roads and delivered everything to the wrong
place in a different district, and so the new school was built there instead.

While we shudder back over the washed-out ruts of the road, the moon rises over
Malungeni and spills silver through the bus. Only across my hands it is still dark.

✧

Today we are in the care of Advocate Sodo. He takes us to the town hall in Umtata, for
our meeting with those in charge of the region. Next to me sits Auntie Laura Mpahlwa.
For years, the community has looked to her for advice and assistance.

The dependency rate in the former Transkei is eighty per cent, the average monthly
income per capita is R115. People stream into Umtata with the desperate hope of
finding work, picking up the crumbs. The most important thing is that jobs must be
created. Auntie Laura puts it carefully. What the Eastern Cape has is a lot of land and
a lot of labour. If farming and the creation of infrastructure were made part of the general plan, South Africa could take the lead in the changes taking place on the continent.
If you can turn your rural areas into places where people live worthy, decent lives, you
have put yourself on the road to changing the world.

Another woman stands up. She works for the Department of Development. There is
a general lack of communication about government strategies and planning, she says.
'We have some of the best laws in place, we get enough money, we have excellent plans
and projects, but people do not know about them. They sit in their isolated villages, they
see that they're not getting water, they don't have electricity, roads, clinics, schools, and
they feel lost and neglected. Government should devise ways of telling people: this is the
area that will receive electricity this month, here are the schools to be built this year, so
that people can know. Government also needs to be monitored. Because between planning and doing, things fall apart. People with experience have been retrenched and
replaced by younger, politically aligned people, who don't know what to do. In the
meantime people are hungry and humiliated. Government should respond.'

Even the people working for the government talk about 'government' as if it is somebody else's.

We ask questions. Where is the first point of contact with the government for people in remote villages? The councillors. They represent wards in the local municipalities, which in turn fall under district municipalities. What are the salaries for these different layers? A district mayor earns R144 000 a year, the speaker of the council R124 000, a committee member R104 000, and a councillor R48 000.

'But some of them can't even write their names, and don't know how to use a telephone,' shouts someone from the back.

And this problem with incorrect IDs?

'Many people do not have the means to come to the city to have their IDs corrected,' says Auntie Laura. 'They don't have money or cars. The government should go to the people. We know that civil servants are being trained to go to the rural areas to correct IDs and issue birth certificates, without all the rigmarole that goes on now. And this makes us very happy. But I want to talk about tilling the land. Do you know what has taken its toll? The fact that people let go of their cattle. Many are saying so openly. People should be able to plough with oxen, like in the old days, but now nobody can do it any more.'

Later we all go for a meal at the pizzeria next to the golf course. 'Are there any whites in Umtata?' I ask. Yes, mainly English and some Greeks. 'Do they mix with you?' Yes, they all have businesses in Umtata and have been living here for years. They do not live all together, but spread out across the city. And when there are parties, people do invite each other.

'The whites in Umtata realize that they are not the decisive factor,' says Mr Sodo. 'Not just realize, they *accept* that they are no longer a factor. They have let go of power, without removing themselves from the society. They participate actively in an environment in which they are an unimportant and powerless minority.'

'I don't know if it is really that,' says Mr Zakade. 'It is more that they live at our pace. They are not better off than we are financially, many of them can speak Xhosa, they eat *umngqusho*. It is only their children, them they send away to East London.'

What about corruption? 'There are two kinds of corruption. The one kind is when people steal and take out of the country. That is the worst. The other kind of corruption is when people steal and spend in the country. If you look at the Eastern Cape, the poverty is overwhelming, yet in general people are fairly well dressed, they often have warm clothes. So the corruption in the Eastern Cape pilfers through to larger parts of the community. You can call it the "trickle-down effect" of corruption, if you like.'

We drop the councillors back at the town hall. The sun is already drawing water, but we still have one more visit ahead of us: Canzibe Hospital.

In the beginning, the road is tarred. But we drive and the road turns to gravel. We drive and the road turns to stone. We drive and the road turns to rut and ravine. We struggle over the stones, rev out of the ditches, spin out of the mud, while the sun sets over the most beautiful, fertile valleys in the country. There is a haze of trees. At the gate the guard stops us. While we're waiting for permission to enter, a young woman in a light-blue candlewick robe saunters past with a two-litre bottle of amasi in her hand. As she passes through the gate we see the letters on the back of her robe: TB.

The guard waves us through. The hospital consists of a series of small buildings housing the various medical units. The grounds are overgrown with old and lovely trees, stretching their branches in gigantic reaches of shade across the complex. Further back are stands of nut and banana trees, and pomegranate hedges. But everything speaks of terrible neglect. Some of the trees have been hacked down. Mildewed walls, cracked windowpanes. The patients are obviously responsible for washing their own clothes, for laundry lies draped all over the mouldering trunks of the felled trees. Everywhere there are pools of water and heaps of rubbish.

In front of the first building is a commemorative stone with an inscription in Afrikaans: 'This hospital was donated by the Dutch Reformed Church congregations of Robertson. For the love of Christ. 1961.'

We go in. In the first ward there are four children suffering from kwashiorkor. They sit with their skinny legs and arms and unblinking little eyes on their mothers' laps on the floor. They are eating pumpkin and pap, and there are orange peels on the plates. To one side a grandmother is sitting. She came here with her four-year-old grandchild, she says. She has to look after eight children and her husband. The mines have never paid out his pension. The only food she can provide is mealie meal thinned with water and then boiled. No vegetables, no meat, no beans. Sometimes she does have money for food, but they live in such a remote place that all she can get hold of is mealie meal.

There are no sheets on the beds. The maternity ward has a single blanket, no pillows, no towels. And everywhere a smell of sewage and neglect. We are indignant. We demand to see the doctor. We don't care that it's half past six. He is still on duty in the administrative section, we are told. So we go there, our outrage mounting with every step. At the top of the stairs we walk slap bang into a short little Indian man with a stethoscope around his neck and a mop of hair so luxuriant it seems to be sprouting from his eyebrows. In broken English he invites us into his neat office. We look questioningly at one another.

'I am Dr Kabir and I want to thank you for your noble hearts,' he says, looking down at his fidgeting little hands, turning us in an instant into the complete fools that we are. 'We have here 140 beds for a population of 169 000 people. From here we also run eleven clinics and ten mobile points. The hospital should have five doctors, but I have been alone here for seven years. This past year, two Cuban doctors have joined me, which made things a lot easier. We have an X-ray machine, but our anaesthetic machine broke down in 1998 so we can no longer do any operations here. Even Caesareans have to be referred to Umtata. We have excellent nursing staff, motivated, hard-working, kind people, and we have a good dispensary with all the medicine we need and an assistant pharmacist, but we do not have enough administrative staff. People with the administrative qualifications do not want to live here because it is so isolated.'

'Why do you live here?' I ask. 'Where did you qualify?'

'I come from Bangladesh. I worked in Western Zambia for some time, then in Mozambique, then here at Canzibe. I ...,' and he gives a half-hearted shrug of his shoulders, 'I like it here. The area is reasonably crime-free. One or two bullet wounds a month, a few stabbings ... Last week some men held up the gate guards with guns and stole two of our six vehicles. But we phoned Umtata and they were caught. Anyway, the bad roads make the maintenance of vehicles impossibly expensive. We usually only keep half of our fleet running.'

'These limitations do not daunt you?'

'Limitations are relative. This hospital is much better than where I worked in Zambia. I believe that motivation comes from within and that this is all part of the challenge.'

The incidence of malnutrition has gone down, he says. There was a stage when the wards were filled with kwashiorkor children. Personnel are frequently sent into the more remote areas to educate people about healthy nutrition. The women who bring their children are also taught about nutrition and what products to use. The provision of clean water and instruction about ways of purifying water have also reduced illnesses from that direction. Aids is a big problem, says Dr Kabir. It is currently the number one cause of death in most hospitals in the district. In 1995, when he first did the different tests in the laboratory, one in five people was positive. Now it is practically everyone. 'You actually get a fright when someone is HIV negative.' The Aids patients are classified as TB cases, and two years ago a new wing was added to house all the patients. Poverty makes it impossible for their families to look after people.

Why are there no South African doctors?

'They don't want to work under these conditions. We had one here from the Medical School in Umtata, he lasted eleven days, then he said: this is not my kind of place. Another one came in the early nineties and stayed for eight months.'

We sit there ashamed of ourselves, trying not to think about the numbers of South African doctors who have left the country.

'Shall I show you the new wing?'

A long passage stretches before us. Dr Kabir walks ahead. He opens a door and leads us into the waste, into this lonely place where death has come to stay. From the ten beds in the first ward stick-thin arms and legs rise. And heat. Some dazedly try to sit up, others just flutter their fingers on the blue bedspreads, one stretches his arms out to the doctor. Falls back into his ribcage. The doctor opens the door across the way. Another ten beds. Heat and fever. Another door. He continues down the passage, door by door, ward after ward, bed following bed, person after person, skinned into thinness, black skulls with staring sockets. The corners of their eyes welted with undignified fear.

Dr Kabir keeps on walking. The helpless, grim anger of the male wards overflows into the female wards, becomes a complete surrender to despair. I see the woman who passed us at the gate, drinking the amasi while tears wash across her cheeks. From her frightened eyes the wish to love still stares. Next to her lies a woman who hardly has skin or flesh left. Black bone splinted there. No need for tongue. Only breath turning the ill blood over and over. Another turns her enlarged gaze on me. Not for help, not for blame, that I realize, but as if remembering herself as a woman, lovely in her bones, living her whole heart's life through days when what she loved was near at hand. They all wait like ferns to die.

This is the end of the world.

And I have nothing to make sense.

And nobody and nothing nowhere to balm them, every one of them, to lift their limbs and sop them into all that is … my lungs search desperately for a word to breathe from … like apple and trellised light. To bathe them for the last time in a world fairer than dreams.

Dr Kabir keeps on opening doors. I turn around and walk back the way we have come, later I am running, down the long passage out of these Novilon-clad vaults of misery and dry death, and gasping out into a night transient with dew.

Around me the flowers have grown fangs, but I breathe.

Coldness comes paring down, but I breathe.

Only the moon. The moon showering silver over Canzibe.

And I breathe, in order not to suffocate in shame. I want to blame. I want to pluck someone from somewhere and shake them for answers. What has happened to us? Where are all the dreams we once had for ourselves? What happened to the desire to change, to release ourselves into more caring lives? Where are we? Have we forgotten so soon what we wanted to be?

How could we ever become that, how could we become whole, when parts of what we are die every day into silently stacked-away brooms of bones?

CHAPTER TWO

MY MOTHER'S COUSIN, Oom Pieta, is a philosopher. He will come and sit peacefully astride our stoep wall, clean his nails with his Joseph Rodgers pocket knife, and say something like: 'To counter the natural tendency towards disorder, the living cell has to take in energy from its surroundings continually.' Then my parents will nod their heads affirmatively. What Pieta says there, sounds right. Oom Pieta knows. His philosophical analyses sprout from his deep insight into – and oversight of – the residents of Kroonstad. Oom Pieta works at the municipality, as we all know. It is only during one family Christmas, after someone has related yet another horrifying toilet experience, that the connection with sewage becomes apparent. This is when Oom Pieta sighs and says: 'During any natural process, in the absence of life, an isolated system will move naturally towards a state of disorder.'

'*Haai* Pieta, what are you saying there?' my mother complains belatedly.

'Sewage talk,' says Oom Pieta, and I prick up my ears.

This is how I end up driving out to the Kroonstad sewage works with Oom Pieta. I had no idea it lay so close to the concentration camp graveyard. 'Yes,' he says. 'And here, next to the camp monument, is the square of wet cement through which your grandfather's Afrikaner oxen pulled the wagon during the commemorative trek in 1938. The man driving the wagon, a Retief nogal, said that those were the largest oxen with the finest humps and horns that they'd come across all the way from the Cape.'

I know about this. I also know that my grandfather, coming back that evening to check on his oxen, heard shuffling noises in one of the wagons, and lifting the tent-flap, found one of the foremost Voortrekker officers making out with a full-bodied matric girl. In the most revered place of the Afrikaner ...

We turn off the main road, and Oom Pieta says, 'Voila!'

There it is: Kroonstad's sewage farm. There are two installations. It seems that Kroonstad makes use of the old trickling filter system as well as the new activated sludge system. The old system processes the sewage from the formerly white town, the new system processes the sewage from the townships.

'Now tell me honestly, Oom Pieta. Is there a difference between the excrement of white people and the excrement of black people?'

He shakes his head vehemently, but I push on.

'People say that in the early nineties, when the townships finally got their sewage hooked up to the white town's system, it was quite a mess here. They say that because black people eat a lot less meat and milk and other proteins, their faeces kept floating on top and therefore did not land up in the processing machinery. They say you had to make these special chopping blades to pulverize the township input, so that it could at least become part of the water. On the other hand, they tell me that the white deposits sank, bull for bull, packing along the bottom like clay pigeons, so that you just had to open the lower sluices and run the water through a stone filter, and it was fit for drinking. They also tell me that the water from the white sewage has to be strained to remove all the disposable nappies, whereas so many dead babies come drifting in with the township sewage that you had to install a special grinder, because nobody wanted to go in and clean the filters.'

Oom Pieta is indignant. He slaps his thighs in fury. What nonsense! What utter lies! He may have been a little bit of a racist himself in the past, but he will not allow the ignorant to twist scientific fact to vent their racist fantasies. Sewage is a science, for God's sake.

'You have to understand how a sewage farm works. The old installation, which was built around 1950, could not cope with the additional load from the townships. And so in 1990 or so, a new installation was built. With this new system, any hardware (if you know what I mean) that arrives here – mostly false teeth and plastic bags, even spoons – lands in a grinder. This speeds up the processing time, because the gravel from the grinder can be disposed of at once by trucks, which cart it off to specially dug holes. The big blades you see churning up the water in the reservoirs here are *not* chopping up human ejecta, they are forcing oxygen into the sludge. This oxygen forms chemical links, which in the end aids the separation of solid matter and fluids.'

'So they lied to me. There is no difference.'

He looks me straight in the eye. 'Actually, there is. The first large movement of sewage from the township arrives between five and six in the morning, while that of the whites only arrives at seven. The sewage from the township is firmer, with more solids, while that of the whites contains much more water, due to extensive bath and washing-up facilities which ease the flow. And that is all.'

Oom Pieta also has statistics. More than 100 000 people live in Kroonstad: 88 000 are black, 16 000 white. Of the 88 000 black people, nearly two thirds have flushing toilets, 15 000 use long drops, 19 000 use buckets.

He shows me the grids in the old system that catch the large objects, the channels that control the flow: if the sewage flows too quickly, the solids do not sink; if it flows too slowly, the wrong kinds of material clump together. Then he shows me the grids that catch stones, gravel, sand, peels. After that, large impellers force everything through pump rooms, where the water and the solids are eventually separated from each other by various processes. Only two of the four pump rooms are functional. The third has been out of order for eight years, while the enormous copper impeller of the fourth was stolen a year or so ago. Nobody knows when or how. It is simply gone. There is no money to replace it, nor to repair the one that is broken. Everything is running down. Even the gigantic iron pipes through which the sewage is pumped are showing serious signs of wear.

'The whole thing with sewage processing is to get more water. The law specifies that we have to give seven per cent of the water we process back to nature. The water is then kept in these reservoirs to be treated, until it is ready to be pumped into the river.'

We walk past a little building with broken windows and a sign: 'Caretaker, Laboratory.' A lab at the sewage farm?

'In earlier years, a trained laboratory assistant had to test the sewage daily to determine the correct chemical additives and the power of the pumps and so on. He also had to add the correct amount of alum and iron salts so that the water did not damage the river. But, well, now that the Department of Water Affairs comes to do the testing ...' and he shrugs. 'Of course, the first thing a cash-strapped town council saves on is the chemicals for the sewage works. I hear that they are already a couple of months behind here. That is why I say: the cell needs to maintain its structure in order to function.'

At the new installation, he shows me the grinder that dumps all the solids into waiting trucks. Enormous blades are churning the water into streams across the dam walls. 'Don't bring your hands close to your mouth,' he warns me urgently. 'In the past, you could use human waste as ordinary fertilizer. But today's human waste is so toxic, so full of pesticides, so crawling with viruses that you can catch deadly diseases here. Look at those dry sludge heaps. Once upon a time sludge was used to fertilize parks and golf courses, rugby fields and traffic-island gardens. Now you have to treat it intensively with heat and oxygen and chemicals to make sure a child does not fall on the grass and pick up a gruesome illness.'

Oom Pieta pushes open the door of a little room full of computer equipment. Lights flash and buttons vibrate, there are levers and digital printouts. All pumping speeds are determined automatically. But he shows me that the main pump gauge is broken. 'What it's throwing out now on these little screens, you can only wonder.'

'What do we need to pull off a big sewage system?' I meant to be more subtle about it, but everything simply rushes to the surface. 'Why are there so few working sewage systems on this continent? What does sewage control say about a nation? And what about the Valsch River!'

'Look, in all cultures there are ways of dealing with sewage that have developed organically from the region and the way of life. Basically, we can classify the systems into wet and dry. A dry system includes everything from disgorging waste in the veld to disposing of it in buckets, but the thing is that water does not play a role. The wet system includes letting go in a stream, septic tanks, and modern flushing toilets. The problem is that Western sewage systems, which generally require a surplus of water, have been imported into this country without rhyme or reason. In Europe it works differently: you build a canal, you let a stream run through the fort or the castle, and it carries everything back into the river or lake or sea, no problem. Here we simply don't have enough water to wash away the entire population's makings and unmakings. Then, during the heavy boycotts in the apartheid years, our sewage experts had to find their own way to sewage salvation. But it wasn't something they boasted about. It was only with the advent of the New South Africa that we realized how much pioneering work had been done in the field of desiccating sewage. Whereas European systems focused on disposal, we had been concentrating on recovering water. And we had achieved formidable results.'

'So why is this system not used in places like Mali? Is it too expensive? Is the science too intensive? More to the point, why is it not working at the King Sabata Dalindyebo Technikon in Umtata?'

'Expensive it is not. We have brought the costs down so much already that the average installation only costs around a million rand. The computerized controls are so simple a child could work them. But there are two things that are indispensable: water and toilet paper.'

What?

'Yes, if you want to win the Nobel Prize, develop an easily degradable newspaper. In other words, a newsprint that will survive the printing rollers, the news, the paging, the wiping, the substance from within, all without tearing in your fingers, and yet will dissolve easily enough not to clog a sewage system. The single greatest obstacle to the development of sewage technology in developing countries is the absence and expense of toilet paper. And water. In the townships there is a further problem. They put in these toilets with cheap plastic flushing mechanisms. When twelve people are sharing a toilet, what you need is a nice strong chain, a decent drop and a supply of soft, dissolvable paper.'

The next day Oom Pieta puts a page in my mother's postbox for me. He says it is an answer to my question about the river, given to him by one of his lecturers long ago:

In Köhln, a town of monks and bones,
And pavements fang'd with murderous stones
And rags, and hags, and hideous wenches;
I counted two and seventy stenches,
All well defined, and several stinks!
Ye Nymphs that reign o'er sewers and sinks,
The river Rhine, it is well known,
Doth wash your city of Cologne;
But tell me, Nymphs, what power divine
Shall henceforth wash the river Rhine.
Samuel Taylor Coleridge

CHAPTER THREE

'He's gone, you know,' says my brother. 'In the early hours.'

When the telephone rang, just after six o'clock, I knew. It is the news you wait for subconsciously all your life, perhaps. At one time or another it will strike most of us. He is gone. Half of what made you is dead. I make coffee. Pick up *Die Burger* from the front steps. Wander through the house. Water the plants. Make the bed. And I know at once: I have to be with them. The others. My mother and my brothers and sister and my place of origin.

Cape Town, Johannesburg, Budget Rent-a-Car. He always phoned, Pa. To say I must come up, he has never seen the red grass as beautiful as this year.

It is dusk when I drive into town from the north. My elder brother waits at the garden gate. The younger one opens the front door, and behind him in the lighted hallway stands my mother. My sister is in the driveway where the flowers seem to lean on one another. And they look, suddenly, mortal. As if what stood between our family and suffering is gone. Grief has reached us, moist in the loam. We are in the front ranks now and we feel loosened.

In his sleep. Ma, who usually sleeps badly, was awake before dawn. 'It doesn't help to roll around and work yourself up. If you cannot sleep, get up and bake a cake.' Thought he had overslept. But then he was lying there, the sheets drawn away from his chest, his eyes closed. Then she phoned her eldest son, and Andries came, and they left him lying like that. Peacefully in his own bed. My mother sat with him a long time, holding his hand. My sister came from Johannesburg. He seemed so peaceful, she said, as if a ring of the phone could wake him at any moment. Kidney failure is the softest way of dying, said the doctor, because the blood moves gradually from the living mixture to the other. Without anxiety. Without terror or suffering.

Before they fetched him, my mother prepared next to him: his woollen jacket, his one hundred per cent wool tie, his best shirt and woollen pants, his leather shoes with the handmade cut-outs. After they carried him out, she got up slowly and beat the sheets over and over as if in a daze.

'I am really bad with death,' she says, while I hold her. We are all in the little sitting room of their house, and I realize for the first time that somewhere along the line every one of us has gone grey. A pair of bifocals hangs around Andries's neck.

'The funeral is Thursday morning,' he says, 'more towards eleven, so that people coming from far away do not have to sleep over, we can give them lunch and they can all go back again.'

'People work during the week. What about Saturday?' I ask.

'Look, I don't want any arguments. It will be Thursday. You will write the funeral address, and you and your sister will sort out the church service and the thank-yous. I will deal with the funeral itself and the undertakers, and he,' pointing to Hendrik, 'will get the grave dug.'

Of course. Where do I think I am? The Krog family has never been a democracy. We work according to a strict patriarchal system, and I am the only one, coming from a far-away place, who has not yet noticed that the mantle has passed to my brother.

'Is the yellow copper bull still on Jurie Botha's grave?'

'Can you believe it! In this era of copper theft that enormous Brahman is still standing inside its bulletproof-glass cage – not even a touch of verdigris on its bronze balls,' says my sister-in-law.

Meanwhile, the telephone rings incessantly. Whoever answers comes back with red-rimmed eyes.

'It is those on the other side who cry so much,' says my sister-in-law.

'If only I was not so bad with death,' repeats my mother. She goes to make tea.

Andries takes me aside. 'It is hard to say all these things in front of Ma. But a white person can't have a funeral on a Saturday any more, because all the black funerals now happen on Saturdays, between eight to twelve a day. As the one hearse drives out of the gates, the next procession is ready to come in. Sometimes there are three services going on at the gravesides simultaneously. I was afraid that we would not be able to get cold-storage space for Pa, because the undertakers that have mushroomed all over Kroonstad do not have their own equipment. They hire everything from Avbob or Saffas, from the cold storage down to the make-up, coffins and hearses. So Saturday is peak hour. The only thing I asked Ma is if she wanted him to be buried next to the blacks of the town or the blacks of the farm. Then she said rather on the farm, so that she can go and visit the grave in peace – here in town several women have been attacked and robbed while they were laying flowers on people's graves.'

'Does Joep Joubert know about it?'

'I told him. He has already cut the fence next to the road, so that we can get to the grave without having to drive all over the farm. But the digging of the grave is our business.'

'Do we really want to bury Pa in land that none of us farm any more? That we might sell soon? Would you like to be buried in somebody else's land?'

'If you want to look at it that way, you can just as well say that the whole country is somebody else's land. If you buy a grave, you buy it from the black municipality to which the cemetery belongs. Cremation, that Pa did not want, nor do any of us, I might add. We all want to be buried on the farm, even if it is no longer ours. We are of it. That farm, that *werf*, that's what made us. I want to be back there when I die. I will give myself back to it – by secret means if needs be. We have no face without that farm.'

I look at him in surprise. Sitting there on Pa's bed, which has been made up neatly, he seems slightly embarrassed by his new-found authority on our belonging. It's not as if we were actually good farmers, or became a prosperous family from the land.

The telephone rings. The cellphones ring. The garden gate squeaks endlessly as people come around to talk and bring food. The kitchen is full of pots of soup and bobotie, rice and pasta, mince and vegetables, flat trays filled with soft triangular sand-wiches, cakes, tarts, and boxes and boxes of meat pies.

'It is terrifying for me that I cannot cook. I would have liked to cook up a storm when your father died, to bake things that rise, lard things, grind and mix herbs, make up bottles of preserves, boil bottles of jam, bake breads, decorate cakes ... now I'm sitting here with my hands folded ...'

'Elmien phoned from Canada,' my sister comes into the room. Her nose red. 'She says she will never be able to think of South Africa in the same way, now that Pa is dead.'

'Your father would never have guessed that Jan Hoender's granddaughter would talk so lovingly about him,' my mother says drily.

Andries and I go to Heilbron, where someone has offered to print the funeral address for free. He drives and I read him pieces about Pa from one of our mother's books. In an essay titled 'Bull of Africa', she describes the Krogs and their sense of style. 'Even if he only had a single suit,' she writes, 'a Krog would wear it as if it was hand-made from Harris tweed – which might quite possibly be the case.' And a bit later: 'I have been the recipient of bottles of kukumakranka brandy, first editions of poetry volumes, hand-crocheted bedspreads and invitations to Bushveld farms simply because of the charming, distinguished manner of the man at my side, my own personal Krog.'

'Do you think Pa felt good about such a piece?' I wonder. 'About being portrayed in such a positive way?'

'He was probably only too pleased that she didn't put down what she always said – that he had the typical legs of the Krogs, spectacular to look at, but useless to use. No good for running, for kicking a ball, for working, not even for dancing.'

His cellphone rings. It is Hendrik. They have dug down half a metre and hit a layer of ironstone. Big hammers and chisels from our cousin the dambuilder are being used, but it is going very slowly. I suspect that Andries's dream of having all of us resting quietly there on the rocky ridge has been dealt a fatal blow by the reality of geology. My mother has already asked whether they've struck water yet, because a dowser once told her there was strong water there on the other side of the stream.

'This morning we asked the undertaker for a Jewish coffin. Then he told us no, your father was too big a man. So I asked him, are you saying it's only the short little Jews who actually die? He was irritated that we want to get off cheaply, I suppose. But apparently they make these coffins in Welkom, so he ordered a bigger one for us.'

At the printing works people start crying when they see us. Your father was so proud of you and we loved him so much. Andries selects a photograph.

'I don't like that one, he seems to be ... averting something, as if he's warding you off as he looks at you.'

'That is why his Sesotho name is Matjama,' says Andries.

We drive back. He drives slowly, as if reluctant to re-enter the zone of grief.

'I once asked Ma why she moved over from fiction to essays. She was busy boiling soap there next to the windpump, I'll never forget it, she had on these thick socks of Pa's and a pair of his pants and a kind of hat with flaps. She sat on a little chair away from the fire, which she and Isak were stoking with mealie cobs, while the big white stirring paddles stood in the pots. Her second book of essays had just been published, you know the one about her family. But a few days earlier my Afrikaans lecturer had given us a whole spiel about the liberating power of the imagination, and how writers who only dig around in the sewers are lacking in imaginative power ... or something like that. When I came home for the weekend, I asked her about it. And she told me something that I'm only starting to understand now.'

I'm surprised to hear him telling me this. 'What did she say?'

'She said that writing and reading give you access to a different, larger world. In the old days, fiction could free you to go to a different place. But nowadays this larger world is so incessantly present in your yard and on your stoep and in your guest room and in your kitchen, it takes up so many seats at your table, it always has a whole mouthful to say about your food. Because of television and newspapers, you are now saddled with this other world. And you want to get rid of this other world, you wonder desperately how you are going to overcome it. Intimacy with your own world is the one thing that enables you to survive this ever-present other world.'

'So why does it only make sense now?'

'Because I realize myself that I prefer more and more *not* to read fiction.'

This is perhaps not the time and place to discuss my view that everything which has been transformed into language has already become fiction. How many times did I not go to town with my mother, and when she told my father about it afterwards, what for me had been a very ordinary excursion became a riveting experience, fraught with meaning and depths of imagery? I take my mother's book from the back seat. 'Let me read the story of the hail storm that drove Ma's first chickens out of the hok and destroyed them in the open.' He switches off the radio and I read:

Isak Mokokoane hands me the young chickens, pounded flat like dried flowers on stiff stalks. I pick up the washing bowl, empty the kettle into it, dunk the first chick in the water and wash the mud from its wilted feathers, dry it off with my apron – and would you believe it, it starts to kick, and when I put it on the floor, it remains standing like a potted flower. When I have the third chick in the bowl, Isak comes back with another load ... and a third ... and a fourth. We fire up the stove with mealie cobs until it's roaring and we wash chicks. Later on, I have nothing left to dry with, and so I take out my best guest towels. We pack newspapers in the stove in order to dry out the most hopeless cases. Some pull through, others lie steaming dead in a growing heap in the corner.

The kitchen is not very big, there are more than two hundred chickens. All the doors and windows have to stay shut and after a while the stove is rattling with heat. I am wet through. Hopeless and sick with sorrow, I keep on washing chickens. Then I start with the heap of dead ones. I pull out their feathers and remove their innards. And now, alone in the light of a paraffin lamp and released from the anxiety of the rescue attempt, I start to recognize them. Here is the little guy with the bent wing, the one with the white spot at the ear, the one that always used to peck at my shoelaces ... tears flow down my cheeks into the bowls filled with the little bodies of those that loved me so impartially and sunnily.

It is after eleven. I bundle the last cobs into the stove, look out over the silent, black-ened crowd, and close the middle door of the kitchen behind me. It is dark before me and I see a pale crack of light from under our bedroom door. I open it and stand in the doorway. My good husband lies reading under the blankets in the little island of the paraffin lamp, quiet and cut off from everything. He looks up at me, drenching wet, dazed from crying and ripe with steam and chicken droppings and entrails. It is a stern test of love, however young and certain. No one can hold it against him that he hesitates before flipping open the bedding for me: 'Clean yourself up a little and come to bed, then I'll read to you what General De Wet says in this book about the battle at Rooiwal.' Not a word about my dead chickens.

Deeply stung, I later climb in with him, definitely not interested in what General De Wet has to say about anything. Then, for the first time I hear the thunder of the spruit outside, I hear the dripping from the roof, and the ice-cold breath of the hailed-out land-scape touches my cheeks.

'Your mealies! Were you out there?' I ask in fear.

He puts the book down. 'No, I know what ...'

I struggle over next to him, across the vast expanse that a double bed can sometimes hold. We lie in one another's arms, vulnerable apart and together before the merciless laws of nature in which we live, find happiness and keep faith. The great dark night, the smell of bruising and pain, the silver death shroud, the erosion of the water, it all lies spread for miles around us. And so we fall asleep.

Andries pulls over and stops at a desolate picnic spot. He lights a cigarette and opens his window. 'Now read the rest,' he says. He knows the story as well as I do.

When I wake up the next morning, it is because of something strange, something like a cherishing peacefulness, as if a blessing hand is stretched over our bed. I lift my head and confront one of the strangest sights I have ever seen in my life. Packed tightly, across our blankets, on top of the cupboards, on the chairs, over the entire floor, stand little black chickens thronging together. Alert like sentries, but motionless, as if they are afraid to violate the silence, there they stand.

Possibly it was the extreme heat and the subsequent fall in temperature that caused the catch on the middle door to come undone. They felt the warmth of our bedroom and moved over. Yes, definitely, that is all it was, I would have to concede – if I accepted that they were chickens. Only they were not. They were people, my people.

✧

The hearse comes slowly across the winter veld. In the back Pa's grainy wooden coffin rocks gently. The driver brings the car to a halt and opens the rear door. My father's sons and grandsons each wrap a handkerchief around a hand and slide the coffin out by its rope handles. Through the grass they carry him to the grave that has taken three days to hack into the ironstone. My brothers cry like people who have lost everything. The smaller grandchildren stumble sobbing amongst the grown-ups who stand so brokenly around the grave. My mother stares blankly in front of her. A freshly shorn fleece is draped softly over the coffin. We sing into the icy wind that cuts from the south. 'Nearer, my God, to Thee, nearer to Thee.'

Death has burst its bonds to be with us.

'O Lord, thou hast searched me, and known me. Thou knowest my downsitting and mine uprising, Thou understandest my thought afar off.' The Dominee reads from the old Afrikaans translation, as my mother wanted. She stands hunched over. 'Thou compassest my path and my lying down, And art acquainted with all my ways. For there is not a word in my tongue, But, lo, O Lord, thou knowest it altogether. Thou hast beset me behind and before, And laid thine hand upon me.'

The coffin starts sinking slowly, and I know that a piece of what I am is leaving with him, going down into the stone. My original blood, my earliest bone, the text of my core.

The coffin scrapes softly down the ironstone flue.

Mooi loop Pa.

We stand here forlornly, your children, lost in a landscape in which we so often feel we no longer belong. A landscape we are bleeding from, generation after generation. You could not safeguard a place for us here. You leave us bereft, unfamiliar with sharing.

There is a quietness spreading over the veld, down to the stream and the willows, the long, naked poplars. Hendrik wipes his face. Suddenly he speaks in Sesotho: 'We, the family, want to thank Isak and Eveline Mokokoane, Ben Nakedi and Laetia, who came with my father many years ago when you were all young. Together you made this farm ...' Then his face explodes into tears.

No one speaks any more. I become aware of how many people are here. Rina and Peet, Ouma Hannie and her sons, Oom Pieta, our cousin the dambuilder ... and yes, Sheridan at the back with his cellphone. An enormous crowd that fills the field and spreads out to the edges of the bull camp. Silent, they stand in the cold Free State air. And for a moment something departs from them, from us, from our Afrikanerhood, our Afrikaansness, our whiteness, and we are filled with confusion, a kind of belated batteredness, disconsolate and vulnerable as we are to inevitable endings.

The prayer is over. My mother's eyes are feverishly dry as she says to my brothers, 'Cover him up yourselves.'

I see Isak in a crumpled jacket, his head grey, his callused hands on his walking stick. He comes forward to throw a handful of grit on the coffin. 'You have left me now, Matjama,' he calls. '*Tsamaya hantle, Ntate Moholo.*'

My brothers drag closer a few bags and pour soft river-sand over the coffin.

Then they take turns to shovel soil into the grave. Sons, sons-in-law, grandsons, cousins. It is hard work and nobody looks completely comfortable with a spade. When Andries straightens up to gasp for air, a black man puts out his hand. It is Kapi, the tractor driver who started working for my father just before the farm was leased out. My brother stares at him for a good few seconds, then hands over the spade.

My mother starts to cry uncontrollably.

Beloved father, guardian of my blood, you lifted yourself clear of us in the small hours of the night, you left us so softly that nothing was torn asunder. Light as a prayer, undamaged as a feather. May you arrive where your place is always certain, may you arrive there covered in fleeces of your finest wool. We have been put together by the many places you have claimed for us, gathered together from all the memories you have maintained for us. Holdfast man. Peacemaker. Unnoticed buckle of our family circle, go well ...

As we walk back to the car, my mother on my arm, I feel something lightly against my hair, something like a blessing. Like the touch, perhaps, of a forefather.

I wheel, slowly. Only the tips of my outstretched wings stir. The wind creaks in my ear hollows. Far beneath me the landscape drifts in flows of brown grass. A dust devil drills the plain. Over the endless, twisting river I turn and glide to where a town spreads like a neglected motherboard. I sink lower, my eyes narrowing. It is, it has to be. Always you – this gravitation of longing. To be with you. Of you. You move as if in pain, and my heart bursts its banks. In a rush I swoop down, I gather you in my arms, I hold you. I rock you. Past spilling and violence and the debris of dreams, I cradle your head in my hand and put your dry lips to my breast. My chest overflows. How I have longed for this. How halved I've been without this. Your eyebrows, your ears, your long neck I flush clean. I buff your shoulders until they gleam like tamboti. I kiss your wrists over and over until the aggressive bulges disappear from your knuckles. I comfort your elbows. I dress your bleeding legs. I soften your thighs and let them rest. Your burdened, beautiful back I caress, vertebra by vertebra, from my deepest memory. I take your blood, so light it could have been dust, and skim from it ages of exhaustion, virus and hunger. I take my own blood and I mix it with yours, as I have always yearned to do – to be of your body, to be surged by your heart, and loved by your skin. I bend over your face. You open your eyes and I see myself for the first time. As you widen your eyes, you see yourself there, compellingly completed.

The rain picks up carefully. The rain has our scent. It clears our throats. Light sifts through. It encompasses everything.

ACKNOWLEDGEMENTS

This book would not have been possible without the storytellers of the Free State – they are really telling the change. Among them are my brothers and my mother who have taught me how the stories around one can lie the truth. Therefore many names and places have been changed – the 'I' is seldom me, my mother and father not necessarily my parents, my family not really blood relatives, and so forth.

It was hard to find a writing space for myself after the success of *Country of My Skull*. Four people, however, made it possible: Stephen Johnson, who adroitly walked the line between encouragement and the kindest pressure possible; Ivan Vladislavić, an unequalled transformer who gave my clutch of many translations its cohesion; my son Andries who made regular back-ups of material on my computer and skilfully translated the original Afrikaans into English; and my husband John, who is, and, since that day in school, always has been my first reader.

Many thanks also to the Gorée Institute, for inviting me on the journey to Timbuktu; the Institute for Justice and Reconciliation, for including me in their visit to the Eastern Cape; and to the SABC, for providing such transformed work surroundings that even the smallest meeting was always something of an eye-opener. I am also grateful to Professors W.J. Botha and Ampie Muller for their particular explorations of the word 'transformation', to Professors Sizwe Satyo, Ncedile Saule and Mpo Mothoagae for their generous exchange during translations, and to the late Sipho Maseko for many a thought-provoking conversation.

Sections of this book have been published before in Afrikaans and Dutch, and sections of Part 2 first appeared in the *Mail & Guardian*. To make sense of these stories I had to interact with a wide variety of texts; some of them are quoted, and the insights gleaned from all are gratefully acknowledged.

Part 1 Breyten Breytenbach, *die ysterkoei moet sweet* (Afrikaanse Pers Boekhandel, Johannesburg, 1964); Jan F.E. Cilliers, *Die Vlakte* (Volkstem Drukkery, Pretoria, 1912); John and Jean Comaroff, *Body of Power, Spirit of Resistance* (University of Chicago Press, Chicago/London, 1985), and *Of Revelation and Revolution*, Vol. 1 (University of Chicago Press, Chicago/London, 1981); Nuruddin Farah, *Yesterday, Tomorrow* (Cassel, London/New York, 2000); J.L. Gili (ed.), *Lorca* (Penguin, Harmondsworth, 1960); John Hayward (ed.), *The Penguin Book of English Verse* (Penguin, Harmondsworth, 1964); Shirley J. Kokot, *Understanding Giftedness – A South African Perspective* (Butterworths, Durban, 1992); Antjie Krog, *Dogter van Jefta* (Human & Rousseau, Cape Town, 1970); Njabulo Ndebele, 'Iph' Indlela? Finding Our Way into the Future', First Steve Biko Memorial Lecture, delivered at the University of the Western Cape in 2000; *Oxford Talking Dictionary* (© the Learning Company, Inc., 1998 – All Rights Reserved); Dot

Serfontein, *Systap onder die Juk* (Human & Rousseau, Cape Town, 1969), *Amper my Mense* (Human & Rousseau, Cape Town, 1974), and *Keurskrif vir Kroonstad* (Perskor, Johannesburg, 1990); Susan Sontag, *Where the Stress Falls* (Jonathan Cape, London, 2002); G. Sterba, *The Aquarist's Encyclopedia* (Blandford Press, London, 1983); Anton van Niekerk (ed.), *Filosoof op die Markplein: Opstelle vir en deur Willie Esterhuizen* (Tafelberg, Cape Town, 1996); N.P. van Wyk Louw, *Die Halwe Kring* (Nasionale Pers, Cape Town/Bloemfontein, 1947); P.E. Vernon (ed.), *Creativity* (Penguin, Harmondsworth, 1980).

Part 2 Yael Danieli, *International Handbook of Multigenerational Legacies of Trauma* (Plenum Press, New York/London, 1998); F. Fanon, *The Wretched of the Earth* (Penguin, Harmondsworth, 1963); Antjie Krog and Ronelle Loots, *The Unfolding of Sky*, a television documentary in the series 'Landscape of Memory' produced by Don Edkins, 1999; Sheila Masote's testimony before the Truth Commission; Deborah Matshoba's testimony before the Truth Commission; Caroline Moser and Fiona Clark (eds), *Victims, Perpetrators or Actors? Gender, Armed Conflict and Political Violence* (Zed, London, 2001); Dot Serfontein, *Rang in der Staten Rij* (Human & Rousseau, Cape Town, 1979).

Part 3 K. Anthony Appiah and Amy Gutmann, *Color Conscious* (Princeton University Press, Princeton, 1996); Margaret Atwood, *Negotiating with the Dead: A Writer on Writing* (Cambridge University Press, Cambridge, 2002); Charles Baxter, 'Literature's Great Divide from Rhyming Action', in *Michigan Quarterly Review* (Fall 1996); Aimé Césaire, *Return to My Native Land* (Penguin, Harmondsworth, 1969); Mahmood Mamdani, *Citizen and Subject* (Princeton University Press, Princeton, 1996); D.B.Z Ntuli, *The Poetry of B.W. Vilakazi* (J.L. van Schaik, Pretoria, 1984); Jeff Opland, *Xhosa Poets and Poetry* (David Philip, Cape Town, 1998) and *Xhosa Oral Poetry: Aspects of a Black South African Tradition* (Ravan, Johannesburg, 1983); S.S. Prawer (ed. and trans.), *The Penguin Book of Lieder* (Penguin, Harmondsworth, 1964); N. Saule, 'Images in Some of the Literary Works of S.E.K. Mqhayi', PhD thesis (Department of African Languages, Unisa); Karel Schoeman, *Verliesfontein* (Human & Rousseau, Cape Town, 1998); D.L.P. Yali-Manisi, *Izibongo Zeenkosi ZamaXhosa.* (Lovedale Press, Alice, 1954).

Part 4 *Connect* (Arts International, New York, Fall 2000); Michael Ignatieff, *Blood and Belonging* (Penguin, Harmondsworth, 1993); Nelson Mandela, *Long Walk to Freedom* (Abacus, London, 1994); N.C. Manganyi, *Being-Black-in-the-World* (Skotaville, Johannesburg, 1973); Christiane Nord, *Translating as a Purposeful Activity* (St Jerome Publishing, Manchester, 1997); Jacqueline Rose, *On Not Being Able to Sleep: Psychoanalysis and the Modern World* (Chatto & Windus, London, 2003); Dot Serfontein, *Serfontein-Atlas* (privately published, 1984).

Part 5 Isabel Hofmeyr, *We Spend Our Years as a Tale That Is Told* (Wits University Press, Johannesburg, 1993); Jim Hudgens and Richard Trillo, *West Africa: The Rough Guide* (Penguin, Harmondsworth, 1999); Ali Mazrui, *The Africans: A Triple Heritage* (BBC Publications, London, 1986); Gabriel M. Setiloane, *The Image of God among the Sotho-Tswana* (A.A. Balkema, Rotterdam, 1976).

Part 6 George Ekama, 'Municipal Waste Treatment in South Africa – Past and Future', Inaugural Lecture, University of Cape Town, 2 September 1992; Dot Serfontein, *Ek is maar Ene* (Human & Rousseau, Cape Town, 1972); M.C. Wentzel, G.A. Ekama, R.E. Loewenthal and G.v.R. Marais, 'Fundamentals of Biological Behaviour', Notes produced by the Water Research Group, Department of Civil Engineering, University of Cape Town.

As I was preparing this text for publication, Kroonstad was placed under heavy water restrictions. A few days earlier, the river practically dried up and the dam closest to the town filled up with dead fish. Investigation revealed that some cattle farmers in the township had opened the manholes and sealed the pipes with plastic cold-drink bottles, so that the sewage would overflow and fertilize the topsoil. On the resultant patches of startlingly green grass, spread all over the township, many a farmer is successfully raising cattle.

GLOSSARY

ACDP – African Christian Democratic Party
Afrikaner Weerstandsbeweging – Afrikaner Resistance Movement; far-right
    paramilitary organization
aikona – no; no way
Amandla! – Power! Populist slogan, with the response *Ngawethu!* To the people!
amasi – curdled milk
ANC – African National Congress
atjar – spicy pickle
AWB – see Afrikaner Weerstandsbeweging

babelaas – hangover
backvelder – hick, country bumpkin
badimo – ancestors
bakkie – pick-up truck
bedonner – mess up, spoil
bietjie – a little bit
biltong – salted and dried meat
bioscope – cinema
boereseun – Afrikaner boy, farm boy
boerewors – spicy sausage
bonga – to sing praises, to perform as an *imbongi*
braai – barbecue
bulletjie – little bull
bunny ears – small portable TV aerial

Casspir – police riot-control and combat vehicle
COSATU – Congress of South African Trade Unions

dagga – marijuana
die Boere is nxa! – the Boers are great!
donga – dry, eroded watercourse
donner – thrash, beat up
DP – Democratic Party
dumela – hello, good day
dumela mongadi – good day, Sir

frikkadelletjies – small fried mincemeat balls

gatkant – arse-end
groot kak – big shit
Groot Trek – Great Trek; great migration of Boer farmers out of the Cape Colony
    in the 1830s

hamba kahle – go well
hanskakie – renegade
Hayi suka wena – Hey, get along with you!
hok – cage or pen for animals
IEC – Independent Electoral Commission
IFP – Inkatha Freedom Party
imbongi (plural *iimbongi*) – praise singer

ja-nee – expression of emphatic or ironic approval (literally 'yes-no')
Jis, Jissis – Jeez, Jesus
joiner – someone who went over to the British forces during the Anglo-Boer
    War; traitor
jol – play, party
joller – party animal
juffrou – miss, schoolmistress
jukskei – game similar to horseshoes played with wooden skittles
    (originally yoke pegs)

kak – shit
kieries – sticks
knobkierie – stick with a knobbed head
kopskote – head shots

lobola – bride price

mageu – drink made of fermented maize-meal porridge
MEC – Member of the Executive Committee (in the provincial government)
meerkat – small mammal similar to mongoose
meneer – mister, sir
Mfecane – period of Zulu and Sotho migration and associated wars
    (nineteenth century)
mfundisi – priest
miesies – missus, the white mistress of the household

MK – see Umkhonto we Sizwe
moederkerk – mother church, main church
moer uit – like crazy
moffies – gays
mos – after all, indeed
muti – traditional medicines and charms

ncinci – small
nè – not so? isn't it?
Nee my magtig – Good heavens, no
Nkosi – Chief
NNP – New National Party
nogal – what's more
nou ja – well then; let's see then

oe, my broe – oh, my brother
Oom – Uncle; used respectfully to address any older man
oubaas – old man; used to address an older white man, especially one in a
    position of authority
oumiesies – old missus; used to address an older white woman, the
    mistress of the household

PAC – Pan Africanist Congress
padkos – food for eating on a journey
Pagad – People against Gangsterism and Drugs; Muslim vigilante organization
pap – mealie-meal porridge
PE – Port Elizabeth
poes – cunt
potjiekos – stew cooked in a pot on the fire

Recces – Reconnaissance Unit

SABC – South African Broadcasting Corporation
SACP – South African Communist Party
sangoma – traditional healer
SAPA – South African Press Association
sjoe! re bapala – really, we play!
Slamse – Cape Malay
snoek – kind of fish
sowaar – really; can you believe it!

spaza – small, informal shop, especially in a private home
spruit – stream
staning – grazing camp
Swapos – soldiers of the South West African People's Organization (Swapo)

takhaar – hick, country bumpkin
Tannie – Auntie; used respectfully to address any older woman
tiekiedraai – fast, spinning dance performed by a couple
toyi-toyi – high-stepping dance performed during protest marches etc
Tsamaya hantle, Ntate Moholo – Go well, Old Man

ubuntu – spirit of fellowship and compassion in African society
UCT – University of Cape Town
UDM – United Democratic Movement
Umkhonto we Sizwe – 'Spear of the Nation', military wing of the ANC
umngqusho – samp (coarsely ground maize) and beans
umqombothi – sorghum beer

velskoene – strong leather shoes
verraier – traitor
vetkoek – deep-fried cake
vleiskamer – meat room

werf – homestead, farmyard
windskerm – windbreak
wors – boerewors, sausage
wragtig – indeed, truly

yebo – yes

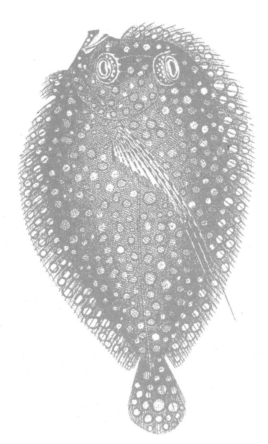